# You Shall Be M



by
Bob and Sandra Waldron

**From Egypt to Canaan**

GUARDIAN OF TRUTH

ISBN 10: 1-58427-109-4
ISBN 13: 978-158427109-3

**Guardian of Truth Foundation**
**P.O. Box 9670**
**Bowling Green, Kentucky 42102**
**1-800-428-0121**
**www.truthbooks.net**

# Table of Contents

# Introduction

Creation Stories
The Flood
Scattering of People
The Patriarchs

*The Exodus
*Wandering

Conquest of Land
Judges
United Kingdom
Divided Kingdom
Judah Alone
Captivity
Return
Years of Silence
Life of Christ
Early Church
Letters to Christians

The book of Genesis closes with the death of Joseph and the placing of his body in a coffin in Egypt. He had assured his people that God would come to their rescue and that He would take them back to the land of Canaan. Joseph asked them to promise that they would take his body with them when they returned, and bury it in the land of his fathers (Gen. 50:24-26).

Since Joseph felt the need to say God would "visit" them, literally "come to their rescue," it seems there was some degree of trouble for the Israelites before Joseph died. Remember that the family had entered Egypt as the honored family of the second ruler of the land. They had come at the special invitation of Joseph, and that invitation had been seconded by Pharaoh himself (Gen. 45:9-11, 16-20). When Jacob died, the family had full permission from Pharaoh to go back to Canaan to bury him in the Cave of Machpelah. A host of Egyptian dignitaries accompanied them and mourned with the family (50:4-9). Afterwards, the family returned to Egypt voluntarily because their condition in the land was still good. Probably Joseph did not remain a ruler very long after the years of famine were over, but he was obviously still an honored man at the time of Jacob's death.

There is no way to know when conditions started to change. We cannot know specifically what was happening in the land of Egypt at this time, because no Egyptian records have been found concerning the famine of Joseph's day, the slavery of the Israelites, or of the subsequent plagues that brought about their release. Moses does not give the personal name of the Pharaoh who made Joseph ruler, or of the one who enslaved the Israelites, or of the one who released them after the plagues. Look into the appendix for information about the political situation in Egypt at this point in history. You will find a discussion of how long the Israelites were in Egypt and of the date of the Exodus, and a description of the Hyksos kings and their role in the history of Egypt.

But by the beginning of the book of Exodus, conditions have changed completely from the way they were when Jacob's family first went to Egypt. The Israelites are still living in the very rich portion of Egypt called Goshen, which they were given in the days of Joseph, but they are now slaves of the king. In spite of their trials, however, God has been with them, because they have multiplied at a phenomenal rate. Indeed, it was that rapid increase in number that began to worry Pharaoh, and that made him decide to afflict the people.

God's providence was also at work in other ways for Israel during these years of their sojourn in Egypt. God had predicted to Abraham that his descendants would live in a land not their own, and that they would be afflicted there, but that God would judge that afflicting nation and would bring the people out with great substance (Gen. 15:13-14). It was not that God wanted the people to be afflicted, but He did want Abraham's descendants to develop into a distinct race of people — not to be absorbed into the tribes that surrounded them. They could do that in the land of Egypt because the Egyptians were a very proud people who did not mix with the peoples who came to sojourn in their land. During these years in Egypt, God has seen to it that the Israelites have grown in number and have developed as a distinct people, even though they are not yet an organized nation. There is no way to know how long the affliction itself lasted.

## Promises to Abraham:

**Promises to Abraham:**
- **Nation**
- **Land**
- **Spiritual**

Do you remember our repeated notice of the promises that were made to Abraham in the book of Genesis? (See Gen. 12:1-3, 7.) God called him to leave his homeland and his family in order to go into a land that God would show him. Abraham obeyed God and moved to the little land of Canaan. God told him that he himself would be blessed abundantly, but then God gave Abraham some promises that would be fulfilled as a part of God's plan for the salvation of mankind. God said that Abraham's descendants would become a great nation; that the nation would inherit the land of Canaan; and that through his seed all nations of the earth would be blessed. As the story progressed in Genesis, those same promises were repeated to Isaac (26:3-4) and then to Jacob (28:13-14).

Paul makes the very specific point in Galatians 3:16 that when God made the promises to Abraham and to his seed, God did not use the plural form of the word "seed." He used a singular word to designate *one* seed, *one* descendant, through whom all nations would be blessed. Paul even identifies that one descendant who would fulfill this promise: *the Christ.* Therefore the rest of the Bible continues to follow this particular promise that was made to Abraham, telling the story of the looking for and of the coming of the Savior into the world.

None of the promises were fulfilled by the end of the book of Genesis. Jacob's family was a very large family by then, but it was not a nation. The only parts of the land of Canaan that belonged to the family were the field that contained the Cave of Machpelah that Abraham bought as a burial place (Gen. 23:1-20) and the piece of land that Jacob bought near the village of Shechem when he returned from Laban (33:18-20). The Israelites (the descendants of Abraham, Isaac, and Jacob) were no longer living in Canaan when the book of Genesis closed. Instead they were living in Goshen in the land of Egypt. But God's plan was right on schedule. When He made the promises into a covenant in Genesis 15, He told Abraham that his descendants would live for a time in a land that was not their own, but that, after a time, God would bring them back to inherit the land of Canaan (15:13-21).

This book, *You Shall Be My People*, will tell how the first of these three promises to Abraham was fulfilled. As Genesis closed, we left the Israelites a very large family. As the book of Exodus opens, there is a vast multitude of people, but they are not yet organized as a distinct nation. By the end of the book of Deuteronomy, they will be a fully organized nation, with a king of their own (God), a law of their own (the Law of Moses), and they will be nearly ready to go in to inherit the land they have been promised. Never lose sight of the continuing thread of the story as we proceed from book to book with the history. God never forgets His overall purpose for the scheme of redemption as He gives the details about a particular period of time.

## Names for these people:

Notice the names that are applied to this group of people in the Bible. The earliest name was *Hebrew,* meaning a "stranger" or "foreigner." It was applied to Abraham because he came from Ur and lived as a foreigner among his Canaanite neighbors (Gen. 14:13). The Egyptians called his descendants Hebrews while they dwelt as foreigners in the land of Egypt. By New Testament days, the word had taken on a new connotation. It was used to contrast one who held devotedly to the old Jewish laws and traditions with one who had accepted the Greek way of life (Phil. 3:5). A Jew who used the term "Hebrew" in this way would be intending it as a compliment.

The terms *Israelite* or *Children of Israel* literally meant descendants of Israel. You remember that Jacob's name was changed to Israel the night he wrestled with an angel (Gen. 32:28), so his descendants were called Israelites instead of "Jacobites." The man named Israel (Jacob) has been dead for many years by the time the book of Exodus begins. From now on, most often, the name *Israel* will refer to the nation of his descendants. These terms were the ones preferred by the people, because they expressed the unique relationship this nation had with God. God had said He would make a great nation of the descendants of Abraham, Isaac, and Jacob. Therefore, the seed of Abraham wanted to be called Israelites as a reminder that they were part of that special nation, and heirs to all the promises made to their fathers. These variations of the name of Israel are the ones used most often in the Old Testament. In the New Testament, these terms are most frequently used to refer to the truly faithful ones within the physical nation, to those who were truly God's people (see Rom. 9, particularly verses 6-9.)

The name *Jew* was not used until very late in Old Testament history (2 Kings 16:6). It was first applied to those living in the southern kingdom of Judah. Since Judah was the last of the divided kingdom to go into captivity, the term came to refer to any Israelite in captivity. Then it was applied to the few who returned to their homeland, and finally, to Israelites scattered everywhere. By New Testament days the term is often used to refer to the Jewish officials who opposed Christ, in contrast to the common people who heard Him more readily (see John 7:1-2). It is, of course, the term most widely used today to apply to individuals of this ethnic group.

Learn the various names thoroughly so that you will never feel confused when one term is used interchangeably with another.

## Suggestions for studying the period of history:

Maps are always of value in any study of Bible history because all the events told were true historical events that happened *in some particular place*, just as all other historical events through the centuries happened at some specific place and at some specific time. But even more than most studies, the study of the route of the Exodus from Egypt to the land of Canaan requires a map study to be able to see where the people were and why they had problems finding water and food. Look at the maps included with this material. One map has all the needed places labeled, while the matching one is blank, waiting for you to label the places as you come to them in your study. You will learn the information much better if you take time to fill in your own map as you proceed.

## You Shall Be My People

*Map assignment: Begin your map work by finding (and labeling) the land of Egypt and the portion called Goshen within that land. Label and color the Mediterranean Sea.*

Our original edition of this book *Ye Shall Be My People,* was divided into two sections. The first section told the narrative of the journey from Egypt to Canaan (Exod. 1:1— Josh. 5:12); the second section was an analysis of the law God gave through Moses. But the book was large, and it was difficult to study enough of the law in order to see what God taught the Israelites, without bogging down in too many details. Therefore, in this revised edition, we have chosen to include a fuller look at the law in the narrative of the story, but we are publishing an analysis of the law of Moses in a companion book called *Jehovah's Covenant With Israel.* In this way, the student can get an overview of the whole law in his study of the story of how God led the Israelites out of Egypt, how He made them His own people with a law directly from Him, and how He prepared them to inherit the land of Canaan. Then, for the student who wants a more in depth study, the new book provides a simple, but comprehensive, analysis of the law with the appropriate passages combined to give all the details the law included on specific subjects — such as details about a feast day, or specific descriptions of the sacrifices, or duties of the priests and Levites.

As you go through the study of the narrative, take time to study the various sections of the law as you come to the appropriate point in your history. Be careful, however, lest by going so deeply into the study of some detail of the law, you lose the general picture of the period of history. The whole book will cover Exodus through Deuteronomy, plus the first five chapters of the book of Joshua. It is a long book, but the events covered fit together so closely they must be studied together in order to understand their place in the overall story of the Bible.

This study can stand alone, just as any study of a portion of the Bible can stand alone. If, however, you are using the book as part of your curriculum in studying Bible history, we have designed the material for two quarters of intensive study (with classes Sunday morning and in midweek). Use the two quarters to study the narrative, with appropriate looks into the details of the law, but leave an intensive study of the law for a later date.

Follow your outline carefully, as found in the Table of Contents, and in the left column at the beginning of each main chapter, to keep in mind the flow of events.

Take time to review often. Try to tie the events together as you move forward in the narrative. Frequent summaries of information help you and your students make sure you are learning the story.

**Quotes and paraphrases:**

As we work on all of our books, we keep more than one translation of the Bible in front of us: the American Standard Version, the King James Version, the New American Standard Version, the New King James Version, and the New International Version. Since this whole set of books is designed to help teachers and students get an understanding of exactly how the Bible story fits together, then more often than not, we paraphrase a passage rather than quoting it exactly from either one of the versions. Or we may use the wording of one translation in one quote, and another translation in the next quote. Try not to let that confuse you.

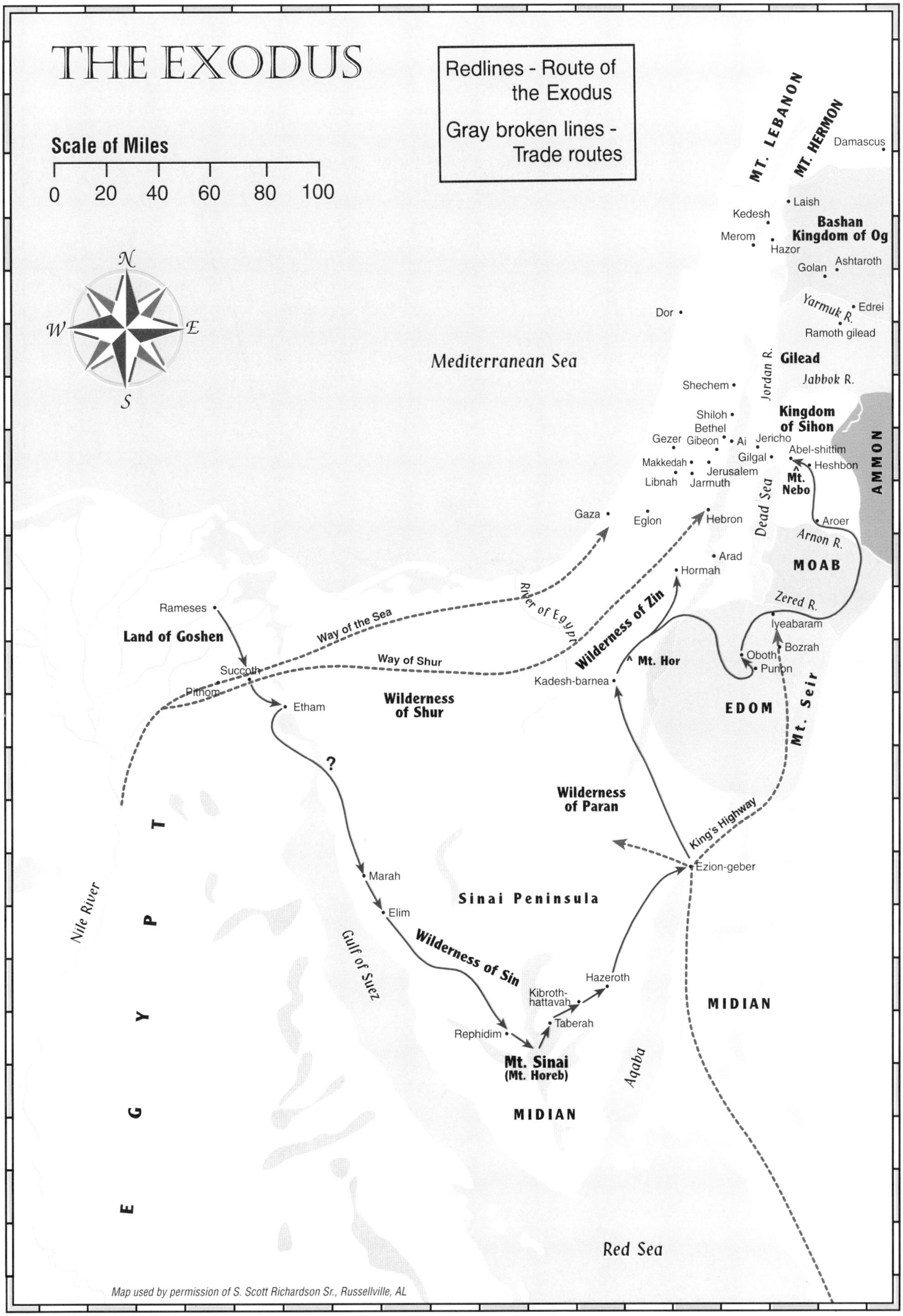
THE EXODUS
Redlines - Route of the Exodus
Gray broken lines - Trade routes
Scale of Miles
0 20 40 60 80 100
N
W
E
S
Mediterranean Sea
MT. LEBANON
MT. HERMON
Damascus
Laish
Kedesh
Merom
Hazor
Bashan Kingdom of Og
Golan
Ashtaroth
Yarmuk R.
Edrei
Ramoth gilead
Dor
Jordan R.
Gilead
Jabbok R.
Shechem
Shiloh
Bethel
Kingdom of Sihon
Gezer
Gibeon
Ai
Jericho
Abel-shittim
Heshbon
Makkedah
Gilgal
Jerusalem
Libnah
Jarmuth
Mt. Nebo
AMMON
Dead Sea
Gaza
Eglon
Hebron
Aroer
Arnon R.
Arad
Hormah
MOAB
Rameses
Land of Goshen
River of Egypt
Way of the Sea
Wilderness of Zin
Zered R.
Iyeabaram
Bozrah
Oboth
Punon
Way of Shur
Succoth
Pithom
Mt. Hor
Kadesh-barnea
Etham
Wilderness of Shur
EDOM
Mt. Seir
?
Wilderness of Paran
King's Highway
Ezion-geber
EGYPT
Marah
Sinai Peninsula
Elim
Nile River
Gulf of Suez
Wilderness of Sin
Hazeroth
Kibroth-hattavah
MIDIAN
Taberah
Rephidim
Mt. Sinai (Mt. Horeb)
Aqaba
MIDIAN
Red Sea
Map used by permission of S. Scott Richardson Sr., Russellville, AL

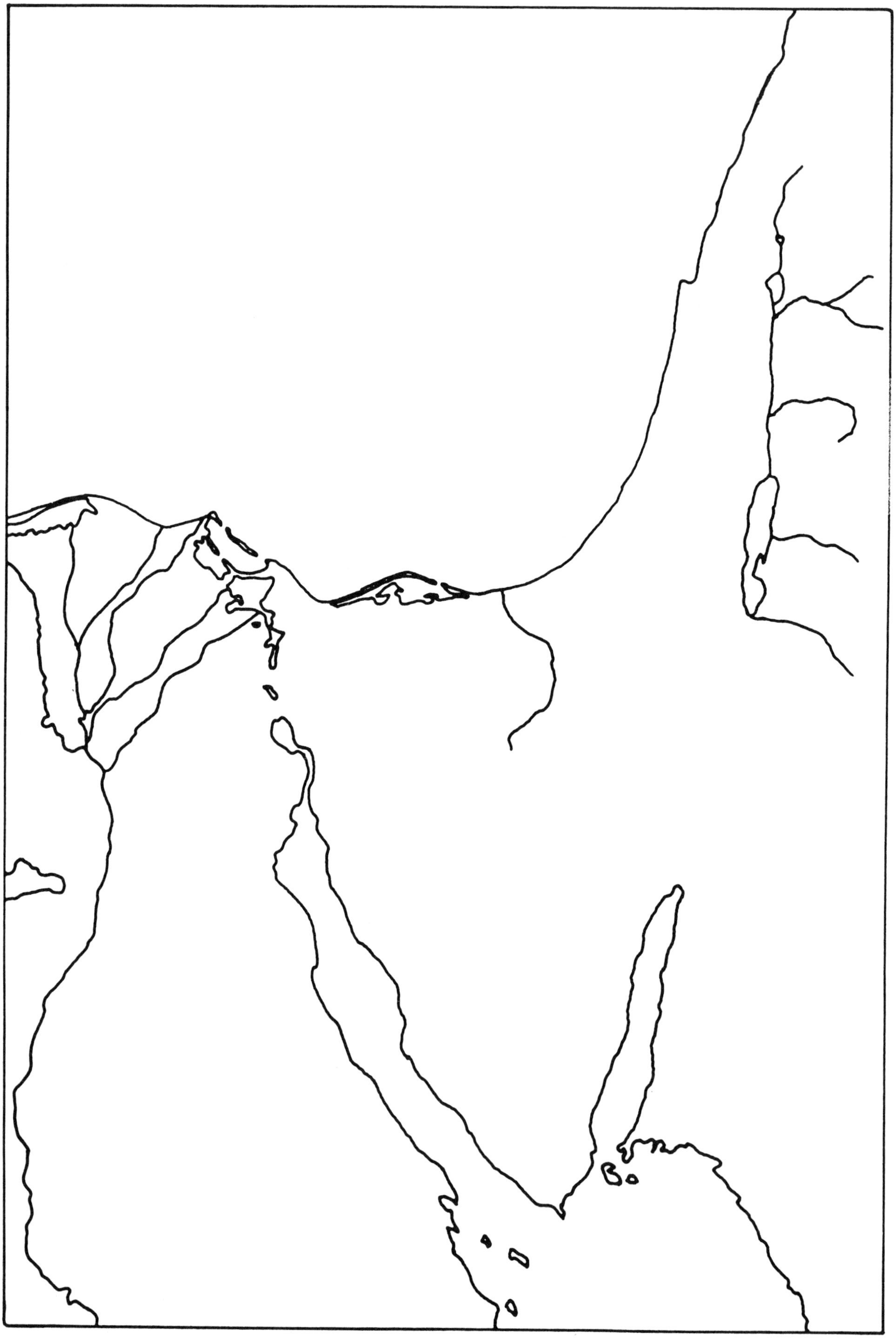

# *The Call of Moses*

## *(Exodus 1:1-7:13)*

## Moses' Early Years

### (Exodus 1:1-2:25)

**Route of the Exodus —**
**From Egypt to Canaan**

***The Call of Moses**
***Moses' Early Years**
***Return to Egypt**
***Request to Leave**

**The Plagues**
**From Egypt to Sinai**
**Jehovah Makes a Covenant**
**More Time at Sinai**
**From Sinai to Kadesh**
**Wandering**
**The Plains of Moab**
**Moses' Speeches**
**Journey's End**

### The affliction of the Israelites (Exod. 1:1-22):

The children of Israel *(that is, the family of Jacob)*, consisting of twelve sons and their families, moved into Egypt during the days of Joseph. At that time the family had a total of only seventy or seventy-five people (see Gen. 46:26-27; Acts 7:14). In Egypt they multiplied and grew exceedingly strong, and they spread over all the land *(of Goshen)*. By God's providence, they grew at a phenomenal rate. Look at how their growth is described in verse seven: they were "fruitful," they "increased abundantly," they "multiplied, waxed exceeding mighty, and the land was filled with them." Since the Holy Spirit inspired the writer to use this many phrases to describe their growth, they must have been growing much more rapidly than the typical group of people.

A new king arose in Egypt who did not recognize *(or acknowledge)* Joseph, or what he had done for Egypt. Afraid that the Israelites *(or Hebrews)* might sometime unite with foreign invaders and help them fight the Egyptians, Pharaoh took steps to subdue them. He told his people, "Come, let us deal wisely with these people. Let us put them to work for us, lest they multiply and join with some enemy and fight against us."

His first measure was to make the Israelites slaves, to place them under taskmasters who would force them to toil at specific projects. Among these projects was the building of the store cities of Pithom and Raamses. From the first, these taskmasters were to "afflict them with their burdens." So the Egyptians made their work harder — making them serve with "rigor." They made their lives bitter with the very hard work set before them. But the more they afflicted them, the more the Israelites multiplied and grew.

Pharaoh attempted to stop the growth of the people by telling the Hebrew midwives, Shiphrah and Puah, "When you go to help the Hebrew women at birth, if the baby is a son, kill him. If it is a girl, you may let it live."

The midwives did not obey the king, however, because they feared God. When Pharaoh asked them why they did not obey him, they answered, "The Hebrew women are not like the Egyptian women; they are vigorous and have their babies before we get to them." God was very good to the midwives because they would not obey the king's wicked command.

Finally, in desperation, Pharaoh commanded the Egyptian people, saying, "Every son that is born to the Hebrews, cast it into the river *(the Nile)*, but every daughter may be spared."

*Why kill the baby boys and not the baby girls? Pharaoh would not have wanted to stop all growth of his slaves, but he did not want boys growing into men who could be soldiers, who might join with an enemy to fight against Egypt. There is no way to know how many babes died, nor how long the ruling stayed in effect.*

*Pithom was located somewhere in the desert that separates the Delta from Ismailia, but scholars are not positive about the exact location. They are reasonably certain that Raamses was at or near Tanis, the Bible Zoan (Num. 13:22). This was the residence of Ramses II (1290-1224 B.C.). See the Appendix for more information about Ramses II.*

***Map assignment:** Label the approximate locations of Pithom and Raamses. Label the Nile River.*

## Baby Moses is rescued (Exod. 2:1-10):

The ruling that all baby boys were to be thrown into the river was in full force when a man named Amram, and Jochebed his wife, had their third child, a boy. Jochebed saw that the baby was beautiful and healthy, and she was in terror that he would be slain. For three months she hid him. When she could hide him no longer, she made a basket of bulrushes *(papyrus reeds)* and waterproofed it with asphalt and pitch. Carefully placing the child in the basket, she laid the precious package in the water among the reeds by the water's edge. Miriam, the baby's sister, stood where she could watch to see what happened.

After a time, Pharaoh's daughter came down to the river to bathe while her maidens walked by the river's edge. Pharaoh's daughter saw the basket floating in the water and sent her handmaid to bring it to her. When the princess opened the basket, she saw the baby, and it cried. Her heart was touched with compassion, and she said, "This is one of the Hebrew children."

Miriam, having seen the baby get a favorable reception, came to the princess and said, "Would you like for me to go and get a Hebrew woman to nurse the child for you?"

The princess replied, "Go." Promptly, Miriam went and called for Moses' own mother to come. Pharaoh's daughter told her, "Take this child away, and nurse it for me, and I will pay you a salary." So Moses' own mother took him to care for, and was paid to do so by the daughter of the man who had decreed that all such babies were to be slain.

Moses was reared by his mother until he was old enough to be taken to Pharaoh's daughter to become her son. Pharaoh's daughter named him Moses, saying, "It is because I drew *(mashah)* him from the water."

*An interesting Jewish tradition says that Pharaoh's daughter had one of her handmaids, who had a baby, to try to feed the infant. He would not have it, so Miriam chose that moment to come up and ask if the princess would like for her to fetch a Hebrew woman to nurse the child. The story is feasible, and would fit into the situation, but there is no way of knowing if it is true.*

*The name of Pharaoh's daughter is never given. Neither is the personal name of the Pharaoh ever given in the story.*

## The Call of Moses

*In his speech to the Jews, Stephen says that Moses was instructed in all the wisdom of the Egyptians and that he was mighty in his words and works (Acts 7:22). The historian Josephus adds that Moses served as a general leading an army against the Ethiopians (Antiquities of the Jews, Book II, Chapter X).*

*Egypt was famous for her learning and wisdom. Her school system was highly developed. Sons of vassal kings came from as far away as the Euphrates River to study and to receive training in Egypt. From the records that have been found, it is possible to have a good estimate of the curriculum Moses studied (Egypt and the Exodus, Pfeiffer, pp. 41-43).*

### Moses goes out to rescue his people (Exod. 2:11-15a):

In spite of his Egyptian education, and his time in the royal surroundings as grandson of the king, Moses did not forget that he was an Israelite. When he was forty years old (Acts 7:23), he went out to see what he could do about the plight of his brethren. He found an Egyptian beating a Hebrew, and after a quick glance around to see that he was not observed, Moses struck the Egyptian, killing him, and buried his body in the sand.

The next day Moses found two of his own people fighting. He asked the one in the wrong, "Why are you hitting your companion?"

The man spat out his words at Moses: "Who made you a judge over us? Will you kill me as you killed the Egyptian yesterday?"

Moses was afraid and said, "Surely what I have done is known." When word came to Pharaoh what Moses had done, he sent to kill him, but Moses had fled to the land of Midian.

*The boldness of Moses when he went out to help his brethren contrasts greatly with his timidity forty years later when God appeared to him in the burning bush and told him to go tell Pharaoh to let the Israelites go. At forty, Moses, perhaps convinced that his life had been spared for a divine mission, went out to deliver Israel singlehandedly, by his own might. However, no man's strength is sufficient for the tasks of God. Moses thought he was ready to deliver his people, but God was not ready, and He could see that Moses was not ready to be used. Later, when Moses had no confidence at all in himself, God was ready to use him as the divine hammer to strike Egypt a mighty blow.*

*Hebrews 11 tells many great things about the role of faith in Moses' life:*

- *There was the faith of his parents who loved him and did not allow the king's command to stop them from doing what was right (11:23).*
- *By faith Moses refused to be called the son of Pharaoh's daughter (11:24).*
- *Instead, he took his stand with the Israelites, though the cost was very high (11:25).*
- *He literally cast away the treasures of Egypt (11:25-26).*
- *In return he looked to God for suitable recompense (11:26).*

*The Hebrew writer says that Moses fled Egypt, not fearing the wrath of the king (Heb. 11:27). In Exodus 2:14, however, the Bible says, "And Moses feared, and said, 'Surely the thing is known.'" How can these two statements be reconciled?*

- *The Hebrew writer carefully observes the chronological order of the events. Beginning with Hebrews 11:23, the writer refers to the act of Moses' parents when they hid him for three months; next, to Moses' refusal to count himself an Egyptian (11:24-25); then to his forsaking Egypt, unafraid of the king (11:27); next, to the keeping of the Passover (11:28), and finally to the crossing of the Red Sea (11:29). This is precisely the order followed in the book of Exodus and in Stephen's speech (Acts 7:20-29).*

- *Therefore, the evidence in Hebrews 11 points more to the idea of his removal to the land of Midian after killing the Egyptian.*
- *One good explanation is found in the parallel between Moses' action and his parents' action. It is said of his parents that by faith they hid Moses for three months, and were not afraid of the king's commandment (11:23). Obviously they were afraid, else why would they have hidden Moses and then put forth the effort to provide a special ark to place among the bulrushes? The point is they did not allow their fear of the king's command to deter them from saving their child, no matter what it took.*
    - *Similarly, Moses feared punishment from the king after killing the man, as Exodus says (Exod. 2:14), but he did not allow his fear of what might happen (and did happen) to deter him from taking the side of his people.*
- *On the other hand, if the reference in Hebrews 11:27 is to Moses' departure from Egypt when he led Israel forth, Moses' confrontations with Pharaoh came when he demanded that the king let the Israelites go. This was when he faced the king bravely, told him of the plagues that would come upon him, and finally led the people forth. Moses was afraid on that occasion also when God first told him what he was to do, but his fear did not stop his obedience to God.*

*The Midianites were a nomadic people. The primary land of Midian seems to have been on the eastern shore of the Gulf of Aqaba, but this does not appear to be where Moses went when he left Egypt. Moses kept sheep near the mountains of Horeb (or Sinai) where the "mountain of God" was (Exod. 3:1). It is highly unlikely that Moses would have taken his flocks a hundred or a hundred fifty miles from home on the east side of Aqaba to Sinai in the southern part of the Wilderness of Sinai. Most likely the land of Midian in Exodus 2 refers to an area east of Mount Sinai where a large family of Midianites had settled. Also note that when Israel left Mount Sinai, it was the area east and north of Sinai through which they traveled (Num. 11-12), and it was this area that Hobab, Moses' brother-in-law knew well (Num. 10:29-32).*

***Map assignment:** Label and color the Red Sea with its two arms at the north: the Gulf of Suez and the Gulf of Aqaba. The land between the two gulfs was desert with only oases spaced widely apart. Find and label the primary land of Midian east of the Gulf of Aqaba and then label Mount Sinai (Horeb) with a group of Midianites living near there. It is this "land of Midian" near Sinai where Moses was.*

## Moses' second forty years (Exod. 2:15b-25):

Moses found a well as he traveled through the desert and he sat down to rest.

The priest of Midian had seven daughters who came daily to this well to draw water to fill the troughs for their flocks to drink. The other shepherds apparently made a habit of letting them draw the water, driving the young ladies away, and watering their own sheep. Normally the women would have to draw water again, but this time Moses was present, and he stood up, rescued them from the shepherds, and helped them water their flocks.

When the sisters returned home, their father Reuel said, "How is it you are home so quickly today?"

They said, "An Egyptian delivered us from the shepherds, and he even drew water for us and watered the flock."

"Well, where is he? Why did you leave him? Go call him to eat bread with us," their father replied.

## The Call of Moses

Moses accepted the invitation and found a home with the family. After a time Reuel gave Moses Zipporah his daughter to be his wife. By her Moses had a son whom he named Gershom *(Sojourner)* because he said, "I have become a sojourner in a foreign land."

A long time after Moses fled Egypt, the king of Egypt died. The children of Israel groaned because of their bondage, God heard their cry, and He remembered the covenant He had made with Abraham, with Isaac, and with Jacob. The time was nigh for deliverance.

*God "remembered" the covenant He had made with Abraham. Did that mean He had forgotten it during these years while the Israelites had been in slavery? No! No, indeed! God's providence had been at work all this time. God accommodates His thoughts to language that men can understand, revealing His plans for the next stage in the development of His purpose. He had not forgotten — but the time for deliverance had not arrived until this moment. God was ready to deliver the people, make them His nation, and take them to the land of Canaan.*

# Moses Returns to Egypt
## (Exodus 3:1-4:31)

*Look at your outline in the left column of the first page of this chapter. The first section of Exodus tells the story of the affliction of Israel at the hands of Pharaoh, the story of Moses' birth and growing up, the story of his effort to help his people, and of his flight to the land of Midian.*

*Next we have the episode of the burning bush, the story of Moses' journey back to Egypt, the account of his first effort to persuade Pharaoh to let the people go, and God's assurance to Moses that He would indeed bring His people out of Egypt. We also will find the genealogy of Moses and Aaron, and the first signs Moses and Aaron showed to Pharaoh. You must have these individual stories clearly fixed in mind as you teach. Help your students keep the overview of the period in mind even as they learn the details of each lesson.*

### The burning bush (Exod. 3:1-4:17):

Moses kept the flock for his father-in-law Jethro *(called Reuel earlier, 2:18)*, and he took his flock through the wilderness to Horeb *(another name for Mount Sinai)*, the mountain of God *(called such in anticipation)*. As Moses kept his flock, the angel of the Lord appeared unto him in a flaming fire that burned in a bush. As Moses watched, the bush was not consumed. This strange occurrence aroused his curiosity, and he said to himself, "I am going to go out of my way to see this great sight, to see why the bush is not burnt."

When the Lord saw Moses turn aside, He called to him out of the midst of the bush, saying, "Moses, Moses."

In astonishment, Moses answered, "Here I am."

"Do not come any closer," the voice said. "Take your shoes from your feet because you are standing on holy ground." The voice continued: "I am the God of your ancestors, the God of Abraham, the God of Isaac, and the God of Jacob."

At these words, Moses hid his face because he was afraid to look upon the face of God.

## You Shall Be My People

Jehovah said, "I know of the affliction of my people in Egypt, and I have heard their cries. I have come down to deliver them from the Egyptians, and to bring them to a good land flowing with milk and honey. It is the place now inhabited by the Canaanite, the Hittite, the Amorite, the Perizzite, the Hivite, and the Jebusite. Having seen the oppression of my people by the Egyptians, I am sending you to Pharaoh that you may bring my people, the children of Israel, up out of Egypt."

Moses replied, "Who am I that I should go before Pharaoh, and that I should bring forth the children of Israel from Egypt?"

God said, "Certainly I will be with you, and you can count on this: you will bring these people out of Egypt, and you will serve God upon this very mountain."

Moses replied, "Well, look, when I come to the children of Israel and tell them, 'The God of your fathers has sent me,' they will ask, 'What is His name?' What shall I tell them?"

God answered, "I AM THAT I AM *(or, "I am because I am")*. Thus shall you tell the children of Israel: 'I AM has sent me to you.' Tell them, 'Jehovah, the God of your fathers has sent me to you.' This is my name forever, and this is my memorial to all generations."

God told Moses, "Go and gather the elders of Israel together and tell them what I have said, that I will come and help you, and I will bring you up out of Egypt into the land of the Canaanites, into a land flowing with milk and honey. They will listen to you; then you and the elders will go in before the king of Egypt and say, 'Jehovah, the God of the Hebrews, has met with us. He wants you to let us go three days' journey into the wilderness to sacrifice to Jehovah our God.' I know that he will not agree to let you go, not by any means. Then I will put forth my hand, and I will strike Egypt with all my wonders, and *after that* he will let you go. And when you go, I will give you favor with the Egyptians so that you will not leave empty-handed."

Moses did not want to accept the charge that God had given him. He said, "They will not believe me. They will say, 'Jehovah has not spoken to you.'"

The Lord asked Moses, "What is that in your hand?"

He said, "A rod" *(a shepherd's staff)*.

God said, "Throw it down upon the ground."

When Moses threw the rod down, it became a snake, and Moses ran away from it. Jehovah said, "Reach out and take it by the tail." Moses did so, and the snake became a rod again. "This sign will help them believe that Jehovah, the God of their fathers, has appeared to you."

God continued, "Put your hand inside your coat." Moses put his hand inside his coat, and when he brought it out again, it was leprous, white as snow. "Put your hand inside your coat again," God said. Moses did so, and his hand was clean.

"If they will not believe the first sign, they will believe the second. If they will not pay attention to either of these signs, then you will take water from the river and pour it upon dry ground, and the water will become blood upon the dry ground."

Moses answered Jehovah saying, "I am not eloquent, neither before nor since you have begun speaking to me. I find it difficult to speak, because my tongue is slow."

The Lord replied, "Who has made man's mouth? Or who makes one mute, or deaf, or seeing, or blind? Is it not I, the Lord? Do as I say, and I will be with your mouth and will tell you what to say."

Moses answered, "Well, Lord, you can send whomsoever you want to send." *(Moses' language was curt and disrespectful. His meaning was, "You can send anybody you want, and there is nothing I can do about it, so if I have to go, I will, but I don't want to." In spite of God's assurances and the signs He had given Moses, the main problem was that Moses did not want to accept such a difficult task.)*

## The Call of Moses

God was angry with Moses, and He said, "I know one thing: your brother Aaron the Levite speaks well, and he is even now on his way to meet you, and when he meets you, he will be glad in his heart. You will speak to him and tell him what to say, and I will speak with you and tell you what to say to him. He will be your spokesman to the people, your mouth, as it were, and you will be to him as God. Take this rod with you, for by it you will do the signs I will give you."

*God has told Moses to go bring the people out of Egypt and Moses has offered these five objections:*

- *Who am I, that I should go to Pharaoh and bring the people out of Egypt? Or, as we would say, Why me?*
- *When I come to the Israelites and say God has appeared to me, they will want to know which God, what is His name?*
- *They will not believe me. They will deny that God has spoken to me.*
- *I am not eloquent.*
- *Send whomsoever you will. I cannot stop you.*

*Be sure you and your students see all these objections, and the answers that God gave to each. Your story line is not complete until these facts are firmly in place.*

*The name Jehovah comes from four Hebrew letters that are without vowel signs in the original Hebrew text. The early Hebrew language was a language of consonants. Vowel signs to show how to pronounce the written word were added much later in history. Therefore no one knows how the name Jehovah was pronounced. During the years of silence between Malachi and the New Testament, the idea arose among the Jews that the sacred name of Jehovah was too holy to be uttered. Therefore they assigned the vowel signs of the Hebrew word "adonai" (Lord) to the name of Jehovah, to signify that wherever the name Jehovah was encountered, the reader would say, "Adonai," pronounced "ah-doe-nah-ee." The King James translators translated the word that was read aloud, which meant "Lord." Therefore, almost always, in the KJV of the Old Testament, when the word Lord appears, it is Jehovah in the original In many editions of the KJV, when the reference is to Jehovah, the letters of the word, Lord, are all capitalized.*

*Jehovah comes from the Hebrew verb "to be." God used this name in dealing with the patriarchs; yet He says, "I appeared unto Abraham, unto Isaac, and unto Jacob, as God Almighty (El Shaddai), but by my name Jehovah, I was not known" — that is, "The true significance of my name, Jehovah, was not known to them" (Exod. 6:2-3). What God did here at Mount Horeb was to designate Himself as the eternal, absolute, self-existent One. He is the God who appears to man in history, but He is the same whenever He appears. The names of God, such as the Almighty, the One Who Sees, and others, were self-explanatory. Though God revealed Himself as Jehovah to the patriarchs (Gen. 14:22; 15:2, 7, 8), He did not reveal to them the significance of that name until He was prepared to become the covenant God of Israel. Such a name would prevent a confused identification with other gods such as Baal, Osiris, and others, but, even more, it would affirm the existence of the true God and the nonexistence of the false gods.*

*It was no surprise to God that Pharaoh refused to let the people go when he was first presented with the proposition. God tells Moses here that Pharaoh will not let them go at first, that God will send great wonders upon the land, and <u>then</u> Pharaoh will let them go. However, we know that Moses was not really listening at this point because he is very upset later when Pharaoh offers his first resistance.*

## You Shall Be My People

*God's plan was still on schedule. When God appeared to Abraham and made His promise into a covenant, He made specific predictions about Abraham's descendants (see Gen. 15:13-16). As we continue the story, observe how each part of the promise is fulfilled completely and literally:*

- *They will live in a land not their own for a while.*
- *They will be mistreated in the foreign land.*
- *The time will come when God will punish that oppressing nation and will bring His people out.*
- *When they leave that country of oppression, they will come out with great possessions.*

*The statement of Moses that he was "slow of speech" does not contradict Stephen's statement that Moses was mighty in word and deed (Acts 7:22), because being mighty in word does not necessarily mean eloquent. Stephen's statement could as easily be translated: "Moses' words carried much weight." God does not argue that Moses was eloquent, but He gave a way to compensate for Moses' inability to speak persuasively to Pharaoh. Aaron would be the spokesman.*

*In keeping with the rest of scripture, God does not take each person before he is born and say, "I think I will make this one blind," or, "this one deaf." God operates by natural laws that He has ordained, and sometimes the operation of these laws results in blindness or deafness, or in some other affliction. This is the consequence of paradise having been lost when sin entered the world in the Garden of Eden. Thus in either a direct way or an indirect way, all things are under the disposition of God, and in this sense, God says, "I make men mute, or deaf, or seeing, or blind." God's point here, of course, was that He could help Moses overcome any defect he had.*

*Watch this shepherd's rod that God has told Moses to take with him to Egypt. It will appear over and over in the story as the various great signs are done to demonstrate God's power.*

### Moses' trip to Egypt (Exod. 4:18-31):

Moses returned to Jethro his father-in-law and said, "Let me go, please, so that I can return to my brethren in Egypt, and see whether they are still alive."

Jethro answered, "Go in peace."

God assured Moses, saying, "Go back to Egypt; all the men who wanted to kill you are dead." *(Remember Moses left Egypt because he feared for his life after killing a man.)*

Moses took his wife and two sons with him as he started toward Egypt. They rode on a donkey, while Moses walked along with the staff of God in his hand.

God warned Moses again, saying, "When you get to Egypt, see that you do for Pharaoh all the wonders I have given you, but I will harden Pharaoh's heart, and he will not let the people go. You will tell Pharaoh, 'This is what Jehovah says: "Israel is my son, my firstborn, and I have told you to let my son go, that he may serve me, but you have refused. Therefore, beware; I will slay your son, your first-born."'"

On their way, as they camped, God met him *(the only "him" in the context is Moses)* and sought to slay him. Quickly Zipporah took a flint and cut off the foreskin of her son and threw it at his feet, and she said, "Surely you are a bridegroom of blood as far as this circumcising business is concerned."

## The Call of Moses

The Lord had spoken also to Aaron, the brother of Moses, in Egypt and had said, "Go into the wilderness to meet Moses." Aaron got up and went out and met him in the mountain of God and kissed him. Moses told Aaron everything that had happened and about the signs God had given him.

When they arrived in Egypt, Moses and Aaron gathered the elders of Israel together, and told them what the Lord had said, and showed them the signs the Lord had given them. The people believed, and when they heard that the Lord had decided to deliver them from their afflictions, they bowed their heads and worshiped.

*Moses' father-in-law is called Reuel when we meet him in 2:18. By 3:1, and again here in 4:18, he is called Jethro. A comparison of Exodus 2:16-18 and 18:1-2 indicates that these two names belonged to the same man, just as the names Jacob and Israel referred to the same man. By the time God appeared to Moses in the burning bush, a full forty years have passed since Moses first met the family, so there is the possibility that the head or chief of this group of Midianites had changed while Moses has been with the group — and that the first man was Reuel and the second one was Jethro. In that case, the term "father-in-law" would refer to the "father (head) of the family," rather than to the literal father of Moses' wife. More likely, though, they are names for the same man.*

*Here as Moses starts on his trip to Egypt to carry out the commission, God gives the first indication of what the final plague will be, the plague that will finally change Pharaoh's stubborn heart — death of the firstborn. And, once again, God has told Moses to expect Pharaoh to refuse to let the people go at first. Moses "hears" what God says, but he does not comprehend all that will be involved in the task God has given him. Watch as Moses' faith and his willingness to depend upon God grow.*

*God speaks of the Israelites as "His firstborn son" here. Continue to note that expression and its significance.*

*Obviously Moses had not followed the decree that all male children belonging to the descendants of Abraham were to be circumcised at the age of eight days (Gen. 17:9-14). By seeking to kill him, God was demanding that the act be done before Moses could continue with the task before him. If Moses were going to be the servant of God, he would have to walk in all His ways.*

*Men typically fail to count the cost of their goals. The elders of Israel were glad to hear what God planned for them, but they were grieved when they discovered the effort necessary to accomplish it. They were very happy to accept blessings; they did not want to have to do anything to get them.*

# Request to Leave
## (Exodus 5:1-7:13)

### Moses and Aaron present God's command to Pharaoh (Exod. 5:1-23):

After telling the Hebrews about God's plan, Moses and Aaron went before Pharaoh and said, "This is what the Lord, the God of Israel, says: 'Let my people go so that they can hold a feast to me in the wilderness.'"

Pharaoh replied, "Who is Jehovah that I should pay any attention to Him? I do not know the Lord, and I will not let Israel go."

*Notice Pharaoh's question, "Who is Jehovah that I should obey Him?" Pharaoh was ruler of the greatest nation in existence in that day, and the gods he knew about were figments of men's imagination, but they were his gods. Why should he, Pharaoh of all Egypt, obey some god that he knows nothing about! The plagues that follow were God's answer to Pharaoh's question. As you continue studying the plagues, notice how often God says that what He is doing is so that Pharaoh, the Egyptians, and the Israelites "may know that I am Jehovah." As they learn the lesson of the power of Jehovah, let us do the same.*

*This first request to Pharaoh was a very reasonable request. Even slaves should have had the right to worship their God, and that was what Moses and Aaron asked for first. They did not, at this point, ask to leave the land, never to return.*

Moses and Aaron said, "The God of the Hebrews has met with us. Please, let us go three days' journey into the wilderness and sacrifice to the Lord our God, lest He send pestilence or the sword upon us."

"Moses and Aaron," Pharaoh said, "why do you try to take the people away from their tasks? Get back to work. The people in the land are many, and you are making them idle."

That same day, Pharaoh commanded the taskmasters of the Israelites and their officers, saying: "You are not to give the people straw to make brick as you have been doing. Let them go and gather straw themselves. And the number of bricks that they make must remain the same or else! The people must have extra time on their hands, because they are saying, 'Let us go and sacrifice to our God.' Therefore, give them more work to do, so that they will not have time to listen to lying words."

The taskmasters went out with their officers, and told the Israelites: "Hear what Pharaoh says: 'I will not give you straw anymore. Go gather your own straw wherever you can find it, and the amount of bricks you make had better not decrease.'"

The Israelites scattered all over the land to gather the stubble they could use for straw, which they mixed with clay to make their bricks. The taskmasters pressed them hard: "Do your work, keep at it. You must make as many bricks as before." But, try as they might, the Israelites could not make the same number of bricks as before, so the Hebrew officers who acted as foremen of the people were beaten. The taskmasters said, "Why haven't you met your quotas of bricks both yesterday and today?"

In terror and desperation, the officers of the people went to Pharaoh and said, "Why are you treating your servants like this? We were given no straw, and yet were told to make brick. Now we have been beaten because we did not make as many bricks as before. It is the fault of your own people, not ours."

Pharaoh answered, "You are idle, idle I say! Therefore you say, 'Let us go and sacrifice to Jehovah.' Now get back to work, because there will be no straw given you, yet the required quota of bricks will remain the same."

The Hebrew officers could see that they were in a bad situation from which there seemed no escape. As they came out from Pharaoh, they met Moses and Aaron, and said, "We hope the Lord will take notice of what you have done, because you have made us to stink to Pharaoh, and you have given a sword into his hands to kill us."

Moses turned to the Lord and said, "Lord, why have you treated this people so badly? Why did you send me? Since I came to speak to Pharaoh in your name, he has treated them very badly. You have not delivered this people at all."

*Do you see that Moses has been ignoring God's warnings that Pharaoh would not listen to him at first? Moses was like so many of us: he did not heed the warnings until he came face to face with the reality. He had not yet learned to rely upon God.*

## God assures Moses He will deliver Israel (Exod. 6:1-9):

Rather than rebuking Moses at this point for his lack of spiritual strength and understanding, God realized he needed assurance so that his faith could grow. He told Moses:

> Now you will see what I will do to Pharaoh; for I will compel him to let the people go. With a strong hand will he drive them out of his land.
>
> I am Jehovah, and I appeared unto Abraham, unto Isaac, and unto Jacob, as God Almighty (El Shaddai), but by my name Jehovah I was not known to them. I made a firm covenant with them to give them the land of Canaan, the land where they stayed. Also, I have heard the groaning of the children of Israel under the hands of the Egyptians, and I have remembered my covenant. Therefore, tell the children of Israel: "I am Jehovah, and I will bring you out from under the burdens of the Egyptians, and I will get rid of their bondage, and I will purchase you by great deeds and judgments that I will bring upon the Egyptians. I will take you as my own people, and I will be your God. *Then you will know that I am the Lord your God* who brought you out from under the yoke of the Egyptians. And I will bring you to the land that I swore to give to Abraham, Isaac, and Jacob. I will give it to you for an inheritance. I am Jehovah."

Moses told these words to the children of Israel, but they paid no attention because of their hopelessness and because of the backbreaking oppression they suffered.

*In verse 1, the KJV uses the expression that, "with a strong hand," Pharaoh will let the people go. The New American Standard version uses the expression "under compulsion" twice in the verse. The "strong hand" and the "compulsion" would come from Jehovah. God is telling Moses that He will force Pharaoh to submit —He will use His strong hand to compel Pharaoh to comply. This is strong reassurance that God is giving to Moses. He is saying, "You can trust me to accomplish what I have set out to do..."*

*"By my name Jehovah I was not known to them." See the note included at the time of the appearance of God at the burning bush.*

*From this point on, begin noticing the expression "I will take you as my own people, and I will be your God." This is a reference to the covenant that God intends to make with these people. As the story proceeds, God uses this expression over and over. Become conscious of how often this exact statement, or one very similar, occurs throughout the Bible. Many years before, when God was giving Abraham the covenant of circumcision, He told Abraham that He would be the God of this special nation that would come through his seed (Gen. 17:7-8). As Moses started to Egypt to rescue the people, God called Israel His "firstborn son"*

*(Exod. 4:22-23). By New Testament days, the relationship is stated in these same warm terms: God is our Father, and we are His sons (see Rom. 8:15-17). At the very end of the New Testament, God is still speaking about "His people." They will be allowed to live with Him forever in heaven, His home (Rev. 21:3). What a blessing!*

## God commands Moses to return to Pharaoh (Exod. 6:10-13):

The Lord said to Moses, "Go to Pharaoh again and tell him that he is to release the children of Israel from his land."

Moses answered, "Look, the children of Israel will not listen to me, why will Pharaoh pay any attention to my clumsy speech?"

Nevertheless, God charged Moses and Aaron to present His demand to Pharaoh that he let the children of Israel go.

## Genealogy of Moses and Aaron (Exod. 6:14-27):

*Moses interrupts the narrative at this point to give us the lineage of himself and of Aaron, to tell who these men were and how they fit into the rest of the families of the Israelites. Look at the lineage long enough to see their family line, but do not forget the thread of the story.*

*"Fathers' houses" (treated as one term in the Hebrew) were the largest divisions of the tribes. To show the position of Moses and Aaron among the tribes, the reckoning starts with Reuben, then Simeon, and then gives the information about Levi and the family of Moses and Aaron.*

*It is not necessary to discuss the families of Reuben and Simeon to get the thread of the story here. We have included most of the facts in this passage that have bearing upon the chronology of the period. Learn these basic facts about the families of Moses and Aaron.*

Levi lived 137 years and he had three sons: Gershon, Kohath, and Merari. Gershon had Libni and Shimei. Kohath lived 133 years and had Amram, Izhar, Hebron, and Uzziel. Merari had two sons, Mahli and Mushi. These are the families of the Levites.

Amram, of the family of Kohath, took Jochebed his father's sister to be his wife, and she bore him Aaron and Moses (they also had a daughter named Miriam — see 2:4-8; 15:20). Amram lived 137 years. We have already learned that Moses had two sons: Gershom and Eliezer; therefore, his children are not described here.

Izhar had three sons, including Korah who later rebelled against the divinely appointed leadership of Moses and Aaron (Num. 16:1). Korah's sons, who did not die with their father (Num. 26:11), were Assir, Elkanah, and Abiasaph. These are the families of the Korahites.

Aaron took a woman named Elisheba for his wife. She was the daughter of Amminadab, the sister of Nahshon (the prince of Judah at the time of the Exodus). She bore Aaron four sons: Nadab and Abihu, Eleazar and Ithamar. Eleazar, who succeeded Aaron as high priest, took a wife of the daughters of Putiel, and she bore him Phinehas, who succeeded Eleazar as high priest.

*See the appendix concerning how long the Israelites were in the land of Egypt. A fuller description and explanation of the tribe of Levi and of the lineage of Moses is found there.*

## Aaron will speak for Moses (Exod. 6:28-7:7):

*The narrative resumes.* The Lord had told Moses and Aaron to go in before Pharaoh and tell him everything God had said. Moses replied, "I am such a clumsy speaker that Pharaoh will not listen to me."

## The Call of Moses

Jehovah said to Moses: "See, I have made you as God to Pharaoh, and Aaron will be your prophet. You will speak everything I have told you, and Aaron your brother will speak to Pharaoh so that he will let Israel go from his land. But I will harden Pharaoh's heart, and will multiply my signs and wonders in the land. Pharaoh will not listen, so I will lay my hand heavily upon Egypt and will bring out my hosts, my people, the sons of Israel, with great judgments. *Then the Egyptians will know that I am Jehovah, when I do these things."*

Moses and Aaron went to do as God had told them. Moses was 80 years old at the time, and Aaron was 83.

*Notice God's use of terms to describe His people here: "My hosts, my people, the sons of Israel..." There can be no doubt that God intends these people to be His in a special way. Observe how it comes to pass.*

### Moses and Aaron return to Pharaoh (Exod. 7:8-13):

God told Moses, "When Pharaoh asks to see a wonder, then you say to Aaron, 'Throw down your rod in front of Pharaoh, and it will become a serpent.'" Moses and Aaron did as they were told, and Aaron threw his rod down before Pharaoh, and it became a serpent.

Then Pharaoh called for his magicians, and they did a similar thing with their secret arts, because they cast down their rods, and they became serpents — but Aaron's rod swallowed up their rods. Pharaoh's heart was hardened so that he did not believe Moses and Aaron had any power beyond his magicians, and he refused to do what the Lord had said.

*Did the magicians of Egypt really turn their rods into serpents? It is not clear whether they did or not. Paul wrote to the Thessalonians of power and signs and wonders of falsehood. He called them "lying wonders" and "strong delusions" so that those who do not want to accept the truth may have lies to believe (2 Thess. 2:9-11). There is no denying the use of trickery and deceit by the servants of Satan. On the other hand, in the days of the New Testament, Satan had the miraculous power to possess men in a special way that went beyond his normal activity. So there is that faint possibility that there may have been men who had access to evil power in Moses' day, in order to show the contrast between Satan's power and God's power. Even if they were using some kind of arcane power, God showed that His power was far greater. He made a similar demonstration in the days of demon-possession, when the Son of God and His servants cast out the demons.*

*Ancient literature, however, tells of those in Egypt who were adept at snake-charming and boasted that they could turn snakes into sticks. The footnote for the word "magicians" is "soothsayer priests." In view of this information, it is much more likely that these were fakers, men who used their wiles to further their control over their people in the name of their false gods. What they claimed to be able to do by trickery, Aaron really did do by the power of God.*

*Another strong indication that these were fakers using tricks is that the magicians were the first of the Egyptians to say these acts came from Jehovah (see 8:19). Magicians using magical arts and trickery would be the first to recognize trickery in another. Instead, they saw true power and true miracles from Moses and Aaron, rather than trickery.*

# The Plagues
## (Exodus 7:14-12:36. 43-51; 13:1-16)



### Water to blood (Exod. 7:14-25):

Jehovah told Moses: "Pharaoh's heart is stubborn; he refuses to let the people go. Go to him in the morning as he goes out to the water, and stand by the river's edge to meet him. In your hand you will have the rod that was turned into a serpent. Say to him that Jehovah, the God of the Hebrews, has sent you to tell him, 'Let my people go so that they may worship me in the wilderness,' and he has not listened. Now this is what Jehovah says: '*By this you will know that I am Jehovah.* Look, I will strike the waters of the river with this rod in my hand, and they will be turned to blood. The fish in the river will die, and the river will become foul, and the Egyptians will find it repulsive to drink the water.'"

Then the Lord told Moses to tell Aaron, "Hold your rod out over the waters of Egypt, over their rivers, their canals, over their lagoons and ponds, that they all may become blood, all over the land of Egypt, both in vessels of wood and in vessels of stone."

Moses and Aaron did exactly as the Lord commanded. In the sight of Pharaoh and his servants, Aaron held up the rod, and all the waters in Egypt turned to blood. The fish in the river died, and the river became foul so that the Egyptians could not drink the water.

When the magicians did a similar thing with their secret arts, Pharaoh's heart was hardened, and he paid no heed to Moses and Aaron. He turned and went to his house and gave it no further thought. All the Egyptians had to dig wells near the river to find water to drink. This situation lasted for seven days.

*Notice that God tells Moses to take with him the rod that had been turned into a serpent. This is the same shepherd's rod that Moses had with him when God first appeared to him at the burning bush. God told him to take it with him to Egypt to use to show signs to Pharaoh and to the Israelites (4:2-4, 17, 20). Now it is the rod by which the plagues are brought upon the land. It is not that this particular rod has some magical power, but God has purposed to use this ordinary stick as a focus of His great power. This rod thus becomes a part of the specific directions Moses is required to follow in order for the various signs to take place.*

*Various authorities cite similar occurrences of the river turning red, saying that the plagues were extensions of natural phenomena, far beyond the point that they would be found normally. Apparently there were other times when the waters of the Nile turned red and the fish died, but it cannot be proven that there was any real similarity. Even the water in vessels and wells was affected this time. There is nothing gained by seeking the roots of the plagues in nature. Of course, rationalists would try to explain the plagues completely in such a manner in order to exclude any place for God. In our study, we need to emphasize exactly what the Bible emphasizes about them: they were chastisements which God was sending upon Pharaoh and Egypt. There is no reason to try to explain "how" God brought about each plague. Each one involved a miracle —and the very meaning of the word "miracle" means there is no physical, natural explanation for it.*

*It is proper, however, to point out that, in the plagues, God turned the things in which the Egyptians trusted into curses. Herodotus called Egypt the gift of the Nile. This plague turned the Nile River, which the Egyptians worshiped, into a foul river of death. One reason they worshiped their river is that, in this land of very rare rains, it was their primary source of water for all their needs, and therefore their source for sustaining life. Now it was a river of death.*

*Jehovah hardened Pharaoh's heart by presenting His demand, knowing that Pharaoh would refuse. The one who was truly responsible for hardening his heart was Pharaoh himself, because he is the one who made himself too stubborn to submit to God's command (7:13, 14, 22-23; 8:15, 19, 32; 9:7).*

## Frogs (Exod. 8:1-15):

The Lord told Moses: "Go to Pharaoh and tell him to listen to what the Lord says: 'Let my people go, that they may serve me. If you refuse to do as I say, I am going to smite your land with frogs. The river will swarm with frogs which will come up into your house, and into your bedroom, and upon your bed, and into the houses of all your servants, into your ovens, and your kneading troughs.'"

Pharaoh did not hearken, so God told Moses to have Aaron stretch forth his rod over the rivers, canals, and over the pools so that frogs would cover the land of Egypt. The Egyptian magicians did a similar thing with their enchantments and brought up more frogs upon the land.

Pharaoh called for Moses and Aaron and said: "Ask the Lord to take the frogs away from me and from my people, and I will let the people go, so that they may sacrifice to Him."

Moses said, "I will let you have the glory of telling the Lord when you wish the frogs to be destroyed. When do you want the Lord to destroy the frogs?"

Pharaoh replied, "Tomorrow."

Moses said, "It will be done as you have said *so that you may know that there is no God like Jehovah our God.* The frogs will depart from your servants and from your people and will remain in the river only."

So Moses cried unto the Lord, and Jehovah did as Moses asked. The frogs died in the houses, in the courts, and in the fields. The Egyptians gathered them in heaps, and the whole land smelled bad. But when Pharaoh saw that the frogs were gone, he changed his mind and did not let the people go.

*The contest between God on the one hand, and Pharaoh, his magicians, the gods of Egypt, and the Egyptian people on the other hand, gradually intensifies. So far, Pharaoh and his people have suffered only inconvenience, yet the hand of the Lord has been clearly revealed. Opportunity for obedience has been given. Watch the struggle intensify.*

*So far, the magicians are doing similar things with their enchantments, and could at least make it appear they could produce frogs or turn water to blood, but they could not use their enchantments to counter the plague. They could do nothing to make the frogs leave. It would have been a more impressive demonstration of their "power" if they could have undone the plague.*

*Even today, frogs abound in the land of Egypt. It takes very little imagination to think how annoying this plague would have been. Most scholars agree that these creatures were frogs as we know them and not some other kind of reptile. Unless there is clear evidence to the contrary, always take the English text literally when it uses terms such as these.*

*Notice that Pharaoh made a promise that he would let the people go if the plague were removed — but he broke that promise when the frogs were gone. Continue watching Pharaoh's responses to each plague.*

## Lice (Exod. 8:16-19):

The Lord told Moses: "Tell Aaron to hold out the staff and smite the dust of the earth, that it may become lice throughout all the land of Egypt." Aaron held out his rod and smote the dust of the earth, and there were lice upon the people and upon their animals all over the land.

This time the magicians were unable to bring lice with their enchantments, and they told Pharaoh: "This is the finger of God." But Pharaoh was stubborn and did not listen, just as God had warned.

*The older English translations (such as the KJV, ASV) use the word lice to describe the insects in this plague. Some of the newer translations (such as the NASV) use the word gnats. This is not a contradiction, but rather a difficulty in knowing exactly what the original word means. There were, of course, lice then just like the lice that exist today, but from the description it is quite possible that these insects were mosquitoes, biting gnats, or some similar insect. The original word meant a "biting insect," — with no further identification. But since we cannot know exactly which insect it was, use the terminology in your classroom that the Bible uses — it was a plague of lice, some kind of biting insect.*

*This episode points strongly to the idea that the magicians were not using real power, because if they were, why could that power call forth frogs but not lice? At first the magicians may have thought Moses and Aaron were also using trickery, but by this time the magicians were convinced that they were dealing, not with competing magicians, but with God Himself. They would have been the first to discover how a trick was done, if it were being accomplished by trickery; instead they are the first to know it was far beyond some magician's trick. Only divine power could accomplish such things.*

*The record tells of no warning to Pharaoh before this plague. He was warned before the water turned to blood, and before the frogs arrived, but then he made a promise that he would let the people go if the frogs left, and he did not keep his word. So the lice come. Neither is anything said about the end of this plague. The Bible does not tell how long it lasted, nor how it came to an end.*

## Flies (Exod. 8:20-32):

The Lord told Moses: "Get up early in the morning and meet Pharaoh. He will be coming to the river. Tell him that the Lord says: 'Let my people go, that they may serve me. Otherwise, I will send swarms of flies *(insects)* upon you, upon your household, upon your servants, and upon your people. The houses of Egypt, as well as the ground, will be full of swarms of flies. And I am going to separate between the land of Goshen, where my people dwell, and the rest of Egypt. There will be no flies in Goshen. *This way you will know that I am Jehovah in the midst of the earth.* I will make a distinction between my people and your people. This sign will be shown tomorrow.'" Jehovah did as He had said, and flies swarmed all over the land of Egypt, and the land was destroyed because of the swarms.

Pharaoh called Moses and Aaron and said, "Go sacrifice to your God in the land of Egypt."

Moses answered, "That won't work, because we will be sacrificing the abomination of Egypt to our God right in front of the Egyptians. Why, they would stone us! We must go three days' journey into the wilderness as Jehovah our God has commanded us."

Pharaoh replied, "Then I will let you go to sacrifice to your God in the wilderness, only don't go very far. Now ask God to get rid of these flies."

"Very well, I am going out of here, and I will ask God to take the swarms of flies away from you, from your servants, and from your people tomorrow. But you, Pharaoh, had better not lie any more about this matter of letting the people go to sacrifice to Jehovah."

Moses went out and asked the Lord, and the Lord did as Moses requested and removed the flies from Pharaoh and his people. But when Pharaoh saw that the flies were gone, he changed his mind and would not let the people go.

*Again, the exact insect under consideration is uncertain from the original language in the Bible text. There are many varieties of flies, some much more serious than others. There is the common housefly, which is a severe nuisance and is germ laden, but likely these were more severe than that. Houseflies might have covered the land, but they would not have destroyed it as verse 24 says these did. There are types, such as the horse fly and the yellow fly, that inflict painful bites. Then there are flies, such as the fruit fly, that can severely harm crops. The two most likely ideas are dog-flies (Keil) or beetles (Blatta orientalis, or kakerlaque, according to Pulpit Commentary). Use the terminology the Bible uses to describe the plague, but help your students see that we ourselves are aware of different kinds of flies.*

*This is the first plague that separated between the Egyptians and the Israelites. At first thought, one might marvel that God allowed His people to suffer the first three plagues, but let us look more closely:*

- *The first plagues did not threaten anyone's life or property (except the fish in the Nile river) so they did not do lasting harm to either the Egyptians or the Israelites.*
- *God's people needed the lessons about God's strength. It had been many, many years since the days when God conversed with Abraham, and these descendants of Abraham, Isaac, and Jacob have been living in the midst of Egyptian idolatry.*
- *God used the opportunity to teach His people some lessons by showing His ability to punish, and then continued to teach His might by showing He could punish the wicked and protect the righteous at the same time.*

*Various authorities have tried to guess what there was about the Israelite sacrifices that would have enraged the Egyptians. Here are some of the possibilities:*

- *Some say the Israelites would not observe the sacred rituals of the Egyptians. For example, Herodotus, the Greek historian, says that an ox could be sacrificed in Egypt if it were found to be clean — that is, totally white. One of the priests would carefully examine the ox, with the animal both standing and lying, to see if there were any black hairs on him. If there were so much as one, he was not clean. The priest inspected the tongue to make sure there were not certain signs present, and inspected the tail to be sure the hairs were arranged in the proper order (Stories From Herodotus, Alfred J. Church, pp. 118, 119). From this illustration it can be seen clearly that the Israelites might well have offered some bullock that was not entirely white, and that was not properly inspected by the priests of Egypt, and the wrath of the Egyptians would have been aroused.*

- *Others say that the abomination would consist of animals which the Egyptians considered sacred. This point comes nearer fitting Moses' statement because it is the thing sacrificed that is referred to as an abomination, not the way in which it would be done.*

*But whatever the objections were that the Egyptians might raise, Moses was on the scene and knew the situation —and the authorities of today who try to guess what those objections might be were not there, even though they are making educated guesses based upon records that have been found. Let it suffice to say that the correct way to offer these sacrifices to Jehovah would have angered the Egyptians. And, it must be remembered, God had commanded them to go three days' journey into the wilderness.*

*This is the second time that Pharaoh offers a compromise, or promises to let the people go —and the second time he breaks his word.*

## Murrain of cattle (Exod. 9:1-7):

The Lord told Moses to go before Pharaoh and tell him: "Hear what the God of the Hebrews says: 'Let my people go, that they may serve me. If you refuse to let them go, then I am going to afflict your livestock in the field: the horses, the donkeys, the camels, the herds, and the flocks. But I am going to make a distinction between the cattle of the Israelites and those of Egypt.'" Jehovah even gave the time when the murrain *(disease or epidemic)* would fall upon the animals: "Tomorrow Jehovah will do this thing in the land."

As predicted, the livestock of Egypt died, but in the land of Goshen, where the Israelites lived, not a single animal died. Pharaoh checked to see whether any Israelite livestock had died, but when he learned the Israelite cattle were safe, he still was stubborn and would not let the people go.

*There are descriptions of plagues or epidemics upon the animals of Egypt in the writings of various travelers even in recent times. The Bible does not say what kind of disease this was. The miraculous nature of it is shown by the extent, by the timing, and by the deliverance of the Israelite cattle from the plague.*

*Until now, the plagues have been inconveniences; severe, but still inconveniences. With this plague, the Egyptians suffer a dreadful loss, even though, since they did not live primarily upon the flesh of their animals, nothing vital has been touched. With each plague, Pharaoh has the option of stopping the chastisement God is administering, but his stubborn heart refuses to submit, even though he has accepted the idea that Jehovah is causing these things.*

## Boils (Exod. 9:8-12):

Jehovah said to Moses and Aaron: "Take handfuls of ashes from the furnace and let Moses throw it up toward heaven in the sight of Pharaoh. It will become fine dust over all the land of Egypt, and it will become boils breaking out in sores upon men and animals." They did exactly as God had said, and sores broke out all over the land on man and beast.

This time the magicians could not stand before Moses because they had boils. The boils were upon the magicians and upon all the Egyptians. But Jehovah hardened the heart of Pharaoh, and he refused to obey, just as God had warned Moses.

*The magicians could not even try to copy this plague, because they themselves were so badly affected by the boils.*

## Hail (Exod. 9:13-35):

God told Moses to get up early, go stand before Pharaoh, and tell him what Jehovah, the God of the Hebrews, says:

> Let my people go, that they may serve me. This time I going to strike your heart with my plagues, and I will send them upon your servants and upon your people *so that you will know that there is none like me in all the earth.* I could already have exerted my power and struck you and your people with disease and wiped you from the face of the earth. Instead, I have let you stand in order to show you my power and to exalt my name throughout all the earth. Do you still exalt yourself against my people? Tomorrow about this time I will cause it to rain hail such as has never fallen in Egypt from the day it was founded until now. Therefore you had better send people to hurry and get your cattle and whatever you have in the field under cover. Every man and every animal that is left in the open will be killed by the hail.

Everyone among the servants of Pharaoh who had learned to fear the word of God made his servants and his animals flee into shelters. Those who had no regard for God left their things in the field.

God told Moses, "Hold out your hand toward heaven that the hail may come upon man, upon the animals, and upon the plants in the field, throughout the land of Egypt."

Moses stretched his hand toward heaven, and Jehovah sent hail upon the land of Egypt. There was thunder and lightning with the hail, a very serious storm, such as had never been before. The hail struck, killing everything in the fields; even trees were broken. Only in the land of Goshen, where the Israelites were, there was no hail.

Pharaoh called for Moses and Aaron and said, "I have sinned this time. Jehovah is righteous, and I and my people are wicked. Please ask God to make the storm stop. There has been enough of these voices of God *(thunderings)* and hail. I will let you go, and you will stay no longer."

Moses answered, "As soon as I am gone out of the city, I will spread out my hands to Jehovah, and the thunder and hail will stop, *so that you may know the earth is the Lord's.* But as for you and your servants, I know that you do not yet fear the Lord."

The flax and the barley were destroyed by this storm, because the barley had already formed ears of grain, and the flax was in bloom. The wheat and spelt were not damaged because they had not developed their ears of grain yet.

Moses went out of the city and spread forth his hands to the Lord, and the thunder and hail ceased, and rain stopped pouring upon the earth. But when Pharaoh saw that the hail had stopped, he and his servants sinned even more and hardened their hearts. Pharaoh continued in his stubbornness and did not let the people go, as God had warned.

*A storm of this magnitude would have been frightening to people anywhere, but it would have been especially terrifying to the people of Egypt because it rained so rarely there. Egypt is surrounded by desert on three sides, with the fourth side reaching to the Mediterranean Sea. It almost never rains in the southern Nile Valley (the part called Upper Egypt), and there are only about eight inches of rain per year in the Delta located on the shores of the Mediterranean. In comparison, Alabama gets an average of about 50 inches of rain in a year.*

### You Shall Be My People

*By now, some of the Egyptian people are taking heed to Moses' word, and they took the precautions called for. First the magicians recognized the power came from God (8:19); now it is the officials of Pharaoh who hear the warning and take heed (9:20) —but Pharaoh himself is too stubborn to see the evidence before him. At the close of this plague of hail, the inspired historian says that Pharaoh sinned yet more, and hardened his heart, he and his servants (9:34). In the next plague, even the servants of Pharaoh beg him to give up his opposition to the will of God and let the Israelites go.*

*The spelt refers to millet, and, according to Herodotus, was the grain from which the Egyptians most commonly made their bread (Stories From Herodotus, p.117). Do you see the intensity of the plagues increasing? This plague has destroyed unprotected people, cattle, and crops. All of their crops are not yet gone, but there has been a major loss.*

## Locusts (Exod. 10:1-20):

Jehovah said to Moses, "Go in to Pharaoh, because I have made his heart stubborn, as well as the hearts of his servants, so that I may show these signs of mine among the Egyptians. I have done this that you may tell your son and your grandson what things I worked in Egypt, *so that you may know that I am Jehovah."*

Moses and Aaron went in before Pharaoh and said, "Hear what the Lord says:"

> How long are you going to refuse to listen to me? Let my people go so they can serve me. Otherwise, tomorrow I will bring locusts upon your land, and they will cover the face of the earth, so that you will not be able to see the ground. They will eat what is left growing after the hail storm, and they will strip the trees that grow in the field. Your houses will be filled, and the houses of your servants, because this will be a locust swarm such as neither you nor your ancestors have seen.

Having given this dire warning, Moses and Aaron turned and left Pharaoh's court.

The servants of Pharaoh said, "How long is this man going to be a trap to us? Let these people go so they can serve their God. Do you not understand that Egypt is destroyed?"

Under pressure, Pharaoh called Moses and Aaron back and said, "Go, serve Jehovah your God; but who is it that will go?"

Moses answered, "We will go with our young and with our old, with our sons and with our daughters, with our flocks and with our herds, because we must hold a feast unto Jehovah."

Pharaoh said, "May Jehovah cooperate with you as I plan to cooperate with you in letting all of you go! If you think I am going to do that, you are crazy. You are planning evil. I will not go along with it. You who are men go and serve Jehovah. That is what you want to do, isn't it?" Then Pharaoh ordered his servants to expel Moses and Aaron from his presence.

God said to Moses, "Stretch forth your hand over the land of Egypt to beckon the locusts so that they can come up to cover the land and eat every plant left by the hail."

Moses stretched out his rod over Egypt, and Jehovah made a wind blow from the east all that day and all that night. When morning came, the locusts came in with the wind from the east and covered the entire land of Egypt. It was a grievous plague; never before or after was there such a locust swarm. They covered the face of Egypt, and the land was darkened. The locusts ate every herb and all the fruit of the trees which the hail had left. Nothing green was left, either tree or plant of the field, through all the land of Egypt.

In haste Pharaoh called Moses and Aaron to him and said, "I have sinned against Jehovah your God, and against you. Forgive, I beg of you, my sins, and ask Jehovah, in my behalf, to please just take away this death and destruction from me."

Moses went out from Pharaoh and asked Jehovah to take away the swarm of locusts. Jehovah turned the wind so that a strong wind blew from the west and drove the locusts into the Red Sea; not one locust remained in the land of Egypt. Nevertheless, Jehovah hardened Pharaoh's heart, and he did not let the children of Israel go.

*The New American Standard Version adds the phrase, "how I made a mockery of the Egyptians," in 10:2. That is the significance of God's words here: "Tell your son and tell your grandson what I did to the Egyptians, tell them what I wrought upon Egypt, the signs I gave; tell them how completely I defeated them."*

*The text does not tell whether the locusts destroyed the crops in Goshen. It would be consistent for God to have spared them this time also, but the Israelites will soon be leaving the land, so the destruction of their crops would not affect them. It may be that their crops were destroyed also so that the whole land of Egypt would be barren when they finally let the Israelites leave.*

## Darkness (Exod. 10:21-27):

The Lord told Moses to hold out his hand toward heaven in order that darkness might be over all the land of Egypt, a darkness so great that men could feel it. Moses stretched out his hand, and for three days Egypt was covered by a thick darkness. For three days, the Egyptians did not see one another, and they could not carry on any activities, but the children of Israel had light in their dwellings.

Pharaoh called Moses and said, "Go and serve Jehovah; only leave your flocks and herds behind. You can even carry your children with you."

Moses said, "No. You must let us carry the sacrifices and burnt offerings we will need to sacrifice to Jehovah our God. Our livestock will have to go with us. Not a hoof shall be left behind when we go out to serve Jehovah, because we do not know what He will want us to sacrifice until we get there."

*The expression, "feel the darkness," is an hyperbole, an exaggeration for emphasis. The miracle stands upon its own strength. The darkness was a miracle. A sandstorm would have given the Israelites the same problem it gave the Egyptians. The light which the Israelites had, and the darkness the Egyptians had, were both of miraculous origin, because any normal darkness or light would have been shared by both. The Bible does not say what means God used to bring the darkness upon Egypt. Notice that there was no warning before this plague. Pharaoh has continued to make promises, and then break them.*

*Take time to notice all the promises or compromises Pharaoh has made during these first nine plagues:*

- *Frogs —He said pray to God to take away the frogs and I will let the people go to offer their sacrifices. The frogs left —and Pharaoh broke his promise (8:8, 15).*
- *Flies —He told them to sacrifice to their God right there in the land, but that would not work because the Israelites would be offering sacrifices that would have been an abomination to the Egyptians (8:25-27).*
- *Flies —After Moses rejected the compromise that they offer in the land, Pharaoh said he would let them go, but "not very far." But when the flies were gone, he broke his promise again (8:28-32).*
- *Hail —Pharaoh was frightened. He said, "I have sinned. Pray to the Lord...and I will let you go; you do not have to stay any longer." But when the plague was over, he broke his promise (9:27,34-35).*
- *Locusts —After being warned that locusts would come, Pharaoh's officials insisted that he let the people go, so he made this compromise: Let only the men go, leaving the wives and children behind. In this way*

*Pharaoh could be assured that the men would return. Moses refused to leave anyone or anything behind. Moses and Aaron were driven out of Pharaoh's presence in anger (10:7-11).*

- *Locusts —After the locusts came, Pharaoh said again, "I have sinned, please pray for me..." But when the locusts were gone he refused to let the people go (10:16-20).*
- *Darkness —Pharaoh said, "Go, take all your people with you, but leave your animals behind." Moses refused because they could not know specifically what Jehovah would require in their sacrifices until they were ready to offer them. Moses stated again that they would leave nothing behind — "not a hoof will be left behind." Pharaoh ordered them from his presence and threatened to kill them if he saw them again (10:24-29).*

# Death of the Firstborn and the Passover Feast
## (Exodus 10:28-12:36, 43-51; 13:1-16)

*Bible students outline portions of the Bible in different ways. Some make chapters 12 and 13 a unit dealing with the consecration of Israel as God's covenant nation. Others have a section consisting of 12:1-42, the institution of the Passover. We prefer to outline in such a way that the first Passover is studied in connection with the last plague. It is dealt with that way in the inspired record, and the Bible places heavy emphasis upon God's consecration of the firstborn of Israel to Himself, because He spared them when He destroyed the firstborn of Egypt. We wait until chapter 19 to study the consecration of the people as God's chosen nation.*

*But we also want to be able to look at the instructions for the last plague itself, and to see why the Israelites were to celebrate the event through all the years to come. So we are going to deal with the story of the first Passover by telling how they prepared for that night when all the firstborn of Egypt were killed, while their own firstborn were spared. Then we will see how Pharaoh and the Egyptians reacted to the plague. There are pauses in the narrative for a description of the rules and regulations by which the event was to be remembered throughout the generations to come (Exod. 12:14-20, 42-49; 13:3-10). We are including those rules and regulations in the chapter called "Be Ye Holy...," under "Special Times," and specifically under the heading of the Passover. Look into our companion book on the law (Jehovah's Covenant with Israel) for a more detailed study of the Passover.*

### Moses and Aaron warn Pharaoh of the last plague (Exod. 10:28-11:10):

When Moses refused Pharaoh's offer to let all the people go into the wilderness to worship the Lord, if they would leave their livestock behind, Pharaoh was very angry. He said, "Get out of my sight, and see to it that you never come here again, because if you do, you will die."

Now God had told Moses, "I will bring one more plague upon Pharaoh and upon Egypt. After that he will let you go, he will thrust you out of the country. Tell all the people to go to their neighbors, both men and women, and let them ask for jewels of silver, and jewels of gold." Jehovah caused the Egyptians to look favorably upon the Israelites, for Moses had gained great respect and stature among the Egyptians.

Moses answered Pharaoh: "You have said it well: I will not see your face again. This is what Jehovah says: 'About midnight I will go out into the midst of Egypt, and all the first-born sons in Egypt will die, from the first-born of Pharaoh to the first-born of the maid-servant behind the mill, and all the first-born of your livestock will die. There will be a great cry throughout the land of Egypt. But against the children of Israel, not even a dog will bark, *so that you may see how Jehovah makes a distinction* between the Egyptians and Israel.' Then all these servants of yours will come to me and bow down to me, saying, 'Get out, you and all your people with you,' and after that I will go out." Then in hot anger, Moses left Pharaoh.

Jehovah had told Moses: "Pharaoh will not do as I tell him, so that I will be able to show many of my wonders in the land of Egypt." Therefore, though Moses and Aaron did all of these wonders before Pharaoh, the Lord hardened Pharaoh's heart, and he would not let the children of Israel go.

*From the KJV it would appear that both male and female first-born were included in this warning, but the word in the original for first-born is masculine and, therefore, refers to each first-born male — here, in the plague itself, and in the description of the consecration of the firstborn to Jehovah.*

*Notice that the common Egyptian, and all of Pharaoh's servants, have learned great respect for this man Moses and for the people he represents. They will be ready to give whatever they have when the moment comes for the Israelites to ask for their possessions.*

## Preparation for the first Passover (Exod. 12:1-14, 21-28):

In preparation for this dramatic event, the Lord told Moses and Aaron:

> This month is to be regarded as the first month of your year from now on. Tell the children of Israel that, on the tenth day of this month, each man is to select a lamb and put that lamb up until the evening of the fourteenth day. Let there be one lamb per household, and if a household is too small for a lamb, then let it join with another household. The lamb shall be without blemish, a male a year old, either a lamb or a kid of the goats. Everyone is to kill his animal at sunset on the fourteenth day.
>
> Take the blood from the lamb and put it on the two side-posts and on the lintel of the door of the houses where the sacrifices will be eaten. The people are to eat the flesh that night, roasted over a fire, with unleavened bread and bitter herbs. Do not eat any of the lamb raw or boiled. The lamb is to be cooked whole, not cut apart. Do not let any of the lamb remain until the morning. Burn any part that is not eaten.
>
> Eat the sacrifice with your clothes girded up, ready to walk, with your shoes on, and your staff in your hand. Eat quickly: it is the Lord's passover. I will go through the land of Egypt in that same night, and I will destroy all the first-born in the land, both man and animals. I will hereby execute judgment upon the gods of Egypt. I am Jehovah.
>
> The blood will be a sign on the houses where you are, and when I see the blood, I will pass over you. No destructive plague will touch you when I strike the Egyptians. This day is therefore to be kept by you as a memorial throughout your generations.

Moses gave God's instructions to the people, both regarding the preparation for the feast, and regarding the putting of the blood on the doorposts and lintels of their houses. He told them that in this way God would see the blood, and the destroyer would not attack those in that house. Moses also said, "In time to come, when your children ask, 'What does this feast mean?' you tell them, 'It is the sacrifice of the Lord's Passover, to remember that He *passed over* the houses of the children of Israel in Egypt, when He destroyed the Egyptians and spared our homes.'"

When the children of Israel heard this message, they bowed down and worshiped the Lord, and they did exactly as they were told.

*Be sure to help students understand what the lintel of the door is: the part of the door casing which goes over the door. The doorposts are the side parts of the casing. Also be sure the significance of the name, Passover, is understood — that is, it is the feast to remember when God "passed over" their houses and spared their first-born.*

## The plague itself — Death of the first-born (Exod. 12:29-30):

**Memorize the Plagues:**
- **Water to Blood**
- **Frogs**
- **Lice**
- **Flies**
- **Murrain of Cattle**
- **Boils**
- **Hail**
- **Locusts**
- **Darkness**
- **Death of the Firstborn**

With all preparations having been made by the Israelites, about midnight, the Lord struck all of the first-born in Egypt, from the first-born of Pharaoh to the first-born of the prisoner in the dungeon, and all the first-born of the livestock. Pharaoh rose up that night, he and his servants, and all of the Egyptians. A great cry was heard throughout all the land, because there was not a house where there was not someone dead.

## The command to leave Egypt (Exod. 12:31-36):

Pharaoh called for Moses and Aaron in the night and told them: "Rise up, get out from among my people: serve Jehovah as you have said. Take your flocks and herds, as you have been saying, and be gone — and bless me also."

The other Egyptians were also eager to see the Israelites leave; they urged them to leave in haste, because they said, "Otherwise, we are all dead men." So they were quite willing to give the children of Israel virtually anything they asked for. As Moses had told them, the Israelites asked the Egyptians for jewels of silver, and jewels of gold, and clothes. The Lord had made the Egyptians look favorably upon the people of Israel. In a sense, therefore, Israel spoiled Egypt as if they had defeated them in battle and had taken their possessions.

The people were in such a hurry, they packed the dough that was mixed in their kneading troughs and carried it on their shoulders, wrapped up in their clothes. *(Bedouins are often seen carrying their possessions this way today.)*

*Look back to God's prediction to Abraham in Genesis 15:13-15. Do you see that things have worked out exactly the way God said they would?*
- *The Israelites have lived in a land not their own,*
- *They have served as slaves,*
- *That enslaving nation has been punished,*
- *And now the Israelites are leaving with great possessions.*

*We need to point out one more time, however, that it was not God's fault that Pharaoh was so stubborn. God knew what kind of man Pharaoh was, and God allowed him to come to the throne at this particular moment so that the Egyptians could be punished for the way they had treated the Israelites. God "hardened Pharaoh's heart" by putting demands before him that Pharaoh was too stubborn to obey. He did not take a good man and make him evil. Rather he allowed an evil man to come to the throne so that He could show His power over the strongest nation in existence at that time. God did not take away Pharaoh's ability to choose right or wrong.*

## The first-born belong to God (Exod. 13:1-2, 11-16):

After 430 years in Egypt *(see Appendix)* the children of Israel left their bondage behind them. Because God had purchased them unto Himself by His mighty deeds done in Egypt, He viewed them as His people. In particular, since He had destroyed the first-born of Egypt, and had spared the first-born of Israel, the first-born of Israel belonged to God in a special way. Therefore Moses told the people:

> When you arrive in the land which the Lord is giving to you, then you are to give to Him the first-born males of both animals and man. If it is a clean animal, it is to be sacrificed. If it is an unclean animal, such as a donkey, it may either be redeemed, or slain. It is not to be sacrificed, nor is it to be kept by the owner for his own profit unless it is redeemed. All first-born sons are to be redeemed.
>
> In time to come, when your sons ask you the meaning of this practice, tell them, "Jehovah brought us out from Egypt from our slavery. When Pharaoh resisted His efforts, Jehovah killed all the first-born males in the land of Egypt, both man and beast. Therefore I sacrifice to Jehovah every first-born male among my livestock, and the first-born among my sons I redeem." This practice will thus be an ever-present reminder of the time when Jehovah brought you out of Egypt.

*As we move forward in the narrative and into the instructions in the law of Moses, we will find out how they could redeem a firstborn child. All we need now is the information given here about the firstborn belonging to Jehovah. Do not forget this point. It will be very important in helping you understand later events.*

# *From Egypt to Mount Sinai*
## *(Exodus 12:37-19:2)*

Route of the Exodus —
From Egypt to Canaan

The Call of Moses
The Plagues

*From Egypt to Sinai
*Crossing the Red Sea
*The Journey South
*At Rephidim

Jehovah Makes a Covenant
More Time at Sinai
From Sinai to Kadesh
Wandering
The Plains of Moab
Moses' Speeches
Journey's End

## Crossing the Red Sea
### (Exodus 12:37-15:21)

### The exodus from Egypt (Exod. 12:37-42, 50-51):

The children of Israel gathered at Rameses *(Zoan or Tanis)* and traveled to Succoth. There were about 600,000 Israelite men with their families. A multitude of people *(a mixed multitude)* from various races and backgrounds went with the Israelites, along with flocks and herds and very many cattle. As they went along on their journey, they baked unleavened cakes of bread from the dough which they brought with them from Egypt. The bread was not leavened because they had been expelled from Egypt with such haste they did not have time to let the bread rise or to prepare other victuals.

*The leavening agent normally used in baking bread was sour-dough. Whatever the agent was, it had to be added early in the day and allowed to rise before time to cook it for the next meal. The significance of the unleavened bread is that they had to leave Egypt in such a hurry they did not have time to add their leavening to their dough, or for it to work, and therefore they baked it unleavened as they traveled along. They were to eat unleavened bread for seven days immediately following the Passover feast in order to remind them, through all generations, of the time when they left Egypt in haste and traveled toward the promised land. Those seven days were called the Feast of Unleavened Bread. Often the name of the one day feast of the Passover is used interchangeably with the name Feast of Unleavened Bread.*

*The identity of the "mixed multitude" who went out of Egypt with the Israelites is uncertain. There are two reasonable explanations. Either, or both, may be correct:*

- *Abraham, Isaac, and Jacob were very wealthy men with many servants (see Gen. 14:14). Jacob's servants traveled to Egypt with the family when they moved there in the days of Joseph but the count given includes only those in the direct blood line of Jacob (see Gen. 46:1-27; Exod. 1:1-5). Those servants would have lived in Goshen; they would have multiplied through the years; and they would have shared the same fate as the Israelites. Likely that is the group referred to here in this expression.*

- *There is the possibility that other Semitic people (those with similar ancestry to the Israelites) had also been living in Goshen during these years and had been sharing the same hardships.*

*Whoever they were, the "mixed multitude" now continues to share the fate of the Israelites as that condition greatly improves. There was plenty of mercy from God and plenty of land in Canaan for these additional people. Since they were all sharing the same conditions, these extra ones would now be worshipers of Jehovah and would be included in the covenant relationship with Him, and therefore, obligated to keep all the rules and rituals of the law of Moses.*

## God takes the Israelites by a surprising route (Exod. 13:17-14:4):

God chose not to take the people to the promised land by the way of the Philistines, that is, around the curve of the seacoast, although that was the nearest way to Canaan *(look on your map)*. He did not want to subject them immediately to the heavy fighting they would have to do if they went that way. Instead God led the people by the way of the Red Sea.

The Israelites moved from Succoth and encamped at Etham. The Lord went constantly before them in the daytime in a cloud shaped like a column or pillar, and at night in a pillar of fire. He was showing the direction they should go by His constant presence. Moses took the bones of Joseph with them, because Joseph had specifically sworn the children of Israel to do so when they left the land (Gen. 50:25).

The Lord said to Moses, "Tell the children of Israel to turn back and encamp by the sea. Pharaoh will say, 'They are confused and are trapped by the wilderness.' I will harden Pharaoh's heart, and he will come after them, and I will gain honor at the cost of Pharaoh and his army. *Then the Egyptians will know I am Jehovah.*" The Israelites did as the Lord commanded.

***Map assignment:*** *It is hopeless to think that we can be exact about the route of the Exodus. Different authorities give different routes. Some of them reflect respect for the Bible record; others completely disregard the facts given in the Bible. Be sure that, when you discuss the route, you honor the inspired record and not the uninspired speculations of men. The map we have included is as accurate as we know how to make it. But think about it: it is difficult to find the site of ancient cities, so think how much harder it would be to find a camping place where someone stayed for one night, or perhaps a few nights.*

*The exact point at which they crossed the Red Sea is unknown. It was somewhere at the very northern end of the Red Sea, probably at the northern tip of the Gulf of Suez as shown on this map, because they crossed into the Sinaitic Peninsula, not into the Arabian Desert, as they would have if they had crossed as far south as our map labels the Red Sea. Wherever they crossed, the water was too deep to wade, and a whole army could drown in it.*

*You should already have the land of Egypt and Goshen labeled on your map. Add:*

- *Rameses,*
- *Succoth,*
- *Etham,*
- *And their camping place on the northwestern edge of the Gulf of Suez.*

## Crossing the Red Sea (Exod. 14:5-31):

As soon as Pharaoh received word that the people were gone, he changed his mind and said, "What have we done, to let Israel go? Now we will not have them to serve us any more!" So he made ready his chariot and gathered a force of six hundred select chariots and their captains, plus all the other chariots of Egypt, his horsemen, and his army. At top speed, Pharaoh's army pursued Israel, overtaking them at their encampment by the Red Sea.

As the army of Egypt approached, the Israelites saw them coming, and they were terribly afraid. They cried out to the Lord, and, in terror, they said to Moses, "Did you think there were no graves in Egypt? Is that why you brought us out here to die? Isn't this what we tried to tell you in Egypt, when we said to leave us alone to serve the Egyptians? It would have been better to serve the Egyptians than to die in the wilderness."

Moses answered the people, "Do not be afraid. Stand still and see the salvation which the Lord is going to accomplish for you today. These Egyptians whom you see today, you will never see again. Jehovah is going to fight for you. Now keep quiet."

Jehovah answered Moses, "Why are you crying unto me? Tell the children of Israel to move forward. As for you, lift up your rod, and hold it in your hand out over the sea and divide it. The children of Israel are going to cross this sea on dry ground. Meanwhile, as for Me, I will harden the hearts of the Egyptians, and they will go into the sea after them. Then I will gain for myself honor upon Pharaoh and upon his army. In this way *the Egyptians will know that I am the Lord.*"

The angel of God, who normally went before Israel, moved from His position in front of the people and stationed Himself behind them, standing between the camp of Egypt and the camp of Israel. God caused darkness to be over the camp of the Egyptians, but there was light in the camp of the Israelites. Therefore, all night, neither camp approached the other.

Moses held his hand out over the Red Sea, and Jehovah caused the sea to be parted by a strong east wind that blew all night. The children of Israel proceeded to cross on dry ground while a wall of water stood on the right and on the left.

When morning came, and the Egyptians could see what had happened, they rose up and pursued the Israelites into the midst of the sea — their horses, their chariots, and their horsemen. The Lord looked down upon the Egyptian army through the pillar of fire and cloud, and He afflicted them: the wheels of their chariots came off *(were bound, swerved — the exact meaning of the original is uncertain)* so that the horses could hardly pull the chariots. The Egyptians said, "Let us run away from these Israelites because Jehovah is fighting for them against us." But it was too late.

Jehovah told Moses: "Hold your hand out over the sea so that the waters may come together upon the Egyptians — over their chariots and their horsemen."

When Moses did so, the mighty waters came crashing back together, even as the Egyptians were trying to flee, and the Lord destroyed the Egyptians in the midst of the sea. Not one of the mighty army was left. The Israelites saw the dead Egyptians lying on the seashore. The same waters that had been a wall of protection on either side of the Israelites were a wave of destruction to the Egyptians. When the Israelites saw the stupendous deed done by Jehovah, they feared Him, and they believed in Jehovah and in His servant Moses.

*As God is about to rescue the Israelites, notice that He gave each participant a task to do: the Israelites were to move forward — even though there was a sea of water directly in front of them. Moses was to hold a shepherd's rod out over the water. And, meanwhile, God was going to harden the hearts of the Egyptians — again, by putting a temptation in front of them that Jehovah knew they would fall for. When each did his part, the people would be rescued, a mighty miracle would be accomplished, and the Egyptian army would be destroyed — thus bringing great glory upon the name of Jehovah. Is that not the way God usually works? There is a task for each participant to play in order to receive His blessings. The Israelites often forgot their part of the equation. As we study their history, let us learn the lesson they often missed.*

## A song of triumph and gratitude (Exod. 15:1-21):

Moses and the children of Israel sang a song of celebration to Jehovah:

I will sing to the Lord because He has triumphed gloriously over the horse and his rider.
This is God, my father's God, and I will praise Him.
Jehovah is a great warrior.
Jehovah is His name.

Pharaoh's chariots and his army Jehovah has cast into the sea.
They stood no chance against the incomparable power of Jehovah.
By the breath of your nostrils you caused the waters to pile up.
The waves stood in a heap.
The enemy said, "I will pursue, I will overcome, I will do as I wish;
I will draw my sword and destroy them."
They sank as lead in the mighty waters.

Who is like you, O Jehovah, among the gods?
Who is like you, majestic in holiness,
Awesome in praises, working wonders?
You stretched out your hand, and they were swallowed up.
You rescued your people in mercy.
You have guided them to your holy habitation.

The other nations have heard, and now they tremble:
The residents of Philistia, the dukes of Edom, and the leaders of Moab.
Those who dwell in Canaan have no courage left at all.
They will be this way till your people pass over, O Jehovah,
Till you bring them into the place of your inheritance,
The place where you will dwell in the sanctuary you will establish.
Jehovah will reign forever!

Miriam the prophetess *(sister of Moses and Aaron)* took a timbrel in her hand, and all the women followed her with timbrels and with dances. They echoed the song which Moses sang:

Sing to the Lord, for He has won a great victory.
The horse and his rider He has cast into the sea.

*The timbrel is what we call a tambourine. The women were dancing in celebration of the occasion, an outpouring of joy and gratitude to God.*

# The Journey South
## (Exodus 15:22-16:36)

### The journey south in the wilderness (Exod. 15:22-27):

Moses led the children of Israel from the Red Sea into the Wilderness of Shur. They traveled three days' journey into the wilderness, and they found no water. With more than 600,000 men and their families, plus flocks and herds, and very much livestock, they were in trouble.

Finally they came to water, but it was so bitter they named it Marah *(bitter)*. The people murmured and complained about Moses' leadership, saying: "What are we going to drink?"

Moses appealed to Jehovah for help, and He showed Moses a tree to throw into the water. When Moses did as God had said, the waters were made sweet. There God made a rule and a promise for Israel: if they would be careful to follow what He told them, He would put none of the diseases common to Egypt upon them.

The people traveled on until they came to Elim where they found a sizable oasis with twelve springs of water and seventy palm trees. There they encamped for a while.

*God is teaching these people to depend upon Him. He led them across the Red Sea on dry land when their enemy was approaching. Now He has made water in the desert suitable to drink. He is teaching the very important lesson that, if they will obey Him, and depend upon Him, He will care for them in every circumstance that confronts them. He expresses the concept here by promising that none of the diseases that plagued the Egyptians will come upon them if they will be careful to obey Him and rely upon Him as they should.*

***Map assignment:*** *Label their camping places in the wilderness so far, and be sure you can tell the characteristics of the place or what has happened there.*

- *Wilderness of Shur*
- *Marah*
- *Elim*

### The Wilderness of Sin (Exod. 16:1-36):

Leaving the oasis at Elim, the children of Israel traveled farther south in the peninsula of Sinai until they came into an area called the Wilderness of Sin. *(The name is derived from Sinai. The word "Sin" has nothing to do with evil in this usage.)* It was the fifteenth day of the second month, which means it had been exactly one month since they left Egypt (see 12:6, 30).

***Map assignment:*** *Look at your maps. They have been traveling for a month, and if they had traveled directly toward Canaan, they would have been there — or very nearly there by now. Since they are just now complaining about food, it must be that during the time of the plagues they had prepared some things for food on their expected journey, but here they are in the wilderness, going in the opposite direction to Canaan, and their food is gone. Hunger would be a constant problem for any large group of people in this desert region. The Bible account freely concedes the difficulties of such a host of people finding enough to eat and drink in such a region, but it also explains that such problems could be overcome because God was with them.*

- *Label the whole peninsula of Sinai and the south-western portion the Wilderness of Sin.*

## From Egypt to Mount Sinai

The whole assembly complained against Moses and Aaron because they had no food. "We would rather have died by the Lord's hand while we were in Egypt. At least there we had our flesh-pots and ate all the bread we wanted. You have brought us out into this wilderness to starve us to death."

The Lord told Moses:

> I have heard the complaints of the children of Israel, and this is what I will do: I am going to rain bread from heaven, and every day the people will go out and gather that day's portion. I will use this opportunity to see whether they will obey me or not. On the sixth day, they will need to gather twice as much as on the other days and go ahead and prepare it.

Moses told Aaron, "Tell the whole congregation to come near before the Lord because He has heard your complaining." Therefore Moses and Aaron spoke to the people and said, "In the evening you *will know that the Lord has brought you out of the land of Egypt, and in the morning you will see His glory,* for He has heard your grumbling against Jehovah. For what are we, that you should grumble against us? Your complaining is not against us, but against the Lord. You will eat meat in the evening, and in the morning you will be filled with bread."

As Aaron told these things to the children of Israel, they looked toward the wilderness, and there was the glory of the Lord in the cloud. God confirmed what Moses and Aaron had just announced by repeating His message directly to the people: "At twilight you will eat meat, and in the morning you shall be filled with bread, and *you will know that I am the Lord your God.*"

As God had said, at evening, quails flew into the camp and covered the ground so that the people had meat to eat. In the morning the dew lay around the camp, and when it had evaporated, there were small, round white flakes all over the ground. When the people saw it, they asked one another: "Man hu" *(Hebrew for "What is it?")*, because they had never seen it before.

Moses told them, "It is the bread which the Lord your God has given you to eat. Now this is what God has commanded: you are to gather an omer *(just over two quarts)* for each member of your family." The Israelites did as Moses said, and measured the manna out with an omer so that the one who gathered a little too much had no excess, and the one who had gathered a little less had no lack.

Moses further instructed them, "Don't leave any of it until the next morning." But some paid no attention and left it overnight, and it bred worms and spoiled. Moses was very angry because of their refusal to do what they were told. Every morning they gathered the manna, and when the sun grew hot, the part that was left on the ground melted.

On the sixth day, when they measured the amount gathered, there was enough for two omers for each person. The leaders of the congregation came and told Moses.

He replied, "Jehovah has said that tomorrow is a solemn rest, a holy sabbath to the Lord. Go ahead and bake what you are going to bake, and boil the part you are going to boil. Then put aside what you do not use today for food tomorrow."

The people did as Moses said, and none of the food they had put aside spoiled. On the sabbath day, Moses said, "Eat what you have put aside for today because today is a sabbath to the Lord. Today you will not find any manna in the field. Six days you will gather it, but the seventh day is the sabbath. On that day there will be none."

Nevertheless, on the sabbath day, there were some who had not laid up manna, and they went out to gather it as usual and found none. About the disobedient ones, the Lord said, "How long will you refuse to keep my commandments and my laws? See that I have given you the sabbath; this is why you have been given twice as much manna on the sixth day. Let no man stir from his place on the seventh day." Therefore the people rested on the seventh day.

The children of Israel called their food manna. Its appearance was like the coriander seed, white, and the taste of it was like wafers made with honey.

Moses said, "The Lord has given us this command: 'Keep an omerful of manna throughout your generations, so that they can see the bread which I fed you in the wilderness, when I brought you out of the land of Egypt.'" So Moses took a pot and put an omerful of manna in it and put it up before the Lord to keep throughout the generations. As Jehovah commanded, Aaron put the pot of manna in the ark of the testimony.

The children of Israel ate the manna for forty years, until they came into the land of Canaan (Josh. 5:10-12).

*In the book of Deuteronomy, Moses reminded the people of how God had tested them during their time in the wilderness, in order to know what was in their hearts, to see if they would obey Him. Moses said God humbled them by letting them get hungry, and then by feeding them with a food never heard of before, so that they could learn that man's greatest need is not food, but obedience. Man does not live by bread alone — but by obedience to the laws which come from the mouth of God (Deut. 8:1-5).*

*The coriander seed was from a plant which grew in Canaan. The seed was pearl-shaped. The manna was small, round white flakes, and therefore, looked somewhat like the coriander seed.*

*Many scholars have attempted to explain that the manna was the "honey-sweet drippings from tamarisk trees whose bark is attacked by a minute insect found only in Sinai" (Keyes). This explanation is utterly fallacious for the following reasons:*

- *Moses had lived in this wilderness for forty years. The question, "what is it," would never have arisen, if the manna had been hardened gum or resin on the bark of tamarisk trees. Even if the people out of Egypt did not yet know what the hardened gum was, Moses could have quickly identified it for them.*
- *There would not have been enough tamarisk trees in all Sinai to have furnished food even once for such a multitude. As numerous scholars have pointed out: there is simply no way that the wilderness, by its natural resources, could have supported such a population. The Bible frankly acknowledges this and then explains that God miraculously sustained Israel.*
- *The theory that the manna was a gum from the local trees would not explain why the manna would ruin if kept over on any of the first five days of the week, but that which was kept over on the sixth day was fine on the seventh day.*
- *Neither does the theory explain how the tamarisk trees kept pace with the Israelites until they invaded Canaan — and then stopped just as they were ready to eat of the food from the land.*

*The only way to advance this or any other naturalistic explanation of the manna is to ignore the details given in the text. Be very careful as you read various commentaries or Bible atlases to be sure you are not led astray by their lack of faith.*

*The quail could have been a natural phenomenon which God made special use of at this time to feed His people. Each year, huge flocks of migrating quail would fly from Africa to Central Europe. After crossing the Gulf of Suez, they would drop to the ground exhausted. Until modern times they were gathered by Egyptians in large numbers, and the meat was dried and preserved. On this occasion, the quail were probably preserved, as they were about a year later (Num. 11:31-32). If the migrating quail came on this particular evening, it was the hand of God that made the timing work out just as He predicted. Of course, God could have caused a huge flock of quail to appear at this moment even if it were not the right time of year at all. We have no other information, and need no other. The people needed meat — and God provided for their need.*

*This is the first time in all Bible history that any mention is made about a sabbath day. Even here, only the barest information is included in the instructions. It is fairly common to refer to this time as "the trial sabbath." The specific laws will soon be given as part of the law of Moses. The rules included here are:*

- *It is the seventh day.*
- *There will be no manna that day. Eat the portion laid up on the sixth day.*
- *Remain in your places today. It is a day of rest.*

# At Rephidim
## (Exodus 17:1-19:2)

### Water from a rock (Exod. 17:1-7):

The children of Israel moved in stages from the Wilderness of Sin and came to Rephidim where they encamped. Again, they found themselves without water. The multitude contended with Moses, saying, "Give us water to drink."

Moses said, "Why do you quarrel with me? And why do you put Jehovah to the test?"

But the people continued to murmur: "Why did you bring us out of Egypt to kill us, and our children, and our cattle with thirst?"

Moses turned to God and said, "Lord, what shall I do? These people are almost ready to stone me."

The Lord told Moses, "Pass on before the people, and take with you the elders of Israel, and your rod, the one with which you smote the river *(the Nile)*, and go. I will stand before you there before the rock in Horeb. Strike the rock, and water will come forth, and the people will drink."

Moses did as God commanded, as the elders of Israel watched. Water gushed from the rock, and the children of Israel were able to drink. Moses called the name of the place Massah *(Contention)* and Meribah *(Testing)* because of the contentions of the children of Israel, and because they tested Jehovah, saying, "Is Jehovah among us or not?"

*Moses asked, "Why do you put Jehovah to the test?" and he called the place "Testing." What was the significance of that question and of that name? As the text first summarizes their contention against Moses for their lack of water it only includes their question about why he brought them out of Egypt. That question was totally inappropriate because their deliverance from Egypt was a rescue from deep trouble, not a forced exodus from a land of ease. But this contention had an another side that added to its seriousness: they were asking, "Is God among us or not?" <u>Is He among us</u>? — and yet they had seen every plague to force the Egyptians to release them; they had seen the Red Sea divide and then come back together to destroy their enemy; they had seen the waters of Marah made sweet; they had seen the quail come at the very moment they needed them; and every day they ate a miraculous bread that God provided. The question itself was an insult to God for all the care He was giving His people.*

## Battle with the Amalekites (Exod. 17:8-16):

While Israel was in Rephidim, the tribe of Amalek came and attacked them. According to Deuteronomy 25:17-19, they preyed upon the weak and the feeble on the outer fringes of the encampment. Moses commanded Joshua, saying, "Choose out men to fight Amalek. Tomorrow I will stand on top of the hill with the rod of God in my hand."

Joshua did as he was commanded and fought Amalek, while Moses went to the top of the hill, accompanied by Aaron and Hur. As long as Moses held the rod of God aloft, Israel prevailed, but when he grew tired and lowered the rod, Amalek prevailed. Therefore, Aaron and Hur seated Moses on a rock and stood one on either side of him and held his arms up until the sun went down. Thus Joshua and the people defeated Amalek with the sword.

Jehovah told Moses: "Write this for a memorial and rehearse it in the ears of Joshua: 'Someday I will completely blot out the remembrance of Amalek from under heaven.'" Moses built an altar there and called it Jehovah-nissi *(Jehovah is my banner)*, and He said, "Jehovah has sworn: He will have war with Amalek from generation to generation."

*These people had been raised as slaves, not fighters. Therefore God chose a visible way to defend His people and to help them fight their battle on this day. Moses was on a mountain overlooking the battlefield, with his rod held above his head. That means each soldier had the opportunity of looking to be reassured that God was still helping all during the battle. God was in the process of teaching these people to rely upon Him in their times of need — whatever that need was.*

*This is the first time we meet the young man Joshua. Watch as we see his name more and more.*

*Remember this decree from God about the Amalekites. The day will come when He will destroy them for their actions, but it will be a long time after this. See 1 Samuel 15 for the fulfillment of this prophecy.*

## Visit of Jethro (Exod. 18:1-12):

Jethro, the priest of Midian, and the father-in-law of Moses, came to visit Moses, and to bring his wife Zipporah and his sons to him. Jethro had heard what God had done for Moses and for Israel in bringing them out of the land of Egypt.

Moses' sons were Gershom and Eliezer. When his first son was born, Moses named him Gershom *(foreigner)* because, as he said, "I have been a sojourner in a foreign land." He named his second son Eliezer *(God of my help)* because he said, "The God of my father came to my aid, and delivered me from the sword of Pharaoh."

When Moses learned that Jethro was coming, he went out to meet him, bowed before him, and kissed him. They asked of each other's welfare and then entered the tent. Moses told Jethro all about what Jehovah had done for the Israelites, and how He had devastated Egypt. He also told him of the trouble and suffering Israel had endured on their journey and how Jehovah had come to their rescue.

Jethro rejoiced at all the good things Jehovah had done and said, "Blessed be Jehovah because of all the wonderful things He has done for Israel in delivering them from Egypt. Now I know that Jehovah is greater than all gods. It was proven when they dealt proudly against Him." Jethro offered a burnt offering and other sacrifices to God, and Aaron and all the elders of Israel came to participate in the meal that accompanied the sacrifices. Thus Jethro was recognized by Moses and Aaron and the elders as a true priest of God, just as Melchizedek had been in the days of Abraham (see Gen. 14:18-20).

## Jethro makes a suggestion (Exod. 18:13-27):

The next day Moses took up his heavy load of work again, and Jethro observed. Every minute, from first light until dark, people came to Moses with their problems. Jethro, being a leader himself, was appalled and said, "What do you call yourself doing? Why are you dealing with these people by yourself all day long?"

Moses replied, "It is because the people come to me to ask what God says. When they have a problem, they come to me, and I settle their disputes, and let them know what God says."

Moses' father-in-law said, "It is not going to work. You will wear yourself out and the people as well, because this is too big a job for you to handle alone. Listen to me and let me give you some advice about how you can continue to intercede between the people and God. You will continue to teach them God's statutes and laws, but you need to choose from among the people able men who fear God, honest men who despise bribes, and put them over thousands, hundreds, fifties, and so forth. Most of the time they will judge the people. Then they can bring only the hardest matters to you. In this way, if God approves, you will be able to do your task, and the people will not go away disgruntled."

Moses took the advice of Jethro and appointed men to judge the people in lesser matters, but the important questions were still brought to Moses. Then Moses bade his father-in-law goodbye and Jethro returned to his own home.

**Memorize the route of the exodus:**

**From Egypt to Sinai:**
- **Rameses - Starting point**
- **Succoth**
- **Etham**
- **Red Sea:**
  - **People murmured**
  - **Crossed on dry land**
  - **Egyptian army drowned**
- **Marah:**
  - **People murmured**
  - **Water bitter**
- **Elim:**
  - **12 springs of water**
- **Wilderness of Sin:**
  - **Murmuring**
  - **Quail in evening**
  - **Manna began**
  - **Test Sabbath**
- **Rephidim:**
  - **People murmured**
  - **Water from rock**
  - **Battle with Amalekites**
  - **Jethro visits**
- **Mount Sinai**

## Israel arrives at Mount Sinai (Exod. 19:1-2):

In the third month after their departure from Egypt, the children of Israel came into the wilderness of Sinai and encamped in front of Mount Sinai. Remember that the Lord had promised Moses that He would bring the people to that spot when He first talked to him from the burning bush (3:12). And now they have arrived in fulfillment of that promise.

***Map assignment:*** *Be sure you have labeled all the places the Israelites have camped on this part of their journey, from Rameses to Mount Sinai. Begin memorizing the list and remember what happened at each of the main places.*

***Chronology note:***

*It is a little difficult to tell whether 19:1 is saying the Israelites had been out of Egypt a full three months by the time they arrived at Mount Sinai, or if it is now into the third month. They left Egypt on the fifteenth day of the first month (12:6, 31-32), arrived in the Wilderness of Sin on the fifteenth day of the second month (16:1), and have now arrived at Sinai "in the third month." The point is not of great significance because the time difference would be only a few days or weeks.*

*Note the times when the Israelites murmured:*

- *They murmured when they reached the Red Sea and saw Pharaoh's army behind them.*
- *They murmured when they reached Marah and the water was bitter.*
- *They murmured when their food was gone by the time they got to the Wilderness of Sin.*
- *They murmured when they found no water at Rephidim.*

*Their faith needed time to grow, they needed time to learn to rely upon Jehovah to care for them when they were in need — but continue to watch their history to see if they learn the lesson. The murmurings do not stop. The people never learn to rely upon Jehovah. Let us learn the lessons they needed to learn from their mistakes.*

# *Jehovah Makes a Covenant*

## *(Exodus 19:1-24:18; 32:1-34:35)*

*Our organization of the text in this section is designed to emphasize that Jehovah was making a covenant with the Israelites. This is one of the most important sections of the Pentateuch in order to help you understand the whole law of Moses, and through it, to understand the rest of the entire Bible. It is necessary to see exactly what is happening in chapters 19-24 and then in chapters 32-34.*



*As we move forward in the study, observe the following very important points in Exodus 19-24, and then in 32-34:*

- *God offers to make a covenant with the Israelites (19:3-6).*
- *They want the covenant and promise to keep all the commandments that God will give (19:7-8).*
- *God speaks aloud to the multitude, giving them the basic rules (the constitution, as it were) that the rest of the law will be based upon (20:1-17).*
- *After He has spoken what we call the ten commandments, but before He finishes giving the rest of the basic rules He wants to include in this covenant, the people ask that Moses talk with God and then report the information to them (20:18-21).*
  - *They promise to keep everything commanded, whether they have heard God speak the commandment aloud or have heard it from Moses' lips (20:19).*
- *So God continues His instructions to Moses, who in turn writes down the portion found in chapters 20 through 23.*
- *By then God was ready to finalize this covenant, and He and the people ratify the covenant (24:1-11).*
- *Less than six weeks later:*
  - *The people sin by making a golden calf (32:1-6). They have broken their covenant with God (32:15-20).*
  - *God is ready to destroy them; they are no longer His people (32:7-10).*
  - *Moses intercedes (32:11-14, 30-35).*
  - *God says He will send the people to the land, but that He will no longer be in their midst (33:1-6).*
  - *Moses intercedes again, asking God to please go with them, to pardon their iniquity (33:12-16; 34:8-9).*
  - *God renews His covenant (34:10).*

*As you study the section, look back often to this overview of these eight chapters (19-24 and 32-34), so that you can see a clear picture of exactly what is happening as each event takes place. It is very important to see that this original covenant that God was offering the people, and that they accepted, was based upon their complete obedience to His commandments. Be sure your students see the point. Look at the basic rules included in this section, but do not bog down in discussing them lest you lose the overall picture. Wait until a study of the main portion of the law before discussing the details.*

# The Covenant is Offered

## (Exodus 19:1-23:33)

### Jehovah offers to make a covenant with Israel (Exod. 19:1-8):

After the Israelites arrived at Sinai and encamped in front of the mount, Moses went to God by approaching the mountain. God called to him, saying:

> This is what I want you to tell Israel: "You saw what I did to the Egyptians. You also see how I have carried you on eagles' wings, and have brought you to myself. Now this is my offer: If you will truly obey my voice and keep my agreement, then you will be my own special people out of all the earth. All the earth belongs to me, but you will belong to me in a special way: you will be to me a kingdom of priests and a holy nation."
>
> This is the message I want you to give to the children of Israel.

Moses returned from the mount, called the elders of the people together, and presented to them what Jehovah had offered. When the message was conveyed to the people they said, "We will do *everything* Jehovah commands." So Moses reported to the Lord what the people had said.

*Understand the points God made in His offer in 19:5-6:*

- *The offer depended upon real, actual obedience, not lip service: "If you will truly obey my voice..."*
- *The opportunity God was offering was a particular way of life, a character God wanted for His people.*
  - *No one can know that life and character without being shown it and taught it,*
  - *Neither can anyone have that life and character without imitating what is shown, or obeying what is taught.*
- *God said that, though the whole earth was His, Israel would be His in a special sense.*
  - *They would be a unique people; unique because, of all the nations, they would be God's special people —a holy people, one set apart.*
  - *The other citizens of earth were God's creatures, but the Israelites would be God's children.*
- *Though the terms of God's covenants with His people has changed with each dispensation, He has always wanted this kind of relationship. The relationship is expressed throughout the Bible as, "I will be your God and ye shall be my people" —or in similar expressions.*
  - *Peter's statement that Christians are to be a "chosen generation, a royal priesthood, an holy nation, peculiar people" corresponds to this point (1 Peter 2:9). Christians are those who have accepted the new covenant offered by Christ.*

- *Those who reach the "holy city, the new Jerusalem" will be His people, and God will dwell among them (Rev. 21:3).*
- *A kingdom of priests and a holy nation: what did God mean by these expressions?*
  - *A kingdom of priests refers to a people under God's direct rule, a people who would present their lives as a holy service unto the Lord (see Rom. 12:1-2).*
  - *They would be a nation characterized by holiness. They would be a special people, one set apart to live by imitating the characteristics of God Himself.*

*This was God's great plan for Israel. What a blessing! It is what God has had in mind for this people since He first promised to make Abraham's descendants into a great nation. Look back to Genesis 17:7-8 and to Exodus 6:7 to see that this was His plan.*

## The people prepare for God to speak to them (Exod. 19:9-25):

Jehovah said to Moses, "I am coming to you in a thick cloud so that the people can hear when I speak with you and may believe you always." Moses reported to the people every word Jehovah said.

The Lord also said, "Go to the people and tell them to prepare themselves for my coming. Let them spend today and tomorrow getting ready. Let them wash their clothes, and let the men refrain from having sexual relations with their wives. On the third day I will come down upon Mount Sinai in such a way that everyone will be able to see. Tell the people to be careful not to go up into the mountain. Whoever touches the mountain is to be put to death, whether man or animal. Do not touch them when you put them to death; stone them or shoot them with an arrow. Then, when there is a long blast from the ram's horn, they shall draw closer to the mount — still being very careful not to come too close or to touch it."

Sure enough, on the third day, when morning came, there was an awesome sight: thunder rumbled, lightning flashed, and there was a thick cloud upon the mountain. There was also the sound of a very loud trumpet blast. Everyone in camp was terrified.

At the sound of the trumpet blast, the signal God had given, Moses brought the people out of the camp to meet God. They stood before the foot of the mountain. As they watched, the entire mountain smoked because Jehovah descended in fire, and the smoke boiled up like the smoke of a furnace, and the whole multitude quaked greatly. The sound of the trumpet grew louder. Moses spoke, and God answered him.

Now that Jehovah had come down upon the mountain, He called Moses up to meet Him. Jehovah said, "Go down and warn the people, lest they charge forward to gaze upon me and perish. Also let the priests who serve me prepare themselves lest I break forth upon them."

Moses answered, "The people cannot come up, because we have set a boundary that cannot be crossed, just as you commanded us."

Jehovah replied, "Go down and warn them exactly as I say. Then you and Aaron come up here, but do not let the priests or the people break through to come up here, lest I destroy them." So Moses went down and warned the people again, telling them exactly what God had said.

## God gives the Ten Commandments (Exod. 20:1-17):

Then God spoke the following words:

> You shall have no other gods besides me.
>
> You shall not make idols, or any likeness of anything in the sky, or on the earth, or in the water. Do not bow down to them or serve them, because I, the Lord your God, am a jealous God. I will

bring the consequences of the iniquity of the fathers upon the children as far as the third and fourth generation of them that hate me and show mercy to thousands of generations of them that love me.

Do not use the name of Jehovah your God for profane and empty purposes. Jehovah will consider the one who does so guilty.

**Memorize the ten commandments:**

- **Thou shalt have no other gods before me.**
- **Thou shalt not make unto thee any graven image.**
- **Thou shall not take the name of the Lord thy God in vain.**
- **Remember the sabbath day to keep it holy.**
- **Honor thy father and thy mother.**
- **Thou shall not kill.**
- **Thou shall not commit adultery.**
- **Thou shall not steal.**
- **Thou shall not bear false witness.**
- **Thou shall not covet anything that is thy neighbor's.**

Remember the sabbath day to keep it holy. You are to work six days, but the seventh day is a sabbath to Jehovah. On that day you are to do no work: no one in your family, your slaves, visitors among you, nor even your animals. God has chosen this day because in six days He created the heavens and the earth and everything in them. Then He rested on the seventh day. Therefore He blessed the sabbath day and made it holy.

Honor your father and mother so that you may dwell in the land that God is giving you for a long time.

You shall not murder.

You shall not commit adultery.

You shall not steal.

You shall not give false testimony or make false charges against your neighbor.

Do not lust after what belongs to your neighbor: his house, his wife, his servants, his ox, or his donkey, or anything he has.

## The reaction of the people to God's appearance (Exod. 20:18-21):

When the people saw the lightning and heard the thunder, when they heard the sound of the trumpet, and when they saw Mount Sinai smoking, and then heard the powerful voice of Jehovah speaking, they were very afraid and moved way back. They said to Moses, "You speak to us, and we will listen, but don't let God speak to us anymore, lest we die."

"Don't be afraid," Moses replied, "because God has come to put you to the test so that you may have respect and awe *(fear)*for Him so that you will not sin." But the people were still afraid and continued to stand way back, while Moses approached the thick darkness where God was.

As Moses tells about this moment in the book of Deuteronomy, he adds these additional details (Deut. 5:23-29). The leaders of the people came, saying, "The Lord has shown us His glory and majesty, and we have heard His voice from the fire. Today we have seen that a man can live even if God speaks with him. But now, why should we die? This great fire will destroy us if we hear His voice any longer, for what mortal man can survive what we have heard and seen today? You go near to God and listen to all He has to say; then tell us, and we promise we will listen and obey."

God heard them and He told Moses: "I have heard everything they have said, and what they have said is good. Oh, that their hearts would be inclined to fear me and to keep all my commandments always, so that it might go well with them and with their children forever!"

## Further ordinances of the Lord (Exod. 20:22-23:33):

*Many laws were added to these first ones, but these laws in chapters 20-23 were the preliminary commandments that the children of Israel promised to keep. They are a cross-section of laws dealing with all areas of life. All commandments in the law are based upon the ten commandments. Therefore the ten commandments are referred to as the Lord's covenant (Deut. 4:13; 1 Kings 8:21), as the tablets of the testimony (Exod. 32:15), and as the tables of the covenant (Heb. 9:4). We group and summarize the laws given in chapters 21-23 in order to show them as concisely as possible.*

*Even if you, the teacher, decide to look at these commandments in a little more detail, please wait until after you have shown how this section (chapters 20-23) fits into the making of Jehovah's covenant with Israel. Its significance is this: When Jehovah proposed this covenant, He said, "If you will obey my voice..." These commandments are a cross section of the law they must obey (24:3, 7). These laws are the terms of the covenant.*

The Lord said to Moses, "This is what you are to say to the children of Israel:"

- You yourselves have seen that I have talked with you from heaven.
  - You shall have no other god in addition to me: gods of silver, or gods of gold.
  - When you sacrifice your burnt offerings and peace offerings to me:
    - You will do so upon an altar of earth.
    - You will sacrifice in the place I appoint.
    - If you make your altar of stone, do not use hewn stones, because when you use a tool upon it, it is polluted.
    - Neither do I want you to go up steps to my altar because I do not want your nakedness to be uncovered upon it.
- If you buy a fellow-Hebrew as a slave:
  - He is to serve you for six years, and then go free in the seventh year.
    - If he comes alone, he goes free alone.
    - If he has a wife when he comes, then she is to be released at the same time.
    - If the master has given him a wife during his time of service:
      - Then only the man goes free;
      - The wife and any children remain with the master.
    - The man may choose to stay with his master and his family by stating his decision to do so.
      - His master will then take him before the judges,
      - And pierce his ear as a sign of his voluntary slavery.
  - If, however, the slave is a Hebrew girl:
    - She is to be treated as a servant wife.
    - If the master is not pleased with her, he must let her be redeemed by her family.
      - He has no right to sell her to foreigners.
    - If he gives her to his son, he is to treat her as a daughter.
    - If he marries another woman:
      - He is not to deprive this first one of her needs or privileges.
      - If he deprives her, she is to go free.
- Laws dealing with personal injuries:
  - If one commits murder, he is to put to death.
    - If he kills accidentally, he is to flee to a place of safety that God will designate.
    - If he has killed deliberately, there is no appeal. He is to be put to death.

        - Anyone who curses his parents or attacks one of them is to be put to death.
        - Anyone who kidnaps another is to be put to death.
        - If one injures another in a fight:
            - He is to be responsible for the other's loss of time.
            - He must see that he is completely healed.
        - If a man beats his slave:
            - So that he dies, the master is to be punished.
            - If the slave is all right after a day or two, the master is not to be punished, because the slave was his own property.
            - If, in punishing his servant, the master knocks out an eye or a tooth, the servant is to go free to compensate for the loss.
        - If fighting men injure a pregnant woman, and cause her baby to be born prematurely, the punishment will be based on how serious the results are.
            - If there is no permanent harm to mother or baby, then the offender is to pay whatever fine the husband demands.
            - But if there is loss of life or other serious injury *(of mother or baby)*, then it is to be life for life, foot for foot, burn for burn, wound for wound, bruise for bruise.
        - If by one person's negligence, another is injured:
            - The negligent one must be punished according to the severity of the injury. For example:
                - If a bull gores someone to death:
                    - The bull is to be killed and the meat not eaten.
                    - But if it had been known to gore, and had not been kept up:
                        - The owner will be held responsible for the death and is to be put to death also,
                        - Unless a specific redemption fee is set for him to pay to the family.
                    - If the ox gores another man's slave, the owner shall pay the master thirty shekels of silver, and the ox must be stoned.
                - If a neighbor's animal:
                    - Falls into a ditch you have dug, and dies, then you pay for the animal, and the dead animal is yours.
                - If your animal kills your neighbor's animal, sell the living animal and split the money.
                - But if your animal was known to be dangerous and it kills your neighbor's animal, your animal replaces his, and the dead animal is yours.
    - Laws concerning the protection of property:
        - If a man steals an ox or a sheep and kills it or sells it:
            - He must repay five head of cattle for the ox, or four sheep for the sheep.
            - If he still has the animal when he is caught, he must pay back double.
        - A thief must make restitution: If he has nothing, he must be sold to pay for his theft.
        - If a thief is killed in the act of robbery:
            - The defender is not counted guilty of murder.
            - But if it is after sunrise, the defender is counted guilty if he kills to protect his property.
        - If by one person's negligence another person's property is damaged, the one responsible must pay for the loss.
            - If your animal eats someone's crop, then you repay with the best from your field.
            - If you set a fire to burn thorn bushes, and it burns another's property, then you pay for the loss.
            - If you have been given money to guard:

        - And it is stolen, then the thief must be found and forced to pay double,
        - Or you must go before the authorities and prove it was not your negligence that caused it to be stolen.
    - If an animal has been left in your care, and it dies:
        - You must prove before the authorities that it was not due to your mistreatment or negligence.
        - If negligence is proven, then the one responsible must pay.
    - If you have borrowed an animal from a neighbor, and it is injured or dies:
        - You must make full restitution,
        - Unless the owner was present; then it was counted as a hired animal.
- Laws concerning social responsibility:
    - If a man seduces a virgin not engaged to be married:
        - He must pay the price set for a bride and take her for his wife.
        - If her father refuses for him to marry her, he still must pay the price for a bride.
- Miscellaneous capital offenses — penalty is death:
    - Do not let a witch live.
    - Anyone having sexual relationship with an animal must die.
    - Anyone who sacrifices to a false god must die.
- Treat others fairly:
    - Do not mistreat a foreigner, for you were foreigners in Egypt.
    - Do not mistreat a widow or orphan, or your own wives will become widows and your children fatherless.
    - If you lend money to one of your own people:
        - Charge him no interest.
        - If you take his cloak as pledge, return it before sunset because he may need it to use as cover for the night.
- Do not blaspheme God or curse the ruler of your people.
- Do not withhold the offerings due God from your crops.
- Give all firstborn unto the Lord.
- You are to be a holy people: therefore do not eat meat torn by wild beasts; throw it to the dogs.
- Laws concerning justice and mercy:
    - Do not give false testimony.
    - Do not follow a crowd to do wrong.
    - Do not pervert justice by siding with the crowd.
    - Do not show favoritism or deny justice to the poor man in his lawsuits.
    - Have nothing to do with a false charge.
    - Do not put an innocent person to death.
    - If you find an animal lost or in trouble:
        - Return the animal or help it bear its load,
        - Even if it belongs to someone you hate.
    - Do not accept a bribe, because a bribe blinds you to justice.
    - Do not oppress an alien; you know how it feels to be aliens, because that is what you were in Egypt.
- Sabbath laws:
    - For six years you are to work your fields as usual:
        - But during the seventh year, let your land lie fallow and unused.

    - Let the poor among you, and the animals, eat whatever grows voluntarily.
  - Do your work in six days:
    - But on the seventh day do not work.
    - Let your animals rest that day and your slaves and servants also.
- Be careful to do all that God has said.
  - Do not let the names of other gods even be heard on your lips.
- Three times a year all the men are to appear before the Lord to celebrate a feast unto Him.
  - Do not come before the Lord empty-handed.
  - Feast of Unleavened Bread:
    - For seven days eat bread made without yeast as you have been commanded.
    - Observe this feast in the month Abib because this is when you came out of Egypt.
  - Feast of Harvest: Bring the first-fruits of your crops to the Lord.
  - Feast of Ingathering: Celebrate this feast at the end of your harvest, when you have gathered your crops for the year.
- Additional rules about sacrifices:
  - Do not offer the blood of a sacrifice with anything containing yeast.
  - The fat from the offerings must not be kept until morning.
  - Bring the best of your first-fruits to the Lord.
  - Do not cook a young goat in its mother's milk.
- God's angel is to go before you to guard you and to bring you to the land God has prepared for you.
  - He will bring you into the land of Canaan and He will wipe out the enemies before you.
  - God will send His terror before you and will throw into confusion all the people of the land.
  - They will turn their backs and run.
  - God will send the hornet to drive them out:
    - But He will not destroy them all at once, lest the land become desolate and be overrun by wild animals.
    - He will drive them out little by little until you have had time to increase enough to take possession of the land.
    - But be assured that He will drive them out, and that He will establish your borders from the Red Sea to the Sea of the Philistines, from the desert to the River Euphrates.
  - In order for God to carry out all these promises, you must:
    - Pay attention to His angel and not rebel against Him.
    - Do not bow down to the gods you find in the land or follow their practices.
    - Demolish every idol and smash every sacred stone.
    - Worship only the Lord your God:
      - His blessings will be upon you.
      - You will not face diseases or be barren.
      - You will have the blessing of a full life span.
    - Do not make a covenant with any of the people of the land nor with their gods.
      - Do not let the people live in your land, or they will cause you to sin against God.
      - Their gods will certainly prove to be a snare to you.

# The Covenant is Ratified
## (Exodus 24:1-18)

When these ordinances had been given, God said, "Moses, I want you and Aaron, Nadab and Abihu, and seventy of the elders of Israel to come to me. All of you but Moses will stand and worship me at a distance. Neither shall the people come up with him. Moses alone will come near me." *(This command was given at this point, but was actually carried out after the next events took place with all the people present.)*

Moses came back and told the people what the Lord had said, and he told them all the commandments and ordinances God had given *(chapters 21-23)*. The people replied with one voice, "We will do everything God has said." *(Note that this was the second time the people have agreed to keep all that God said — 19:8; 24:3.)*

Moses wrote all the words Jehovah had given *(chapters 20-23)*. Early the next morning, he arose and built an altar beneath the mountain and set up twelve pillars to represent the twelve sons of Israel. He sent young men of the children of Israel to offer burnt offerings and to sacrifice peace offerings of oxen to the Lord. *(Burnt offerings were burned completely, but peace offerings were partly burned and partly eaten by the one offering the sacrifice. It is portions of the peace offerings that will be eaten by the leaders of the people in verses 9-11.)*

When the oxen were killed, they were bled, and half of the blood was caught in bowls. The other half was splashed upon the altar. With the burnt offerings consumed, and the peace offerings ready, and half the blood of the oxen in bowls, Moses took the scroll of the covenant and read it in the hearing of the people. They said, "All the Lord has said we will do, and we will be obedient." *(This was their third time to make this promise.)*

Upon the basis of this promise by the people, Moses took the blood that was in the bowls and sprinkled it upon the people, saying, "Look, this is the blood of the covenant which the Lord has made with you upon all these conditions."

After Moses had sprinkled the people with the blood of the covenant, he, Aaron, Nadab and Abihu, and the seventy elders of Israel did as God had commanded (24:1-2) and approached the Lord. God let them see a throne scene in which they saw the God of Israel, and under His feet was a floor paved with bright sapphire clear and blue as the sky. And though the nobles of Israel ate before Him, God did not destroy them, and they looked at God and ate and drank.

*Now the agreement between God and Israel was official. The covenant had been made and ratified. The Israelites were ready to be the chosen people of God. Notice the exact steps that had been taken to make and ratify this covenant:*

- *God offered to make a covenant with the Israelites (19:3-6).*
- *Moses told the people what God had offered, and they agreed that they wanted His covenant, and promised to obey all the laws that God gave (19:7-8).*
- *So God came down upon the mount and started giving the laws orally (20:1-17).*
- *The people were afraid of His voice and of His manifestation on the mount, so they asked Moses to go to God in their place, let Him tell Moses the laws, and Moses would tell the people. Again, they promised to listen carefully to Moses and obey the instructions given (20:18-21).*
- *God gave Moses the rest of the ordinances He wanted included in this original covenant (21:1-23:33).*
- *Moses gathered the people together and told them what God had said. The people promised again that they would obey. They were agreeing to keep their side of the covenant. (24:3)*
- *Moses made a written copy of the commands and ordinances God had given (chapters 20-23).*
    - *He set up an altar, and young men from Israel offered burnt offerings and peace offerings (24:4-5).*

- *Moses divided the blood of the peace offerings in half:*
  - *He sprinkled half of the blood upon the altar, symbolizing God's part in ratifying the covenant (24:6).*
  - *Then he read the written portion of the law to the people, and again they promised to obey all that God had said (24:7).*
  - *Moses took the other half of the blood that had been preserved, and he sprinkled it upon the people —thus signifying the people's part in the covenant (24:8).*
- *As a final act to ratify the covenant, Moses, Aaron, Nadab, Abihu, and seventy elders (as representatives of the people) went up into the mount and ate a portion of the meat of the sacrifice before the throne of Jehovah (24:9-11).*

*Thus Israel's covenant with Jehovah was made the way all ancient covenants were made and confirmed: the covenant was offered, the terms were decided, and then they offered sacrifices, and the parties involved in the covenant shared the sacrificial meal. It is to this way of making a covenant that the Lord refers in Jeremiah 34:18 (cf. Gen. 15:7-11, 17-21; 31:44-46, 54). The words translated, "make a covenant," in the Hebrew language literally mean to "cut a covenant" and likely refer to this ancient method of making an agreement.*

*We cannot avoid seeing the connection between the words of Moses, "Behold the blood of the covenant," and the words of Christ when He instituted the Lord's Supper: "...for this is My blood of the covenant, which is poured out for many for forgiveness of sins" (Matt. 26:28). Moses referred to the blood of the peace offerings which were subsequently eaten by the representatives of the people of Israel. Jesus referred to the fruit of the vine which He chose to be a memorial of the blood which He shed in His death upon the cross. Just as the subsequent eating of the peace offering by the representatives of the people was a ratifying, or sealing, of the agreement between Jehovah and Israel, so our eating of the Lord's Supper is a ratifying, or a re-affirming, of the agreement we have with the Lord. According to the example found in the New Testament (Acts 20:7), we eat the Lord's Supper each first day of the week as a way of reminding ourselves of the sacrifice Christ made for our sins, and by eating, we re-affirm that we have a covenant — an agreement —with Him that we must remember to fulfill. For a full discussion of this important lesson, see another of our books, Christ In You, The Hope of Glory.*

*Who were the priests mentioned in 19:24, and who were "the young men" who offered the sacrifices in 24:5? The Levitical priesthood had not been ordained yet. Nevertheless, the function of priest had to be carried on because sacrifices are being offered in behalf of the people. There are really only two choices. One is that these men had been chosen indiscriminately from among the tribes to serve as temporary priests, or, two, Aaron and his sons were already acting as provisional priests. There is no positive proof, but the evidence points to the latter. Look at some of the evidence that these priests were Aaron and his sons:*

- *It would have served as an uncertain precedent to have priests chosen generally when God planned to limit them to one tribe.*
- *God called Aaron, and his two sons, Nadab and Abihu, to Himself along with Moses and seventy elders in chapter 24.*
- *Aaron was already very much in the role of leadership with Moses, so it would be quite logical for his family to be already in this role of acting priests even though the laws concerning the priests were just now about to be given.*

- *The law itself will be quite specific about the rules for priests and for the identity of those eligible. So, if these men were from various tribes, they will be used only until the Levitical priesthood can be established.*
- *The text does not identify the young men beyond the verses cited.*

*The New Testament specifically says that "no man has seen God at any time" (John 1:18). This means that no man has seen God in His real spiritual essence. There were several times during Old Testament history when men "saw" God, but in each incidence, it was when He manifested Himself to them in some form they could see and understand. The only man who has seen God in His real spiritual essence is that One who came down from heaven, and has now returned to the bosom of the Father —Jesus Himself.*

*It must have been a day of great joy when God and the Israelites ratified their covenant. But the story does not end here. As we continue our study, we will find that Israel did not measure up, they did not achieve the great aim of God for them. The opportunity they had to do so, and the reasons why they failed, not only furnish the substance of the Pentateuch, but also the substance of all Old Testament history. Our understanding these points from the Old Testament gives us a clearer understanding of our opportunity, and what we must do to achieve God's plan for us under the new covenant.*

## God calls Moses into the mount (Exod. 24:12-18):

The Lord said to Moses, "Come up to me on the mountain and remain there, and I will give you stone tablets with the law and the commandments that I have written for instructions for the people."

So Moses and his servant Joshua arose and went up to the mountain of Jehovah. But before he left, he said to the elders of the people, "Wait here for us until we return. Aaron and Hur are here with you, and if any of you has a legal matter to be decided, let him come to them."

Moses went up into the mountain, and the cloud covered the mountain for six days. On the seventh day Jehovah called to Moses from the midst of the cloud. To the eyes of the sons of Israel who were camped at the base of the mountain, the glory of God was as a consuming fire on the top of the mountain. So Moses went up into the cloud upon the mountain, and remained in the mount forty days and forty nights. No one was with Moses except Joshua, his minister. Joshua did not go all the way to approach God with Moses, but he was somewhere on the mountain as Moses' helper.

## Our organization of the material to follow:

*Chapters 25 through 31 give a portion of the information Moses received in the mount during these forty days he was gone from the people. But before we look at the instructions Moses is receiving, let us keep our attention focused on this covenant between God and Israel. For the moment, we will skip chapters 25-31 and come to the breaking of the covenant and take up our story there. Please be sure that your students see the making of the covenant at Mount Sinai, and then see that it is broken by Israel. Put the two parts together as a connected story. The story is a beautiful one when the two parts are seen together. Usually this point is not seen, and it is for this very purpose that we now proceed to chapter 32. We will come back to chapter 25 when we discuss the building of the tabernacle.*

*Look again at an overview of what is about to happen in chapters 32 through 34:*

- *The people sin, and their covenant is broken (32:1-6).*
- *God is ready to destroy the people; they are no longer His (32:7-10).*

- *Moses intercedes, so God does not destroy them (32:11-14).*
- *Moses comes down the mountain, sees their idolatry, and breaks the stones that contain the terms of the covenant that is now broken (32:15-19).*
- *Moses realizes the serious consequences of their sin, and he leads in punishing the guilty (32:20-29).*
- *Moses intercedes again through prayer to God (32:30-32).*
- *God responds by saying He will send the people to inherit the land, but that He will not go with them as He had intended (32:33-33:6).*
- *Moses will not accept these terms. He pleads with God to go with them; to accept these people as His people again (to renew His covenant) (33:12-16).*
- *God hears Moses' prayer, and renews the covenant (33:17-34:28).*

# The Covenant is Broken
## (Exodus 32:1-33:6)

### Israel breaks her covenant with God (Exod. 32:1-8):

Moses had been gone for almost six weeks *(40 days)* when the people gathered themselves and came to Aaron, whom Moses had left in charge, along with Hur (24:14). The people said, "Get up and make us a god to go before us, because we do not know what has become of this fellow Moses who brought us up out of Egypt."

Aaron said, "Tear off *(literally, jerk off)* the golden earrings of your wives, of your sons, and of your daughters, and bring them to me."

All the people promptly broke off their earrings and brought them to Aaron. He took the gold and fashioned it with an engraving tool and made it a molten calf. Aaron brought forth the idol for the people to see, and they said, "O Israel, this is your god which brought you up out of the land of Egypt."

Aaron built an altar and made a public proclamation: "Tomorrow will be a feast to the Lord."

Early the next morning, the people got up and offered burnt offerings and peace offerings before their golden calf. They sat down to eat and drink, and then rose up to play, celebrating with singing and dancing (32:18-19).

*This "playing" may have included immoral acts, because so many of the false religions of the day did include such things, but the text does not say or necessarily imply such. Any kind of worship to a golden calf broke at least the second of the ten commandments, and was therefore very serious, even if they claimed it still represented Jehovah.*

*The word for god or gods is elohim which may be singular or plural. When referring to false gods, it is most often plural, but here it is the singular sense because there was only one calf (32:4, 19-20, 24, 35; cf. Ps. 106:19-20). Probably Aaron was saying, "This is an image of Jehovah who brought you out of Egypt," but whether he was saying this was a new god they could depend upon, or whether he was saying this was an image of Jehovah, it was sinful. The first of the ten commandments forbade their having any god besides Jehovah, and the second commandment forbade their making an image of Jehovah.*

*By this deed, the children of Israel broke their covenant with the Lord. Even if the people did not view themselves as worshiping another god by saying they were worshiping the God who brought them out of Egypt, this sin was idolatry (see Ps. 106:19; 1 Cor. 10:7). They had promised to "obey all that the Lord commanded," yet here they were constructing and worshiping an idol within six weeks of making that covenant. Remember that their covenant had been based upon their obedience to God: "We will obey all that God has commanded" (19:8; 20:19; 24:3, 7). The covenant is broken — and there is nothing the people themselves can do to restore that covenant, unless God chooses to forgive them.*

## God threatens destruction (Exod. 32:9-14):

*A cloud covered the top of the mountain, so Moses could not see down into the camp. He knows nothing about what is happening with the people until God tells him. God's anger, therefore, must have come as a shock to Moses.*

Jehovah told Moses, "Go, get back down to the camp, for your people that you brought up from Egypt have corrupted themselves. So quickly they have turned aside from the way I commanded them and have made themselves a molten calf and have worshiped it. They have said, 'This is your god, O Israel, which brought you forth from Egypt.'"

Jehovah continued, "I have observed that these people are very stubborn and hard-headed. Now allow my wrath to grow hot against them so that I may destroy them. Then I will make of you a great nation."

*When God called Israel Moses' people, was He merely saying, "These are the people for whom you intercede," or was He saying, "They are my people no longer"? Since God made it clear that He was ready to destroy the people, and since He said that these were the people Moses had brought up from Egypt, we conclude that God no longer recognized Israel as His covenant people. Consider this: if the terms of the covenant were serious to God, then, at this point, Israel could not be regarded as His people — because they had broken their promise to keep their side of the covenant. By this statement, God put the fate of Israel into the hands of Moses. By saying nothing to dissuade God, he could have had Israel destroyed, and God would have begun again developing His promises — this time through Moses. But Moses loved his people and filled his place as their mediator.*

Moses entreated the Lord his God, saying, "Lord, why will you let your wrath grow hot against your people, the ones you brought out of Egypt by such a mighty display of power? Why should the Egyptians be able to say that God brought Israel out of Egypt to slay them in the mountains, to wipe them off the face of the earth? Please turn from your fierce wrath, and change your mind about what you will do with these people. Remember Abraham, Isaac, and Jacob, your servants. You swore to them by your own self and said, 'I will multiply your descendants as the stars of heaven, and all this land I have described I will give to your descendants, and they will inherit it indefinitely.'"

God listened to Moses' intercession and changed His mind about the calamity He had threatened to bring upon His people.

*Look at the points Moses made in his intercession:*

- *They are your people, your people whom you brought out of Egypt (not Moses' people).*
- *The Egyptians will say you brought Israel out of Egypt in order to destroy them.*
- *You promised, with an oath, to Abraham, Isaac, and Jacob that their descendants would be the nation to inherit the land of Canaan.*

## The people are punished (Exod. 32:15-29):

Moses turned and went down from the mountain. In his hands were the two tables of stone upon which were written on both sides the words of the testimony *(the covenant)*. The writing was done by the finger of God, engraved upon the stones (31:18; 32:15-16).

As Moses and Joshua drew nearer to the camp *(but before they could see through the cloud)*, they heard the noise the people were making, and Joshua said, "It sounds like war in the camp." Remember that Joshua had been in the mountain as Moses' helper, but he had not been communicating with God.

Moses replied:

It is not the sound of the cry of triumph,
Nor is it the sound of the cry of defeat;
But the sound of singing I hear.

As soon as Moses and Joshua could see the camp, Moses saw the golden calf and the dancing. Moses was very angry, and he threw the tables of stone upon the ground, breaking them there at the foot of the mount. Moses demonstrated the serious nature of the situation by the intensity with which he dealt with the sin. He took the calf and burned it with fire and ground it to powder and cast the dust upon the water and made the Israelites drink it.

Moses asked Aaron, "What did these people do to you to cause you to bring such a great sin upon them?"

Aaron made the lame reply, "Let not my lord be angry. You know this people, that they are bent on doing evil. They said, 'Make us a god which will go before us, because we do not know what has become of this Moses who brought us up from the land of Egypt.' So I told them, 'Whoever has any gold, let him bring it.' They gave me the gold, and I threw it into the fire, and this calf came out." *(No reply is recorded. What reply would fit an excuse such as that from a man like Aaron?)*

The people had been allowed by Aaron to become completely unrestrained. A state of anarchy prevailed, a state that would soon cause Israel to become an object of scorn among the nations. So Moses stood at the entrance of the camp and said, "Whoever is on Jehovah's side, let him come to me." All the sons of Levi gathered themselves unto Moses.

Moses told them, "This is what Jehovah says, 'Let every man put his sword on his side and go back and forth through the camp and slay every guilty person, whether they be friends or relatives.' Dedicate yourselves wholly to God. Let your hand be against even your son and your brother so that God may bestow a blessing upon you today."

The Levites obeyed Moses and killed about 3,000 men.

*The breaking of the stone tablets by Moses was not a thoughtless act of frustration and anger. Moses was not that kind of man. Rather, he knew that what he saw meant that the Israelites had broken their covenant with God, and that covenant was based squarely upon what was written upon those tablets (Deut. 4:13). Moses knew better than anyone else that the covenant was broken. He knew that God had been ready to destroy the people, and he had been the one who had interceded with God not to wipe Israel from the face of the earth, but he did not know where the matter would go from here (32:30). The breaking of the tablets was, therefore, symbolic of what Israel had done.*

*Sin is never a matter for complacent behavior. Sin is a serious breaking of man's relationship with Jehovah. Moses realized this as he stood watching the worship around the golden calf. He dealt with the matter immediately and severely. He made sure the people realized the enormity of what they had done. Then, after the punishment that he could bring upon the people, it was time to pray to God for His* *forgiveness. Notice that the time for prayer for forgiveness came <u>after</u> the people had been made aware of how serious their offense was to God and when they were ready to grieve over their sin.*

*These tables contained the text of the ten commandments given in 20:1-17, but not just the bare commandments, because four sides of the stones would not have been necessary to write the basic commandments themselves. We know the ten commandments were on the stones, but we have no way of knowing how many additional ones from those found in chapters 21-23 were there also. All of the commandments in chapters 20-23 formed the basis of that original covenant with God.*

*Though the details are not given, almost certainly the idol was made with a wooden core and overlaid with gold plate. The plate was melted, or at least heated, in the process and then shaped and smoothed with a "graving tool" (see verse 4). The wooden core of the idol would have burned. The gold would have been left to grind into powder. When cast upon the water, the dust would have sunk quickly, but the point of the act was clear: the children of Israel would have to accept the consequences of their sin.*

## Moses prays for the people (Exod. 32:30-32):

The next morning Moses told the people, "You have sinned a great sin. And now I will go up to Jehovah. Perhaps I will succeed in making atonement for your sin." At this point, though Moses had persuaded God not to destroy Israel, he did not know how far God would be willing to go in restoring Israel to His mercy.

So Moses returned to the Lord. He prayed, saying, "This people have sinned a great sin and have made them a god of gold. Even so, if you will forgive their sins — ."

*Moses stopped for a moment. How could he finish? What deal could he make? What offering could he give to persuade God to forgive Israel? What price could he pay? It has been well said that only Jesus could complete the sentence: "If thou wilt forgive them, I will pay their penalty with the sacrifice of my blood."*

Moses concluded his prayer: "And if not, blot me, I beg of you, out of the record you have written."

*In God's first threat to destroy the people, He had said He would spare Moses and would make a great nation through him. But Moses is saying that if the people cannot be spared, then let him die with them.*

## God's answer (Exod. 32:33-33:6):

God answered, "Whoever has sinned against me, him will I blot out of my record. Now, go on and lead the people into the place I have told you about. My angel will go before you. Nevertheless, in a day of my choosing, I will make an accounting for this sin which they have done." And the Lord struck the people with a plague because of what they had done in building the golden calf.

*No specific description is given of this plague or its results. Some, therefore, think the reference may be to the 3,000 who were killed by the Levites. Others say that the wording of 32:34-35 indicates God is saying He <u>will</u> punish them for the sin on this occasion "in the day when I punish." In that case, "the day of visitation" probably refers to the day when God told Israel they would wander in the wilderness until that generation was dead (Num. 14:20-25, 26-35). The wandering in the wilderness was not only because of Israel's lack of faith at Kadesh-barnea, but also because they had tempted God "these ten times" (Num. 14:22), and because of their "whoredoms" (Num. 14:33).*

Jehovah proceeded to tell Moses what His plan was: "My plan is for you and your people that you brought out of Egypt to leave and go to the land that I swore to Abraham, to Isaac, and to Jacob, saying, 'To your seed I will give it.' I will send an angel before you, and I will drive out the inhabitants of the land, a land flowing with milk and honey. But I will not go up in your midst because you are a hard-headed people, and if I dwelt among you, I would destroy you on the way."

When the people heard God's reply, they were deeply grieved. None of them put on their ornaments.

God sent word to the Israelites and said, "You are a hard-headed people. You will not do as you are told. If I came into your midst for even a moment, I would destroy you. Take off your baubles and bracelets till I know what to do to you." The children of Israel were dismayed that God was not to be in their midst, and they mourned. They obeyed God and stripped off their ornaments there at Mount Horeb *(another name for Sinai)*.

*This news was very discouraging to Moses and to the people. When this great adventure had begun, God was present, and He was in charge. He gathered His people into His arms, as it were, to deliver them, and to make them what He wanted them to be. Moses was called from his quiet life as a shepherd to undertake an enormous task, a task which he could do only with God's help. Now God has withdrawn Himself. Now He is not near the people. They are Moses' people, not God's. God will send an angel, but He will not be among the people. The wonder and the glory of this whole great saga was gone, and it had become rather ordinary. Without God's personal involvement, what else could it be? The covenant is broken! They are no longer God's special people!*

*The most basic issue involved in God's dealings with mankind was at the heart of this crisis. God made man because of His love for him. He wanted nothing more than to bless man, to love him, and to be loved by him. But how could a sinless and pure God tolerate sinful, defiled man who, in his wickedness, was a travesty of God? And how could God bring about His great plan when the material He had to work with were sinful people? It would be only as a means was given by God whereby men could be forgiven. These were the great lessons that had to be taught to Moses, to the Israelites, and through them to all mankind.*

# The Covenant is Renewed
## (Exodus 33:7-34:35)

### Moses uses a tent of meeting (Exod. 33:7-11):

To save the time necessary to climb up the mountain to speak with God, Moses took a tent, apparently with God's approval, and pitched it outside of the camp, a good distance away, though it could still be seen from camp. Moses called the tent, "the tent of meeting," for there God would meet to speak with him. When Moses would go out to the tent, all the people would get up and stand at their tent doors and watch Moses approach the tent. When he entered, the pillar of cloud would descend and stand at the door of the tent, and Jehovah would speak with Moses. The people were filled with awe and worshiped. Jehovah spoke to Moses face to face, as a man speaks to his friend. Then Moses would go back into the camp, but his assistant, the young man Joshua, remained at the tent *(presumably to guard it)*.

*This tent of meeting was not the tabernacle:*

- *Even though the word tabernacle means tent, it is from a different Hebrew word than the one used for tent in this passage.*
- *The tabernacle had not been built at this point.*
- *When the tabernacle was built, it was surrounded by a court, so the entrance was not easily visible to the people.*
- *This was, therefore. a strictly temporary tent of meeting.*
- *After the tabernacle is built, set up, and the worship is set in order, the expression "tent of meeting" always refer to the tabernacle itself.*

*It seems evident that the purpose for this tent of meeting was to provide Moses with a more convenient place to meet with God. Even so, the evidence is clear that Moses did go up into the mountain again after this first discussion with God that is recorded in 33:12-23. In verses 17-23 God tells Moses what He is going to do for him, and how He is going to do it, but He waits until Moses comes up on the mountain to fulfill His promise.*

## Moses continues to intercede (Exod. 33:12-34:9):

Moses said to Jehovah, "See, you say to me, 'Bring up this people,' but you have not let me know whom you will send with me. Yet you have said, 'I know you by name, and you have found favor with me.' If this be so, tell me clearly what your intentions are so that I can find favor with you, and please consider this nation to be your people." *(He is saying, "Let me know your plans for us, and please renew your covenant to make these people your special possession.")*

God heard Moses' heartfelt cry and He replied, "My personal presence will go with you, and I will give you rest."

Moses continued to press his case, "If you yourself do not go up with us, then do not send us from this place, because how shall it be known that I and your people have found favor in your sight, unless it is by the fact that you go with us? In this way we are distinguished from all other people of the earth."

The Lord then said, "I will do this thing that you have asked because you have found favor in my sight, and I know you by name."

Moses said, "Show me, I beg of you, your glory!"

God answered, "I will make all my goodness to pass before you and will proclaim the name of Jehovah before you, and I will be gracious to whom I choose, and I will show mercy to whom I wish. But you cannot see my face, for man cannot see me and live. There is a place by me, and you will stand upon the rock. When my glory passes by, I will put you in a crack in the rock, and I will cover you with my hand until I have passed by. I will take away my hand, and you will see my back, but my face will not be seen."

The Lord said to Moses, "Hew two tablets of stone like the first ones, and I will write upon them the words which were upon the tablets which you broke. And be prepared by tomorrow morning to come up into Mount Sinai and present yourself to me on the top of the mountain. Do not let anyone come with you or even be seen anywhere upon the mountain. Do not allow even your flocks and herds to graze in front of the mountain."

So Moses chiseled out two tablets of stone like the first ones, and arose early the next morning to go up onto the mountain. Jehovah descended upon the mountain and stood with him there and proclaimed the name of Jehovah. The Lord passed before Moses and proclaimed, "Jehovah, Jehovah, a God merciful and gracious, slow to anger, and abundant in mercy and truth, remaining merciful to thousands, forgiving iniquity and transgression. But He will by no means clear the guilty, visiting the iniquity of the fathers upon the children even to the third and fourth generation."

Quickly Moses bowed himself to the earth and worshiped God. With this demonstration of God's favor given to him, he said, "If now I have found favor with you, O Lord, please go up among us. I concede that it is a stiff-necked people, but pardon our iniquity and our sin, and take us for your inheritance."

*There is much that we cannot understand about this story, because there is much we cannot know about God Himself. God manifested Himself on occasion as simply an ordinary man (Gen. 18 e.g.). At other times He manifested Himself in a fearsome way, such as in the pillar of fire by which the Israelites were led at night or in the throne scene the leaders of Israel saw as they ratified their covenant. But this was a special plea from a man who had drawn very close to God. The closer one gets to God the more one wishes to know of Him. Moses wanted assurance that he had God's favor; he wanted to know more of this God for whom he was mediator.*

*When Moses said, "Show me thy glory" (33:18), he did not mean, "Show me a bright light." He wanted to see the divine character or nature of God. How the divine goodness can be shown to the physical eye by a mere display is incomprehensible. For this reason it is likely that when the glory of Jehovah passed by Moses, His goodness was somehow displayed to the mental or spiritual eye of Moses while in some way there was a physical manifestation of God's presence as well (33:23). It is best just to tell the story and not attempt to "explain" very much, because, frankly, there is little we can explain. But tell the event vividly enough to be awed by the blessing God gave Moses on this occasion.*

*Even in the midst of his glorious experience, Moses does not forget his task, which is to intercede for his people. In the face of Israel's iniquity and unworthiness, think of the enormity of asking Jehovah, the God of heaven and earth, to take them for His inheritance. In his intercession, Moses voices the only means by which man can sustain a relationship with God, that is: "I know the people are obstinate, but please pardon and forgive our iniquities and sins." Since man sins, it is only through God's forgiveness that man has a hope of approaching God. How blessed Israel was — and how blessed we are — that God is merciful, that He forgives iniquity! This was a most important lesson that Israel — and all mankind — had to learn.*

## Jehovah renews His covenant with Israel (Exod. 34:10-28):

*Exodus 34:4-28 covers the forty days that Moses was in the mountain the second time. Which part of the law was given to Moses the first time he was in the mount and which part was given the second time is unclear. The natural assumption is that chapters 25-30 were given to him the first time. Chapters 35-40 contain the record of the building of the tabernacle and its furniture, the making of the garments for the priests, and the setting up of the completed tabernacle. Nearly all of Leviticus and parts of Numbers also contain laws and regulations which were almost certainly given to Moses during these two sessions in the mount.*

The Lord said unto Moses:

- Look, I am making a covenant with you.
  - I will do amazing things before all your people, things that have not been wrought in all the earth among any nation.
  - All these people whom you lead will see the work of Jehovah because I am going to do awesome things.
  - Be careful to do what I tell you today.

## Jehovah Makes a Covenant

- I am going to drive out the Amorite, the Canaanite, the Hittite, the Perizzite, the Hivite, and the Jebusite.
    - Be careful that you make no covenant with the inhabitants of the land where you are going, or they will be a snare to you.
    - Break down their altars and smash their obelisks. Cut down their sacred poles *(Asherim)*.
    - You are to worship no other gods:
        - For Jehovah, whose name is Jealous, is a jealous God and will not tolerate such a thing.
    - Do as I say lest you make treaties with these people and become unfaithful to me:
        - If you take their daughters as wives for your sons, and those daughters prostitute themselves with their idols, they will lead your sons to do the same.
    - Do not make molten gods.
- You are to keep the feast of unleavened bread.
    - For seven days you will eat unleavened bread, in the month Abib, as I commanded, because that is the month you came out of Egypt.
- Remember that every male that opens the womb is mine:
    - Including all your firstborn livestock that is male.
    - The firstling of a donkey you will redeem with a lamb, or else break its neck.
    - You will redeem all the firstborn among your sons.
- No one is to come before me without an offering.
- You are to work six days and rest on the seventh day.
    - Even during plowing and harvest, you will rest.
- Observe the feast of weeks *(called Pentecost in the NT)*, the first reaping of the wheat harvest.
- Observe the feast of final harvest at the year's end.
- Three times a year all your males will appear before the Lord Jehovah, the God of Israel.
    - As long as you appear before me these three times a year:
        - I will drive out the nations before you,
        - I will enlarge your territory,
        - And no man will make designs on your land.
- Bring the first of your harvest unto the house of God as an offering.
- Do not boil a kid in its mother's milk.
- Write these words, because according to these words I have made a covenant with you and with Israel.

Moses was in the mount with God forty days and forty nights. During that time Moses did not eat bread or drink water. He wrote upon the tables the words of the covenant, the ten commandments. As we mentioned in the note above, almost certainly during these two trips into the mountain, Moses received the full law, plus full instructions about building the tabernacle, the worship to be conducted there, and the role and duties of the priests.

*Some of the information in 34:10-27 is found in chapters 21-23, particularly in 23:10-33. It is not surprising to find the repetition of thoughts since God is making a new covenant with the same people that He had before.*

*Many argue that the ten commandments are binding upon us today. They say that the law of the Jews contained ceremonial laws and moral laws. According to this argument, the ten commandments are the moral law and did not pass away when the old covenant was done away; it was only the ceremonial law that was done away. In 34:28 the "words of the covenant" are the ten commandments (see also Deut. 4:13).*

*Therefore, for the covenant made at Sinai to be done away, the laws upon which it rested, the ten commandments, had to be done away also. In the new covenant of Christ, all of the ten commandments are repeated except the sabbath commandment, and we obey them because they are a part of that new law.*

*Who wrote the words of the covenant upon the tables of stone, Moses or God? The pronoun references in 34:27-28 point to Moses, but pronoun references are often unclear, especially in the Old Testament. Regarding the first tables of stone, God told Moses, "I will give you tables of stone, and the law and the commandment, which I have written, that thou mayest teach them" (24:12). Also, "He gave to Moses...the two tables of the testimony, tables of stone, written with the finger of God" (31:18). When God tells Moses to come up into the mount the second time, He tells him to hew two stone tablets, but He says, "I will write upon the tables the words that were on the first tables" (34:1). When Moses later tells Israel what happened, he says, "I hewed two tables of stone like unto the first, and went up into the mount, having the two tables in my hand. And He wrote on the tables, according to the first writing, the ten commandments" (Deut. 10:3-4). It seems clear, therefore, from the evidence that the "He" of Exodus 34:28 is God.*

## Moses returns with the tables of stone (Exod. 34:29-35):

When Moses came down from the mount with the tables of stone, the skin of his face shone because God had been speaking to him, but Moses did not realize his face was shining. When Aaron and the Israelites saw him, they were afraid of him because his face was so bright. Nevertheless, Moses called Aaron and the leaders of the congregation to him and spoke with them. Afterwards, he spoke with all the Israelites, telling them all that Jehovah had said to him. When he finished speaking to them, he put a veil upon his face. From that time forward, when Moses went in to speak with the Lord, he would remove the veil. After communing with the Lord, he would come out and speak with the people. Then he would put on the veil again until he went in to speak with the Lord.

*Some have had the idea that Moses put on the veil to cover his shining face so that the children of Israel would not be frightened. It is clear from verses 33-35, however, that he did not wear the veil when he spoke with the people, but that he put the veil on after he spoke to the people. He wore the veil over his face until he went in to commune with the Lord again. Paul says that Moses put on a veil so that the children of Israel would not be able to gaze on the glory upon his face as it passed away, in other words, so they would not see the shining of his face fade away (2 Cor. 3:13). He (and God) wanted the people to be impressed that Moses had indeed been in direct communication with God so that they would listen to his words.*

# An Overview:
# The Months at Mount Sinai
## (Exodus 19:1-Numbers 10:12)



When God first appeared to Moses in the burning bush and told him to go to Egypt to deliver the Israelites from bondage, He gave Moses a sign that He would be with him to help him accomplish the difficult task before him: He promised to bring the people to Mount Sinai to worship Him (Exod. 3:12). God has kept His promise. Just as God predicted (3:19; 4:21-23), Pharaoh was stubborn and would not grant the request to let the people go into the wilderness to worship their God (5:2). God used Pharaoh's stubbornness as a way to show His power and to punish the Egyptians for the way they had mistreated the Israelites (9:13-16). He sent ten mighty plagues to show Pharaoh, all the Egyptians, and the Israelites who Jehovah was and why they should obey Him (5:2; 6:7; 7:5, 17; 8:10, 22; 9:14, 16, 29; 10:2; 11:7). Finally Pharaoh ordered his slaves to leave his land before it was completely destroyed (12:31-33). Even then, he changed his mind and pursued them with his army, but God was watching over His people, and He divided the waters of the Red Sea, letting His people cross safely on dry ground, and then destroyed Pharaoh's army when they tried to chase them — in order to prove one more time that Jehovah is indeed the Lord (14:4, 17-18).

By the third month after they left Egypt (19:1), God had led the Israelites through the wilderness of the Sinaitic peninsula and had brought them to Mount Sinai — just as He had promised Moses. He had rescued His people from their enemies (14:21-30; 17:8-16); He had given them water to drink when they needed it (15:22-26; 17:1-7); He had given them food to eat when their supplies from Egypt were gone (16:1-36). Indeed, He had borne them on eagles' wings to bring them to Himself (19:4).

At Mount Sinai, God made His covenant with Israel in order to make them His special people out of all the earth. We have studied the making of that covenant very carefully in the preceding chapter. It is the most important event that took place at Mount Sinai. But remember, that covenant was based squarely upon the law that God was in the process of giving. The people have promised to keep that law, and, before they leave Sinai, God will have given the law in its entirety. The account tells of their arriving at Sinai in Exodus 19:1, and they will not leave there until Numbers 10:11-12. They will have been at Sinai nearly a year by that time. They arrived in the third month after leaving Egypt, and they leave on the twentieth day of the second month of the second year.

Many important things happened during the year at Sinai. It is beyond the scope of this particular course to study the details of the whole law of Moses, but we want to look at the most important events and at enough of the laws for you to understand what God did for Israel and what His reasons were for doing each thing. Take this study as a foundation for a later, more detailed study of the law of Moses. As you study each thing, look at it only long enough to see what was happening (and to get a visual picture in your mind of the tabernacle), but do not bog down in the details.

In order to keep the whole picture before us, let us look very briefly at an outline of the major things that took place at Sinai. Then as we study each major event in more detail, each event will become richer and fuller in your understanding. After a brief study of the law, we will leave Sinai with the Israelites and travel on to the land of Canaan. Do not lose sight of the history. Look back to this chapter often to see that less than a year passes while all these events are taking place.

***Map assignment:*** *Look back at your map to remind yourselves where Mount Sinai was located. See Egypt and see the land of Canaan. The people are in the wilderness, but they are there because God has particular things He is doing with them. They have not yet refused to go into the land, so we are still in the period of the exodus from Egypt instead of the period of the wandering in the wilderness. They are not "wandering" now, because God is still moving forward with His plan for them.*

## Months at Mount Sinai:

- Jehovah makes a covenant with Israel. We studied the making of that covenant in detail in our last chapter. With the covenant now in place, let us see how the details of the law fit into the framework of the covenant:
  - In the simplest terms, the covenant was, "I will be your God, and you will be my people."
  - The covenant was based upon the people's obedience of the law ("If you will obey me...), for in this way they would learn how to live as the people of God.
  - Therefore, the law, which centered around the ten commandments, was given to them.
  - As the people lived in accordance with God's law:
    - He would dwell among them in their lives, in their words, and in their deeds.
    - The tabernacle was built as a visual reminder to Israel that their God dwelt among them.
  - But Israel was sinful; they needed God's forgiveness.
    - Therefore, God designed a priesthood to mediate between Himself and Israel.
    - The priests would offer the sacrifices the law called for when sin occurred,
    - And through those sacrifices, the sins of Israel could be forgiven, and their relationship with God could remain intact.
  - By noting these points it is easy to see their relationship to each other and to remember what God did for Israel at Mount Sinai. In order to stress these points, we will follow the lead of the narrative which gives attention to:
    - The building of the tabernacle,
    - Then to the priesthood and the sacrifices,
    - And finally to the details of the law itself.

## The Months at Sinai

- They build the tabernacle (Exodus 25:1-27:21; 30:1-10; 30:17-31:11; 35:4-38:31; 39:32-40).
- They make garments for the priests (Exodus 28; 39).
- God gives rules for the sacrifices (Leviticus 1-7).
- They set up the tabernacle (Exodus 38:21-31; 39:32-43; 40:1-38).
- They consecrate the priests (Exodus 29; 40:9-16; Leviticus 8).
- They set the worship in order (Leviticus 9:1-10:20; 24:10-16, 23; Numbers 7:1-89).
- The remainder of the law is given. (Details are found in Exodus through Deuteronomy.)
- They observe the Passover (Numbers 9:1-14).
    - One full year has passed since the last plague in Egypt, and the Israelites were ordered to leave the land. It is the fourteenth day of the first month of the second year, time for the Passover.
    - Some were unclean, so God gave instructions for those few to observe the feast one month later.
- While they are waiting for that month to pass, God commands them to take care of additional matters.
    - The soldiers are numbered and organized (Numbers 1:1-2:34).
    - The Levites are numbered and organized (Numbers 1:47-53; 3:1-4:49; 6:22-27; 8:5-26).
    - God sets blessings and curses before His people (Leviticus 26:1-46).
- The cloud lifts from over the tabernacle (Numbers 10:11-13).
    - It is time to leave Mount Sinai and travel on to inherit the land of Canaan.
    - It was the twentieth day of the second month of the second year.

**Chronology note:**

- 15th day, 1st month, 1st year: the Israelites left Egypt (Exod. 12:6, 31, 37-40).
- 15th day, 2nd month: they arrived in the Wilderness of Sin (Exod. 16:1).
- "In the 3rd month": they arrived at Mount Sinai (Exod. 19:1).
- A few days passed:
    - God made His offer of a covenant and the people prepared to hear God speak. He came down upon the mountain and spoke the ten commandments orally.
    - The people were afraid and asked that God speak to Moses and let him tell them the requirements from God.
    - God gave Moses the overview of the law that formed the original covenant (Exod. 20-23).
    - Then the covenant was ratified.
- Moses went into the mountain for 40 days (Exod. 24:18).
- At the end of the 40 days:
    - The people build a golden calf, breaking their covenant (Exod. 32).
    - Moses intercedes, and the covenant is renewed (Exod. 32-34).
- Moses returns to the mount for another 40 days and nights (Exod. 34:28).
- Next 6 months:
    - The people build the tabernacle and all its furnishings.
    - They prepare garments for the priests.
- 1st day, 1st month, 2nd year: they set up the tabernacle (Exod. 40:1, 17).
- Next 7 days:
    - Aaron and his sons are consecrated (Exod. 40:12-15; Lev. 8:33-35).

- $8^{th}$ day, $1^{st}$ month: Aaron and his sons begin their work as priests (Lev. 9:1).
- $1^{st}$ through $12^{th}$ day of $1^{st}$ month: The princes of each tribe come bringing a gift to provide the necessities for the worship. They begin on the day the tabernacle was set up, and one prince comes each day for the next 12 days (Num. 7:1-2).
- $14^{th}$ day, $1^{st}$ month, $2^{nd}$ year: the people observe the Passover. It has been exactly one year since the night of the last plague in Egypt (Num. 9:1-5).
- $1^{st}$ day, $2^{nd}$ month, $2^{nd}$ year: they begin counting and organizing the people (Num. 1:1).
  - They count the soldiers (Num. 1:1-46).
  - They organize the tribes in their correct camping order and marching order (Num. 2).
  - They take the Levites in the stead of the firstborn (Num. 3).
  - They count and organize the Levites in the age bracket to work (Num. 4).
- $14^{th}$ day, $2^{nd}$ month, $2^{nd}$ year: those unclean in the first month partake of the Passover feast (Num. 9:11).
- $20^{th}$ day, $2^{nd}$ month, $2^{nd}$ year: it is time to leave Mount Sinai (Num. 10:11-12).

Look back to this chronology note frequently to keep on track with what is happening to the people of Israel. All of these things happen in barely more than one year since they came out of Egypt. When God has completed all He wants them to do at Sinai, it will be time for them to go inherit the land of Canaan. Do not forget the thread of the history. Do not bog down in a study of the details of the law at this time.

## The nation promise is fulfilled:

By the time the Israelites leave Mount Sinai, they are no longer a group of slaves. They are a separate, distinct nation with its own law and its own king (Jehovah Himself). *The promise to Abraham that his descendants would become a great nation has come true (Gen. 12:2).*

# The Tabernacle: God's Dwelling Place Among the People

## (Exodus 25-31; 35-39)

**The Route of the Exodus: From Egypt to Canaan**

**The Call of Moses**
**The Plagues**
**From Egypt to Sinai**
**Jehovah Makes a Covenant**

***More Time at Sinai**
***Building the Tabernacle**
***The Tabernacle**
***The Furniture**
***Additional Rules**

**From Sinai to Kadesh**
**Wandering**
**The Plains of Moab**
**Moses' Speeches**
**Journey's End**

*While Moses was in the mount, God gave him detailed instructions about how to build a dwelling place for Him that would serve as a constant reminder to the people that God was indeed in their midst. It was to be a beautiful, very costly, moveable structure. The Hebrew word for tabernacle means a tent, but it was much more than a typical tent. Most of it was built of wood and then covered with costly metal. Even the coverings and curtains were specially designed and woven to fit the prescribed pattern. All metal inside the tabernacle itself was either gold or silver, except for the sockets for the entrance poles. Those sockets were of bronze. The metal outside was either silver or bronze.*

*Where did all the wealth of gold, silver, brass, and costly fabrics come from? The gold came from bracelets, earrings, rings, and necklaces (Exod. 35:22). Gold, silver, and brass were also probably offered in bulk in the form of coins, wedges, or ingots. Brass (or bronze) mirrors were one source of that metal (Exod. 38:8). Everyone who had blue, purple, and scarlet, and fine linen, goats' hair, rams' skins, and sealskins brought them. Anyone who had acacia wood donated it. The women spun goats' hair, while the rulers brought onyx stones and other gem stones for the priestly garments, and spices and oil with which to make the oil for the light and the sweet incense. The donations came from a large host of many individuals (35:20-29). Each individual gave liberally, and, together, their contributions amounted to a vast amount.*

*But where did the people get these precious things? As Jehovah was planning to bring the last plague upon Egypt, remember that He told Moses to tell each man and each woman of Israel to ask the Egyptians who lived nearby for jewels of silver and jewels of gold. The Lord gave the Israelites favor in the sight of the Egyptians so that they gave in abundance (11:2-3; 12:35-36). Jehovah did not tell the Israelites to get these things from the Egyptians so that they would have nice jewelry. He was looking ahead to the need the Israelites would have to build His tabernacle.*

*Take time to study the details of the tabernacle, its furnishings, and their purposes carefully. All the worship described in the Old Testament is based upon the tabernacle and the instructions given here. The temple that will be built in Solomon's day will be designed like the tabernacle, except that it will be a permanent structure, not moveable; everything will be bigger; and it will have treasure rooms all around the inner sanctuary.*

*It is necessary to know about the tabernacle in order to understand the concept of the church and heaven in the New Testament. The book of Hebrews is impossible to understand without an understanding of the Old Testament tabernacle and the sacrifices offered there. God "showed Moses a pattern" for the tabernacle, and the book of Hebrews makes the point that the whole structure —the whole concept of the tabernacle of the Old Testament —was a pattern of the true tabernacle of the New Testament. The rooms of the tabernacle and all the rituals of their service foreshadowed the day of the new covenant. Sometimes we think the old physical structures were the true tabernacle, and the church, its worship, and heaven as figures of the old. But the exact opposite is true. God was revealing and developing His ultimate plan for redemption from the time sin first entered the world. The physical structure was the figure to help mankind learn what God would accomplish in the sacrifice of the Christ. Let us be sure to learn the lessons God intended for us to learn.*

*God gave Moses instructions in Exodus 25 through 31 about how to build the tabernacle and all its furniture, how to make the special garments for the priests, and many other details connected with the tabernacle worship. When Moses returned from the mountain, he gave the instructions to the people, and they worked carefully to obey all that God had said. Therefore, some details about the various pieces are recorded in chapters 25 through 31 and then are repeated in chapters 35 through 39 as the people do the work. We combine the information as we describe each item so that we can have all the details together.*

*The measurements for the tabernacle and its furnishings are given in cubits in the Bible text. According to dictionaries, a cubit was usually about 18 to 21 inches long. Since we do not know the exact length of the cubit they used, we are using the 18 inch cubit for our description of the measurements.*

*Look into our companion book about the law, Jehovah's Covenant With Israel, for a full description of the tabernacle. There we have the specific details outlined for easy reference when you are studying and teaching the information.*

*Look for a model of the tabernacle, or transparencies, or some other visual aid, to help get the plan of it in mind. We cannot know exactly how all the details looked, but we can visualize the overall design from the descriptions given.*

## Instructions to the people (Exod. 25:1-9; 31:1-11; 35:4-36:7):

As Moses records the law the Lord gave him in the mount, the first thing he describes is the tabernacle (25:1-9). God gave exact instructions for how to build each piece, how it was to be used, and how it was to be cared for. He said, "I will show you a pattern of the tabernacle and a pattern for all its furniture, and you are to construct each piece exactly according to its pattern." More than once, God stressed that it must all be done according to the pattern (25:9, 40).

After Moses returned from his second trip into the mountain, he spoke to all the people, saying, (35:4-19): "This is what the Lord has commanded:

> Take up from among yourselves an offering for the Lord. Whoever is willing to give freely, let him bring the Lord's offering, whether it be gold, silver, brass, blue, purple, scarlet, fine linen, goats' hair, rams' skin dyed red, sealskins, acacia wood, oil for the light, spices for the anointing oil and

BAdgerskin

> for the sweet incense, and onyx stones and other precious stones to be set for the ephod and for the breastplate.
>
> Also let every skillful person among you come forward to make the tabernacle and the things which pertain to it. Make the structure itself, the coverings, and the curtains for it; make the furniture with all the vessels that pertain to each piece and the coverings for those pieces; make the posts and curtains for the courtyard; and make all the garments for the priests. Make this sanctuary for me, *and I will dwell among you.* Make this tabernacle and all its furnishings exactly like the pattern I will show you.

The work was to be done by the Israelites, led and supervised by Bezalel and Oholiab. For Moses told the congregation (see 31:1-11; 35:30-35):

> See, the Lord has chosen Bezalel the son of Uri, the son of Hur, of the tribe of Judah, and has filled him with the Spirit of God. He has given Bezalel skill, ability, and knowledge in all kinds of crafts so that he can make artistic designs for work in gold, silver and bronze; so that he can set stones, work in wood, and engage in all kinds of artistic craftsmanship. And He has given Bezalel and Oholiab, the son of Ahisamach of the tribe of Dan, whom He has appointed with him, the ability to teach others. They will be filled with the ability to do all kinds of work as craftsmen, and designers, and weavers; and He will show them how to do embroidery work in yarn and in linen. Also God has given skill and understanding to other craftsmen who will work with them so that they can build the tabernacle, all its furnishings, and the garments for the priests exactly as God has commanded.

Thus Bezalel and Oholiab were to be the master craftsmen, the ones who would be able to understand and to build exactly what God had in mind, because God was placing His Spirit upon these men, thus inspiring them to understand every detail. Other skilled craftsmen, and the rest of the people, were to work under their guidance.

The people all went away and determined what each one would give. All who were willing, both men and women, came bringing gold jewelry of all kinds as an offering to the Lord. Everyone who possessed any of the other items needed, from rams' skin to bronze, brought what they had to be used in the work. The women willingly spun goat's hair, fine linen, and the blue, purple, and scarlet yarn needed. The leaders of the people brought onyx stones and other precious gems to be used in the priests' garments. Others brought spices, oil, and incense. All the Israelite men and women offered their things freely and willingly.

Moses summoned Bezalel, Oholiab, and the other skilled craftsmen, and delivered into their hands all the offerings the people had brought to carry out the work. The people continued to come with their offerings, and they gave so freely that those who were doing the work finally went to Moses and said, "The people have brought much more than enough to make everything."

So Moses proclaimed throughout the camp, "Let neither man nor woman any longer perform work for the contributions of the sanctuary." Thus the people refrained from bringing more, and the work was begun.

# The Tabernacle

## (Exodus 25:1-8; 26:1-37; 31:1-11; 35:4-36:38)

### The tabernacle itself:

Though the walls were made of boards, the whole tabernacle could be taken apart and moved. Exact instructions were given for how each piece was to be handled, how it was to be moved, and how it was to be set into its place.

The overall size of the tabernacle was thirty cubits long by ten cubits wide *(45 feet by 15 feet)*. It was divided into two sections: the Holy Place and the Most Holy Place. The Holy Place was the first room a priest entered when he came through the entrance curtain. It was 20 cubits long and 10 cubits wide *(30 feet by 15 feet)*. The Most Holy Place was a cube: as wide as it was long and as high as it was wide and long *(10 cubits or 15 feet)*.

There were very strict restrictions concerning who could enter the tabernacle. It was not an auditorium for the congregation of the people. Only the priests could enter it at all, and only the High Priest could enter the Most Holy Place. Even they could enter the structure only when there were specific tasks to be performed.

**A. The boards with their sockets for the walls (Exod. 26:15-30; 36:20-34):**

Huge boards to form the walls were made from acacia wood *(shittim in the Hebrew language)*. Each board was ten cubits long and one and one half cubit wide *(15 feet high by 27 inches wide)*, but their thickness is not told. Some scholars believe that instead of these "boards" being solid planks, they were box-shaped frameworks made of comparatively small strips of acacia wood which were then overlaid with gold plate. This seems to be a reasonable explanation of the boards, although, of course, we cannot be sure.

Each board had two projections *(tenons)* on its base which fitted, each one, into a silver socket. Each silver socket weighed about 75 pounds, and there were a total of 100 of these sockets (Exod. 38:25, 27). The total silver used in building the tabernacle weighed about three and three fourths tons.

The boards had gold rings attached to the outside surface through which long poles were slid to lock the boards together. These poles were made of acacia wood also and were overlaid with gold plate. There were five long poles to put through the rings on each of the three sides of the tabernacle that had the boards. The center pole extended the full length of the side. Though the exact position of the other poles is not given, since they were designed to give stability to the boards, they would either have reached the full length of the wall, or they would have been staggered so that they overlapped to give the most strength possible.

The sockets and boards were designed so that the boards stood side by side vertically, with the tenons of each board fitting into the two sockets under it. There were twenty boards for the south side, twenty for the north side, and a total of eight for the west side. Since every single board had two sockets of silver under it, there were ninety six sockets for the walls. Since the boards were twenty seven inches wide and there were twenty on each of the long sides, the tabernacle was forty five feet long *(30 cubits)* and the short walls were approximately fifteen feet *(10 cubits)*. This adding of the size of the twenty boards on each long side is how we determine the overall length, because there is no passage that specifically gives the overall length and width of the tabernacle.

There were a total of eight boards on the west side of the tabernacle, but their exact arrangement is hard to know. Six stood vertically, side by side, just as the boards were arranged on the other two sides. But that seventh and eighth board stood in some way that helped strengthen the corners.

Notice 26:22-25 and 36:27-30. The boards on each end were "double" from top to bottom, fitting into one ring, to form the corners.

*There are many details, like the arrangement of the corner boards, that we simply cannot know for sure about how the tabernacle looked. That is why the people needed Bezalel and Oholiab to whom God had given special understanding so that they could know exactly how God intended each detail to be. Do not get into prolonged discussions on the details we cannot be sure about. Work to get the overall picture of the tabernacle in mind.*

**B. Posts with their sockets (Exod. 36:36, 38):**

The other four silver sockets that are described were for the posts upon which was hung the veil that divided the tabernacle into the Holy Place and the Most Holy Place. These four posts were also made of acacia wood overlaid with gold. All other poles had chapiters *(metal caps)*, on top and were connected by a rod *(fillet)*. The four inside poles had hooks of gold, but there is no description of metal caps and rods. The mechanical requirements for hanging the curtain imply that they had them.

The tabernacle was always set up so that the entrance was on the east side. There were five pillars *(posts)* upon which an entrance curtain was hung. These pillars were made of acacia wood overlaid with gold. Their capitals *(chapiters, metal caps)* were overlaid with gold also, and the hooks were gold, but the sockets on the ground into which these pillars fitted were of brass *(bronze)* instead of silver. A rod *(fillet)* overlaid with gold probably connected these poles at the top, though it is not described.

## The coverings and curtains for the tabernacle (Exod. 26:1-14, 31-37; 36:8-19, 35-38):

Although this tabernacle had wooden walls, it was still a tent *(the meaning of the word tabernacle)*, therefore the outer coverings were very important as part of the structure. The exact shape of the structure with these coverings is uncertain. A ridgepole is never mentioned, but tent pegs are (38:20). Since water would pool if the coverings lay flat across the boards, it seems logical that there was a ridgepole over which the coverings were stretched and were then held taut by the tent pegs. But, if so, the details are not given.

**A. Fine linen (Exod. 26:1-6; 36:8-13):**

The coverings for the tabernacle consisted of four layers. The innermost layer was of "fine linen." It was white. Figures of cherubim were woven into the fabric in colors of blue, purple, and scarlet. The text uses the expression "embroidered" as it describes the workmanship, but it seems the designs were actually woven into the fabric of the cloth rather than being stitched onto the cloth as we would define embroidery work. According to *Keil and Delitzsch,* the blue was a "purple of a dark blue shade, approaching black rather than bright blue." The purple was "true purple of a dark red color," and the scarlet was "scarlet-red purple, or crimson" (see *Keil and Delitzsch* on Exodus 25:1-9).

What the figures of the cherubim looked like is not clear. For practical purposes, we can say cherubim are special servants of God, supernatural figures as are angels. These cherubim were woven into the fabric of the innermost covering of the tabernacle, the layer seen from inside, and into the veil which divided between the Holy Place and the Most Holy Place.

This first innermost covering was called the tabernacle (26:1) because it was largely what one saw from inside the structure. It was made into ten panels, each twenty eight cubits long and four cubits wide *(42 feet by 6 feet)*. Then five panels were sewed together to make two panels twenty cubits wide *(30 feet)*. These two large panels were fastened together along their edges by fifty clasps of gold hooked onto fifty corresponding loops of very dark blue thread. The ten panels sewed and hooked together would, therefore, be forty cubits long and twenty eight cubits wide *(60 feet by 42 feet)*. Possibly this layer hung down on the inside of the walls. If these curtains hung down on the outside, then the cherubim woven into the cloth would not be seen at all in the part that hung down, because only the part overhead would be seen. Yet the symbolism of the cherubim suggest that the tabernacle was the dwelling place of God, surrounded by His special servants. No details are given about how the covering was suspended overhead.

**B. Goats' hair (Exod. 26:7-13; 36:14-18):**

The second covering of the tabernacle was of goats' hair. That is, it was cloth woven from thread made from goats' hair. It was likely black because that was the usual color of fabric made of goats' hair. This layer was made into eleven panels, each one thirty cubits by four cubits *(45 feet by 6 feet)*. Then the panels were sewed together in one set of five and one set of six panels. These two big panels were fastened together with fifty loops and fifty bronze clasps. The goats' hair layer is referred to as the tent *(the ordinary word in the Bible for tent)* (26:7). The over-all dimensions of the goats' hair layer was forty four cubits by thirty cubits *(66 feet by 45 feet)*, so this layer extended beyond the front, the back, and the sides to give the tabernacle extra protection.

Since the goats' hair layer is called a tent (Num. 3:25), it was probably the layer arranged like a tent with a peaked roof, and was held around the edges by ropes and stakes. Indeed, these ropes and stakes are referred to in Exodus 27:19, in 38:20, and in Numbers 3:26, 37, though no ridge pole for a peaked roof is ever specified.

**C. Rams' skin and badgers' skin (Exod. 26:14; 36:19):**

The next two layers were rams' skins dyed red and what the KJV refers to as badgers' skins. The rams' skins was leather made from the skin of male sheep with the wool left on.

One thing virtually all scholars agree upon is that the outermost layer was not what we would call badgers' skins. The overwhelming majority of scholars say it was the skin from some aquatic mammal, but there is no way to know which one the Hebrew word means. And since we do not know which specific animal was used, we will use the term the Bible text uses and call the layer badgers' skin, or one of the other terms used in another translation (e.g. seals' skin - ASV).

No details are given about their size or how these skins were put together. It is assumed that since these layers were outermost, they would have been at least as big as the goats' hair layer. These layers gave protection against rain and served as insulation against both heat and cold.

**D. The veil (Exod. 26:31-33; 36:35-36):**

The veil between the Holy Place and the Most Holy Place was made of the same fine white linen as the innermost layer of the coverings, and like that covering, it had cherubim woven into the fabric with the colors of blue, purple, and scarlet. It was suspended from hooks of gold upon four poles overlaid with gold. It was hung on the side of the poles next to the Most Holy Place. We are not told how high this curtain reached, but likely it was no higher than arm's reach, because when the priests prepared the ark for travel, they went to the veil, unhooked it, and walked forward to lay the veil over the ark of the covenant (Num. 4:5).

When the Bible speaks of "the veil of the tabernacle" *(or temple)*, it is referring to this curtain because of its importance in dividing the Most Holy Place from the Holy Place. Therefore it was the veil at this place in the temple which tore when Jesus died on the cross (Mark 15:38).

**E. The entrance curtain (Exod. 26:36-37; 36:37-38):**

The veil or curtain at the entrance of the tabernacle was made of white linen, but instead of having figures of cherubim of blue, purple, and scarlet woven into it, these colors were intermingled with the white *(no particular pattern is specified)*. It was fastened on hooks of gold and hung on five poles overlaid with gold. The five sockets for these poles were of bronze.

## The courtyard (Exod. 27:9-19; 38:9-20):

The tabernacle was surrounded by an open *(no covering over the top)* court one hundred cubits long and fifty cubits wide *(150 feet long and 75 feet wide)*. That means the courtyard was over three times as long as the tabernacle itself, and five times wider, but only half as tall, because the tabernacle was thirty cubits long, ten cubits wide, and ten cubits high *(45 feet by 15 feet by 15 feet)*. The walls of the court were curtains five cubits high *(7½ feet)* and made of finely woven white linen. The cloth was suspended from silver rods and silver hooks upon posts set in sockets of bronze. The north and south sides had twenty posts with their twenty sockets, while the east and west sides had ten posts with their ten sockets. On the east side of the court there was an entrance curtain made like the front curtain of the tabernacle with blue, purple, and scarlet intermingled with the white. It was the only part of the court hangings that had any color. All the tent pegs for the tabernacle and the surrounding courtyard were made of bronze.

# The Furniture

### (Exodus 25:10-40; 26:35; 27:1-8, 20-21; 30:1-10, 17-21; 37:1-38:8; Leviticus 24:1-9)

Just as with the tabernacle itself, instructions are given first for how the pieces of furniture were to be built and how they were to be used; then a description is given about how the people did the work; and later the rules for caring for and moving the items will be given (see Num. 3:31-32; 4:1-20). Every piece of furniture, except for the candlestick, was made with rings for staves to be run through to make it possible to carry. The candlestick was wrapped and moved within a cloth bag. The Kohathites, a particular clan of the Levites, were responsible for moving the furniture. The priests themselves were Levites, of the family of Aaron, from the clan of Kohath.

## The ark of the covenant (Exod. 25:10-22; 37:1-9):

Within the Most Holy Place there was one article of furniture, the ark of the covenant. It was a box two and a half cubits long, one an a half cubits wide, and one and a half cubits high *(45 inches long, 27 inches wide, and 27 inches high)*. It was made of acacia wood and overlaid with gold plate. The lid was called the mercy seat and was made of solid gold. Two cherubim which faced each other with their wings extended toward one another, formed the top of the mercy seat. It was from this space above the mercy seat and between the cherubim that God promised to have fellowship with Israel as their God; this is where He would "meet with them" (25:22). The box was designed to hold the tables of stone, the Testimony, that God was giving them — thus, it was literally, the "box of the testimony."

The ark had four feet *(projections on the bottom)* with a ring in each of the four feet. Through these rings two staves of acacia wood overlaid with gold were placed by which the ark was carried. These staves were to be left in place always. The top edge of the ark had a rim, a molding, into which the mercy seat fit to keep it from sliding off.

## The altar of incense (Exod. 30:1-10, 34-38; 37:25-29):

The little altar of incense stood just outside the veil which divided the Most Holy Place from the Holy Place. Even though it stood on the front side of the veil in the Holy Place, it was regarded as belonging to the Most Holy Place (Heb. 9:3-4), because it was here that incense was offered directly to Jehovah. The altar stood two cubits high *(3 feet)* and its top formed a cubit square *(18 inch)*. It was made of acacia wood and covered with gold. There was a gold molding around the top that formed a "horn" at each corner. Just below the molding, there were rings on the four corners through which gold covered poles of acacia wood were placed for carrying it.

Aaron was to burn incense upon this little altar every morning when he came into the tabernacle to trim the lamps in the lamp-stand, and then again in the afternoon when it was time to trim the lamps again. It was to be done regularly so that incense would burn before the Lord through all the generations to come. Nothing else was ever to be offered upon this altar — no burnt offering, no grain offering, no drink offering, nor even any other kind of incense. Once a year, on the Day of Atonement, Aaron *(and every high priest after him)* was to bring blood from the atonement sacrifice and put some of it on the horns of the altar of incense.

Even the recipe for the special incense to be offered on this altar was specified. The Lord told Moses, "Take fragrant spices — gum resin, onychia, galbanum, and pure frankincense, all in equal amounts. Make a fragrant blend of incense, the work of a perfumer. It is to be salted, pure, and sacred. Grind some of it into powder and spread it in front of the Testimony in the Tent of Meeting, where I will meet with you. Do not make any incense like this for your own use. Consider it holy *(set apart)* to the Lord. Whoever makes any like this for his own use is to be cut off from his people."

## The table of shewbread (Exod. 25:23-30; 26:35; 37:10-16; Lev. 24:5-9):

On the north side of the Holy Place there was a table called the table of shewbread *(or table of the Presence)*. It, too, was made of acacia wood and overlaid with gold. There was a border around the sides of the table and a rim above that. A ring of gold was on each of the four legs of the table, through which two staves were placed for carrying it.

The vessels which accompanied the table of shewbread were of gold. They included dishes *(platters or bowls)* in which the loaves were probably placed, spoons or small scoops used to hold the incense which was offered with the shewbread, vessels to dip out the wine and pour it (Exod. 37:16), and bowls *(chalices or goblets)* which were used for drinking vessels.

They were to take finely ground flour and bake twelve loaves of unleavened bread and place them on the table in sets of six *(possibly in two stacks of six each)*. Frankincense was placed on top of each stack of shewbread, and was burned in the fire as an offering to the Lord. Every sabbath day the shewbread was replaced with twelve fresh loaves. The old bread was to be eaten by the priests in a holy place, for it was a holy sacrifice unto God.

The twelve loaves were for the twelve tribes, and the Bible says, "It is on the behalf of *(or from)* the children of Israel, an everlasting covenant" (Lev. 24:8). The bread was probably a symbol of Israel's presence before God, suggesting that they would ever stand before His face to do His bidding.

## The golden candlestick (Exod. 25:31-40; 26:35; 27:20-21; 37:17-24; Lev. 24:1-4):

On the south side of the Holy Place stood the golden candlestick. It and the mercy seat on the top of the ark of the covenant were the only articles of gold that did not have a core of acacia wood. The candlestick was made of a talent of gold *(about 75 pounds)*. Apparently, the snuffers and snuff dishes were made of that same talent of gold (Exod. 25:39). No dimensions are given, but it is speculated that it was about a cubit and a half *(27 inches)* in length and a cubit and a half *(27 inches)* in width from outside branch to outside branch.

There was a base, a pedestal, and seven branches. Each branch consisted of three cups shaped like almond blossoms, followed by a knop *(pomegranate)* and a flower *(lily blossom)*. There is no point in trying to decide exactly what the details of the candlestick looked like.

It is important to understand that, though many translations of the Bible use the word "candlestick," the object referred to was actually a lamp-stand with lamps on the end of the branches which held olive oil with wicks (25:37; 27:20). The Israelites were instructed to bring pure olive oil so that the lamps could be kept burning regularly.

The lamps were not perpetually lit *(in the sense of never being extinguished)* because, when traveling, the Israelites carried the lamp-stand with its vessels in a bag suspended from a frame or bar (Num. 4:9-10). "Continually" means regularly, when the tabernacle was set up. The Bible says the lamp-stand was to be "kept in order" from "evening to morning." Every morning Aaron was to dress the lamps *(clean the lamps and put in fresh oil)*, and every evening he would light *(or trim)* the lamps (Exod. 30:7-8). It was at these times, while the priest was inside the tabernacle, that the incense was to be offered upon the golden altar of incense (30:7-8).

## The altar of burnt offering (Exod. 27:1-8; 38:1-7):

Outside of the tabernacle there were two objects which stood in the courtyard: the altar of burnt offering and the bronze laver. The altar was a big square frame, with the inside hollow so that a fire could be built and animals burned upon it. The boards were of acacia wood overlaid with bronze. A "horn" was made into each corner of the altar. There was a grating of network (*net,* 27:4) which reached from the bottom half-way up under the ledge round about the outside of the altar. The altar was five cubits long, five cubits wide, and three cubits high *(7½ feet by 7½ feet by 4½ feet)*. The priests would stand upon the ledge to work over the altar. They used various vessels and flesh hooks to do their work, and each of these vessels was made of bronze. This is the altar where all sacrifices were offered except for the incense that was offered inside on the little altar. This altar also had four rings to hold the bronze covered poles for carrying it.

## The bronze laver (Exod. 30:17-21; 38:8):

The other article in the courtyard was a large bronze bowl which sat on a base. At this brazen laver, the priests were to wash their hands and their feet so they would not die when they came to do service for Israel before God. They were to wash each time they entered the Tent of Meeting or approached the altar to offer a sacrifice. The laver was made from the mirrors the women had donated to the work of the tabernacle. Its size and exact shape are not told.

All of these things were made by Bezalel and Oholiab, assisted by skilled helpers (Exod. 36:1-8). And all the items — the structure itself, the coverings, the courtyard, the furniture, and all the vessels — were made exactly according to the pattern Moses was shown in the mount.

*Notice that every part of the tabernacle was designed so that it could be moved. The boards stood separate, and they and their sockets could be moved. Each piece of furniture was designed with staves so that it could be carried.*

## Additional Rules Related to the Tabernacle Worship
### (Exodus 30:11-16, 22-33; 31:12-17; 35:1-3)

As we described the altar of incense, we noted that a specific recipe was given for the incense to be used on it. The people were not to make the identical recipe for use at home (30:34-38). The exact kind of oil was specified to be used in the seven lamps on the golden candlestick (27:20-21). Details were given for how to make the shewbread for the table, how it was to be placed on the table, when it was to be changed, who was to eat it, and where it was to be eaten. It was to be counted as holy because it had been offered before the Lord (Lev. 24:5-9).

In addition to the specific details concerning the incense, the oil for the light, and the shewbread, there are details given about two other things in the very midst of the details about building the tabernacle. Therefore, before we describe the garments for the priests, let us look at those items.

*Although we do not live under the law of Moses, and there are not as many minute prohibitions given in the new law, perhaps we need to learn some lessons from the principles here. Let us be careful to show respect toward the things that have been dedicated to the Lord —for example, to the "leftovers" from the Lord's Supper. The point is not that the unleavened bread that is left is holy, but that if we allow our children to eat freely the bread that is left, it tends to blur the distinction in their minds between the very special use of that bread in the Lord's Supper, and its use as common food. One of the greatest lessons we learn from a study of the old law is that of respect for things sacred.*

### The atonement money (Exod. 30:11-16):

The Lord told Moses, "When you take a census of the people, each one is to pay the Lord a ransom for his life so that no plague will come upon you. As one passes from the group of the uncounted to the group of the counted, he is to pay a half shekel, according to the sanctuary shekel *(about 1/5 ounce, or 6 grams)*. This half shekel is an offering to the Lord and is to be paid by everyone who is counted, all those twenty years old and above. The rich is to pay no more, and the poor is to pay no less. Receive the atonement money from the people and use it for the service of the tabernacle. It will be a memorial for the Israelites before the Lord, making atonement for their lives."

*This was the "temple tax" that the Jewish officials asked Peter if his Lord paid. Peter was quick to answer "Yes," but then he wondered whether it was necessary for Jesus to pay it, because it was money for supplying the needs of the tabernacle (or temple) for worshiping Jehovah. Jesus knew about the conversation, and He asked Peter whether kings collected taxes from their sons. When Peter replied correctly, Jesus told him, "But, lest we cause them to stumble, go catch a fish and take the shekel in its mouth to pay the tax for you and for me." Why should the Son of God be required to pay a temple tax? (See Matt. 17:24-27.)*

## The anointing oil (Exod. 30:22-33):

The Lord also told Moses, "Make a sacred anointing oil from the following recipe:

500 shekels *(about 12½ pounds)* of liquid myrrh
250 shekels of fragrant cinnamon
250 shekels of fragrant cane
500 shekels of cassia
One hin *(probably about 4 quarts)* of olive oil

Make these ingredients into a sacred oil, a fragrant blend, the work of a perfumer. Use the oil to anoint the Tent of Meeting, the ark of the covenant, the table and all its articles, the candlestick and all its accessories, the altar of incense, the altar of burnt offering and all its utensils, and the laver. You shall consecrate them so that they will be holy, and whoever touches them will be holy.

Then take some of the oil and anoint Aaron and his sons so that they will be consecrated and can serve me as priests. But tell the rest of the Israelites that this is God's sacred anointing oil for all generations to come. Do not make any oil by this same formula to use for any personal use. Whoever makes a perfume like it and whoever puts it on, other than a priest, must be cut off from his people.

## Study the schematic drawing:

*Look at the schematic drawing of the tabernacle on the next page. Study it carefully. Learn it well enough to make one of your own. Know which way the tabernacle faced; know how much bigger the courtyard was than the tabernacle itself; know where every piece of furniture stood and what it was used for. Try drawing one to scale for yourself.*

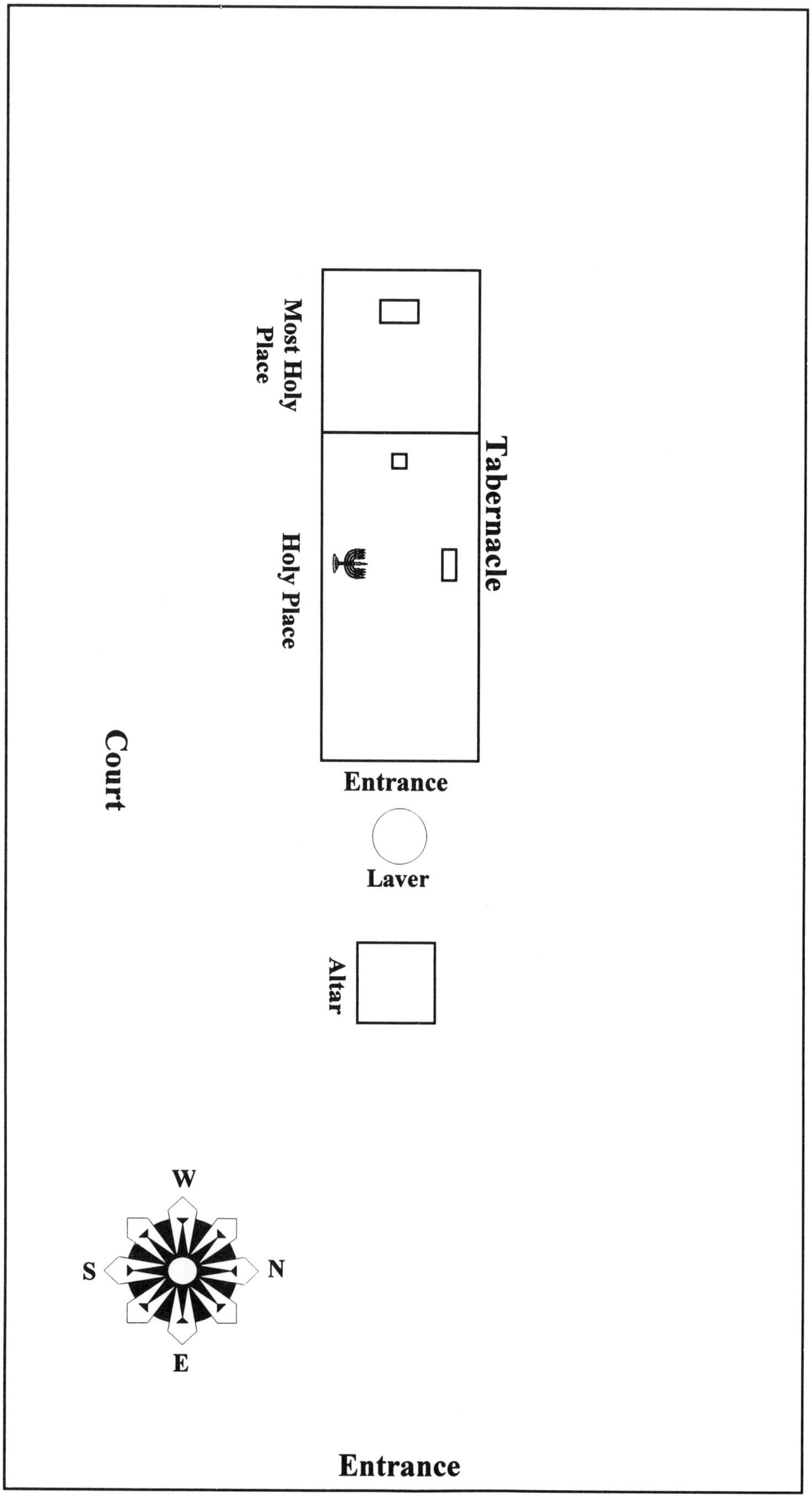
Tabernacle
Most Holy Place
Holy Place
Entrance
Laver
Altar
Court
W
S
N
E
Entrance

# *Garments for the Priests*

## *(Exodus 28 and 39)*



The Lord instructed Moses, "Have Aaron your brother brought before you from among the Israelites, along with his four sons: Nadab, Abihu, Eleazar, and Ithamar, so that they can serve me as priests. Make sacred garments for Aaron to give him dignity and honor. Tell all the skilled men to whom I have given wisdom in such matters to make the garments exactly as they have been instructed, so that Aaron may be consecrated, and may serve me as priest. Have them use gold, blue, purple, and scarlet yarn, and fine linen to make the garments."

The garments of Aaron *(the High Priest)* were made for glory and for beauty (28:2, 40). Since Aaron was the first High Priest, and his garments were specially made at this time, they were to be kept for future generations of High Priests. Each new High Priest was to wear Aaron's garments for the seven days of his consecration (29:29-30). It is, therefore, the garments for the High Priest that are described in the most detail.

### Mediators between God and Israel:

*God ordained that there be priests to mediate between Himself and the people. From the time sin entered the world, God no longer walked and talked freely with man. There is proof that by the days of Cain and Abel God had ordained that men approach Him by means of a sacrifice (Gen. 4:3-5). During the patriarchal age, the father of each family offered the sacrifices for his own family. The word "Patriarch" means "father-ruler" and refers to the way the father was the mediator between God and his family. For example, see the story of Job who was a patriarch. When his sons and daughters met to eat and drink together, Job offered burnt offerings "according to the number of them all," saying, "It may be that my sons have sinned, and renounced God in their hearts" (Job 1:4-5).*

*Now, here as the Law of Moses is being given, God is setting apart specific men who will serve as mediators between Himself and the Israelites. The intercessory nature of the work of the priests is set forth in several ways. In God's instructions describing the garments of the high priest, twice Aaron is said to* <u>*bear*</u> *the names of the tribes of Israel. Upon the onyx stones of the shoulder pieces of the ephod the names of the tribes of Israel were to be engraved, "and Aaron shall bear their names before Jehovah upon his two shoulders for a memorial" (Exod. 28:6-12). Then on the breastplate that was to be affixed to the front of the ephod, there were twelve stones upon which were engraved the names of the twelve tribes of Israel, "And Aaron shall bear the names of the children of Israel in the breastplate of judgment upon his heart, when he goes into the holy place" (28:29). When God gave instructions about the work of the priests and Levites He said that He chose the Levites to be His special tribe in the place of the firstborn that He had claimed as His own after the last plague in Egypt (Exod. 13:2; Num. 3:41).*

*The sacrifices to be offered under the law of Moses were much more complex than they were during the patriarchal period. It was essential to have people set apart who would have nothing else to occupy their attention but the offering of the "holy things" of the Lord. Therefore the priests were charged not to drink wine or strong drink that they "might make a distinction between the holy and the common, and between the unclean and the clean," and they were commanded to teach Israel all the statutes of the Lord (Lev. 10:10-11; Mal. 2:7).*

*It was their task "to keep the charge of the sanctuary, and the charge of the altar; that there be wrath no more upon the children of Israel" (Num. 18:5). In the New Testament the Hebrew writer says of the high priest, "And by reason thereof is bound, as for the people, so also for himself, to offer for sins" (Heb. 5:3; cf. 7:27; 9:7). Perhaps the clearest proof of the intercessory role of the priests is that Jesus became our High Priest, and in a context emphasizing the effectiveness of His priesthood, the Hebrew writer says, "He ever liveth to make intercession for them" (Heb. 7:25).*

*The role of the priests was very important in God's scheme of things under the law of Moses. They stood between God and the people, so it was a position of honor, but also one of great responsibility. A priest who did not take his position seriously was in a dangerous position before the Lord. He was to obey God carefully in his own life, to be an example of obedience before the people, and he was to instruct the congregation so that they could continue in their faithfulness to Jehovah. The High Priest even stood as the supreme court if a matter of wrong was done that was too difficult for the local judges and officials to handle. As you continue your study of Old Testament history, watch for God's emphasis upon the responsibilities of the priests. Observe the rebukes to the priests as the nation as a whole turns away from God, and as the prophets come along to warn of impending doom. The priests were held responsible for the sins of the nation, because they failed to teach the people and to punish the wrongdoer.*

*The Levites will soon be numbered, organized, and presented to Aaron as his assistants. But though the Levites will serve as assistants to the priests, God was quite specific in saying that the priests themselves were to be Aaron, his sons, and his direct descendants after him (Exod. 28:1, 43; Num.3:10; 18:1-7.) That is, all priests were Levites, but none of the Levites except the direct descendants of Aaron could offer sacrifices or perform any of the other duties specifically assigned to priests. There were times in their history when some of the Levites themselves objected because they were not allowed to offer sacrifices, and they were punished severely for their rebellion (Num. 16-17).*

*Before any specific instructions about the work of the priests or the tribe of Levi are given, Moses is told to bring Aaron and his sons before the assembly as God's chosen priests. Moses received instructions how to make special garments for the priests at the same time he received the instructions for building the tabernacle, and the garments were being made while the tabernacle and its furniture was being built. We will follow the pattern of the text and describe the priests' garments first. Then there will be the story of their consecration and the beginning of their work. Finally, as the rest of the law is recorded, all the rest of the instructions for the priests will be given. There will be chapters that are filled with special rules and regulations for the priests; their portions from the sacrifices will be specified; cities will be given to the priests and Levites as their inheritance. We will include summaries of this information as we look into the law in this book, but you might find it useful to look into our companion book, Jehovah's Covenant With Israel, for a more detailed look at all the information about the priests, the Levites, their duties, and their portions.*

*Look for some form of visual aid to help you visualize the garments for the High Priest and the other priests who served with him. As you find a visual aid, compare it with the information in the Bible text, and choose the one that is most nearly accurate.*

## Garments for the High Priest (Exod. 28:1-43; 39:1-31):

The garments of Aaron *(the High Priest)* were made for glory and for beauty (28:2, 40), and it is his garments that are described in the most detail. Just as He did with the instructions about the tabernacle and its furnishings, God gave Moses detailed instructions about how the garments were to be made (chapter 28), and then chapter 39 tells how the people carried out those instructions. Again, we combine the information to make it as concise and clear as possible.

The Lord told Moses, "And these are the garments which they shall make: a breastplate, an ephod, a robe, a coat of woven work, a mitre, and a girdle. They shall make holy garments for Aaron your brother and for his sons so that he may minister unto me in the priest's office. They shall make them of gold, blue, purple, scarlet, and fine linen."

*As God listed the garments, He listed them from the outermost garment in, but we are starting with the simplest item first, so we are describing the items from the innermost out. The passages are given here for each item, so it should not be confusing.*

**A. The linen undergarment (Exod. 28:42-43; 39:28):**

All the priests *(high priest and regular priests)* were to wear linen breeches *(underwear)*, reaching from their waist to their thighs. The garment was designed "to cover their nakedness." They were forbidden to enter the tabernacle or to approach the altar without this garment on, lest they incur guilt and die. Just as all the other instructions for the priests and their duties, this was to be a lasting ordinance for all the generations of priests to come. No other details are given about the design of this item.

**B. The coat (Exod. 28:39; 39:27):**

The first garment worn over the underwear was a coat *(a tunic)* of woven work *("embroidered" —KJV; "checker work"—NASV)*. It was made of fine linen and woven in some kind of pattern. No other details are given in the text about this coat.

*Josephus says that this garment for the priest reached to the feet and had tightly fitting sleeves. He also says that the fabric of the coat was made of white linen that was woven in a pattern and embroidered with flowers of scarlet, purple, and blue. The text, however, says nothing of such figures or colors. (Antiquities of the Jews, Book III, Chapter VII, Para. 2)*

**C. The robe (Exod. 28:31-35; 39:22-26):**

Over the coat the high priest wore a robe made of blue. It was called the robe of the ephod because the vest-shaped ephod was attached to this garment. A strong band — strong enough that it would not tear — was woven around the neck of the garment. Pomegranates *(a ball shape)* of blue, purple, and scarlet alternated with gold bells around the hem at the bottom of the robe. The purpose was for these objects is uncertain, but Aaron was commanded to wear the robe when he did his work — "lest he die." The sound of the bells was to be heard as he went in and out of the tabernacle. The bells' jingling may have been a reminder that the high priest was going about his business of intercession.

**D. The ephod (Exod. 28:6-14; 39:2-7):**

Next there was the ephod. The background of the word *ephod* is uncertain. There are times it may refer to a simple tunic (2 Sam. 6:14), but it is clear that, most of the time, when the word is used, it is describing an ephod of the pattern described here.

This article was worn only by the high priest. It had two flaps, a front and a back. Two pieces were used to join the two flaps upon the shoulders. An onyx stone was fastened in a setting *(filigree)* of gold onto each shoulder piece, and on the stones were engraved the names of the twelve tribes of Israel — six on one stone and six on the other "according to their birth" — so that "Aaron may bear their names before the Lord on his two shoulders for a memorial."

The fabric of the ephod was of fine twined linen interwoven with threads of gold, blue, purple, and scarlet. The gold was not merely gold colored thread — it was pure gold. They hammered out gold sheets and cut them into threads to weave in with the blue, purple, and scarlet thread in the fine linen, "the work of a skillful workman" (39:3).

A sash called a "skillfully woven band" *(a curious girdle —KJV)* was woven into one piece with the ephod, and by this sash the ephod was fastened about the body *("wherewith to gird it on" —ASV, 28:7; 39:5)*. It, too, was made with pure gold threads interwoven with blue, purple, and scarlet into the fine linen.

Two chains of gold made to resemble a heavy cord were fastened to the shoulder pieces. They were made to hold the breastplate in place.

**E. The breastplate (Exod. 28:15-30; 39:8-21):**

The breastplate was the most important part of the high priest's attire — it is called "the breastplate of judgment." Aaron was to wear it as he went in and out before the Lord. It was made of the same mingled colors as the ephod — gold, blue, purple, and scarlet — "the work of a skillful workman." The fabric of the breastplate formed a perfect nine inch square *(a span)* and it was folded double to form a pocket in which were kept the Urim and the Thummim (28:30). Four rows of three precious stones each were set in gold filigree upon the breastplate. Engraved upon these twelve stones were the names of the twelve tribes. Thus Aaron bore "the names of the children of Israel upon his heart, when he went into the holy place, for a memorial before the Lord continually" (28:29).

Two golden chains were fashioned to resemble cords. These chains were fastened to rings attached to the upper end of the breastplate at each of the two corners. The other ends of the chains were fastened to the front part of the shoulder-pieces *(which held the onyx stones)* of the ephod. There were two other rings on the lower end of the breastplate, on the back side next to the ephod (28:26), by which the breastplate was bound to rings on the ephod with a lace *(a cord)* of blue. Thus bound by chains at the top and blue lace at the bottom, the breastplate was regarded as permanently bound to the ephod.

"And you shall put in the breastplate of judgment the Urim and the Thummin, and they shall be over Aaron's heart when he goes in before the Lord..." (28:30). It is uncertain what the Urim and the Thummim were. The terms are used very few times in the Bible (Exod. 28:30; Lev. 8:8; Num. 27:21; Deut. 33:8; Ezra 2:63; Neh. 7:65). The words themselves mean Lights *(Urim)* and Perfections *(Thummim)*. They were some sort of device by which God could give a yes-or-no answer to a question. Some have speculated that they were two stones of differing colors. To reach into the pocket formed by the breastplate and draw out one would mean yes; the other would mean no. By this means the priests could inquire of God. In this capacity the priest could almost be thought of as a prophet. It may be for this reason that David asked Zadok, one of the high priests in his day: "Aren't you a seer?" (2 Sam. 15:27). According to the law, the High Priest stood as the one with the ultimate say-so in the case of a dispute about a detail in the law. When there was a dispute, the ones involved took the matter to the local Levitical judge who was supposed to know the law in detail; if he could not settle the matter, it was taken to the priests, and finally to the High Priest. If one refused to listen to the judgment of the High Priest, he was to be put to death (Deut. 17:8-13). Presumably the High Priest was given that position by God because he could inquire of God by means of the Urim and Thummin (see Num. 27:21).

**F. The miter and the girdle (Exod. 28:36-40; 39:27-31):**

On his head, Aaron wore a miter, or turban, made of fine linen *(therefore white)*. On the front of the miter was a gold plate with the words, "Holy to Jehovah," engraved upon it, engraved like the engraving on a seal. It was attached to the miter with blue lace *(cord)*. By these words Aaron was designated as the one who, through the offerings he made for the people, atoned for their sins: "...and Aaron shall bear the iniquity of the holy things, which the children of Israel shall hallow in all their holy gifts... that they may be accepted before Jehovah" (28:38).

## Garments for the ordinary priests (Exod. 28:40-43; 39:27-29):

The garments of the ordinary priests were distinctive and were also made "for glory and for beauty," but theirs were much simpler than those of the High Priests. Theirs consisted of the linen breeches commanded for all priests, plus the coats or long tunics which, in the high priest, was the innermost garment next to the linen breeches. In addition, the ordinary priests wore a colorful girdle *(sash)* such as the one the high priest wore around the ephod and blue robe. For their head gear, they wore simple caps of white linen. The only break from the stark white of the ordinary priests' clothes was the colorful girdles they wore.

# *Rules for the Sacrifices*
## *(Leviticus 1-7. Numbers 15.)*

**The Route of the Exodus:
From Egypt to Canaan**

**The Call of Moses
The Plagues
From Egypt to Sinai
Jehovah Makes a Covenant**

***More Time at Sinai
Building the Tabernacle
Garments for the Priests
*Rules for the Sacrifices**

**From Sinai to Kadesh
Wandering
The Plains of Moab
Moses' Speeches
Journey's End**

*Sacrifices to Jehovah have been part of God's law for His people since sin first entered the world, but there are no rules recorded for the sacrifices that were offered under the Patriarchal Code. It is evident from the story of Cain and Abel that God had given rules that He intended to be obeyed precisely, because He was pleased with Abel's sacrifice and displeased with Cain's (Gen. 4:3-5). The writer of Hebrews says that Abel offered his sacrifice "by faith," which confirms that there had been instructions from the Lord because faith comes by hearing God's word (Heb. 11:4; Rom. 10:17).*

*The sacrifices under the Patriarchal Code were offered under a variety of circumstances — to "call upon the name of the Lord" (Gen. 12:8), to confirm a covenant between God and Abram (Gen. 15), to confirm covenants between men (Gen. 21:22-34; 26:26-33), as a burnt offering (Gen. 22:13), and perhaps for other purposes as well. But God did not choose to leave the precise instructions for any of these sacrifices, or any details about whether there was a difference in the way the sacrifices were offered under different circumstances.*

*In the Law of Moses, however, there are very precise instructions given for the kinds of sacrifices God wanted and for exactly how each of those sacrifices was to be offered. It was absolutely necessary for the instructions to be followed exactly in order for the sacrifice to be pleasing to God.*

*Though many rules are given concerning sacrifices and offerings in the Law of Moses, we will focus here on the rules given in Leviticus 1-7, and then include a few additional passages and points to make the information reasonably complete. These were the rules given as God was preparing His people to set up their worship to Him. Here in the narrative, we describe each kind of sacrifice as concisely as we can. Look into our companion book on the law of Moses to find an entire chapter devoted to the sacrifices. The details are set forth there in outline form for easy reference.*

*Certain laws in the Law of Moses are easy to understand, because human reasoning says that it is necessary for there to be rules about how to treat our fellow men. Other laws deal directly with the relationship of the people to Jehovah Himself. These laws recognize who God is and what is due Him —such as the laws concerning their worship of Him, those concerning their reverence for Him, and those forbidding their giving other gods the praise and worship that He alone deserves. No human reasoning explains laws of this kind. They are to be obeyed simply because God commands them.*

*The commanded sacrifices fall into the second category. Human reasoning can understand that offerings, such as the sin offerings, were necessary, because when one disobeyed a law of Jehovah, it was necessary to pay the price He demanded in order to be in His favor again. But the details of what was to be offered in each kind of sacrifice, when it was to be offered, and how it was to be offered, was entirely God's prerogative to set. The choice man had was whether to accept God's terms and receive the blessings, or to refuse the terms and face the consequences. God has always been the One sinned against when man disobeys, and He, therefore, is the One with the right to set the demands and penalties.*

# The Types of Sacrifices
## (Leviticus 1-7)

*The English words, offering, sacrifice, and oblation, are all used generally of sacrifices. Leviticus 1-7 lists and describes five distinct kinds of sacrifices: the burnt offerings, the meal offerings (translated as "meat" offering in the King James' Version), the peace offerings, the sin offerings, and the trespass offerings. Then under each major category, there are more specific offerings described. For example, under the major heading of peace offerings there were thanksgiving offerings, vow offerings, and freewill (voluntary) offerings.*

*The passage here in the first part of Leviticus does not tell when each of these sacrifices was to be offered. That information will be given as various topics are discussed in the law. Here the rules are about how the offering was to be performed. In other words, when there were certain prescribed sacrifices to be made to fit a specific occasion, this is the section of the law where the priest would learn exactly how each one was to be offered. Therefore, the rules in this section tend to be general in nature. It will list all the animals that might be used for a burnt offering, and then a particular animal will be specified when the details are given that fit for a particular circumstance.*

*Each of these offerings might be made by the priests on behalf of the whole congregation, or some individual might bring one of the offerings. The rules were different, depending upon whom it was for and what its purpose was. If it were a sacrifice for the whole congregation, the prescribed animal was selected from the flocks and herds that were kept specifically for that purpose. It was killed by the priest, and the sacrifice was done in the prescribed order. If it were a sacrifice by an individual, he selected the animal from his own flocks and herds, brought it to the tabernacle, and killed it there before the priest, and then the priest finished the task of offering it according to all the prescribed details. Notice that the details are given about where one was to stand while he killed the animal (1:11); details are given about which parts were to be laid directly upon the fire after the animal was killed, and which pieces were to be washed first (1:8-9). The sacrifice was not acceptable if all the rules were not followed.*

*As we study the law, we will come to passages that list the many regular sacrifices that were commanded for the whole congregation. One duty of the Levites was to see that the animals were available and ready for each assigned sacrifice —but they could not provide the animals if the people themselves did not pay their temple taxes and their other charges that kept up these supplies. The law also includes instructions about when individuals were to bring offerings: for example, as an atonement for a specific sin, as a payment of a vow, or as an offering after a baby was born. If an individual needed to bring a sacrifice, he was obligated to bring one of his own animals from his own flocks. The law provided for different animals to be offered if the individual were poor.*

## Burnt offerings (Lev. 1:3-17; 6:8-13):

The burnt offering was the most ancient of sacrifices (Gen. 4:4; 8:20). The animal was completely burned, except for the hide, which went to the priest who prepared the sacrifice (Lev. 1:9, 13; 7:8). The word translated "burnt offering" means a "going up." It signified complete dedication of oneself to the Lord. The idea of atonement was also definitely associated with the burnt offering (see 16:24). If there were a series of sacrifices to be offered for some particular event, there was almost always a burnt offering included in the required list.

God gave instructions to the priests (6:8-13):

> These are the regulations for the burnt offering: It is to remain on the altar throughout the night, and the fire is to be kept burning. In the morning, the priest is to put on his regular linen garments, including the undergarment so that his nakedness will not be seen when he approaches the altar, and he is to remove the ashes from the burnt offering that has been consumed upon the altar and place the ashes in front of the altar. Then he is to change his clothes and take the ashes outside the camp to a place that is ceremonially clean. The fire on the altar is to be kept burning all the time, it is not to go out. Each morning the priest is to add firewood and arrange the burnt offering for the congregation upon the fire. The fire must be kept burning continuously.

Burnt offerings might be bullocks, sheep, goats, turtle doves, or pigeons. The text is specific about which animal was to be offered when it describes the burnt offering to be made for a specific reason. This list is a summary of animals that could be used. Notice that it was always a "clean" animal, and it was to be a male without defect.

The one offering the sacrifice laid his hands upon the animal's head to convey the concept that the animal stood in the place of the offerer. The offerer then killed and flayed *(stripped the skin off)* the animal. The priests and Levites performed this part of the process for the regular burnt offerings for the congregation (see 2 Chron. 29:32-34). Then the priest sprinkled the blood "round about upon the altar" *(the altar of burnt offering).* He cut the animal into pieces, and laid some of the parts, including the head and the fat, directly upon the wood on the altar. He washed the inward parts and the legs before laying them upon the fire also. Then he burned the entire animal in the fire as a sweet savor unto the Lord. Except for the skin, the animal was entirely burned, and the ashes were taken outside the camp to a clean place. No one ate any portion of a burnt offering.

## Meal *(grain)* offering (Lev. 2:1-16; 6:14-23; Num. 15:1-16):

*The translation, "meat offering," has caused great confusion, because, today, "meat" does not mean merely "food" as it did in Shakespeare's day when the King James' Version was translated — it means flesh. Yet the meat offering of the law of Moses was never a sacrifice of flesh; it was a grain offering. In the Law of Moses the word translated "meat offering" always refers to bloodless sacrifices, although it occasionally refers to blood sacrifices elsewhere in the Bible (e.g. Gen. 4:4, where the word is rendered "offering").*

## Rules for the Sacrifices

When a flesh offering was made, whether a burnt offering or any other kind of sacrifice, a meal offering had to be given with it. The instructions were to be followed with each animal offered, no matter how many sacrifices were offered that day, and everyone, whether home-born or a sojourner, had to follow the rules. Drink offerings were also required with the meal offerings. Just as there was a specified amount of meal for each animal, there had to be a corresponding drink offering of a specified amount. The exact proportions for the meal offering and the drink offer for each animal are given in detail in Numbers 15:1-16.

Though sometimes offered by itself (Lev. 5:11-13; Num. 5:15, 25-26), the meal offering most often accompanied other sacrifices (Num. 15:1-16). The priest brought the offering before the Lord, in front of the altar. He took a handful of the flour and oil, along with all the incense, and burned that portion as a memorial to the Lord — "as an aroma pleasing to the Lord." A meal offering given by a priest was all burned because it was counted as the Lord's share.

Details of exactly what was to be offered, and how it was to be offered, differed with the purpose for the sacrifice. For example, if the meal offering were an offering of early ripened grain *(first fruits),* the fresh ears of grain were to be roasted in fire and then rubbed to obtain the grains. The priest then burned a portion of it as a memorial to the Lord, along with its oil and all of its incense.

As in the other descriptions, the information in Leviticus 1-7 about the meal offerings is a summary. Sometimes the requirement was for raw flour or meal; or it might be for cakes baked with flour in an oven or before a fire, cakes cooked in a pan or skillet, cakes fried in deep oil, or roasted grain. Salt was an indispensable ingredient. God said, "Do not leave the salt out of your grain offerings. Add salt to all your offerings." According to Numbers 18:19, salt signified a covenant that could not be dissolved. Oil was either mixed with *(stirred into it)* the flour, or poured upon the flour. Frankincense always accompanied the meal offering, except in the meal offering of jealousy that is described in Numbers 5:11-31. The incense was given in such a way that it could be taken separately from the meal offering and burned completely upon the fire on the altar of burnt offering. Yeast and honey were both forbidden as ingredients in the meal offering.

Except for the memorial portion of the meal offering that was burned upon the altar, all of this kind of offering went to the priest. The priests were to eat their portion, cooked without yeast, in the courtyard of the tabernacle. It could not be baked with yeast, and it was to be eaten in the place specified, because, like the sin offering and the trespass offering, it was the priest's portion of the sacrifice and it was most holy. Whatever touched the offering was to be counted as holy. Any male descendant of Aaron's had a right to share in the meal offering. It was their regular share of the offerings made to the Lord, and was to be so considered through all the generations to come. The only exception to the rule that the priests were to eat the meal offering was if the offering came from a priest himself.

When it was time for a priest to be anointed, a special meal offering was to be brought. It consisted of about two quarts of fine flour prepared with oil on a griddle. The son who would later succeed the priest about to be anointed was the one who prepared the offering. It was to be brought before the Lord, half of it in the morning and the other half in the evening. It was to be broken in pieces and burned in its entirety to the Lord — a sweet-smelling aroma to the Lord. It, just like all other meal offerings from a priest, was to be burned completely, because it was counted as the Lord's share.

The significance of the meal offering is uncertain.

### Peace offering (Lev. 3:1-17; 7:11-21; 19:5-8; 22:29-30):

The name "peace offering" comes from the Hebrew word *"shelem,"* a derivative of the word peace. Therefore, this sacrifice signified that all was right between the worshiper and God. It could be offered as a supplication that things *be right*, or as praise that they *were* right. When a combination of sacrifices was required, they were always offered in this order: a sin offering in order to gain forgiveness, then a burnt offering as an expression of complete dedication to the Lord, and finally a peace offering as an expression of joy that all was well again in the fellowship between God and man.

The law describes three classes of peace offerings: thanksgivings, vow offerings, and freewill *(ASV)* or voluntary *(KJV)* offerings. A few times the peace offering as an offering of thanksgiving is rendered "thank offering" (2 Chron. 29:31; 33:16). The details of how each kind of peace offering was to be offered are as specific as any of the other laws concerning the sacrifices. Again, these chapters in Leviticus give a summary of how each kind was to be done. Then, as the various situations are described where a specific offering was required, the details are given as to exactly which animal was to be offered.

The peace offerings could be offered at the impulse of the worshiper — particularly the freewill offerings and the thanksgiving offerings. Vows were made at the impulse of the worshiper, but then there were prescribed sacrifices, including peace offerings, that were to be offered when the vow was completed. In addition, peace offerings were called for during the Feast of Firstfruits (Lev. 23:19). It is strongly implied that peace offerings were to be a part of the other set feasts, and at the new moons (Num. 10:10).

An interesting detail is told in connection with the peace offering: if it were a sheep, the "fat tail entire" was burned upon the altar, plus the portions of fat that were common to the other animals. The sheep that were common in Canaan had enormous tails, composed of fat, and the fat from the sacrifices were always burned as the Lord's portion. In connection with this point, God takes time to specify that "all fat is the Lord's." As a perpetual statute throughout their generations, the Israelites were forbidden to eat any fat or any blood. All fat was to be burned from any sacrifice, and the blood was poured out or sprinkled around the altar. (3:9, 11, 16-17.)

To make the information easier to understand, we are dividing descriptions of the peace offering under two headings. The vow offerings and the freewill offerings were done alike, so we describe them together. There are a very few differences between these and the thanksgiving offering.

**A. Freewill offerings and vow offerings (Lev. 3:1-17; 7:28-34):**

Male or female animals without defect from the cattle, sheep, or goats could be used for this offering. Pigeons would not suffice for this sacrifice, because the worshiper always ate a portion of the sacrificial meat as part of the ceremony, and the pigeon would not have been large enough to suffice.

The offerer laid his hands upon the animal to convey the representative nature of the sacrifice; then he killed the animal, and the priests sprinkled the blood upon the altar. With his own hands, the offerer brought the fat from the abdominal cavity of the animal and the breast or brisket to Jehovah as the offerings made by fire. The priest burned the fat upon the altar, but the brisket was given to him *(the presiding priest)* as a wave offering before the Lord.

The breast or brisket of the sacrifice was first given to the Lord and then to the priests. This portion was called the *wave-breast* because the offerer took the meat in his hands and extended the offering toward the altar and back to signify that the portion was given to God who then gave it back for His servants the priests. The word translated *"wave"* signifies a moving back and forth. Though some disagree, the most likely and fitting idea is that of extending the wave-breast, as to the Lord, and then drawing it back, as if receiving it back from the Lord.

The officiating priest also received the thigh, or the ham of the right leg. The term *heave-thigh* signified that this portion was *heaved* or *lifted* from the sacrifice and given to the priest. The wave-breast and the heave-thigh were appointed the portions of the priest by law. The primary difference between the two kinds of offerings, "wave" and "heave," was that the wave carried the idea of what was offered to the Lord and given back by Jehovah to the priests, while the heave offering was an offering from the offerer to the priests as commanded by the Lord.

The parts of the animal left after burning the Lord's portion, and after giving the thigh and brisket to the priests, were eaten by the offerer and his family or companions. All members of the family or associates were allowed to share in the sacrificial feast, unless some member of the party were unclean. Then that one was forbidden to eat. If by some accident, some of the meat touched something unclean, that portion was not to be eaten. If there were more meat than was needed for the one meal, some could be kept and eaten on the second day, but under no circumstances could it be kept to be eaten on the third day (7:15-18; 19:5-8).

**B. The thanksgiving offering (Lev. 7:11-15):**

The same animals listed above were appropriate for the thanksgiving offering, because it was a kind of peace offering. In addition, there had to be unleavened cakes mingled with oil, unleavened wafers rubbed with oil, and cakes mingled with oil, made of fine flour soaked. Cakes of leavened bread also accompanied this offering. This leavened bread, along with the two loaves of leavened bread offered at the Feast of Firstfruits (Lev. 23:17), were the only offerings of leavened bread made in any of the sacrifices.

In addition to the above procedures described in the freewill offerings, the offerer gave to the Lord one cake or piece of each kind of bread mentioned in Leviticus 7:12, 13. This offering was then given to the priest who sprinkled the blood of the peace offering *(to the presiding priest)*.

The same ones who could eat the freewill offerings could participate in the sacrificial meal that followed. But there was another important difference: the flesh had to be eaten on the day it was offered, with none left till morning (7:15; 22:29-30).

## Sin offerings (Lev. 4:1-5:13):

Sin offerings and trespass offerings are described in more detail than the others, partly because the requirements were so specific with these. The procedure was different if the offering were for the whole congregation, for a priest, for a ruler, or for an ordinary individual. That means there were fewer rules that could be summarized. We follow the pattern of the text and describe these in more detail — giving their purpose and the basic procedures that were to be followed.

Sin offerings and trespass offerings had basically the same function, which was to expiate sin. The sin offering was commanded for sins of error: "If any one shall sin through error, in any of the things which Jehovah hath commanded not to be done, and shall do any one of them," then he was to offer a sin offering for it (4:2). The sin offering was to satisfy the judicial wrath of God and to remove the guilt of sin. The shedding of the victim's blood *(symbol of life —17:11)* signified that the death of the transgressor was deserved for sin but that, by the mercy of God, the death of the victim was accepted instead. The primary ideas in propitiation and expiation are appeasement *(restoring one's favor)* and removal *(of guilt)*. Of course, ultimately, the removal of guilt was through the blood of Christ (Rom. 3:25; Heb. 9:15).

The idea was this: When men under the law of Moses offered the sacrifices called for when they sinned, they met the conditions God imposed for them to receive forgiveness, but their sacrifices were acts of faith in God who would provide the redemption. Indirectly, therefore, when they sacrificed, they were expressing their faith in Jesus. It was when the Jews offered their sacrifices as mere rituals that their sacrifices became vain. Then, of course, when they rejected Christ, their sacrifices became vain because they did not believe on the Only Begotten of the Father (John 1:11).

The ordinances regarding the sin offering are given under four categories:

- The sin offering for a priest,
- For the whole congregation,
- For a ruler,
- For the common people.

**A. The priest (Lev. 4:3-12):**

"The anointed priest" may mean the high priest in particular, but it is a little difficult to prove that this is the case. Some say that the high priest was the only anointed priest, based on Leviticus 8:10-13 (*Keil and Delitzsch*, e.g.). Also, since the text says *the* anointed priest, rather than *an* anointed priest, it may be true that these instructions particularly applied to the high priest. Yet in Exodus 30:30 God says, "Thou shalt anoint Aaron and his sons." Therefore, the reference may have been to any priest — and that would fit the circumstances of reality, because there would be many times when any priest might sin and need a sin offering.

For his sin, the priest was to offer a young bullock without blemish. This sacrifice was to be made anytime a priest sinned in his official capacity. His was the most valuable of the sacrifices, indicating how serious God considered it when a priest failed to carry out his prescribed duties in the worship ceremonies.

The procedure for offering the sacrifice was somewhat similar to that of the burnt offering (Lev. 1:3-5). The offerer *(the priest)* brought the animal and laid his hand upon its head and killed the animal. In the burnt offering the blood of the animal was splashed upon the altar round about (1:5), but in the sin offering for a priest, the blood was taken into the tabernacle and sprinkled before the veil. Some of the blood was rubbed onto the horns of the altar of incense; the rest of the blood was poured out at the base of the altar of burnt offering. The same portions that were taken from the peace offerings and burned upon the altar were taken from the sin offerings as well. The rest of the animal was taken to the place outside of the camp, where the ashes from the altar of burnt sacrifice were emptied, and burned upon wood.

The priests normally received a portion of a sin offering, but no one ate of the sin offering if the blood were carried into the tabernacle. This was one more way of showing the serious nature of a sin committed by one of the mediators for the people. (See Leviticus 6:30; 10:18. Compare Leviticus 4:6-7, 11-12, 17-18, 20-21, with Leviticus 4:25, 26, 30-31.)

The only time a sin offering for a priest was specified was on the Day of Atonement (Lev. 16:6). On that occasion, the High Priest offered a sin offering for himself, before he offered the sin offering for the congregation. Otherwise, this sin offering would have been offered as the need arose. It, like the other sin offerings, was to remove the sin of a priest and to restore him to God's favor (4:20, 26, 31, 35).

**B. The congregation (Lev. 4:13-21):**

A sin offering for the whole congregation also required a bullock, and the procedure for offering it was almost identical to the ritual carried out for the priest. The elders laid their hands on the animal's head in behalf of the congregation, and the blood was taken inside the tabernacle. Therefore, no one ate any of the meat.

The only other detail we need to add is a list of the times when a sin offering was required for the whole congregation. Notice that most of the occasions were feast days or other special days when there was a series of sacrifices to be made.

- At new moons *(the first day of each month)* (Num. 28:15).
- On each day of the Feast of Unleavened Bread (Num. 28:22, 24).
- On the day of the Feast of Weeks (Num. 28:30).
- On the first day of the seventh month (Num. 29:1, 5).
- On the Day of Atonement (Num. 29:11).
- On each day of the Feast of Tabernacles (Num. 29:16, 19, 22, 25, 28, 31, 34, 38).
- Anytime the congregation was guilty of transgression in omitting a specific command of God (Num. 15:24).

**C. A ruler (Lev. 4:22-26; 6:25-30):**

If a ruler sinned unwittingly regarding something God had said, and someone brought it to his attention, he was to offer a he-goat without blemish. The procedure was similar to the previous examples except that the blood of the sacrifice was not carried into the tabernacle.

The ruler laid his hands on the head of the animal and killed it. Part of the blood of the sacrifice was smeared on the horns of the altar of burnt offering, and the remainder poured out at the base of it. The same parts of the animal specified in the peace offering were burned on the altar, but the rest of the sacrifice was given to be eaten by the priests (Lev. 6:25-26, 29; Num. 18:9).

In those sin offerings where the blood was not carried into the tabernacle, the priests were to eat the flesh of the sin offering. Any male in the priest's family could eat of the meat. It could be roasted or boiled, but if it were boiled in a pottery vessel, the vessel was to be broken afterward because it was made holy by its contact with the sin offering and could never be used for any common purpose. A brazen vessel had to be thoroughly scoured and rinsed before use for anything else. The sacrifice was to be eaten by the priests in the courtyard of the Tent of Meeting.

There is no specific time given for a sin offering for a ruler. Therefore, it was to be offered as the need arose. It, like all the other sin offerings, was to remove the guilt of sin and to restore the ruler to the favor of Jehovah.

**D. One of the common people (Lev. 4:27-35):**

The sin offering for an ordinary person was a female goat or lamb. The procedure for offering it was exactly the same as for the sin offering for a ruler, and the flesh of this sin offering was also eaten by the males among the priests because it was they who "bore" or "took away" the iniquity of those for whom they offered sacrifices (6:26, 29; 10:17).

The text here in Leviticus describes three different circumstances that would cause an individual to need to make a sin offering:

- If someone heard an oath made, and a situation arose where a witness to that oath were needed, and he did not speak up, then he would be guilty. When convicted of his wrong, he was to confess his sin and offer either a female lamb or goat for a sin offering (5:1).
- If a man touched something that was unclean and thus unwittingly defiled himself, upon learning of it, he was to offer a female lamb or goat (5:2-3).
- If a man were careless in his speech and swore an oath and then sinned in regard to something he had sworn the oath about, when he learned of it, he was to offer a sin offering (Lev. 5:4-6).

One interesting feature about the sin offerings in these three situations is that, unlike the sin offerings specified in Leviticus 4, provisions were made for one's financial situation. If the offerer could not afford a female lamb or goat, then he was to offer two turtle doves or two pigeons, one for a sin offering and one for a burnt offering. If the person could not afford even two birds, then he could bring a tenth part of an ephah *(between two and three quarts)* of fine flour. There was to be no oil and no frankincense with it because it was a sin offering and not a meal offering. A handful of the flour was burned upon the altar as the token that a sacrifice was being made, and then the rest of the flour belonged to the priest.

## Trespass offerings (Lev. 5:14-6:7):

In Leviticus 5:6 the term *trespass offering* is used interchangeably with *sin offering*. The original Hebrew means, "He shall bring for his *guilt (expiation of his guilt)* unto Jehovah for his sin which he hath sinned, a female from the flock, a lamb or a goat, for a sin offering." Therefore the trespass offering was a special kind of sin offering. Three situations are described in which one caused another to be deprived of his rights, whether God or man. In each case, it was a trespass offering that was called for.

- If a man sinned in not offering to God what was commanded, then he had to bring a ram of a certain value in shekels to offer as a trespass or debt offering. He also had to pay a penalty of twenty per cent, in addition to that which he had failed to give originally (5:14-16).

- The precise nature of the sin involved in the second case is not specified, but since it is describes two situations in which the sin was to deprive someone of what was rightfully his, and because common crimes were covered elsewhere, this trespass likely involved Jehovah more directly and concerned the depriving of God of what was owed to Him in some way not involved in offerings. This trespass involved the kind of things where restitution could not be made. The trespass offering was a ram of a certain value to be set by the priests. The point is made abundantly clear that ignorance did not at all prevent guilt (5:17-19).

- The third trespass involved wrongfully keeping a deposit given one by his neighbor, or wrongfully seizing a possession. For example a man finds a thing belonging to another, and when asked, denies that he has it. Or, when asked for a loan, collateral is taken and then denied to the borrower when the loan has been paid. In all such matters, not only was the trespass offering of a ram to be offered, but the property was to be restored, or the loss compensated, with a twenty percent penalty added (6:1-7).

## Three categories of sin offerings not included in Leviticus 1-7:

### A. Sin offerings on the Day of Atonement (Lev. 16:1-34):

Obviously, if the person did not learn of his sin, no sin offering was given. What was done to atone for those sins which remained unknown to a person? The Day of Atonement was a day of sacrifice for all the sins of the nation: one goat for a sin offering (16:15), and one goat for removal (Azazel, 16:8, 20-22). The Day of Atonement is discussed much more fully in the chapter describing the special days for the Israelites. It was one of their most important days out of their year.

### B. Sins of omission (Num. 15:22-26):

The sacrifices described in Leviticus 1-7 were for transgressions of commandments. Some sins, however, are failures to obey — sins of omission — failures to obey "all that the Lord has commanded." If the congregation had failed to keep some commandment, there was to be a burnt offering of a young bull with its prescribed meal and drink offerings, followed by a sin offering of one he-goat. If an individual neglected one of the commandments, he was to offer a she-goat a year old for a sin offering. When the priest made atonement through these sacrifices, the congregation or the individual was forgiven.

**C. Law of restitution (Num. 5:5-10):**

*The laws given in this passage are general. These are for the situations where a more specific law does not fit. Take note that there was to be restitution made, even if the wronged person were now dead. One did not ignore a wrong he had done.*

If a person commits a wrong, he must confess his sin, and make full restitution for his guilt. He must add twenty percent to its value, and give it to the one he has injured. If the man sinned against is now dead, the restitution must be given to his next of kin. If there is no next of kin, then let it be given to the Lord, and it becomes the property of the priest, along with the ram of the atonement sacrifice.

**D. A presumptuous sin (Num. 15:30-31):**

These sacrifices did not cover one who sinned "with a high hand," that is, one who sinned deliberately, willfully, and arrogantly. There was no sacrifice for such a sin. That person had blasphemed the Lord and had to be completely cut off from his people. He had despised God's law and had broken His commandment; therefore his guilt remained upon him.

## Additional rules about sacrifices:

**Take your sacrifices to the place God chooses (Lev. 17:1-9; Deut. 12:1-28):**

- All sacrifices were to be taken to the tabernacle to be killed, so that the people would no longer offer sacrifices in the open field as the people before them had done (Lev. 17:1-9). *(This law was given to keep down temptation to offer the sacrifices to the idols of the land.)*
    - They were to offer such animals as peace offerings before Jehovah.
    - Anyone who did not take his animal to the tabernacle to be offered was to be cut off from his people.
- But if they were killing an animal merely for food, they could kill it and eat it in any of their towns, just as if it were a deer or gazelle (Deut. 12:15-16, 20-25).

**Unacceptable sacrifices (Lev. 22:17-28):**

- No blemished animal could be offered.
- No sacrifice from the hand of a foreigner could be offered.
- No animal less than eight days old could be offered.
- A mother and her young could not be offered on the same day.

**Prohibition against eating the fat or the blood of an animal (Lev. 3:17; 7:22-27; 17:10-16):**

- No one could eat the fat of any animal (3:17; 7:22-25).
    - They could use the fat for other purposes, but they could not eat it.
    - Any one who did so, was to be cut off from his people.
- No one could eat blood from any animal or bird (3:17; 7:26-27; 17:10-16):
    - Any person who did so was to be cut off from his people. God said, "I will set my face against him... and I will cut him off from among his people."

- "For the life of the flesh is in the blood... I have given it to you to make atonement for your souls... its blood is identified with its life... Therefore I said no one could eat the blood."

## Firstfruits (Lev. 19:23-25; 23:9-21; 27:30-33; Num. 15:17-21; Deut. 26:1-11):

- Firstfruits were to be offered on behalf of the whole congregation in connection with the Feast of Unleavened Bread and at the Feast of Weeks (Lev. 23:9-21).
- In addition, the people were to offer individual offerings of their firstfruits — both in the form of the fresh grain and in the form of loaves of bread (Num. 15:17-21).
- When they planted a fruit tree, they were to eat no fruit from it for the first three years, the crop from the fourth year was given to the Lord; in the fifth year, they could eat of its fruit (Lev. 19:23-25).
- They were to take a basket of firstfruits to offer before the Lord, express their gratitude for God's blessings, and then worship and rejoice before the Lord (Deut. 26:1-11).

## Tithes (Lev. 27:30-33; Deut. 14:22-29; 26:12-15):

- In addition to the congregational and individual sacrifices that were offered, the people were commanded to give a tenth of all their increase to the Lord.
- The rules were specific (Lev. 27:30-33):
  - One tenth of all the increase of both crops and animals went to the Lord.
  - Any portion of the vegetable tithe could be redeemed by adding one fifth to its value and paying the full redemption price into the treasury.
  - The animal tithe could not be redeemed.
    - It was to be given without selection or substitution.
    - That is, every tenth animal in the count belonged to Lord — whether it was good or bad.
      - If a substitution were tried, then both animals must be given to God.
- A portion of the tithe was to be eaten by the offerer; the Levites were to be invited to share the meal (Deut. 14:22-27).
- Every third year, the tithes were not to be taken to the sanctuary; they were to be left in the gates of each city (Deut. 14:28-29; 26:12-15).
  - It could be shared by the Levites, the alien in their midst, the widows, and the orphans.

## Portions for the priests (Num. 18:8-20; Deut. 18:1-8):

*Priests were highly regarded by God and were richly rewarded for their work. They were given no tribal territory, because special portions were given to them as an inheritance in return for their service to God. Parts of nearly all the sacrifices belonged to the presiding priest. Exact rules were given for which portions belonged to the priests, exactly what steps were to be done before it was given to them, and exactly who could share in eating the meat.*

- The Lord said, "Tell Aaron and his sons to treat the sacred offerings with respect. These things were consecrated to me, and you must not profane my holy name. I am the Lord" (Lev. 22:1).
- Portions from the sacrifices that belonged to the priests:
  - The hide of every burnt offering (Lev. 7:8).
  - Every meal offering and drink offering (Num. 18:9).
  - Every sin offering in which the blood was not taken inside the tabernacle (Lev. 6:25-30; Num. 18:9).
  - Every trespass offerings (Lev. 7:6).

## Rules for the Sacrifices

    - The breast and right thigh from the peace offerings (Lev. 7:31-34; Num. 18:11).
    - The shoulder, cheek, and maul from animals offered on feast days (Deut. 18:3). .
- All firstfruits went to the priests: the best of the oil, the best of the vintage of the grapes, the best of the grain, and the first of the fleece of the sheep (Num. 18:12-13; Deut. 18:4).
- Every firstling went to the priests (Num. 18:15-18).
- The Levites were given the tithes of all Israel for their portion; in turn, they were to give a tithe of their income from the tithes of Israel to the priests (Num. 18:21-34).

There were rules about who could eat the sacred things (Lev. 6:16, 29; 21:21-22; 22:1-16):
- The priest and "his sons," "every male among the priests" were allowed to eat of the sin offerings (6:16, 29).
- If a priest, or any member of his family, were unclean for any reason, he could not touch the holy things until he was cleansed.
- No priest was to defile himself by eating anything unclean.
- No visitor, or hired servant of the priest could eat of the holy things; but a slave purchased by the priest, or a servant born into his household could share the food.
- If a daughter married one not a priest, she could no longer eat of the holy things. But if she were widowed or divorced, and had no child, and returned to her house as she was in the days of her youth, she could eat of the holy things again.
- If anyone ate of the holy things unknowingly, then he was to repay the amount he ate, plus one fifth more to compensate for it.
- The priest must not desecrate the sacred offerings by allowing an unauthorized person to eat of it.
- A member of the priestly family who had a defect and could never perform the duties of a priest, could still eat of the holy things (21:21-22).

# *The Worship is Set in Order*

## *(Exodus 38-40; Leviticus 8-10; Numbers 7, 9)*

## The Tabernacle is Set Up

**(Exodus 38:21-31; 39:32-43; 40:1-38)**

**The Route of the Exodus: From Egypt to Canaan**

**The Call of Moses**
**The Plagues**
**From Egypt to Sinai**
**Jehovah Makes a Covenant**

***More Time at Sinai**
**Building the Tabernacle**
**Garments for the Priests**
**Rules for Sacrifices**

***Worship Set in Order**
***Tabernacle Set Up**
***Consecration of Priests**
***Worship Begun**
***Passover Observed**

**From Sinai to Kadesh**
**Wandering**
**The Plains of Moab**
**Moses' Speeches**
**Journey's End**

### Total of the metals used in building the tabernacle (Exod. 38:21-31):

Moses commanded the Levites under the direction of Ithamar, the son of Aaron, to record all the materials used in building the tabernacle. When the work was finished, the totals of the metals used was determined.

Twenty nine talents, plus 730 shekels *(one metric ton)*of gold had been used. Gold covered all the boards, posts, and items of furniture inside the tabernacle. The mercy seat and the golden lamp stand were of solid gold.

Three and three/fourths tons of silver had been used. The silver had come from a half-shekel tax that had been collected from the community as the men over twenty years old had been counted *(603,550 men)*. The total collected was 100 talents, plus 1,775 shekels. The 100 talents of silver had been used to make the bases for the boards that formed the walls of the tabernacle and for the bases of the poles that held the veil that divided the Most Holy Place from the Holy Place. The extra shekels had been used to make the hooks for the posts in the courtyard, to overlay the tops of the posts, and to make their bands.

Seventy talents, plus 2,400 shekels *(2.4 metric tons)* of bronze had been used. The bronze was used to make the bases for the entrance poles for the tabernacle itself, the brazen altar *(the altar of burnt offering)* with its bronze grating and all its utensils, the bases for all the posts in the courtyard, and all the tent pegs.

*The value of the tabernacle is beyond our calculation in today's currency. The expense and the task of doing the work was an enormous undertaking for the Israelites, but God had blessed them, and they had the things they needed to perform what He asked them to do.*

*The details about counting the people are not given until Numbers 1, and the date for that counting is after the tabernacle was built and set up. Yet it is obvious they had this silver (called the atonement money) in time to use it in the building process. Therefore the command must have gone out for each man above twenty years old to bring his half-shekel and to be counted at the time the call went out for building supplies, but then after the building was done, the men were counted again by tribes, and the numbers totaled for specific groups.*

## Moses inspects all the work (Exod. 39:32-43):

The work of building the tabernacle and preparing the garments for the priests was finally finished. The Israelites had made everything exactly the way the Lord had commanded Moses. When they were through, they brought everything to Moses for his inspection. They brought the tent with all its furnishings, its clasps, its frames, crossbars, posts, and bases. They brought all the coverings — the outer layers, the inner curtain for overhead, plus the veil to divide the two rooms, and the entrance curtain. They brought the ark of the covenant with its poles and the mercy seat to go on the top of it. They brought the table of shewbread with all the articles that went with it and the bread prepared for its use. They brought the golden candlestick with all the vessels that accompanied it, plus the oil for the light. They brought the altar of incense with its anointing oil, and its fragrant incense. They brought the large bronze altar with its bronze grating, its poles, and all its utensils. They brought the laver with its base. They brought all the curtains for the courtyard, the posts, their bases, and all the ropes and tent pegs. They also brought all the sacred garments that had been made for Aaron the high priest, and for his sons who would serve as the regular priests.

Moses inspected all the work and saw that the Israelites had made everything exactly according to directions. So Moses blessed them.

*So often there is reason to feel critical of the Israelites for their failure to obey God. Let us take time to note that on this occasion they should be praised. They had grown up as slaves, so they understood hard work. They brought the expensive supplies for the work so generously they had to be told to stop, because there was more than enough to accomplish everything that was needed. They willingly joined in and worked hard on whatever task fell their lot. When the work was finished, Moses was very pleased to find it all done exactly according to the pattern God had given. There is no mention of the murmuring of the people during the time they were building the tabernacle.*

## The Tabernacle is set up (Exod. 40:1-38):

The Lord said to Moses:

> Set up the tabernacle on the first day of the first month. Place the ark of the covenant in its place and shield it with the veil; bring in the table and set out what belongs upon it; set up the candlestick and light the lamps; place the golden altar in front of the veil before the ark of the covenant; and put the entrance curtain at the door.
>
> Place the altar of burnt offering in front of the entrance to the tabernacle, and place the laver, with water in it, between the altar and the door of the tabernacle. Set up the courtyard around it all and put the curtain at the entrance of the courtyard.
>
> Take the anointing oil and anoint the tabernacle and everything in it so that it will be holy. Then anoint the altar of burnt offering and all its utensils; consecrate it so that it will be most holy. Anoint the laver and its base to consecrate them.
>
> Then bring Aaron and his sons to the entrance of the Tent of Meeting and wash them with water. Dress Aaron there with the sacred garments, anoint him, and consecrate him so that he may serve

me as priest. Dress his sons in their tunics and anoint them just as you anointed their father, so that they may serve me as priests. Their anointing will be for a priesthood that will continue for all generations to come.

*Notice that the people could observe each step of the process of setting up the tabernacle. They could watch the walls going up, the coverings going on, and the furniture being moved inside. The courtyard was to be the last thing put into place so that it all could be seen.*

*By this point in your study, both teacher and students should know the tabernacle and its furniture well enough to be able to visualize each piece as it is put into place. If you are not to that point in your understanding, study the details of the tabernacle more before setting it up with Moses and the Israelites. If you are using a model of the tabernacle as a visual aid, set it up as Moses sets up the true one. It will be a very effective picture of what is happening.*

Moses did everything just as the Lord commanded him. Notice how many times this sentence occurs in Exodus 40:16-33. He set up the tabernacle on the first day of the first month of the second year. He put the silver bases in place, erected the boards, inserted the crossbars, and set up the posts. Then he spread the tent over the tabernacle and put all the coverings over the tent, just as the Lord had commanded him.

Moses took the tables of stone on which the covenant was written and placed them in the ark of the covenant. He attached the poles to the ark and set the mercy seat on top of it. Then he took the ark into the tabernacle and placed it in its place, and hung the veil to hide the ark and to divide the Most Holy Place from the Holy Place. From that moment on, the people could no longer see the ark of the covenant.

Moses placed the table of shewbread on the north side of the Holy Place and set out the bread before the Lord, just as God had commanded. He placed the candlestick on the south side, opposite the table, and set up the lamps before the Lord. He placed the altar of incense in front of the veil and burned fragrant incense upon it. Then he put the curtain at the entrance of the tabernacle, and, from that moment on, the people could no longer see into the Holy Place.

Next Moses set up the altar of burnt offering in front of the entrance to the tent of meeting and offered burnt offerings and grain offerings upon it, as the Lord commanded him. Then he placed the laver between the altar of burnt offering and the tent of meeting and put water in it to be used for washing. Moses, Aaron, and Aaron's sons were to use it to wash their hands and feet. They washed themselves whenever they entered the tabernacle or approached the altar, just as the Lord commanded Moses.

Then Moses set up the courtyard around the tabernacle and the altar, setting all the posts in place and hanging the curtains. Finally he hung the colored curtain at the entrance of the courtyard. So Moses finished the work of setting up the tabernacle.

At that moment the cloud representing God's presence among His people settled upon the tabernacle, and the glory of the Lord filled it. Moses could not enter because of the cloud. What an impressive sight to see God symbolically moving into the Tent of Meeting that had been prepared for Him!

From that time forward, in all the travels of the Israelites, whenever the cloud lifted from above the tabernacle, they knew it was time to move. But if the cloud did not lift, they remained in camp until the day it lifted again. So the cloud of the Lord was over the tabernacle by day, and fire was in the cloud by night. Thus the Lord was in the sight of all the house of Israel during all their travels.

***Chronology note:***

- *1st day, 1st month, 2nd year: The tabernacle was set up (Exod. 40:17).*
- *Remember that the first Passover in Egypt marked the beginning of the Jewish religious year (12:2).*
  - *They ate that first Passover on the evening of the fourteenth day of that first month and were ordered to leave the land (12:6, 31-32).*
  - *The next morning (the fifteenth day of the month) they left Egypt and traveled to Sinai, arriving in the third month (19:1).*
  - *Nine more months have passed during which all the events from Exodus 19-40 transpired.*
    - *That includes God's appearing to them on Mount Sinai and making a covenant with them.*
    - *Moses' going into the mount for the first forty-day session,*
    - *Their making the golden calf,*
    - *Moses' return to the mount for the second forty-day session with Jehovah,*
    - *And all the work of building the tabernacle.*
- *When the tabernacle was set up, it lacked only two weeks being a full year since they left Egypt.*

*Notice that Moses acted as priest as he set up the tabernacle and carried out the function of each piece of furniture as he set it into its place. The priests had not yet been consecrated for the work. That will be their next step as they set up their worship as the Lord has commanded.*

# Consecration of Aaron and His Sons
## (Exodus 29; 40:9-16; Leviticus 8)

### Instructions for the consecration (Exod. 29:1-46; 40:9-16):

In Exodus 40:1-16 Jehovah commanded, not only that the tabernacle and its furniture be set up, but that Aaron and his sons be consecrated to their priestly office (40:12-16). Instructions were given earlier about exactly how the consecration was to be done (Exod. 29). The instructions are as detailed as the description of how they carried out the consecration, so for our purposes, we combine the two accounts. As you study the consecration, carefully compare Leviticus 8 with Exodus 29.

The particulars of Aaron's consecration, however, are not given immediately after describing the setting up of the tabernacle. It is set up in the last chapter of Exodus, and the book of Leviticus begins with seven chapters devoted to the various sacrifices, and the priests' role in offering those sacrifices. Then the account of the consecration of Aaron and his sons is given. But the anointing of the tabernacle and of the altar of burnt offering was done in connection with the consecration of Aaron and his sons.

God said (29:38-46):

> This is what you are to offer on my altar: two one year old lambs every day, continually *(the daily burnt offerings for the congregation)*. Offer them with their appointed grain offerings mixed with oil and with their drink offering. Offer one lamb in the morning and the other at twilight. They shall be for a soothing aroma, an offering by fire to the Lord. It shall be a continual burnt offering throughout your generations at the doorway of the tent of meeting before the Lord, where I will meet

with you, to speak to you there. And I will meet there with the sons of Israel, and it shall be consecrated by My glory.

I am doing all this to consecrate the tent of meeting, the altar, and the priests, so that they may serve me. Then I will dwell among the Israelites and be their God. They will know that I am the Lord their God who brought them out of Egypt, so that I may dwell among them. *I am the Lord their God.*

*Though the details given here are about the consecration of Aaron and his sons, the rules for consecration were the rules to be followed hereafter in consecrating all priests. Look into our companion book on the law of Moses, in the chapter on the priests, for a fuller description of which rules were for this first consecration and which were for later consecrations. The book of Leviticus derives its name from the many laws it includes for the priests and Levites.*

## The people gather (Lev. 8:1-5):

In compliance with God's command in Exodus 40:1-16, Moses set up the tabernacle and started the process of consecrating Aaron and his son as priests. The ceremonies consecrating the priests lasted for seven days, and on the eighth day the final sacrifices were offered. Moses officiated in the sacrifices during the seven days of consecration, but on the eighth day Moses instructed Aaron and his sons, and they offered the sacrifices from that time forward.

The Lord said to Moses, "Take Aaron and his sons, and the priestly garments, along with the anointing oil, a bullock for the sin offering, two rams, and the basket of unleavened bread, and call the whole congregation together at the door of the tent of meeting."

Moses did as he was instructed and gathered the congregation together, saying to them, "We are now going to carry out what the Lord has commanded."

*The door of the tabernacle itself was inside the court, but the whole congregation could not have fit inside the court. There are two possible explanations:*

- *As in other places, the congregation may have been represented by its leaders (e.g., Exod. 24:1, 11), and only they saw the consecration begin.*
- *Or, the Lord may have used the expression, "door of the tent of meeting," to refer to the entrance curtain at the front of the courtyard on occasions when the whole group was expected to assemble.*
- *God said call "all the congregation," so the second explanation seems the logical one — and all the people were gathered at the entrance of the courtyard.*
- *The exact number present has nothing to do with the consecration itself, but this was a very important event for all the congregation to see and to be impressed that Aaron and his sons were specially chosen by God as their priests, and that the order of the priesthood was not to be changed.*

## Aaron and his sons are bathed, dressed, and anointed (Lev. 8:6-13; Exod. 29:1-9):

Moses had Aaron and his sons to come near, and he bathed them with water. Then Moses dressed Aaron in all the special garments that had been made: the inner tunic, the special sash that went about his waist, then the robe of dark blue with pomegranates alternating with bells around the hem. Then the ephod was put on and tied with its skillfully woven sash. Next Moses fastened the beautiful breastplate onto the ephod, and, into the pouch formed by the doubling of the breastplate, Moses put the Urim and the Thummim, by which the high priest served as the voice of Jehovah to the people. Finally, Moses placed the miter, or turban, of the high priest upon Aaron's head, and, on the front of it, the golden plate with the words, "Holy to Jehovah," inscribed upon it. Remember that this ceremony was done before the eyes of the congregation. This official putting on of the high priest's garments symbolized his entrance into the office which God had provided for him.

Moses took the specially prepared anointing oil, and anointed the tabernacle and all the furniture. He sprinkled the oil upon the altar of burnt offering seven times, and anointed the altar and all its vessels, and the laver and its base, to sanctify them. Then he poured the anointing oil upon Aaron's head, and anointed him to sanctify him. Thus Aaron became a functioning part of the tabernacle and its system.

Now Moses brought forward Aaron's sons and clothed them with the plain white tunics which the ordinary priests were to wear. About their waists went the brightly colored sashes, and on their heads were placed the simple white caps which the regular priests were to wear.

*The scriptures clearly say that both Aaron and his sons were to be anointed (Exod. 28:41): "Anoint them just as you anointed their father" (40:15). So, not only was Aaron to be anointed, his sons were to be anointed also. But the manner of their anointing differed. Several times the scriptures specifically say that the anointing oil was "poured" on Aaron's head (Exod. 29:7; Lev. 8:12; see also Ps. 133:2). No scripture says anything about pouring oil upon Aaron's sons, though they were anointed. The high priest is designated as "the high priest among his brethren, upon whose head the anointing oil was poured" (Lev. 21:10, 12). He was "the anointed one." It seems clear, therefore, that there was some kind of difference between the anointing of the high priest and the ordinary priests. Most likely the anointing of Aaron's sons consisted of smearing some of the anointing oil upon their foreheads. A combination of the anointing oil and of the blood of the ram of consecration was sprinkled upon Aaron and his sons (Exod. 29:21; Lev. 8:30), but this sprinkling is not referred to as anointing.*

*In Zechariah 4, the prophet sees a vision of a lamp stand of gold with a bowl or reservoir on top. On either side there is an olive tree. Zechariah asked what the two olive trees were. The Lord answered, "These are the two anointed ones who are standing by the Lord of the whole earth" (Zech. 4:14). The only two offices involving an anointing by pouring oil upon the head were those of the high priest (Exod. 29:7) and of the king (1 Sam. 10:1). In Zechariah 6 the prophecy is made that when the man, whose name is "Branch" comes, He shall be a priest upon his throne (Zech. 6:12-13). In this prophecy through Zechariah the Lord is saying that, in Jesus the Messiah (the Anointed One, the Christ), the offices of priest and king would be combined.*

## Special sacrifices are offered for the priests (Lev. 8:14-36; Exod. 29:1-37):

### A. The bullock for the sin offering (Lev. 8:14-17; Exod. 29:10-14):

*(This sacrifice follows the instructions for a sin offering for a priest in Leviticus 4:1-12.)*

The bullock which had been provided for a sin offering was brought over, and Aaron and his sons laid their hands upon its head. Moses killed the animal, took the blood and smeared some of it upon the horns of the altar of incense, and poured the rest of it at the base of the altar of burnt offering to sanctify it and to make atonement for it. Moses took the various internal organs, which the law required to be burned upon the altar, and offered them before the Lord; but the rest of the bullock, with the hide, the flesh, and the entrails, was burned with fire outside the camp as the Lord commanded Moses.

*The passage in Leviticus 8 does not specify which altar Moses smeared the blood upon and at which altar the blood was poured around the base in order to purify it. According to the rules for a sin offering for a priest, the blood was to be taken inside the tabernacle, sprinkled before the veil, smeared on the horns of the altar of incense, and then the rest was poured out around the base of the altar of burnt offering (Lev. 4:6-7). Almost certainly, this is the procedure followed here, although there may have been blood smeared on the horns of the altar of burnt offering and its vessels also on this occasion to symbolize its purification.*

**B. The ram for the burnt offering (Lev. 8:18-21; Exod. 29:15-18):**

*(This sacrifice follows the instructions for a burnt offering in Leviticus 1:3-17.)*

One of the rams was brought forward and Moses presented it for a burnt offering. Aaron and his sons laid their hands upon it, and Moses killed it, and sprinkled its blood all around the altar of burnt offering. He took certain internal parts from the ram and burned the head, and the selected pieces, and the fat. He washed the insides and the legs with water and then burned the whole ram upon the altar.

**C. The ram of consecration (Lev. 8:22-36; Exod. 29:19-34):**

*(This sacrifice was treated as a peace offering as described in Leviticus 3:1-17, except it was more specialized than usual because it was offered for the consecration of the priests.)*

The other ram was a ram of consecration. Again Aaron and his sons laid their hands upon this ram. Moses, having slain the animal, took of its blood and rubbed it upon the lobe of Aaron's right ear, upon his right thumb, and upon the big toe of his right foot. He applied the blood similarly to Aaron's sons and sprinkled the rest of the blood round about the altar. Then he took some of the blood and some of the anointing oil and sprinkled them upon Aaron and upon his garments, upon his sons and upon their garments, that they and their garments might be hallowed before God.

Moses took the various internal parts of the animal called for, the right shoulder, and, from the basket of unleavened bread, he took one unleavened cake, one cake of oiled bread, and one wafer. Moses placed these items upon the hands of Aaron and his sons and had them wave them for a wave offering before the Lord. Then he burned the items upon the altar. In other words, on this occasion, Aaron and his sons surrendered to the Lord, as an offering by fire *(an ordination, or consecration offering)*, a portion which afterward would belong to them from a peace offering.

Moses took the breast of the ram and waved it before the Lord; it belonged to Moses for his portion, as Jehovah commanded. From this time forward, both the right shoulder and the breast from a peace offering would belong to the priests as their portion.

Moses told Aaron and his sons exactly how to prepare the portion of the meat of the ram of consecration which they were to eat. "Boil the flesh at the door of the tent of meeting, and eat it there with the bread that is in the basket of consecration. No one else may share the food, because it is holy. What is left of the meat and of the bread by morning you will burn with fire; it must not be eaten because it is holy."

**D. A bullock for a sin offering each day for seven days (Lev. 8:33-36; Exod. 29:35-37):**

Moses instructed the men, "Do not go out of the tent of meeting for seven days, until the days appointed for your consecration are over. The things we have done today have been commanded by the Lord to make atonement for you, and you are to remain at the door of the tent of meeting day and night for seven days to carry out what Jehovah has charged you to do so that you do not die."

According to Exodus 29:35-37, there was to be a bull offered for a sin offering on each of the seven days that the priests were to remain at the tabernacle. The altar was to be cleansed and anointed each day also as a way of purifying it to sanctify it. The altar would thus be made holy, and everyone who touched the altar was to be holy.

And Aaron and his sons did all the things Jehovah told Moses to tell them

*The Hebrew writer was probably alluding to this "washing of water" (Lev. 8:6) and "sprinkling of blood" (Lev. 8:30) when he spoke of us, the priests of God, under the new covenant, having our bodies washed with pure water (in baptism) and having our hearts sprinkled from an evil conscience (Heb. 10:22).*

# The Worship is Set in Order

## (Numbers 7:1-89; Leviticus 9:1-10:20; 24:10-16, 23)

### The offerings of the princes of Israel (Num. 7:1-89):

When Moses had completed the setting up of the tabernacle and the anointing of it, the princes of the tribes brought special offerings that had been prepared for the service of the Lord. First they came bringing six covered wagons, and twelve oxen, a wagon for each two princes and an ox for each prince. They presented these before the tabernacle, and God told Moses, "Take these wagons and give them to the Levites as each man's work requires." Moses dealt the wagons out, according to the need for them. He gave two wagons and four oxen to the Levites of the family of the Gershonites, and he gave four wagons and eight oxen to the Levites of the family of the Merarites, but he gave none to the Levites of the family of Kohath, because their work was to carry the furniture on their shoulders rather than in wagons.

Then God said, "The princes will offer their oblation, each prince on his day, for the dedication of the altar." So for the next twelve days, the princes came bringing the gifts from the tribes.

*We will study the duties of the Levites as we come to the information in its chronological order. It will be clear at that time why the wagons and oxen were distributed as they were.*

*The first eight of these twelve days when one prince from a tribe came each day to present his tribe's gift, were the exact eight days when the priests were going through their eight-day consecration process. The last prince brought his gift on the twelfth day of the month, only two days before time for the Passover feast.*

The order of the tribes from which the princes came with their offering is listed below, with the name of each prince:

Judah - Nahshon
Issachar - Nethanel
Zebulun - Eliab
Reuben - Elizur
Simeon - Shelumiel
Gad - Eliasaph
Ephraim - Elishama
Manasseh - Gamaliel
Benjamin - Abidan
Dan - Ahiezer
Asher - Pagiel
Naphtali - Ahira

The offering of each tribe and each prince was precisely the same:

- One large silver platter full of fine flour
- One silver bowl full of fine flour
- One golden spoon (or cup with a handle) full of incense

- Burnt offerings consisting of one young bullock, one ram, and one he-lamb a year old
- A sin offering of one male goat
- Peace offerings consisting of two oxen, five rams, five he-goats, and five he-lambs a year old

The total offerings from the tribes was: twelve silver plates, twelve silver sprinkling bowls, and twelve gold ladles. Each silver plate weighed 130 shekels, and each sprinkling bowl weighed 70 shekels. Altogether, the silver dishes weighed 2,400 shekels *(about sixty pounds)*. The twelve gold ladles weighed ten shekels each, making a total of 120 shekels *(about three pounds)*. The total number of animals for burnt offering came to twelve bulls, twelve rams, and twelve male lambs a year old — each with its grain offering. The total number of animals for the peace offering was twenty-four bulls, sixty rams, sixty he-goats, and sixty male lambs a year old. These were all offered at the time of the dedication of the altar.

*It seems that these animals were sacrificed each day as they were brought. Some have wondered if these animals were to form the flock from which the regular daily sacrifices could be made. This is unlikely, because the animals are brought as a specific class of sacrifice, as special sacrifices to dedicate the altar, not as an animal that might be used for a variety of sacrifices. We will come to a passage that will show where the first animals came from to form the first flocks and herds needed for the community sacrifices.*

When Moses would enter the Tent of Meeting to talk with the Lord, he would hear God's voice speaking to him from between the cherubim above the ark of the covenant. Thus God would speak with Moses there.

## Aaron begins his work on the eighth day (Lev. 9:1-24):

On the eighth day, Moses called Aaron and his sons, and the elders of Israel, and he told Aaron, "Take for yourself a calf of the herd *(a bull)* for a sin offering, and a ram for a burnt offering, both without defect, and offer them unto the Lord. Then tell the children of Israel, 'Take a he-goat for a sin offering, and a calf and a lamb, both a year old, without blemish for a burnt offering. Take an ox and a ram for peace offerings, and a meal offering mingled with oil, because today Jehovah is going to appear to you.'"

Everything that was commanded was brought, and all the congregation drew near and stood before Jehovah. Then Moses said, "This is what Jehovah has commanded you to do, so that the glory of Jehovah will appear to you."

He told Aaron, "Come to the altar, and offer your sin offering, and your burnt offering, and make atonement for yourself, and for the people."

*Notice that, whereas before, Moses was officiating, now it is Aaron's role to officiate in offering the sacrifices.*

### A. The sin offering and burnt offering for Aaron himself (Lev. 9:8-14):

So Aaron came to the altar and killed the calf for the sin offering for himself *(following the rules for a sin offering for a priest)*. His sons presented the blood to him, and he dipped his finger in the blood, smeared it upon the horns of the altar *(of incense)*, and poured out the rest of the blood at the base of the altar *(of burnt offering)*. He burned the internal parts on the altar, but the flesh and the skin he burned with fire outside the camp, as Jehovah had commanded Moses,.

Next he slew the burnt offering, and his sons again presented him the blood of the sacrifice, and he sprinkled it on the altar. They delivered the burnt offering to him — giving him the internal parts and the head. Then he washed the inside of the carcass and its legs and added them to the fire upon the altar.

**B. The sacrifices for the people (Lev. 9:15-21):**

Now it was time for the offerings for the people, so Aaron took the goat of the sin offering and offered it for sin *(following the rules for sin offerings for the congregation)*. He also offered the burnt offering according to the ordinances. He presented the meal offering, dipping a handful out to burn upon the altar. Next he killed the ox and the ram, the sacrifices for the peace offerings for the people. His sons brought the blood to him, and he sprinkled it upon the altar and burned the various internal parts of the animal upon the altar, but the breasts and the right thighs of the animals, he waved as a wave offering before the Lord, as Moses commanded. It was the priests' portion.

When all the ceremonies were completed, Aaron lifted up his hands toward the people and blessed them, and he came down from offering the sacrifices. Moses and Aaron went into the tent of meeting, then came back out and blessed the people. Suddenly the glory of the Lord appeared to all the people, and fire came forth from the Lord and instantly consumed the burnt offering and the fat *(sacrifices which were already burning upon the altar)*. When the people saw this, they shouted and fell on their faces.

*During the preceding week, many sacrifices had been offered. Earlier in the account of Leviticus 9, Aaron had burned sacrifices upon the altar even on this particular day (9:10, 11, 13-17). Therefore the miracle here was not that God ignited the fire which burned the sacrifices, but that a fire came forth which greatly intensified the fire which was already burning and caused the sacrifices to be consumed instantly. God was signifying that He accepted the worship and all the acts of consecration of the priests. The priests were performing their work, and God accepted their sacrifices.*

*The Hebrew writer makes the point more than once that the priests of the Old Testament had to offer sacrifices for their own sin, and then for the people (see Heb. 5:1-3), unlike Jesus, who was blameless and did not need to offer for His own sins (Heb. 7:26-28). Here at the end of the consecration ceremonies and at the beginning of the work of the priests for the people, it is very vivid that the priests had to offer first for themselves. What a blessing we have in the sacrifice of Christ!*

## The priestly blessing (Num. 6:22-27):

The Lord said to Moses, "Tell Aaron and his sons that this is how they are to bless the Israelites:

The Lord bless thee and keep thee;
The Lord make His face shine upon thee and be gracious unto thee;
The Lord lift up His countenance upon thee and give thee peace.

The Lord continued, saying, "So they will put my name on the Israelites, and I will bless them."

## Death of Nadab and Abihu (Lev. 10:1-20):

*The tabernacle had been set up and consecrated; God's presence had moved in to the place provided; the priests had been consecrated and had offered their first sacrifices; God had sent fire to consume the sacrifice to show He approved of all that had been done. Now it was time to start the normal process of offering all the prescribed sacrifices.*

Nadab and Abihu, two of Aaron's sons, each took his censer *(a metal bowl)* and put coals in it, added incense, and offered strange fire which the Lord had not commanded. Promptly fire came forth from before the Lord and burned them to death.

Moses told Aaron, "This is what the Lord was talking about when He said, 'I will be held in high regard by those who are intimate in their service to me, and I intend to be respected before all the people.'" *(Aaron made no response. What could he say? His sons had disobeyed the instructions and had been punished by the Lord.)*

Then Moses said to Mishael and Elzaphan, Aaron's first cousins: "Come and carry these bodies of your kinsmen away from the sanctuary, out of the camp." The two men came and carried the dead men out in their linen tunics as Moses commanded. *(That is, Nadab and Abihu were not completely consumed by the fire, but were killed by it as by a flash of lightning. Therefore their tunics were not destroyed.)*

*The death of Nadab and Abihu occurred between the offering of the goat for the sin offering (Lev. 9:15) and the eating of the flesh of the sin offering by the priests (10:16-20). That means it occurred immediately after the consecration process was ending, and as the normal priestly duties were beginning.*

Here in connection with the deaths of Nadab and Abihu, Moses gave Aaron and his other two sons strict instructions about how they were to show their grief. They were on duty as priests, and their brothers had died because of disobedience, therefore they were not to show any outward sign of grief. All the rest of the Israelites could grieve for the dead men, but Aaron, Eleazar, and Ithamar were not to leave the tabernacle or interrupt their work.

Moses continues by warning them that they were never to drink any kind of fermented beverage when they were on duty, "Lest you die." This was to be a lasting ordinance for the priests through all the generations to come. Priests must be able to distinguish between things holy and unholy, between things clean and unclean, and must be able to teach all the Israelites the differences.

Then Moses reminded them exactly which portions of the sacrifices were their portions to eat, exactly where the meat could be eaten, and who might share in the meal. But when Moses looked for the portion of the sin offering that they were supposed to eat that day, he found they had burned it. He was very angry with Eleazar and Ithamar and said, "Why didn't you eat the sin offering in the sanctuary area? This meat was most holy, and it had been set aside for you to eat in order for you to bear away the guilt of the congregation, to make atonement for them before the Lord. Since its blood was not taken inside the sanctuary *(as it would have been if it were a sin offering for a priest),* you should have eaten it, exactly as I commanded."

*Moses thought the command on this matter had been disregarded the same way the instructions about the incense had been disregarded. He was thinking the priests were being very negligent about learning that God demanded obedience in even the details of offering the sacrifices.*

But Aaron stepped forward with the explanation for the burned meat. He said, "Today they sacrificed their sin offering and their burnt offering before the Lord, because such dreadful things have happened to me today. Would the Lord have been pleased if I had eaten the sin offering today?" His answer satisfied Moses.

## The Worship is Set Up

*The sin of Nadab and Abihu was in "offering strange fire which the Lord had not commanded." Yet, it was after the death of Aaron's two sons (Lev. 16:1) that God's instructions are recorded that the coals to burn the incense were to come from the altar of burnt-offering (16:12). These instructions are given in the context of the Day of Atonement (16:2-3, 6-10). The high priest was to take the incense in with him when he took the blood of the bullock that was the sin offering for himself into the Most Holy Place (16:11-14). Now it may be inferred that this command meant that, under ordinary circumstances as well, the coals for burning incense had to come from the altar of burnt-offering, but there is no specific command to that effect recorded before these men died. There is therefore uncertainty about exactly what made the fire used by Nadab and Abihu "strange" fire except that it was not what God commanded. "Strange" incense would be incense prepared differently from the way God had prescribed (Exod. 30:9). There are two possible explanations:*

- *One is the more traditional one: that Nadab and Abihu sinned by using fire from some source other than the altar of burnt offering. This position is supported by the fact that the sin was in the offering of "strange fire" which the Lord had not commanded.*
  - *The problem with this position is that we find no command given on the subject until after the deaths of Nadab and Abihu.*
  - *Nevertheless, it could be inferred that since they offered fire which God had not commanded, that there was also a fire which God had commanded, a commandment which the priests already knew even though it is not yet in the text as it is arranged today, and Nadab and Abihu did not follow God's instructions.*
- *The other position is that Nadab and Abihu, awestruck by the fire that came from the Lord and consumed the burnt offering and the fat which were upon the altar, took their censers to offer incense when God had not commanded that any such thing be done — thus a "strange burning," an unauthorized offering.*

*In either case, the sin was in doing what God had* <u>*not*</u> *commanded. It is very important to see that doing what God did not say is as bad as doing what He has specifically forbidden. There is no question about God's right to destroy these men — they had been disobedient, they had ignored God's rules, so they deserved punishment. The only question we raise is exactly which rule they had disobeyed. Do not bog down in your class on a prolonged discussion over the exact explanation of what they did wrong. The point we are making is that there is not enough information given for us to know exactly what was wrong, but we have enough faith in God to know that He did know what was wrong, and that He was just in punishing these men.*

*When Moses asked why the meat of the sin offering had not been eaten, any reason that sounded as if Aaron were saying, "We did not feel like it," would not have been accepted by Moses. The point was that Aaron, along with Eleazar and Ithamar, felt defiled by the sins of Nadab and Abihu, and did not feel worthy to eat the sin offering. This answer was the only one that would have satisfied God and Moses.*

*God did not continue striking priests dead every time they disobeyed Him. The point was that this sin occurred immediately after the consecration and just as the priests were beginning their new work. If God had not made His point now, that He demanded careful observance of His rules about sacrifices, then the negligence would have multiplied from the first. A parallel incident occurs in the New Testament when Ananias and Sapphira were struck dead when they lied about the money they had received for land they had sold (Acts 5:1-11). Again, that event was very soon after the new covenant had been set into effect, and God was making the point that He demanded that His children act the part.*

### A blasphemer is stoned (Lev. 24:10-16, 23):

At some point during the months at Sinai *(the time is not given)*, the son of an Israelite woman and an Egyptian man got into a dispute with an Israelite man. In the dispute, the son blasphemed the Name *(Jehovah)* and cursed. Those who had heard him curse brought him to Moses, and they put him into custody until the Lord declared what should be done with him.

Jehovah said, "Bring the one who has cursed outside the camp, and let all who heard him lay their hands on his head *(the witnesses)*, and let the whole congregation stone him. Tell the children of Israel that whoever curses his God will bear the consequences. Anyone who blasphemes the name of Jehovah will surely be stoned to death by the congregation, whether he is a sojourner or a native Israelite."

Moses relayed these instructions to the children of Israel, and they brought the man out and stoned him to death.

*Again, God was making the point that He intended for His people to keep His laws. They could not expect His special blessings if they did not keep their side of the covenant. If the people had continued to administer the assigned punishments when sin occurred, then sinful practices would have been sharply reduced, and their whole history could have been different.*

## The Passover is Observed
### (Numbers 9:1-14)

The tabernacle was set up on the first day of the first month of the second year (Exod. 40:2). The priests were consecrated during the next eight days (Lev. 8:33-9:1). During those same eight days, plus four more, the princes of Israel came bringing the offerings from the tribes (Num. 7:1, 10-83). By then the first two weeks of that first month of the second year were almost over — and God reminded Moses that it was time to keep the Passover.

God said, "Have the Israelites celebrate the Passover at the appointed time, at twilight on the fourteenth day of this month, according to all the rules and regulations that have been given about the day."

Moses reminded the Israelites that the time had come for the celebration, and they made all preparations and observed the feast there in the Desert of Sinai, in front of Mount Sinai where they had been camped since they arrived there in the third month after leaving Egypt. Exactly one year had passed since that night of sorrow for the Egyptians and release for the Israelites.

Part of the rules for the Passover included a week immediately following the Passover itself when they were to eat unleavened bread. So, in reality, the Passover and the Feast of Unleavened Bread fit together and lasted a total of eight days.

*Take time to think of all that has happened in this one year:*

- *They crossed the Red Sea on dry land;*
- *They found the bitter water at Marah, and God made it sweet for them;*
- *The manna began when they had been out of Egypt one month;*
- *They received water from a rock and fought the Amalekites at Rephidim;*
- *They arrived at Mount Sinai in the third month.*
- *Since that time, here at Sinai:*
    - *God has spoken to them from the mount, and has made a covenant with them.*

- *The people promised to do all that God said, even though they asked that God never speak directly to them again.*
- *The covenant was ratified, and Moses went into the mount to receive the complete law.*
- *He was gone so long the people gave him up for lost and demanded that Aaron make them a god — and he made the golden calf.*
- *That broke their covenant with God, and God was ready to destroy them all.*
- *Moses interceded for the people, and the covenant was finally renewed.*
- *Moses returned to the mount for another forty days while the people waited at the foot for more instructions.*
- *This time when Moses returned, they were ready to build their tabernacle.*
- *They worked hard on their structure, giving freely of their own possessions, and made everything exactly according to the pattern God had given Moses.*
- *Now, the tabernacle is finished, it is dedicated, and the priests have been consecrated and have started their work.*
- *Each tribe has sent its gift of vessels and sacrifices.*
- *One year is complete.*

## A second Passover observance for those unclean (Num. 9:6-14):

There were some in the company who could not partake of the Passover at the proper time, because they had handled a dead body and were ceremonially unclean according to the law. So they came to Moses and Aaron to inquire about what they should do. Should they ignore the laws of ceremonial cleanliness and go ahead and eat the Passover, or should they ignore the Passover because of their circumstances? They said, "We have become unclean because of a dead body, but why should we be kept from participating in the Lord's offering at the appointed time?"

God had not yet given instructions on such matters, so Moses did not know the answer. He said, "Wait until I find out what the Lord commands for you."

Then God told Moses, "Tell the Israelites: 'When any of you or your descendants is unclean because of a dead body, or is away on a journey, that one may celebrate the Passover one month late. He is to celebrate it on the fourteenth day of the second month, and he is to observe all the rules exactly as if he were observing it on time. But if a man who is ceremonially clean, and not on a journey, fails to celebrate the Passover, then that person is to be cut off from his people. He did not obey the Lord and present the Lord's offering at the appointed time. He will bear the consequences of his sin."

The Lord continued, "And if any alien comes among you and wants to celebrate the Lord's Passover with you, he must do so in accordance with all the rules and regulations that have been given. The same rules apply for the stranger and for the native-born."

The Israelites remain at Mount Sinai for one more month, waiting until this second group could observe the Passover. We will continue to observe the dates given for the various activities, and we will see what happens between the first observance of the Passover and the second one for this group of unclean men.

*In a company that size, there would often be a dead body that had to be buried, so it was not surprising that this problem arose. There will be other feasts described as we proceed with our study of the law. Those, too, were to be kept on certain dates with certain rules and regulations. There is no evidence that there were similar provisions for them. But the principle is laid down here that if one failed to partake due to neglect, he was counted as a sinner and punished accordingly. If he had a legitimate reason why he could not partake, then at least in the Passover Feast, he was to be given a second opportunity.*

# *"Be Ye Holy For I The Lord Am Holy"*
## *(Leviticus 11-16. 18-27: Numbers 5. 6. 19. 28-30)*



*The consecration of the priests, the death of Nadab and Abihu, and the death of the one guilty of blasphemy, are the only bits of history found in the book of Leviticus. The rest of the book is a detailed look at the law telling how God intended for the Israelites to live as His people. Over and over He uses the expression, "Be ye holy for I the Lord am holy," or, "I am the Lord your God who makes you holy." God was saying that if they were to be His special people out of all the world, then they were to be like Him, they were to be different to all other people, because He is different. The word "holy" means to be different, to be consecrated, devoted, set apart for something. These were God's people, they were set apart unto Him —and they were to demonstrate this fact in their lives by copying the nature of God through the laws He gave. The law not only gave rules for the people to follow, it showed what God is like, so that they could know how to imitate Him. Most of the people failed to see this underlying message of the law and thought of the law as merely a set of rules to be obeyed, rather than a guide for their way of life. We must be careful not to make the same mistake in our understanding of the law of Christ.*

*If you are studying this material in sequence as an overview of all Bible history, there is not time to include a detailed study of the law at this time. So, look at the major laws, grasp the scope of the laws covered, but do not bog down in minute details in this study. Save that kind of study for a later date. Our companion book on the law includes all these laws, organized and outlined under a wide range of topics. Use it and this chapter as a reference source for a detailed study of the law.*

*Do not lose sight of the history. The Israelites set up their tabernacle on first day of the first month of the second year, and then observed their Passover feast on the fourteenth day of that same month. Some were unclean, and God told them to wait one month, and then they could partake of the feast by following all the rules prescribed. During that month while the congregation was waiting for the second group to eat of the feast, God had some very important things for them to do. We will discuss those things in our next chapter, but let us look at an overview of the law before we look at more history.*

# Clean and Unclean
## (Leviticus 11-15; Numbers 19)

Perhaps the best way to describe the concept of "clean and unclean" in the law of Moses·is to quote from Leviticus 11:43-45 and 15:31:

> Do not render yourselves detestable through any of the swarming things that swarm; and you shall not make yourselves unclean with them so that you become unclean. For I am the Lord your God. Consecrate yourselves therefore, and be holy; for I am holy... For I am the Lord, who brought you up from the land of Egypt, to be your God; thus you shall be holy, for I am holy... Thus you shall keep the sons of Israel separated from their uncleanness, lest they die in their uncleanness by defiling My tabernacle that is among them.

*The passages like this could be multiplied in our quotations (see Lev. 20:25-26). As you study the section, mark the passages where God says "Be ye holy, for I am holy," or "for I am the Lord your God," particularly in the book of Leviticus. God did not tell them to avoid certain meats because they had "too much fat content," or because they might be contaminated, or to avoid a house that was desecrated by disease lest they find germs. No. There was no reason to describe germs to the Israelites. They were to be holy, clean, undefiled, because they belonged to God, and their holy God dwelt among them. Therefore do not argue over whether God should or should not have described something as unclean; take His statements at face value, and move on to the next point. That is what He asked the Israelites to do.*

*God considered sin to be the greatest defilement which His people could suffer. Extensive instructions were given about sacrifices which would cleanse from sin in order that the holiness God expected of His people could be maintained. A sin offering was to be handled carefully so that the presiding priest would not be defiled by another person's sins.*

*The laws of cleanness that are included in this chapter, however, are not dealing with sinful matters. There was nothing sinful about eating pork (until God forbade it in His law). There was nothing sinful about having a baby; or sexual intercourse, or menstruation; there was nothing sinful about mildew or leprosy. All of these things in the second group involved either a disfiguring blight or something which soiled whatever it touched, and, therefore, had to be cleansed. Even though it was not sinful to become defiled in any of these ways, it was a sin to neglect the cleansing process prescribed (Lev. 5:2-3, 5-6).*

*There were secondary benefits the children of Israel derived from the practice of the laws of cleanness. Quarantine of those with skin diseases protected others from getting them. Lawful sanitation and the proper disposal of human waste kept infectious diseases from spreading among them. The diet the law required was a healthy one. One of the promises God made when they first left Egypt was, "If you will listen carefully to my word, and do what is right in my eyes, I will not bring on you any of the diseases of the Egyptians, for I am the Lord who heals you" (Exod. 15:26). There are several ideas included in that promise: one was that God would not send plagues upon them as He had sent upon the Egyptians; second, He would bless them and make them a healthy people. But it is also true that if they would follow the laws that He gave them concerning cleanliness, they would not face the severe scourges that often swept through ancient civilizations. But health reasons are never the ones given for the laws of cleanness in the law of Moses.*

*The primary purpose of the laws of cleanness was to impress the concept that they were the people of God and were to be holy. God said, "I live in your midst, and I am holy, so I do not intend to tolerate filth or defilement" (Num. 5:3b; Deut. 23:14). Perhaps it is in understanding the laws of cleanness that we come to our clearest understanding of what God meant by telling the Israelites they were His people. "You are mine. I bought you as my possession. Therefore you are to be as different to other people as I am to other gods. I am holy; I am unique. You are to be holy; you are to be unique —therefore, you must not defile yourselves. If something happens that defiles your body, wash it to remove the defilement. If it cannot be washed away, then move outside the camp. My camp must not be defiled."*

*If a person was unclean for any reason, he could not touch any holy thing; he could not be a part of any public assembly of the people; and he could not partake of any religious feast. These restrictions enhanced the importance of God's requirements for cleansing after one was defiled. In many circumstances, one was unclean only until evening. At that time, after he had bathed and put on clean clothes, he could return to his normal activities. In more severe circumstances, he might be defiled a week, or longer. In the case of long term illness, such as leprosy, he might be defiled for the rest of his life.*

## Clean and unclean animals (Lev. 11:1-47; see Deut. 14):

**Clean animals (Lev. 11:3, 9, 21-22):**

- The Israelites could eat any beast which had a split hoof and chewed the cud.
- Anything in the water which had fins and scales could be eaten.
- They could eat winged creatures *(insects)* that have jointed legs for hopping on the ground — such as, the locust, katydid, cricket, and grasshopper.
- They could eat most birds (Deut. 14:11).

**Unclean animals (Lev. 11:4-7, 10-20, 23, 27-43):**

- Any animal that did not meet both qualifications — having a split hoof and chewing the cud — was to be counted unclean and could not be eaten. The expression, *chewing of the cud*, in Hebrew, means "bringing up the cud" and strictly applies only to true ruminants. For example:
  - The camel could not be eaten, because though he chewed the cud, he did not have a split hoof like a cow or a deer.
  - The rock-badger, or hyrax, and the rabbit were unclean because they were not cloven footed. Actually, neither the hyrax nor the rabbit chews a cud, but they were popularly thought to do so because they move their mouths as if they were chewing the cud.
  - The hog was unclean because, although his hoof is parted, he does not chew the cud.
- Any water creature which did not have both fins and scales was an abomination.
- In some cases the exact bird referred to by a Hebrew word is uncertain. But, in general, the prohibition of birds for food included birds of prey such as the eagle and the hawk, and eaters of carrion such as vultures and ravens.
- All flying insects that walk on their feet *(instead of hopping)*, or swarm, were unclean.
- Hunters of prey, such as dogs, cats, or bears, were unclean.
- Animals that move about low upon the ground — such as, lizards, reptiles, weasels, and rats were unclean, and their dead bodies defiled anything they touched.
- Everything that crept or groveled upon the earth, such as snakes and moles, worms and weasels, were unclean. They were an abomination and were not to be eaten.
- Nothing which died of itself could be eaten.

**Defilement from unclean animals (Lev. 11:9, 11, 24-26, 31-40):**

- Anyone who ate one of these unclean animals, fish, or insects was defiled. "They shall be abhorrent to you... their carcasses you shall detest" (11:11).

- Anyone who touched the carcass of the unclean animal, insect, or creeping thing was unclean until evening. The one who picked up the carcass had to wash his clothes and be unclean until evening.
- Vessels of wood, raiment, skin, or sack, defiled by contact with the dead body of one of these creatures had to be washed and remained unclean until evening.
    - A pottery vessel was to be broken if defiled *(one that could not be washed)*.
    - Any food or water contacted by the dead body was unclean.
- Springs or wells that a carcass fell into would not be considered unclean because the constant fresh supply of water flushed the uncleanness away.
    - Whoever removed the dead body from the spring would, however, be defiled.
- Grain seed, if dry, was not defiled by contact with the dead body of one of these creatures.
    - If the grain were wet, then it would be unclean.
- If a clean animal dies of itself, it defiles the one who touches it until evening.
    - Anyone who eats it must wash his clothes and be unclean until evening.
    - The one who picks it up must wash his clothes and be unclean until evening.

Failure to follow the correct procedure for cleansing was counted as sin, even if one were unaware of defiling himself. When it was brought to his attention, he was to:
- Confess his sin (Lev. 5:5).
- Bring a female lamb or goat to the priest for a sin offering (5:2-3, 5-6).

## Uncleanness after childbirth (Lev. 12:1-8):

A woman was unclean after giving birth to a baby, and certain procedures were to be followed:
- If it were a son, she was unclean for seven days. On the eighth day the child was to be circumcised, and she would continue her purifying process for thirty-three days after the original seven.
- If she bore a girl, she was unclean two weeks, and would continue her purifying for 66 days.
- During the time of her uncleanness, she was not to touch any holy thing *(eat a part of a peace offering, or the Passover, for example)*, or come to the sanctuary.
- After her days of purification were over:
    - She was to bring a lamb a year old for a burnt offering, and a young pigeon or a turtle-dove for a sin offering to the door of the Tent of Meeting where the priest would offer them for her. Thus she would be cleansed.
    - If she were very poor, she could offer two pigeons or two turtle-doves: one for a burnt offering and one for a sin offering.
        - It is indicative of the financial status of Joseph and Mary that they brought two birds for their sacrifice at the time of her purification after Jesus was born (Luke 2:24).

## Uncleanness from skin diseases (Lev. 13:1-46; 14:1-32):

*The word leprosy in the Bible covered a variety of skin ailments. The medical term for leprosy today is Hansen's disease, which is still dreaded in parts of the world where modern medicine is scarce. Leprosy, in its worst form, was the most dreaded disease of ancient people. But it is difficult to know from the Hebrew word, or from the descriptions given, exactly which kind of skin disease is under consideration in all passages. One disease which fits the description is elephantiasis. As this disease begins, there is a spot or pimple and, in its last stages, it becomes a truly gruesome affliction. It was particularly severe in those days before modern medicines. (See the description in the footnote of* Pulpit Commentary*, Vol. II, p. 186.)*

*However, any occurrence of what is today called leprosy, as well as other skin diseases —some mild, some severe, possibly even some skin cancers — are included under the heading of leprosy. We use the term leprosy as we find it in the text, but understand that it included more than one kind of disease. Instructions were given to help the priests know how to diagnose leprosy, so that they would know how to determine whether a skin blemish or condition was serious or not. The people were warned to be very careful to do exactly as the priests instructed them on the matter of these various kinds of skin diseases.*

**Ways to detect leprosy in people (Lev. 13:1-46):**

*If one had a skin blemish, and it was suspected of being leprosy, he was to go before a priest to be examined. The priest made his diagnosis based upon the rules set forth in the law. A skin blemish might arise from various causes, and the law told the priest how to determine whether it was a dangerous condition or not. If the diagnosis was uncertain at the time of the first examination, the person was confined for a week at a time, the priest examined it after each week, and then made his diagnosis on the basis of whether the spot was improving, getting worse, or remaining the same.*

**Skin blemishes that must be examined (13:1-44):**
- Leprosy which arose from a skin blemish (13:1-8).
- Leprosy which first shows itself as a blemish (13:9-17).
- Leprosy arising from a boil (13:18-23).
- Leprosy which began from a burned place (13:24-28).
- Leprosy originating on the head from a mole (13:29-37).
- False leprosy (13:38-39).
- Leprosy of bald heads (13:40-44).

**Conduct of a leper (Lev. 13:45-46):**

"As for the leper who has the infection, his clothes shall be torn, and the hair of his head shall be uncovered *(disheveled, unkempt)*, and he shall cover his mustache and cry, 'Unclean! Unclean!' He shall remain unclean all the days during which he has the infection; he is unclean. He shall live alone; his dwelling shall be outside the camp."

**Cleansing of a leper (Lev. 14:1-32):**
- In the day that a leper was cleansed *(illness healed)*, word was brought to the priest. The priest was to go out of the camp to inspect him.
  - If the plague of leprosy were healed, the priest and the leper were to follow a very carefully prescribed procedure for cleansing.
  - On the next day after he was clean, and ready to enter into fellowship with Jehovah:
    - He was to take two he-lambs without blemish and a ewe-lamb a year old without blemish, along with meal, and a little over a cup of oil, to the priest.
    - The priest who had pronounced him clean brought the man and his offerings to the door of the Tent of Meeting and offered his sacrifices in a prescribed way.
    - If the person were poor, he might bring for his offerings a he-lamb, a smaller meal offering, a cup of oil, and two turtle-doves or two pigeons. The lamb was slain as his trespass offering, but one of the birds was killed as his sin offering and the other as his burnt offering. Otherwise the procedure was the same.

- After all the procedures were completed, and all the sacrifices were offered, the person was counted clean and in full fellowship with the holy people of God.

## Leprosy in garments and houses (Lev. 13:47-59; 14:33-57):

*Leprosy affecting material things was a blight caused by the growth of fungus, probably what we call mildew or some similar thing. We use the term leprosy as it is in the Bible text. It was not sinful for leprosy to show up in one's garment or in his house, but the blight caused by the fungus disfigured whatever it was upon. The people were to be holy, and their possessions holy. The blight had to be controlled.*

### Leprosy in garments (Lev. 13:47-59):

*The garments specified are those of wool, linen, and leather. The "warp and woof" were the threads running lengthwise and crosswise in the woven cloth (13:48-49, 51-52). Before weaving, the yarn to be used for the warp was accumulated in one place, and the woof was gathered in another, so that before the weaving was begun, the warp and the woof were separate. If the finished woven garment had leprosy in it, the yarn used to weave it was subject to inspection also, in order to find the source of the problem.*

If a spot showed up in a garment made of wool or linen, or in yarn to be woven, or in leather, it was to be examined by a priest. A greenish or reddish color indicated it was leprosy.

- The priest put the garment away for a week.
    - If the plague *(scourge)* had spread, it was leprosy. The garment had to be burned.
    - If the spot had not spread, the garment was to be washed and put up for one more week.
    - If, after the second week, the spot was still there, though it had not changed color, and had not spread, it still must be burned.
- If the spot faded after washing, the priest removed the spot from the garment or from the yarn by tearing or cutting it out.
    - If it broke out again, burn the garment or the yarn.
- If the spot was gone from the garment after washing it, then wash it a second time and it could be counted clean.

### Leprosy in a house (Lev. 14:33-57):

When the people went into the land God promised them, if one of them found an outbreak of leprosy *(mildew)* on or in his house, the owner was to go and tell a priest, "It seems there is a plague *(of leprosy)* in my house." They would empty the house and the priest would make an inspection.

- If the walls had streaks of green or red, and the marks were more than surface deep, the priest closed up the house for seven days.
    - Upon a second inspection, if the condition had spread, the priest would have the affected stones removed and cast into an unclean place. The plaster was scraped off and cast into an unclean place. New stones were inserted, and fresh plaster was put on the walls.
- If the plague came again, the priest was to inspect the house and declare the condition leprosy.
    - The house must be torn down, and the stones, timbers, and plaster carried out to an unclean place.
    - Anyone who went into the house while it was shut up was unclean till evening.
    - Anyone who spent the night in the house or ate in the house had to wash his clothes.
- If the corrective measures worked, and the leprosy did not return, the priest pronounced the house clean.
    - To complete the cleansing:
        - The priest took two birds and the special waters of purification (see Num. 19:1-10).

- He killed one of the birds in an earthen vessel of water from a spring or brook.
- He sprinkled the house with the blood of the bird and the water of purification.
- He released the living bird in the open field.
- So atonement was made for the house, and it was clean.

## Uncleanness from discharges (Lev. 15: 1-33):

### A person with a discharge (Lev. 15:1-15):

*The discharge in this first section was one caused by a disease or infection. It might be a long-lasting illness, or a short one. The masculine word "man" is used in the description, but since either a man or a woman could have an illness that caused a discharge, the text may be using the word "man" in the sense of a person —as is true in many other passages.*

- Whether the issue *(the discharge)* was active, or stopped by a blockage, the man was unclean.
- Every bed the man lay upon, or every place where he sat was unclean.
- Anyone who touched the infected person, his bed, or any place where he had sat was unclean and must wash his clothes, bathe himself, and be unclean until the evening. *(This would include the care-taker.)*
- The one upon whom the infected person spat was unclean.
- Whoever the infected man touched without first washing his hands had to bathe and be unclean till evening.
- Any vessel the infected man used must be washed or broken.
- When the man was healed of his issue:
    - He must number seven days and then wash his clothes, bathe in a spring or brook, and be clean.
    - On the eighth day he must take two turtle-doves or pigeons to the Tent of Meeting.
    - The priest offered one bird for a sin offering and one for a burnt offering.
    - Thus atonement would be made for him.

### Uncleanness from sexual intercourse (Lev. 15:16-18):

- Any time semen went forth from a man he had to bathe and be unclean until the evening.
- All garments or skins contacted by the emissions had to be washed and were unclean till evening.
- After sexual intercourse, both the man and the woman had to bathe and be unclean until evening.

### Uncleanness from a woman's menstrual cycle (Lev. 15:19-33):

- During a woman's normal menstrual period:
    - She was unclean for seven days.
    - Whoever touched her during that time was unclean until evening.
    - Everything she lay upon or sat upon was unclean, and anyone who touched her bed or anything she sat upon must bathe and be unclean until evening.
    - If any man had sexual intercourse with her during this time, he was unclean for seven days, and every bed he lay upon was unclean.
- Uncleanness from abnormal menstruation:
    - If a woman bled at a time that was not during her period, or if the bleeding went beyond the normal limits of her period, she was unclean as long as the condition lasted, and all the rules of defilement regarding uncleanness during her period applied to her abnormal condition.
    - When, however, the issue stopped:
        - She was to count seven days, and then she would be clean.

- On the eighth day she was to take two turtle-doves or two pigeons to the priest. He would offer one bird for a sin offering and the other for a burnt offering, thus making atonement for her.

## Uncleanness from contact with a dead body (Num. 19:11-22):

*Contact with a dead body caused serious defilement. It not only defiled one for a week, but if the waters of purification were not applied at the proper times, and the proper requirements were not met, the person defiled would not be cleansed. He must be cut off from among the people — either be put to death or completely lose his fellowship with the congregation (Num. 19:12-13, 20-21). It was not sinful to take care of the body of a dead friend, or to participate in a battle that God had decreed, but human life was to be counted valuable, and thus death was important. Stringent methods of cleansing were required.*

- Anyone who touched a dead body was unclean for one week.
- When someone died in a tent, everyone already inside the tent, or who came into the tent, was unclean seven days. Every open vessel was unclean.
- In the open field, whoever touched someone slain by the sword, the body of one dead from a natural cause, a dead man's bone, or a grave, was unclean for a week.
- In all cases the defilement caused by death required more than the usual remedy for cleansing. The special waters of purification (see Num. 19:1-10) must be sprinkled upon him on the third and seventh days. Otherwise, he would not be clean at the end of the week. If a man did not apply the water for purification, he was to be cut off
  - The unclean person must take ashes from the sin offering, put them into a jar, and pour fresh water over them *(verse 17 merely repeats instructions for the special waters for purification)*.
  - A clean person took hyssop and dipped it into the prepared water and sprinkled it upon the tent, upon all the vessels, and upon the people who were there; or upon anyone who touched a bone, or the slain, or the dead, or the grave in the field.
  - This was to be done on the third day and the seventh day.
  - On each of those days, the unclean person must wash his clothes, bathe with water, and be unclean until evening.
  - Whoever sprinkled the water for impurity, or touched it, was unclean until evening. Thus the water for impurity constituted a sin offering which, because of its connection with sin in atoning for it, defiled those who contacted it (Num. 19:21).
- Anything that an unclean person touched became unclean, and anyone who touched the object the unclean person had touched became unclean also. He was unclean until evening.

## Cleanness in the Camp (Num. 5:1-4; Deut. 23:9-14):

*These laws dealt with sanitation in their regular camps or towns, and in their army campaigns.*

- In their regular camps or towns (Num. 5:1-4):
  - While they were still at Mount Sinai, shortly before the tribes set forth on their march north, Jehovah said to Moses, "Command that the children of Israel put out of the camp every leper, and everyone who has an issue, and whoever is unclean by reason of contact with the dead. Put out both men and women, lest they defile the camp, where I dwell among them."
- In their army camps (Deut. 23:9-14):
  - When they set out on a campaign, they were to keep themselves away from anything unclean.

    - If a man had a nocturnal emission, he had to go outside of the camp. He must bathe and remain where he was until the sun was gone down; then he could return to camp.
    - They were to designate a place outside the camp where they were to go for elimination. Each soldier was to have a paddle to dig with among his weapons. He was to dig a hole, and after elimination, he was to cover the hole.
- Reason given: "For the Lord your God moves about in your camp to protect you and to deliver your enemies to you. Your camp must be holy, so that He will not see among you anything indecent, and turn away from you" (23:14).
    - Though this law served a sanitary function, the reason continually emphasized by God, was that by this means the people were taught the utmost reverence for God and His holiness. And since God's holiness was an example for the holiness of His people, these laws were designed to create in them a recognition of the need for holiness in their lives.

## Water of Purification (Num. 19:1-10):

**Instructions for preparing the waters of purification:**

- The people were to provide a red heifer without blemish, upon which no yoke had ever been placed.
- The heifer was given to the priest who was successor to the high priest *(in this case, Eleazar),* but not to the high priest himself, because the procedure defiled the priest involved in the preparation — and the high priest was not to defile himself.
- The heifer was taken outside the camp and slain before Eleazar. He took the blood of the heifer upon his finger and sprinkled it toward the front of the Tent of Meeting seven times.
- While the priest watched, someone *(not Eleazar, see v. 8)* burned the entire heifer. The priest threw cedar-wood, hyssop, and scarlet onto the burning heifer.
- Then the priest washed his clothes, bathed himself, and was unclean until evening because he had touched the blood of the sin offering which became defiled in behalf of those who sinned, and therefore rendered the priest unclean.
- The man who burned the heifer would likewise be unclean and had to wash his clothes, bathe himself, and be unclean until evening.
- A man who was clean gathered the ashes into a container and put them in a clean place without the camp.
    - He, too, was made unclean and had to wash his clothes, bathe himself, and be unclean until sunset.
    - These ashes were kept for a long period of time for use in making the waters of purification.
- This sacrifice was a sin offering, so it had to be offered outside the camp (Num. 19:9; Lev. 4:11, 12, 21).
- When the need arose for waters of purification *(for example, when the priest was cleansing a house from leprosy, or cleansing a person who had been defiled by a dead body)*, they took some of these ashes and added water from a spring to make a solution that could be sprinkled upon the unclean object (see Lev.14:51; Num. 19:12, 17-18).

# Special Times
## (Leviticus 16, 23, 25; Numbers 28-29; Deuteronomy 16)

*Just as there were specified sacrifices the people were to offer because God commanded them, there were special times they were to observe because He commanded it. God had the right to set the rules and regulations for these special times, and it was man's choice to obey or disobey —and experience the consequences of his choice. The Lord commanded, "These are my appointed feasts, the ones the Lord has set apart, which are to be proclaimed as sacred assemblies" (Lev. 23:1-2).*

*Even though it was God's prerogative to set special times that the people were to observe, for whatever reasons He chose, He revealed those reasons and He taught the people the lessons He wanted them to remember. These times were reminders of the blessings God had given them. The occasions themselves were to be blessings: for their rest, for feasting together, for times of rejoicing.*

## Sacrifices for the congregation (Num. 28:1-29:40):

*Numbers 28 and 29 summarize the instructions for the sacrifices the priests were to offer on a regular basis on behalf of the congregation. These animals were chosen from the flocks and herds kept for this purpose. All of these sacrifices for the congregation were in addition to the individual sacrifices for vows, freewill offerings, burnt offerings, grain offerings, drink offerings, and peace offerings —or whatever else was required of some individual to fulfill a specific law. Each feast day required individual offerings as well as these community sacrifices. The Israelites were to give freely to their God.*

Look briefly at the number of animals to be offered regularly for the congregation:

- Daily: 2 lambs *(one in the morning and the other in the afternoon)*.
- Sabbath day: 2 additional lambs.
- New moons *(1st of each month)*: 11 additional animals.
- Passover and Feast of Unleavened Bread: 18 additional animals on each of the eight days.
- Feast of Weeks: 11 additional animals.
- Feast of Trumpets: 10 additional animals.
- Day of Atonement: 10 additional animals, plus the special atonement sacrifices.
- Feast of Ingathering: an eight-day feast with special sacrifices each day:
    - 1st day: 30 extra animals.
    - 2nd day: 29 extra animals.
    - 3rd day: 28 extra animals.
    - 4th day: 27 extra animals.
    - 5th day: 26 extra animals.
    - 6th day: 25 extra animals.
    - 7th day: 24 extra animals.
    - 8th day: 10 extra animals.

## The sabbath day (Lev. 23:1-3):

- The sabbath day was the most frequent time to be observed because it came once a week.
    - It was given to Israel as a blessing.
- The sabbath law was one of the ten commandments: "Remember the sabbath day to keep it holy" (Exod. 20:8; Deut. 5:12).

- As the rest of the law was given, the command was repeated and amplified (Exod. 31:12-17; 34:21; 35:1-3; Lev. 19:3, 30; 23:3; 26:2).
- The sabbath was a day of rest: "Six days you may work, but the seventh day is a sabbath to Jehovah. No one is to work on that day... neither you, nor your son or daughter, nor your servants, nor your animals, nor the stranger within your gates" (Exod. 20:9-10; 23:12; Lev. 19:3, 30; 23:3; Deut. 5:13-14).
  - This command was to be obeyed even during plowing season and harvest time (Exod. 34:21).
  - As an example of work that might be done, they were forbidden to kindle a fire in their dwellings on that day (Exod. 35:3).
- Anyone who desecrated this holy day, or did any work, was to be put to death (Exod. 31:14-15).
  - While they were in the wilderness, a man was found picking up sticks on the sabbath. He was put into custody until God commanded what to do with him. God said, "This man must die. The whole congregation must stone him to death" (Num. 15:32-36).
- God ordained a day of rest for His people in order to remind them that they had been slaves without the privilege of rest, but He rescued them. They were now free, with the right to rest (Deut. 5:15).
  - He said they must observe His sabbaths as a sign between Himself and the people for all generations to come, so that they might know that He was the Lord who made them holy (Exod. 31:13).
  - The sabbath day served as a weekly reminder that they were a people who had been redeemed from bondage by a loving and powerful God who had taken them for His special possession.
- God chose the seventh day as the day of rest, rather than some other day of the week, because it was on the seventh day God rested after the creation (Exod. 20:11; 31:15-17).
  - There was no observance of the seventh day until the Israelites came out of Egypt.
  - The first mention of the day is in Exodus 16:23-26, when the Israelites were encamped in the Wilderness of Sin, and the manna was beginning. God told them the manna would be on the ground every day for six days, but that the seventh day was to be a day of rest, and there would be no manna to gather on that day.
- The sabbath was to be "a day of holy convocation" (Lev. 23:3).
  - The expression "holy convocation" is found only in the books of Exodus, Leviticus, and Numbers. It meant a holy assembly, a gathering to worship or to fulfill some specific purpose set forth by God.
- The priests had special duties to perform on the sabbath.
  - Two extra lambs were to be offered as burnt offerings each sabbath day. These were in addition to the regular daily sacrifice of two lambs (Num. 28:9-10).
  - New shewbread was to be baked and put on the table of shewbread in the Holy Place of the tabernacle. The old was to be removed, and the priests were to eat it in a holy place as one of their shares in the offerings to the Lord (Lev. 24:5-9).

*By New Testament days, there is abundant evidence that the Jews met each sabbath in their synagogues. In the Old Testament, there were special sabbaths in connection with their feast days when the Israelites met for "holy convocations." But the passage in Leviticus 23:3 speaks of regular assemblies on the sabbath. As we follow their history through the Old Testament, there are many times when the people are rebuked for not keeping their sabbath days, but the sin mentioned is their continuing with their normal work (see Neh. 13:15-22; Jer. 17:19-27).*

*There is no historical information about these assemblies on the weekly sabbath days. There is never a mention of a synagogue (or an equivalent Hebrew term) as a place of meeting. It seems, therefore, that these assemblies were informal during most of Old Testament history. During the captivity, after the kingdom of Judah fell, the people began to meet more regularly in the lands to which they had been taken. There, they read from their law and from their prophets, and were exhorted to return to the Lord with their full hearts. They were reminded of their unique position before God. The synagogues of the New Testament grew out of these regular assemblies of the captivity.*

## New Moons (Num. 28:11-15):

- The next most frequent time the Israelites were to observe was the new moon — that is, the first day of each new month.
- In addition to the daily sacrifices, on the first day of each month, the priests were to offer a burnt offering of two young bullocks, one ram, and seven he-lambs a year old without blemish, with their appropriate meal and drink offerings, and one he-goat for a sin offering.
- The silver trumpets Moses made were to be blown over the sacrifices on the new moons (Num. 10:10).

*Very little is said in the law about the new moon. There is no law for any kind of special assembly or feasting on those days, but there is more historical evidence concerning gathering on new moons than there is about the sabbath gatherings. For example, when David was first beginning to flee from Saul, he knew there would be a feast the next day because he said, "Tomorrow is the new moon, and I should not fail to sit with the king at meat." Instead of going, he hid while Jonathan went to the feast and learned of his father's hatred for David (1 Sam. 20).*

*Later in Israelite history the new moon grew more and more into a feast day. Trade was suspended (Amos 8:5), and it became a time associated with special religious endeavors such as inquiring of a prophet (2 Kings 4:23). Therefore, in the prophets it is treated as a day similar to the sabbath, and is usually mentioned in the same breath as the sabbath (see Isa. 1:13-14; Ezek. 46:1; Hos. 2:11).*

## Yearly Feasts:

"Three times a year all the men are to appear before the Lord to celebrate feasts unto Him" (Exod. 23:14, 17; 34:23; Deut. 16:16). "Do not come before the Lord empty-handed" *(that is, without gifts and offerings)* (Exod. 23:15; 34:20). "Each must bring a gift in proportion to the way the Lord has blessed him" (Deut. 16:17).

*The three primary feasts included in the basic covenant were the Feast of Unleavened Bread (immediately following the Passover), the Feast of Harvest (or Feast of Weeks), and the Feast of Ingathering (or Tabernacles) which came at the end of their harvest. Much information is given in the law about each of these feasts. We are including enough information here to help you see what was to be done, and the purposes for each feast, but we will not go into detail about exactly how each thing was done. Our companion book on the law has a more detailed analysis. Since there is so much information given about these feasts, we are making a separate heading for each one.*

*Notice that the women and children were not required to present themselves for these yearly feasts. They were welcome, and did attend on most occasions, because it was a time of feasting and rejoicing for the whole family, but they were not required to do so because there were times when a woman was not physically able to make the journey, or she would be unclean due to the birth of a baby, or some related reason.*

## The Passover Feast and the Feast of Unleavened Bread (Lev. 23:4-14):

### The Passover:

*God gave precise instructions about how they were to keep the Passover Feast every year to remember the great night when God passed over the firstborn of the Israelites. Look into the chapter on the plagues to see the details of how the Israelites ate their feast in the middle of the night as the firstborn of Egypt were dying (Exod. 12). At that time, they put blood on the doorpost and on the lentils at each house, and they ate the feast dressed for a journey because God had told them they would leave the land after that plague. It all came to pass as God had predicted. The later feasts were to remember that night, but they never again needed the blood on their doorposts, nor did they need to eat it in a hurry in order to be ready to leave on a journey.*

To remind them of the night of the last plague:

- God commanded them to observe the feast every year, throughout their generations (Exod. 12:14, 17).
  - "When you enter the land God is giving you, do not forget to keep this service in the first month of your year, because it was by the Lord's strong hand that you were delivered. Explain to your sons why you keep the day. Let it be a sign upon your hand and between your eyes, lest you forget how God brought you out of bondage" (Exod. 13:3-10).
- God commanded that this month become the first month of their religious year (Exod. 12:2).
  - The month was called Abib (Exod. 13:4), which means "green ears of corn" (Deut. 16:1). It was the month, equivalent to our March 15 to April 15, when the green ears of wheat appeared on the stalks.
  - The Israelites had two calendars that they used regularly. Their religious year began with Abib and the keeping of the Passover Feast, and ended with the month Adar. The other calendar was for their civil year, and it began six months later, in the fall, at the beginning of the seventh month of their religious calendar. The seventh month was also an important month of their religious calendar, as we will see as we proceed with our study of their special times.
- Look at the listing of the sacrifices for the congregation at the beginning of this section. On the day of the Passover itself, and on each of the seven days of Unleavened Bread that followed, the priests were to offer the prescribed sacrifices according to all the rules God had given (Num. 28:16-25).
- Each family came to the feast bringing the necessary ingredients for the Passover meal they would eat before the Lord.
  - The animal for the feast was to be a year old male, without defect, from either the sheep or the goats.
    - It was to be the size needed for one family, or for two or more families sharing it (Exod. 12:3-5).
    - On the tenth day of the month, they were to put up the animal, and then kill it on the evening of the fourteenth day (Exod. 12:3, 6; Lev. 23:5; Deut. 16:6).
    - The lamb was to be roasted or broiled (Exod. 12:8; Deut. 16:7). No bone was to be broken (Exod. 12:46), nor was it to be boiled in water (Exod. 12:9). All the food was to be eaten that evening, inside the house, and any leftovers destroyed (Exod. 12:10, 46; 34:25; Deut. 16:4).
    - The rest of the menu included bitter herbs and unleavened bread (Exod. 12:8).
    - In the days of Jesus, the fruit of the vine was drunk with the feast (Matt. 26:26-29). It was probably drunk with the original feast since, universally, men have drunk beverages at their meals, but it is not mentioned.

**The firstborn belongs to God:**

- Very closely related to the Passover was the command that the firstborn belonged to Jehovah. God spared the firstborn of Israel when He destroyed the firstborn of Egypt. "Every firstborn must be given to the Lord, both animals and man" (Exod. 13:1-2, 12; 22:29; 34:19-20).
- The Levites took the place of the firstborn of the generation that left Egypt (Num. 3, 4, 8).
- The law told exactly how to give each firstborn to God, or how to redeem it if it were not an animal that could be sacrificed (Num. 18:15-19; Deut. 15:19-23).
- God said, "Tell your sons the meaning of the practice. Tell them of the plague, of how God saved the firstborn of Israel, and therefore claimed them for His own. Let it be an ever-present reminder of the time Jehovah brought you out of Egypt" (Exod. 13:11-16).

**The Feast of Unleavened Bread:**

- The Passover Feast was immediately followed by a week of eating unleavened bread — called the Feast of Unleavened Bread.
  - The names are used interchangeably to refer to the eight-day celebration — sometimes called Passover, referring to the whole period, and sometimes called the Feast of Unleavened Bread, referring to the whole time (see Luke 22:1).
  - Technically, the Passover was a one-day feast, immediately followed by the Feast of Unleavened Bread which was a seven day feast.
    - The Passover began at twilight on the fourteenth day of the first month, and then on the fifteenth day of the month the Feast of Unleavened Bread began and lasted through the twenty-first day (Exod. 12:18; Lev. 23:5-6).
- On the first and seventh days of the Feast of Unleavened Bread, there were to be holy assemblies. On those days they were to do no work of any kind except the necessary preparations for meals (Exod. 12:16; Lev. 23:7-8; Deut. 16:8).
- For all eight days, the people were to eat unleavened bread (Exod. 12:15; Lev. 23:6; Deut. 16:3).
  - On the first day *(the 14th of the month)*, they were to put all leaven out of their houses: whoever ate leavened bread during those eight days was to be cut off from the people (Exod. 12:15; Deut. 16:4).
- Even though unleavened bread was eaten at the Passover meal (Exod. 12:8), the significance of keeping a memorial seven-day period of eating unleavened bread went beyond the memory of the last plague.
  - When they left Egypt, they were in such a hurry there was no time for their bread to rise. They had to bind up their kneading troughs and carry them on their shoulders, so when they stopped to eat, it was unleavened bread that they had (Exod. 12:34, 39). The feast was a reminder of those days.
- The Feast of Unleavened Bread was to be observed as regularly as the Passover feast itself, because it, too, was a reminder of the day God brought their armies out of Egypt.
- All the congregation of Israel was to keep the feast *(the 8-day celebration)*, but no stranger, no uncircumcised person, could eat of it (Exod. 12:43-49; Num. 9:14.)
  - After a bought servant was circumcised, he could partake of the feast, but no foreigner or hired servant who had not been circumcised could eat of it.
  - If a stranger came to live among them, and wanted to keep the feast, all the males in his family had to be circumcised before he could partake of the feast. After he was circumcised he was like one born in the land.
  - It was by the rite of circumcision that a foreigner expressed his desire to become part of the special nation of God. It was his way of becoming a part of the family of Abraham (see Gen. 17).

- The rules for observing the feast were the same for the one born at home or the stranger who had come into their midst (Exod. 12:15-20; 13:6-7).

*Unleavened bread is simply bread without any agent to make it rise, such as a sourdough starter, baking powder, or yeast. We use unleavened bread regularly today in our pie crusts and in other kinds of flat bread. Many have had the idea that unleavened meant unsalted, but salt is not a leavening agent. Leaven was forbidden in almost all their sacrifices, but salt was a necessary item in those same sacrifices (Lev. 2:11-13).*

**Firstfruits of barley (Lev. 23:9-14):**

*Though the wording is a little uncertain, almost certainly the sacrifices described in Leviticus 23 were those the priests offered on behalf of the whole congregation. The book of Leviticus gives the rules for how the priests and Levites were to perform their duties for the congregation. From Jewish historical records, there was a public offering of the sacrifice described here, the priests ate from that sacrifice, and then the people ate of their own firstfruits.*

- First fruits of barley were offered on the day after the first day of holy convocation during the Feast of Unleavened Bread.
  - That would make it the sixteenth day of the month *(the Passover on the fourteenth day, a holy convocation on the next day as the beginning of the Feast of Unleavened Bread, and then the offering of the firstfruits on the next day).*
  - The law does not specify which grain was offered on this occasion, but it was their barley that ripened first, and was therefore ready at this time of the year.
- The priest waved a sheaf of the new grain before the Lord *(that means it was presented before the Lord, but not burned).*
  - At the same time, he offered a he-lamb as a burnt offering. With it they were to give a meal offering of two tenths of an ephah *(twice the normal amount —Num. 15:4-5)* of fine flour mixed with oil. The drink offering was one-fourth of a hin *(normal amount).*
- The people were forbidden to eat either bread, parched grain, or fresh ears from the new harvest until this sheaf was offered.

**Second opportunity (Num. 9:6-14):**

At Sinai, when it was time to observe the Passover, the question arose about what to do if one were unclean when it was time to keep the feast. God gave His answer: "Anyone who is unclean, or is away on a journey, may keep the Passover in the second month on the fourteenth day of the month. All rules and regulations apply just as if it had been at the right time. A man who is clean, however, and not on a journey, who does not keep the Passover, is to be cut off from his people."

## Feast of Weeks (Lev. 23:15-21):

*In the Old Testament, this feast is called the Feast of Weeks (Exod. 34:22; Deut. 16:10, 16), the Feast of Harvest (Exod. 23:16), and the Day of the Firstfruits (Num. 28:26). It was called the Feast of the Fifty Days in the writings of Josephus. It is from that name "fifty days" that the term Pentecost comes (Acts 2:1). The word Pentecost was a Greek term and is never used in the Old Testament. Still other names were used in non-Biblical Jewish writings.*

- "Celebrate the Feast of Harvest with the firstfruits of the crops you sow in your fields" (Exod. 23:16).

- The time of the feast was determined by counting seven sabbaths from the day on which the sheaf of the wave offering was presented during the Feast of Unleavened Bread. The Feast of Weeks was the next day, the fiftieth day, after the seventh sabbath.
- It was a one day feast, a time of rejoicing before the Lord — "you, your sons and daughters, your men-servants and maid-servants, the Levites in your towns, the strangers, the fatherless, and the widows among you" (Deut. 16:10-12).
- It was a day of holy assembly before the Lord, and no rigorous work was to be done.
- The feast was to be a reminder that they were once slaves and were now free. That memory should make them careful to obey all the decrees carefully. (See Deut. 16:9-12.)
- All the men were to present themselves at the sanctuary for the feast (Exod. 23:17; Deut. 16:16).
- A special meal offering was made on this Feast of Weeks consisting of two leavened loaves, each made of one tenth of an ephah *(a little over half a gallon)* of flour.
    - Leavened bread was never burned on the altar. Leavened bread accompanied other thanksgiving offerings, but like these two loaves, they were eaten instead of burned (Lev. 7:11-15).
    - The bread for this occasion was made like the common bread eaten in homes. Made from the just completed wheat harvest, these loaves were symbolic of the provisions God had made for His people to have good things to eat in the land He had given them.
- Burnt offerings of seven lambs, without blemish, a year old, one young bullock, and two rams, were to be given along with the appropriate meal and drink offerings; one he-goat was to be given for a sin offering; two he-lambs a year old were sacrificed for peace offerings.
    - The two he-lambs, along with the two loaves, were given to the priest.

*Just as we said in connection with the firstfruits offering during the Feast of Unleavened Bread, the offering of the two loaves of bread on this occasion was by the priests on behalf of the whole congregation. But when we put all the information together, seemingly each family brought bread made from their new wheat crop and other items from their homes to eat at this time of thanksgiving before the Lord. The priests offered the loaves and the other sacrifices for the congregation, and then they and their families ate the loaves and the lambs as their portion for the feasting.*

## The Seventh Month

*The seventh month completed the cycle of feasts which began with the Passover. This month was the time for the Feast of Trumpets, the Day of Atonement, and the Feast of Tabernacles (Ingathering). The year which began with Abib did not end with this Feast of Tabernacles, but it was the last great feast in the year. Abib was equivalent to our March 15-April 15, and the Feast of Tabernacles was in October.*

*Remember that the Israelites had a religious year and a civil year — thus two calendars they used regularly. The religious year began with the month Abib and concluded with the month Adar. The civil year began with the first day of Tishri, which was the seventh month of the religious calendar. It was counted as a very important month, partly because it began their civil year, but mostly because of the importance of the Day of Atonement and the Feast of Ingatherings that took place that month. The word "end" found in Exodus 34:22 means revolution and may refer to the fact that the Feast of Ingatherings was at the time of the changing of the civil year ("at the turning of the year").*

**Feast of Trumpets (Lev. 23:23-25; Num. 29:1-6):**

- There was to be a holy assembly on the first day of the seventh month. This assembly marked the day as more special than the normal "new moon" days.

- No rigorous work was to be done.
- It was to be a day for the blowing of trumpets.
  - It was because of this blowing of the trumpets that the day got its name.
  - Moses commanded that the silver trumpets be blown on days of rejoicing, at set feasts, and at the beginnings of the months (Num. 10:2-10).
    - Since there is special mention of the blowing of the trumpets on this first day of the seventh month, there must have been some unusual way they were blown that set the day apart from the first day of the other months.
- Ten specified animals were to be offered, with their meal and drink offerings. These were in addition to the regular sacrifices offered on the first day of each month and to the regular daily sacrifices (Num. 29:2-6).

## Day of Atonement (Lev. 16:1-34; 23:26-32; Num. 29:7-11):

The Day of Atonement was one of the most important days in the whole year. It is described in detail in Leviticus 16:

- "This is to be a lasting ordinance for you: Atonement is to be made once a year for all the sins of the Israelites" (16:34).
  - On this day atonement was made for the priest and for the people before Jehovah, so that they would be clean from all their sins (16:30; 23:28).
  - Atonement was also made for the holy sanctuary *(the Most Holy Place)*, the tent of meeting *(the Tabernacle)*, and for the altar (16:33). *(These objects had to be "atoned" or "cleansed" because they had been defiled by the sins of the people.)*
- Special animals were selected for the Day of Atonement:
  - For the special occasion, there was to be a burnt offering of a young bullock, a ram, and seven he-lambs a year old without blemish, with the appropriate meal and drink offerings, and one he-goat for a sin offering. These were in addition to the daily burnt offering and the special sin offerings for the atonement (Num. 29:9-11).
  - For the special atonement sacrifices:
    - For the high priest: A bull was selected for a sin offering and a ram for his burnt offering (Lev. 16:3).
    - For the congregation: Two male goats were selected for sin offerings and a ram for their burnt offering (16:5).
- The day of the atonement was the tenth day of the seventh month (16:29-30; 23:27).
- The people of Israel were to afflict their souls *(fast and deprive themselves of amusements)* from sunset on the ninth day until sunset on the tenth day (16:29; 23:32).
  - This was the only "fast" God ever commanded His people. It was to be done on this solemn day when atonement was made for them before the Lord their God.
- It was to be a sabbath of solemn rest in which no kind of work could be done (16:29; 23:28, 30; Num. 29:7).
  - Most special days that included sabbaths stated that "no rigorous work" was to be done. On this day, there was to be no work at all done. It was therefore comparable to a seventh day sabbath.
  - Anyone who did not afflict himself or who did any work on this day, was to be cut off from his people (Lev. 23:29-30).

**Atonement for the high priest:**

- Aaron was warned that the high priest was not to enter into the holy place within the veil *(the Most Holy Place)* at any time he chose (Lev. 16:2).
  - Only on the Day of Atonement was he permitted to enter through the veil (Exod. 30:10; Heb. 9:7).
- The ceremonies for the Atonement Day began with the high priest bathing and clothing himself, not in the normal attire of the high priest, but all in white (Lev. 16:4).
  - These garments were similar, but not identical, to those of the common priests. He wore linen underbreeches, a tunic or body-coat of white, a sash, and a turban. The garments all of white symbolized holiness in this all-important task of making atonement for the people.
- The first sacrifice offered was a bull for the priest's sin offering to atone for him and his house (Lev. 16:6, 11; see Heb. 7:27; 9:7).
  - When the bullock had been slain:
    - The high priest took a censer full of coals of fire from the altar of burnt offering and his hands full of sweet incense beaten into small pieces into the Most Holy Place and there offered the incense before the mercy seat (Lev. 16:12-13).
    - He brought the blood of the bull within the veil, and sprinkled it with his finger upon the front of the ark and then sprinkled it upon the ground before the mercy seat seven times (16:14).

**Atonement for the people:**

- The two he-goats and the ram for the congregation were brought forward.
  - The priest cast lots over the two he-goats. One goat was selected for Jehovah, and one for Azazel *(Removal)*. The goat for Jehovah would be slain as a sin offering, while the goat for Azazel would be sent into the wilderness. (16:5, 7-10).
- The high priest slew the sin offering *(the he-goat)* for the people and brought the blood within the veil and sprinkled it, as he had done the blood of the bullock, upon the mercy seat and before the mercy seat (16:15).
  - Thus the high priest made atonement for the Most Holy Place because of the children of Israel and because of their transgressions (16:16).
    - This atonement extended to the whole Tent of Meeting (16:16).
    - No one but the high priest was present during these procedures (16:17).
- The high priest went back out to the altar, took more of the blood of the bull and of the goat, and smeared the blood on the horns of the altar before the Lord and sprinkled the blood upon the altar with his finger seven times and thus cleansed and hallowed it from the uncleanness of the children of Israel (16:18-19).
  - Since the priest went "out" to this altar (16:18), it is the altar of burnt offering (cf. Lev. 4:25).
- Having made atonement for the Most Holy Place, the Tent of Meeting, and the altar, the high priest presented the live goat (Azazel) and confessed over him all the iniquities and transgressions of the children of Israel (16:20-21).
  - Their iniquities were thus put upon the head of the goat, and the goat was led away by the hand of a man appointed, into the wilderness into a deserted area and released, symbolically "removing" the sin from the camp (16:21-22).
  - Afterward this man washed his clothes, bathed, and returned to camp (16:26).
- Now the high priest returned to the Tent of Meeting and put off the linen garments *(16:23 — nothing further is said about what was done with these linen garments)*.
  - He bathed again and put back on his official garments of the high priest (16:24).

- He came out and offered the ram for his burnt offering and the ram for the burnt offering of the people (16:24, 3, 5). He burned the fat of the sin offering upon the altar (16:25).
- Then the bullock of the sin offering and the goat of the sin offering were carried without the camp where their skins, their flesh, and their entrails were burned (16:27).
    - The one who burned them was to wash his clothes, bathe his flesh in water, and afterward he could return to camp (16:27-28).
- The atonement was complete for another year.

## Feast of Tabernacles or Ingatherings (Exod. 23:16; 34:22; Lev. 23:33-44; Num. 29:12-38; Deut. 16:13-17):

- "Celebrate the Feast of Ingathering at the turning of the year" (Exod. 23:16; 34:22; Deut. 16:13).
    - This month marked the end of the previous agricultural cycle and the sowing of the new crop.
- It was a seven day feast, beginning on the fifteenth day of the seventh month (Lev. 23:34).
- There were two primary purposes for this feast, thus its two very different names:
    - It was a time of thanksgiving, a time of celebration, for the harvest Jehovah had made possible for them (Lev. 23:39; Deut. 16:13-15). Therefore the feast was called the Feast of Ingathering.
    - It was also a time to remember the years they spent in the wilderness (Lev. 23:40-43). Thus the feast was called the Feast of Tabernacles *(tents)*.
        - On the first day of the feast, simple arbors or shelters were to be made from the branches of palm trees and the leafy boughs of other trees.
        - In these huts the children of Israel were to rejoice for seven days.
        - This week would be a reminder to them of the years they dwelt in booths *(temporary shelters)* when God brought them out of the land of Egypt.
- The first day and the eighth day of the feast were to be days of holy assembly, and no rigorous work was to be done (Lev. 23:35-36; Num. 29:12, 39).
- Special sacrifices were to be offered. The number of sacrifices was incredible during these seven days:
    - Look at the list of sacrifices for the congregation at the beginning of this section (Num. 29:13-38).
        - On the fifteenth day, thirteen young bullocks, two rams, and fourteen he-lambs were offered as burnt offerings, plus the required meal offerings and drink offerings, and a he-goat for a sin offering.
        - Each day, for the next six days, the same sacrifices were offered except that one bullock less was offered each day.
        - Then on the eighth day, one bullock, one ram, and seven he-lambs were offered as burnt offerings, along with meal and drink offerings, plus a he-goat for a sin offering.
        - All sacrifices required by the feast were in addition to any other sacrifices called for by the law on any day which fell within that feast, and in addition to any individual offerings to pay some vow or to give some freewill offering.
- One hundred and fifty-nine animals were offered for the congregation in the seventh month alone, not counting the daily burnt-offerings *(two each day)*, the regular new moon offerings *(eleven on the first of the month)*, and the sabbath offerings *(two additional ones each sabbath)*.

## The Sabbath Year:

**Plant no crops (Exod. 23:10-11; Lev. 25:1-7):**

- The land itself was to have a sabbath of rest, a sabbath to the Lord.
- For six years they planted their crops and gathered the harvest, but on the seventh year, they were to let the ground lie fallow, growing only what came up from seed left in the ground from previous crops.
  - Vineyards and olive trees were treated the same way.
- Whatever the land produced could be food for the owner, his family, his servants, his animals, the poor, any stranger living among them, and for the wild animals (Exod. 23:11; Lev. 25:6-7).
  - But they could not reap or harvest any of the produce to keep for later use.
- God warned that if they did not keep these and other laws, then they would someday be driven away into captivity. "Your land will be laid waste, your cities will be destroyed, and the land will enjoy the sabbath years that you failed to give it" (Lev. 26:33-35; see 2 Chron. 36:21).

**Let Hebrew slaves go free in the seventh year (Exod. 21:2-11; Deut. 15:12-18):**

- If an Israelite bought a fellow-Hebrew man as a slave, he was to serve his master for six years, and then go free in the seventh year.
  - The man might choose to stay with his master and family by stating his decision to do so. In that case the master took him before the judges and pierced his ear as a sign of his voluntary slavery.
- When a Hebrew servant was released, his former master must not send him away empty. He must furnish him liberally with livestock, grain, and wine. These provisions gave the servant a good chance to establish himself.
- If the slave were a Hebrew girl, she must be treated as a servant wife.
- All these rules of kindness toward slaves were reminders that they had been slaves in Egypt and the Lord their God had redeemed them.
- They were not to consider it a hardship to set a servant free, because his service during those six years was of more value than a hired servant would have been.
- If the masters obeyed the Lord in this command, God promised to bless them in everything they did.

**Release debts to fellow-Hebrews in the seventh year (Deut. 15:1-11).**

- Every seventh year, each creditor must release what he had loaned to his fellow Hebrew. He could not require repayment.
- There would always be poor in the land, so that is why God was giving the instruction. It was a way to help each poor person regain his ability to prosper.
- The Lord promised, "If you will do as I have commanded, you will have no poor among you."
- As you see the seventh year approaching, do not have a base attitude and say, "The seventh year, the year of release is at hand. If I loan this to my brother, I may not get it back." The Lord will bless you so that you will have enough, so loan liberally to your brother.

**Read the law aloud to the whole assembly in the seventh year (Deut. 31:9-13).**

"In the seventh year, at the Feast of Tabernacles, in the place the Lord chooses, you will cause this law to be read in the hearing of the men, the women, and the children, and the strangers within your gates, so that they can hear and learn, and fear Jehovah your God, and do according to all He has said. Each generation of children must hear the law and learn to fear Jehovah for as long as you live in the land."

## The Year of Jubilee (Lev. 25:8-55):

- "Number seven sabbaths *(sevens)* of years, that is, forty nine years. Then on the tenth day of the seventh month, on the Day of Atonement, sound the trumpet *(ram's horn)* throughout the land as a signal of the beginning of the Year of Jubilee... Consecrate the fiftieth year and proclaim liberty throughout the land to all its inhabitants. It is a Year of Jubilee to you and it is to be holy...." (25:8-12)
  - The name *Jubilee* comes from the word *jobel* which means a loud blast on a ram's horn.
- It was to be a year of release from work and debt, a year of celebrating the blessings of God, a year of returning every man's possessions to him.
- As in the sabbath year, nothing was to be planted or reaped.
  - Jehovah said, "If you will serve me, you will dwell in the land in safety. If you say, 'What will we eat the seventh year, since we are not sowing or reaping?' then I will command blessings for you in the sixth year, and your fields will provide enough for the sixth, seventh, and eighth years, until the crops planted in the eighth year are harvested in the ninth year" (25:18-22).
- Everyone was to return to his own property — to the land his forefathers inherited when the land was divided among the tribes.
  - If the land had been sold, in the Year of Jubilee, every man's property was to be returned to him.
  - The land could not be sold permanently, because the land belonged to the Lord, and all the people were merely pilgrims and tenants of the Lord's land (25:23). Therefore, whatever land one held, he must provide for the redemption of that land in the Year of Jubilee.
- Since the land was redeemed every fifty years, they were to be fair in their pricing of it.
  - Any field sold *(in reality, leased)* had to be sold in relationship to the nearness of the Jubilee.
    - If it were a long time until Jubilee, the price was greater.
    - If it were a relatively short time until Jubilee, then the price was less, because what was really being sold was the number of crops that could be raised in the field till Jubilee.
    - The figuring was done according to the years since Jubilee, and the price was set in terms of the years to the next Jubilee.
- If a man sold his property because of poverty, there were ways to redeem it.
  - His nearest kinsman could redeem it.
  - If the man who sold it gained enough money to buy it back, he could buy it by paying the purchaser an amount equal to the profit that one could expect to make in the years remaining to Jubilee.
  - Even if he could not redeem it before, the possession went back to him at Jubilee.
- Exceptions to the laws of redemption:
  - A house sold within a walled city could be redeemed for up to one year after the sale. Then it became the property of the purchaser in perpetuity. It did not return to the original owner at Jubilee.
  - Houses located in the fields, however, were reckoned with the land, and were treated as the land so far as the right of redemption and the law of Jubilee were concerned.
- The exception to the preceding rule was that the Levites could redeem their houses in their cities at any time with no limit. So neither the houses nor the fields in the suburbs of the Levitical cities could be sold permanently, because those were the only inheritance the Levites had.
- When vows were made regarding the dedication of houses or lands from one's family property to the Lord, the value was assessed in reference to the Jubilee (Lev. 27:17-21).

### Treatment of the poor:

In connection with the rules concerning the year of Jubilee, God gave additional details about how they were to treat their fellow Hebrews who were poor.

- "If your brother becomes poor and unable to support himself, you must help him as you would help a needy stranger among you, so that he can continue to live in the land with you" (Exod. 22:25; Lev. 25:35-38).
    - You must charge him no interest on loans.
    - You must not sell him food at a profit, because the Lord who brought you out of Egypt demands your kindness to him.
- If your brother becomes poor and sells himself to you:
    - Do not make him work like a slave; treat him as a hired servant.
    - He is to work for you until the Year of Jubilee.
    - Then he and his entire family are to be released *(even those who had an ear pierced as a sign of voluntary service —Exod. 21:5-6).*
    - He is to go back to his clan and to his own property.
- They could buy male and female slaves from the nations around them or from the temporary residents in their land.
    - They became their property and could be left as an inheritance for their children.
    - They could be made slaves for life, but not their fellow Israelites.
- If an Israelite sold himself to a non-Israelite resident of the land:
    - He could be redeemed by any relative.
    - If he came into money, he might redeem himself.
    - In either case, he would be redeemed, or could redeem himself, at a price in keeping with the years left till Jubilee *(the same law applied to the seventh year).*
    - If he were not redeemed, or did not redeem himself, he went free in Jubilee.
- These rule regarding the slavery of Hebrews was true because God said, "All the Israelites are mine. They belong to me as servants. I brought them out of Egypt and they cannot be sold as slaves. Do not make them serve with rigor; fear the Lord your God. I am the Lord your God" (25:39-43, 55).

*Do you see that the laws of property ownership and of kindness to their fellow Israelites were not given for purely humanitarian considerations? God did not say, "your fellow human being is special" He said, "These are MY people, therefore you are to treat them kindly... This is MY land, you are only using it while you live." God gave every law of the Old Testament based upon the covenant He had with them as His people.*

# Vows
## (Leviticus 27; Numbers 6, 30)

*The word vow means a solemn promise. When we think of vowing, we think of promises we make to one another, and of our obligation to keep our promises. But that kind of vowing, or promising, is not what is emphasized in the law of Moses. The vows discussed in the law were voluntary sacrifices to God. The vows might involve property —whether people, lands, houses, animals, or actions —and were essentially freewill offerings. In order to invoke the Lord's favor, or perhaps to express gratitude for the Lord's blessings, the worshiper promised to give something of value to the Lord.*

*The expression "redemption of vows," does not mean changing one's mind about fulfilling the vow — it meant fulfilling the vow. One could actually give the thing itself to the Lord, or pay the prescribed value into the treasury. Either way was an acceptable way of fulfilling the vow. If the vow concerned a person, then in almost all cases, the vow was fulfilled by paying the prescribed amount of money, and all parties went back home. But in the case of property, there were additional consideration. An animal might be sacrificed, it might be given into the work of the sanctuary (such as a pack animal that could help haul wood and water), or the owner could choose to pay the assessed value as his gift. If he chose to pay the assessed value, however, in order to take the animal back home with him, he must add one fifth more to the assigned value.*

- Since vows were voluntary, no one was obligated to make one.
  - But if a vow were made and not kept, it was counted a sin.
  - Moses expresses the thought very clearly in Deuteronomy 23:21-23: "If you make a vow to God, be quick to pay it, for the Lord will certainly demand it of you, and you will be guilty of sin if you do not fulfill it. But if you refrain from making a vow, you will not be guilty. Whatever your lips have vowed, you must be sure to do, because you made your vow freely before the Lord with your own mouth."
- If a person made a vow without thinking through the consequences, and then realized he could not keep his vow, it was a sin, and he must offer a prescribed sacrifice to God for making such a rash vow (Lev. 5:4-6).
  - He must confess the sin he had committed, and he must take a female lamb or goat from his flock to the priest and offer it as a sin offering for an atonement.
- God demanded that His people be careful about what they vowed and how they carried out their vows.

**Kinds of vows and how they were to be fulfilled (Lev. 27:1-25):**

- Vows could take many different forms. One might vow to give property, a person, or even one's self to the Lord.
  - The vow could be satisfied in either of two ways:
    - By actually giving the property or person into the service of the Lord,
    - By paying a prescribed sum of money representing the value of the object named.
      - The value was given to the Lord by donating it to the treasury of the sanctuary.
- Vowing of persons (27:1-8):
  - The assessed "value" of a person was based upon age and sex. That is, it was based upon the value that person's work would be. The one making the vow paid the assigned price in order to fulfill his vow. The law was specific about the price to pay.
  - The story of Samuel shows another way of fulfilling a vow concerning a person. Hannah literally gave her son into a lifetime of service to Jehovah with a Nazirite vow (1 Sam. 1, 2).
- Vowing of animals (27:9-13):
  - If the animal vowed was one that could be sacrificed to God, it was holy and could not be redeemed or exchanged.
    - If an exchange were attempted, then both the first animal and the second belonged to Jehovah.
  - If the animal was unclean *(and therefore could not be sacrificed)*, the priest set a moderate price for it as the assessed value of the gift.
    - If the offerer wanted to redeem the animal *(that is, take it back home with him)*, then he paid the assigned value plus twenty percent more as the redemption price.
- Vowing of houses or land (27:14-25):
  - If a man vowed a house, the priest assessed it, and that value must be accepted.
    - The house could remain a permanent part of the inheritance of the priests and Levites.

- Or the person could add twenty percent to the assigned value of the house, pay the total amount into the treasury, and he continued to own the house.
- If a man vowed a field, the priest assessed its value based upon the number of crops that could be raised on it before the Year of Jubilee.
  - He could give the land to the Levites as part of their permanent inheritance, or he could redeem it as his own by adding twenty percent to the assessed value and paying the money into the treasury.
  - If he did not redeem it before the Jubilee, the land automatically became the property of the Levites.

**Which vows were binding? (Num. 30:1-16):**

- Generally vows were considered binding.
  - If a man made a vow, he must keep it.
  - Any vow taken by a widow or a divorced woman was binding on her.
- But there were exceptions:
  - The determining factor about whether a vow was binding was whether it was made by a responsible person. God gave very specific laws regarding the vows of wives and daughters.
  - The vows discussed in Numbers 30 include both positive vows to do something, and vows to deny oneself something: "to afflict the soul."
  - If a young woman still in her father's house made a vow with her father's knowledge, and he did not reject or disallow the vow, then it was binding.
    - But if, when her father heard of the vow, he forbade her to keep it, then none of the vows or pledges she had made would stand. The Lord released her because her father had forbidden her.
  - The situation of a wife with a husband was the same. Whether it was binding depended upon the action of the husband.
    - If when he learned of it, he said nothing to stop her, the vow was binding.
    - But if he forbade her to take the action, he nullified the vow she had made. The Lord released her.
  - If a widow vowed before her husband's death, and he did not disallow it, the vow stood even after his death, and it had to be fulfilled.
    - If he had forbidden the action when he heard it, then God counted her released from the vow.
  - If, however, the husband heard of the vow and did not speak day after day, he confirmed the vow.
    - If he later decided to forbid his wife to fulfill her vow, she was released, but he would bear her iniquity. That is, he would be the one counted as sinning by breaking the vow.

**Things which could not be vowed (Lev. 27:26-34):**

- If something were already commanded to be offered to Jehovah, it could not be counted as a voluntary sacrifice, a vow.
  - The giving of the item was in direct fulfillment of a commandment, not a free gift from the giver.
- Firstlings of animals that could be sacrificed could not be vowed. They belonged to Jehovah and had to be given.
  - The firstling of an unclean animal could be redeemed *(taken back home with the owner)* by adding one-fifth to the assigned value and giving the money to the Lord.
  - If the owner chose not to redeem it:
    - It could be sold by the sanctuary at its set value (27:27).

        - It could be redeemed with a sheep, or have its neck broken (Exod. 13:13; 34:20).
- Devoted things (27:28-29):
    - Nothing that was devoted was eligible to be offered as a vow since it already belonged to God..
    - The basic idea of a devoted thing was that of a compulsory dedication of something because of a direct command of God. For example, the city of Jericho will soon be declared "devoted," or "under the ban" to God (Josh. 6:17-19). No person could take some object from the spoils and "vow" to give it to God. It already belonged to God.
    - No one devoted to destruction could be redeemed. He must be put to death.
        - That is, one who deserved death as punishment could not be vowed as sacrifice to God. The ordained punishment must be completed.
- Tithes (27:30-37):
    - A tithe *(a tenth)* of all increase belonged to the Lord. It could not be vowed as a voluntary offering because it was already holy to Jehovah.
    - If a man wanted to use the portion tithed, he must add one-fifth of the value of it to pay the redemption price.
    - The entire tithe of the herd — every tenth animal that passed under the shepherd's rod — was the Lord's.
        - The owner must not pick out the good from the bad or make any substitution.
        - If he attempted to make a substitution, then both the original animal and the substitute became holy and could not be redeemed.

**The Nazirite vow (Num. 6:1-21):**

*The Nazirite vow is the best known of the vows of the Old Testament. It was a vow of special dedication of one's own self to God. Usually the vow was for a limited time, but there are three cases in the Bible of men who were Nazirites all their lives: Samson (Judg. 13:4-5), Samuel (1 Sam. 1:11), and John the Baptist (Luke 1:15). The rules for a Nazirite vow were specific — how to begin the vow, how to live during the period of the vow, and what to do at the end of the vow.*

Rules for a Nazirite vow:

- Anyone who chose to do so could take the Nazirite vow, man or woman.
- During the time of the vow, the person was consecrated to the Lord.
- These were the requirements:
    - He must not eat anything that had to do with grapes: wine, grape juice, grapes, or raisins.
    - During the entire period of the vow, no razor was to be used on his head. He was counted as holy unto the Lord, and he must let his hair grow long throughout the whole period.
    - He must not go near a dead body, not even for his closest relatives.
- If the vow were interrupted:
    - If a man were to die suddenly beside the one with a vow, so that he was defiled:
        - He was to count off seven days, and on the seventh day shave his head.
        - On the eighth day he had to bring two turtle-doves or two pigeons to the priest.
        - The priest offered one for a sin offering, and the other for a burnt offering.
        - The person then brought a he-lamb one year old for a trespass offering, and he began his Nazirite vow anew, and the time he had already spent did not count because he had been defiled.
        - *(Notice that he was to renew his vow, not just count it finished early.)*
- When the time for the vow expired:

- The Nazirite went to the door of the Tent of Meeting, bringing:
  - One he-lamb a year old for a burnt offering, one ewe-lamb a year old without blemish for a sin offering, and one ram for a peace offering.
  - Plus a basket of unleavened bread, cakes of fine flour mixed with oil, and unleavened wafers rubbed with oil, with the meal offerings and drink offerings which pertained to the burnt offering and the peace offering.
  - And, in addition, whatever he could afford and had vowed to give to the Lord (6:21).
- The priest offered the sin offering and the burnt offering, then the peace offering, with the basket of unleavened bread, and the meal and drink offerings.
- Then, at the entrance to the Tent of Meeting, the Nazirite shaved his hair which had grown during the days of his separation and burned it in the fire that was under the sacrifice of peace offerings.
- The priest then took the broiled shoulder of the ram, and one unleavened cake and one unleavened wafer out of the basket, and put them into the hand of the shaved Nazirite.
  - The priest waved these items for a wave offering before Jehovah, likely putting his hands under the Nazirite's hands and moving his hands holding the sacrifice back and forth.
  - This portion was now holy *(set apart for)* for the priest, in addition to the wave breast and heave thigh that was already part of the peace offering that belonged to the priest.
- After this the vow was counted as complete, and the Nazirite could drink wine.

# Miscellaneous Laws
## (Leviticus 18-20, 24:16-22; Numbers 5)

Leviticus 18 begins with a direct message from God to the sons of Israel:

"I am the Lord your God. You shall not do what is done in the land of Egypt where you lived, nor are you to do what is done in the land of Canaan where I am bringing you; you shall not walk in their statutes. You are to perform my judgments and keep my statutes, to live in accord with them; I am the Lord your God. So you shall keep my statutes and my judgments, by which a man may live if he does them: I am the Lord."

*From Leviticus 18:1 through the end of the book, the expression "I am the Lord your God," or a very similar wording appears over forty times. God is saying, "I am different; my laws are different. You are mine; therefore, you are to be different by obeying my laws." We are including a wide variety of laws under this heading. Our companion book has many more of these laws, classified and organized under logical headings.*

**Sexual sins (Lev. 18:6-30):**

Chapters 18 and 20 fit together. Chapter 18 forbids the action and chapter 20 gives the penalty if one broke the law. Study them closely together.

- All forms of incest were forbidden:
  - Father or mother
  - Father's wife
  - Sister, half-sister, step-sister (18:9, 11)
  - Granddaughter

- Aunt, uncle, or uncle's wife
- Daughter-in-law
- Brother's wife *(unless she is his widow, Deut. 25:5-10)*
- You shall not marry:
  - A woman and her daughter
  - Your wife's granddaughter
  - Your wife's sister while your wife is alive, as a rival
- You shall not approach a women during her menstrual impurity.
- You shall not take your neighbor's wife.
- You shall not offer your children to Molech, nor profane the name of God.
- You shall not commit sexual perversions:
  - Homosexual acts; it is an abomination.
  - You shall not lie with a beast; it is a perversion.

God warned (18:24-30):

"Do not defile yourselves by any of these things; for by all these the nations which I am casting out before you have become defiled. For the land has become defiled, therefore I have visited its punishment upon it, so the land has spewed out its inhabitants. But as for you, you are to keep my statutes and my judgments, and shall not do any of these abominations... (for the men of the land who have been before you have done all these abominations, and the land has become defiled), so that the land may not spew you out, should you defile it, as it has spewed out the nation which has been before you. For whoever does any of these abominations, those persons who do so shall be cut off from among their people. Thus you are to keep my charge, that you do not practice any of the abominable customs which have been practiced before you, so as not to defile yourselves with them; I am the Lord your God."

**Sins that deserve death as punishment (Lev. 20:1-27; 24:16-22):**

- Anyone who offers a child to Molech shall be put to death.
  - "I will set my face against that man... he has defiled my sanctuary and profaned my holy name..." (20:1-5).
- A man or a woman who is a medium or a spiritist shall be put to death (20:27).
  - "I will set my face against the one who turns to mediums or spiritists... I will cut him off from among his people... consecrate yourselves and be holy, for I am the Lord your God" (20:6-8).
- Anyone who curses his father or his mother shall be put to death.
- If a man commits adultery with another man's wife, both the man and woman shall die.
- The one who commits incest with his father's wife or his daughter-in-law shall die.
- If a man lies with a man as with a woman, both shall be put to death.
- If a man marries a mother and her daughter, all three shall die.
- If a man or a woman lies with an animal, the person and the animal must die.
- If a man takes his sister or his half-sister, they shall both be cut off from their people.
- If a man lies with a woman in her menstrual period, both shall be cut off from their people.
- If a man takes his aunt, or his uncle's wife, they shall be childless.
- If a man takes his brother's wife, it is abhorrent; they shall be childless.
- The one who blasphemes the name of the Lord shall surely be put to death (24:16).
- If a man takes the life of any human being, he shall surely be put to death (24:17-22).
  - If he kills an animal, he shall make it good: a life for a life.

- If a man injures his neighbor, as he has done, it shall be done to him: fracture for fracture, eye for eye, tooth for tooth.
- But if he kills the man, he must die.

God warns again (20:22-26):

"You are to keep my statutes... and do them, so that the land to which I am bringing you to live will not spew you out...You shall not follow the customs of the nations which I shall drive out before you, for they did all these things, and therefore I have abhorred them... I separated you from all the peoples... Thus you are to be holy to me, for I the Lord am holy, and I have set you apart from the peoples to be mine."

**Test for adultery (Num. 5:11-31):**

*God was so determined that the land be kept pure from sins that would defile, He gave orders about what to do if a man suspected his wife of adultery, but had no proof of her guilt. The rules were stringent and the punishment was severe. This law was the only "trial by ordeal" that is found in the law of Moses. The test worked because God said it would work —not because of some function of psychology.*

The husband took his wife whom he suspected of adultery to the priest.

- He took a meal offering of barley with no oil or frankincense.
  - This was different to the normal meal offering, because it was an effort to uncover sin, not an effort to seek the grace of God.
- The priest set the woman before the Lord; took water kept at the tabernacle for this use, added dust from the floor of the tabernacle to make it "bitter water."
  - The woman's hair was let down unadorned as she swore to her innocence.
  - The priest performed the commanded rituals, and then the woman drank the water.
    - If she were guilty, the waters caused her body to swell and her hip to rot away.
      - She would thus be a curse among her people.
    - If she were innocent, the water had no effect, and she was capable of bearing children.

**Miscellaneous laws (Lev. 19:1-37):**

"You shall be holy, for I the Lord your God am holy:"

- Respect your parents.
- Keep my sabbaths.
- Do not turn to idols or make molten gods for yourselves.
- Offer your sacrifices as the law prescribes, so they will be accepted by God.
- When you reap your harvests, do not reap the corners of your fields; neither shall you glean your fields or your vineyards.
  - Leave them for the poor and the stranger among you.
- You shall not steal, or deal falsely, or lie to one another.
  - You shall not swear falsely by my name, so as to profane the name of your God.
- You shall not oppress your neighbor, or rob him.
  - The wages of a hired man must be paid each day — not kept until next day.
  - Do not curse a deaf man, or put a stumbling block in front of the blind.
- Judge fairly:
  - Do not show partiality to poor or rich.
  - Do not slander your neighbor, or act against his life.

- Do not hate your fellow countryman.
  - You may reprove him *(that is, if he is truly in sin),* but you must not incur sin because of him.
  - You shall not take vengeance, or bear a grudge.
  - Instead, you shall love your neighbor as yourself.
- Keep my commandments:
  - Do not cross-breed two kinds of cattle.
  - Do not sow your fields with two kinds of seed.
  - Do not mix kinds of fabric in your clothes.
- If a man commits fornication with a slave girl who belonged to another man, and yet had not redeemed her:
  - There must be punishment, but not death, because she was not free.
  - He must offer a trespass offering, and the sin will be forgiven.
- You shall not eat anything with its blood.
- Do not practice divination or soothsaying.
  - Do not turn to wizards and to those with familiar spirits, or seek them out to be defiled by them (19:26, 31).
- Do not mar your appearance:
  - By cutting your hair or beard in an unusual way.
  - By cutting your body for the dead, or by putting tattoo marks on your body.
- Do not profane your daughter by making her a harlot... lest the land become full of lewdness.
- You shall keep my sabbaths and revere my sanctuary.
- Rise up *(show respect)* to the gray-headed; honor the aged.
- Revere your God.
- When a stranger lives in your land, treat him as a native; love him as yourself:
  - For you were strangers in Egypt.
- Do no wrong in judgment *(justice in courts).*
- Use true weights and measurements:
  - Have just balances, weights, and measures.

"I am the Lord your God, who brought you out from the land of Egypt. You shall thus observe all my statutes, and all my ordinances, and do them: I am the Lord."

**Idolatry:**

*Notice that we have not made a separate section for laws about idolatry. There are many such laws, but the whole idea of an exclusive relationship with Jehovah permeates the whole law and narrative. Be alert to how often the point is made.*

# *Numbered and Organized*

## *(Numbers 1-6, 8, 10; Leviticus 26)*



## The Soldiers: Numbered and Organized
### (Numbers 1:1-2:34)

*The book of Numbers derives its name from the numbering of the people here at Mount Sinai, and then again in the plains of Moab just before they enter the land (Num. 26).*

### Counting the soldiers (Num. 1:1-46):

Exactly one month after the tabernacle was set up, on the first day of the second month of the second year, Jehovah spoke to Moses, saying, "Take a census of the whole community of Israel. Count every male above the age of twenty who is able to go to war. You and Aaron are to number them. One man from every tribe, each one the prince of his tribe, will assist you."

The counting of the soldiers was done with the following results:

| | |
|---|---|
| Reuben: | 46,500 |
| Simeon: | 59,300 |
| Gad: | 45,650 |
| Judah: | 74,600 |
| Issachar: | 54,400 |
| Zebulun: | 57,400 |
| Ephraim: | 40,500 |
| Manasseh: | 32,200 |
| Benjamin: | 35,400 |
| Dan: | 62,700 |
| Asher: | 41,500 |
| Naphtali: | 53,400 |

The total number of soldiers was 603,550. The Levites were not counted among the other tribes (1:47-49). There was a separate count made of them, however, and we will discuss why in a moment.

*This first group counted was of the men: "those able to go forth to war." In other words, these were the soldiers. The women, children, old men, and disabled were never counted. Keep this group in mind because we will mention them again later.*

***Chronology note:*** *Since the events are not recorded in chronological order through Leviticus and Numbers, let us look again at the dates given:*

- *1st day, 1st month, 2nd year: The tabernacle was set up (Exod. 40:1).*
- *1st day through 8th day: The priests were consecrated (Lev. 8-9).*
- *1st day through 12th day: The princes of the tribes brought their offering to the tabernacle (Num. 7).*
- *14th day through the 21st day, 1st month, 2nd year: The observation of the Passover began, immediately followed by a week of the Feast of Unleavened Bread (Num. 9:3).*
- *1st day, 2nd month, 2nd year: God commanded a census to begin (Num. 1:1).*
- *14th day, 2nd month: Those who were unclean in the first month observed the Passover (Num. 9:6-11).*
- *Therefore, this census and the organizing of the people took place between the regular observance of the Passover and the observance in the second month by those unclean in the first month.*

## The arrangement of the tribal camps (Num. 2:1-34):

The Lord instructed Moses and Aaron, "The Israelites are to camp around the Tent of Meeting, each man under the standard of his tribe with the banners of his own family." Even the positions of the tribes were specified by God. As the camping location is given, their marching orders for moving is given also.

On the east side, counting from those closest to the tabernacle to the outside, were the tribes of Judah, Issachar, and Zebulun. These three tribes were designated the "camp of Judah." The number of soldiers in the camp totaled 186,400. This camp would be the first to move out when the nation traveled.

On the south side was the camp of Reuben, which included the tribes of Reuben, Simeon, and Gad. The number of soldiers in this camp totaled 151,450. These tribes would move out after the camp of Judah.

The Tent of Meeting would go next with the camp of the Levites in the midst of the other camps. They were to move out in the same order as they encamped, each under his own flag.

On the west side of the tabernacle was the camp of Ephraim consisting of Ephraim, Manasseh, and Benjamin. The total number of soldiers on the west was 108,100. They were to set forth after the Tent of Meeting and the Levites.

The camp of Dan was on the north side with the tribes of Dan, Asher, and Naphtali. Their soldiers totaled 157,600. They would bring up the rear.

*Note God's providence and wisdom in the placement of the tribes for camping and for traveling:*

- *Each family knew exactly where his position was, whether they were traveling or camping, so that everything could be done in an orderly way.*
- *They were all camped around the tabernacle so all could be closely involved in the worship activities.*
- *And the very expensive tabernacle was right in the middle where it could be well protected.*
  - *Any band of marauders who might have wanted to steal the wealth, would have had to fight their way through over 100,00 soldiers, no matter which side of the camp they approached.*

# The Levites:
# Numbered and Organized
### (Numbers 1:47-53; 3:1-4:49; 6:22-27; 8:5-26)

## The Levites were not included in the census of the soldiers (Num. 1:47-53):

When the Lord told Moses and Aaron to count the soldiers, He said, "Do not include the tribe of Levi in the census with the other Israelites. Instead, appoint them to be in charge of the tabernacle, over all its furnishings, and over everything belonging to it. They are to carry the tabernacle and all its furnishings when it is time to move from one place to another, and they are to take care of it and encamp around it. Whenever the tabernacle is to be moved, the Levites are to take it down, and then they are to set it up again. Anyone else who goes near it is to be put to death. The Israelites are to set up their tents by divisions, each man in his own camp under his own standard. The Levites, however, are to set up their tents around the tabernacle so that wrath will not fall on the whole community."

## The clans of the Levites (Num. 3:1-4, 17-20):

*Before going further in looking at the counting of the Levites and at their duties, look at the family tree of Levi and at how Aaron and his sons fit into the picture. All four sons of Aaron were appointed priests at first, but remember that Nadab and Abihu, the two oldest sons of Aaron, have already died because they disobeyed God (Lev. 10:1-2). They had no sons, so only Eleazar and Ithamar served as priests during the lifetime of their father Aaron.*

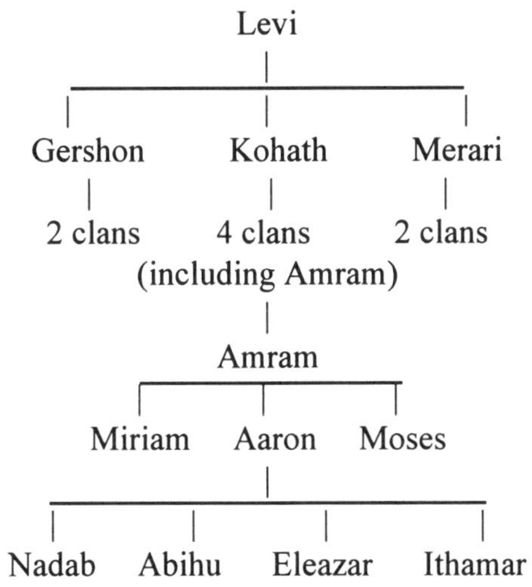


## The Levites are presented to Aaron as his assistants (Num. 3:5-10):

The Lord told Moses, "Bring the tribe of Levi and present them to Aaron as his assistants. They are to perform duties for him and for the whole community by doing the work of the tabernacle. They are to take care of all the furnishings, fulfilling all the obligations of the Israelites by doing the work of the tabernacle. The Levites are the only Israelites who are given wholly to the High Priest, but, out of the Levites, only Aaron and his sons are to serve as priests. Anyone else who approaches the sanctuary must be put to death."

*Be sure you understand what the Lord is saying at this point.*

- *Out of all the Israelites, only the Levites could help around the tabernacle.*
  - *They were to be sure the animals and wood were ready when it was time for a sacrifice.*
  - *They were the only ones who could handle the parts of the structure or the furniture, to move them or to set them up.*
  - *They were to repair the various parts when it was needed.*
  - *They did other jobs directly related to the tabernacle worship.*
- *But, even the Levites could not offer sacrifices,*
  - *Whether on the altar of burnt offering or on the little altar of incense inside.*
- *Only the Levites who were in the specific family of Aaron could serve as priests and offer sacrifices.*

## God takes the Levites instead of the firstborn (Num. 3:11-20, 39, 40-51):

The Lord continued, "Look, I am taking the Levites from among the children of Israel instead of all the first-born males. When I struck the first-born of Egypt, I made the first-born of Israel special because I did not strike them to kill them. They are mine, man and beast. Since I am substituting the Levites for the first-born of Israel, then the Levites are mine. Therefore count the children of Levi, every male from one month old and up." (See Exodus 13:1-16.)

Moses did as God said. He counted the three divisions of Levi — Kohath, Gershon, and Merari — with the clans that fit under each division. There was a total of 22,000 males (3:39).

Then God said, "Now count all the first-born males of Israel from one month old and up, and make a list of their names." The count was made, just as the Lord commanded, and there were 22,273 — two hundred and seventy-three more first-born among Israel than there were Levites.

The Lord said, "Now, take the Levites instead of all the first-born among Israel. Also take the livestock of the Levites instead of the firstlings of the livestock of the children of Israel. As for the 273 first-born males of Israel over and above the number of the Levites, for their redemption, collect five shekels per head for each of them. Give the money you collect to Aaron and his sons."

These things were done as the Lord commanded.

*This substitution was to take care of the existing situation. In the future, God's laws concerning the treatment of first-born sons would have to be obeyed (see Num. 18:15-16; Deut. 15:19). Each time a first-born son was born, a special sacrifice was to be offered for him, and the parents were to pay five shekels to redeem him. In the same way, these measures did not mean that the Levites would henceforth provide all the animals required for sacrifices, but rather their animals were taken on this occasion to replace the firstlings already in the flocks of all Israel. After this, each time a first-born animal was born, it was to be offered to God. If it were clean, it was to be sacrificed upon the altar (Num. 18:17-18). If the clean animal were blemished, then it was not to be sacrificed, but was to be eaten within the gates of the Israelites (Deut. 15:21-23). If it were an unclean animal, then it was to be redeemed by offering a clean animal to the Lord in its place, or it could be donated to the tabernacle to be sold or used as a work animal, or it was to be killed.*

*Notice that God has now provided flocks and herds of animals to be used regularly for the sacrifices for the congregation. This would give a large enough group of animals to keep up with all the supply needed if the Israelites continued to follow the rules they had been given.*

## The Levites are organized and their duties are specified (Num. 3:21-38; 4:1-49):

As they counted the Levites, Moses and Aaron also specified where they were to camp and which specific jobs each clan was responsible for. The clans of Gershon were to camp on the .west, behind the tabernacle, between it and the camp of Ephraim. The clans of Kohath camped on the south side, between the tabernacle and the camp of Reuben. The clans of Merari camped on the north side between the tabernacle and the camp of Dan. Moses, Aaron, and his sons camped on the east side of the tabernacle, between the tabernacle and the camp of Judah. Since the tabernacle was always set up with its entrance facing east, Moses and the priests were camped directly in front of the entrance. One of the primary duties of the Levites was to protect the tabernacle, so that is why they were placed next to it, all the way around it.

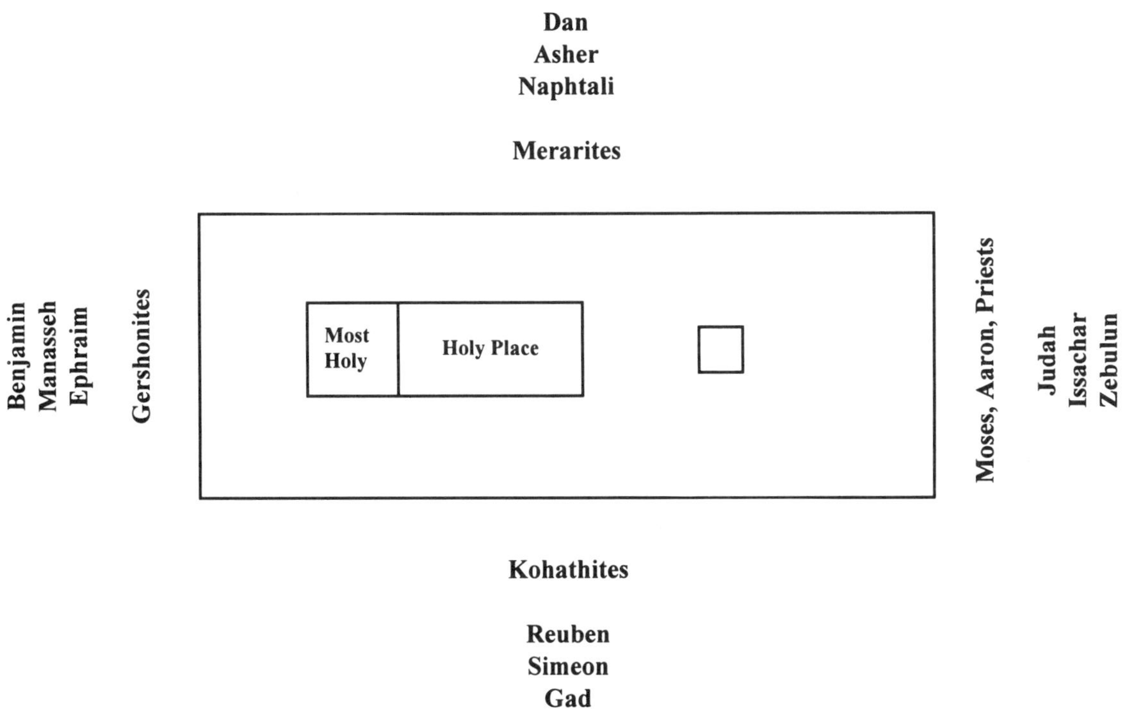


When Moses and his assistants counted the Levite males, they counted them from one month old and upward because they were counting them in order to replace the first-born. But then they counted them again, by clans, to determine how many there were to carry out the duties to be performed. The three great clans of Levi: Kohath, Gershon, and Merari, were each given specific responsibilities.

The work of transporting the tabernacle was to be done by the men between thirty and fifty years of age (4:1-3, 21-23, 29-30). They could, however, serve in other capacities from 25 to 50 years of age (8:23-26), that is, at the standing tabernacle. In David's day, Levites were employed from the age of 20 upward. The explanation is given there that the Levites no longer had to carry the tabernacle and its furniture (1 Chron. 23:24-27).

Chapter 3 of Numbers tells of the counting in order to replace the firstborn, but it also tells how many males fit into each clan, where it was to camp, and summarizes the duties for that clan. Chapter 4 tells of another counting, this time to determine how many men fit into the age category of 30 to 50, and then it gives the duties in much more detail. Look briefly at what each clan was to do. Look into our companion book on the law *(Jehovah's Covenant with Israel)* in the chapter about priests and Levites for a more detailed look at the duties of the Levites.

**A. The Gershonites (3:21-26; 4:21-28; 7:7):**

The Gershonites were in charge of transporting all the curtains and hangings of the tabernacle and of the court. Two wagons and four oxen were given to them to help them in their work. The Gershonites were placed under the supervision of Ithamar, one of Aaron's sons.

**B. The Kohathites (3:27-32; 4:1-20; 7:9):**

The Kohathites, the clan of Moses and Aaron, were given the weightiest responsibility of all: the care of the furniture within the tabernacle. The Kohathites were to carry the ark, the altar of incense, the candlestick, the table of shewbread, and the altar of burnt-offering. Sometimes the priests themselves, who were Kohathites, carried the ark (see Deut. 31:9; Josh. 3:6, 13, 17; 4:3, 9-11, 17, 18), but the Bible makes it clear that ordinarily this task was done by other Levites of the clan of Kohath (see 1 Chron. 15:2, 15, 26, 27; Num. 4:15).

Since the Kohathites had the most sensitive job of all, there were special preparations the priests had to make before the Kohathites could do their work. When it was time for the camp to resume its journey, the priests would go in and take down the veil which divided between the Holy Place and the Most Holy Place. Holding the veil before them, they went to the ark of the covenant and covered it with the veil. Over this went a covering of sealskin, and over this a cloth of blue. Then the staves, which had to be removed to wrap the ark, were replaced (Exod. 25:15; Num. 4:6).

The priests spread a blue cloth upon the table of shewbread and placed on it all the vessels, plates, flagons, and scoops which were used in its service. They spread over the whole a cloth of scarlet. Last, an outer covering of sealskin was placed over the table. Its staves were likewise replaced.

The lamp-stand with all its instruments — snuffers *(tongs)*, snuff-dishes *(dishes to hold the tongs),* and all the oil vessels — were put into a blue cloth and wrapped with sealskin and suspended from a frame *(a bar or pole).*

The altar of incense was covered with a cloth of blue, then sealskin, and the staves were replaced. All the vessels of the altar — censers, incense containers — were placed in a blue cloth, covered with sealskin, and hung on a frame *(a bar or pole, possibly the same one from which the candlestick hung)*.

Last of all, the altar of burnt-offering was cleansed of its ashes, and a purple cloth was placed on it. Onto this purple cloth they placed the fire-pans, flesh-hooks, shovels, and the basins. Then its sealskin covering was put over everything, and the staves were replaced.

Since the Kohathites were to carry everything upon their shoulders, they were provided no wagons (Num. 7:9). God gave solemn warnings regarding the very sacred nature of the items they were to carry. He said, "Be sure not to cause the families of the Kohathites to be cut off from the Levites. Be sure to follow the directions I have given, for the Kohathites are not to go in to see the sanctuary even for a moment lest they die."

Eleazar, the son of Aaron, was given charge of the work of the Kohathites and of all the things of the tabernacle.

C. **The Merarites (3:33-37; 4:29-33, 42-45; 7:8):**

The Merarites were given the responsibility of carrying the boards, silver and bronze sockets, tent stakes, cords, the pillars of the tabernacle, and the posts of the court. The work of the Merarites was also placed under the supervision of Ithamar. Due to the bulky, heavy nature of what they had to carry, the Merarites were given four wagons and eight oxen.

## Consecration of the Levites (Num. 8:5-26):

After the Levites had been counted and organized, the Lord commanded that they be brought before the Tent of Meeting and consecrated to make them ceremonially clean and to set them apart for their work. He said:

> Take the Levites from among the Israelites and cleanse them. Sprinkle purifying water on them. Let them shave their whole bodies, and wash their clothes, and they will be clean. Let them bring two bulls with their grain offerings as special sacrifices to be made. Assemble the whole congregation and present the Levites before the Lord in front of the tent of meeting. The sons of Israel shall lay their hands upon the Levites, and Aaron shall present them as a wave offering to the Lord from the sons of Israel, that they may qualify to perform the service of the Lord.
>
> Then the Levites are to lay their hands on the head of the bulls, and offer one bull for a sin offering and the other for a burnt offering to the Lord, to make atonement for the Levites. Have the Levites stand before Aaron and his sons so as to present them as a wave offering to the Lord.
>
> Thus you shall separate the Levites from among the sons of Israel, and the Levites shall be mine. After the consecration, the Levites may go in to serve the tent of meeting. But you shall cleanse them and present them as a wave offering first, for they are wholly given to me from among the sons of Israel. I have taken them for myself instead of every first born of the womb of all the sons of Israel. For the first-born is mine — every man and every animal— because I spared them in the land of Egypt, and I sanctified them for myself. But I have now taken the Levites in their place. And I have given the Levites as a gift to Aaron and to his sons from among all the Israelites to perform the service of the sons of Israel at the tent of meeting, and to make atonement on behalf of the people, so that there will be no plague among the sons of Israel by their coming near to the sanctuary.

Moses, Aaron, and the whole congregation carefully carried out all of God's instructions concerning the Levites, and the Levites themselves cleansed themselves from sin and washed their clothes so that Aaron could present them before the Lord. Thus Aaron made atonement for them to cleanse them, and then the Levites were ready to begin their service in the tent of meeting, exactly as the Lord had commanded.

And the Lord spake again:

> These rules apply to the Levites from twenty-five years old and upward. They shall enter to perform service in the work of the tabernacle; but at the age of fifty they shall retire from service and work no more in the tabernacle. They may assist their brethren in the tent of meeting, to fulfill some obligation, but they themselves will not do the work. Thus you shall deal with the Levites in all their obligations.

## Rules for priests (Lev. 21:1-24):

God said, "Tell the priests:"

- No one shall defile himself for a dead person among his people,
  - Except for his nearest relatives: his parents, his children, his brother, his virgin sister.
  - He may not defile himself for a relative by marriage.
  - He shall not mar himself by cutting his hair or beard, or cut his flesh, for the dead.
  - The priests shall be holy to God, and must not profane the name of their God, for they present the offerings before Jehovah; so they shall be holy.
- Do not marry a profane woman:
  - One profaned by harlotry.
  - One divorced from her husband.
  - For he is holy to his God.
- If the daughter of a priest profanes herself by harlotry, she profanes her father: she shall be burned with fire.
- No man with a defect may be a priest:
  - Blind, lame, disfigured face, a deformed limb, a broken bone, a hunchback, a dwarf, one with a blemish in his eye, eczema, scabs, or crushed testicles.
  - He could share in eating the holy things, but he could never serve as priest.

- Rules for a high priest (21:10-15):
  - He must not uncover his head, tear his clothes, or approach a dead person — even for a close relative.
  - He shall not go out of the sanctuary, nor profane it.
  - He must take a virgin from his own people for his wife, so that he will not profane his children.
    - He must not take a widow *(unless it was the widow of a priest, Ezek. 44:22)*, a divorced woman, or a harlot.

*Look carefully at the symbolism of what God has commanded on this occasion:*

- *God spared the first-born, so they were His.*
- *But He chose to let the Levites take their place to serve before Him.*
- *Therefore, the congregation assembled, put their hands upon the Levites, and presented them to Jehovah as a wave offering to Him.*
  - *The Levites were a gift from the Israelites to God — to replace their first-born whom God had spared.*
- *In turn, God gave the Levites to the priests as their assistants.*
  - *But the Levites had to be cleansed and their sins atoned for before they could begin their work.*
    - *So they had to wash their clothes, shave their bodies, and have purifying water sprinkled upon them as a symbol of cleanness.*
    - *Then there was a sin offering, followed by a burnt offering given before God.*
- *By that time the ceremony was complete, and the Levites were ready to begin their work.*

*Why was the tribe of Levi chosen to play this special role?*

- *Of course, Moses himself was from the tribe of Levi, and from the first, Aaron was given the role of leadership along with Moses (Exod. 4:14-17).*

- *When Israel first arrived at Mount Sinai, and the covenant was being ratified, it was Aaron and two of his sons who went up to eat before the Lord along with Moses and the seventy elders of Israel (Exod. 24:9-11).*
- *From the time the instructions were given about the priestly garments, it was specified that they were being made for Aaron and his sons. They were set apart as priests at that time (Exod. 28:1-5).*
- *One important reason why this honor was given to the tribe of Levi goes back to one specific occasion when the Levites, as a tribe, were praised for their actions.*
  - *When Moses came down from the mount and found the golden calf, he called for those on the Lord's side to come to him.*
  - *It was the tribe of Levi that rallied to him. Each man took his sword and went through the camp killing the guilty — even if it were a relative.*
  - *God was pleased with their actions, and Moses told them, "Consecrate yourselves today to the Lord...that He may bestow upon you a blessing this day" (Exod. 32:26-29).*
  - *Then in Deuteronomy 9-10, when Moses was recounting the persistent wickedness of the people, he told of the golden calf that was made at Horeb, and says, "<u>At that time</u> Jehovah set apart the tribe of Levi to bear the ark of the covenant of Jehovah, to stand before Jehovah" (Deut. 10:8). In the context, "that time" goes back to the rebellion at Mount Sinai.*

# Signals for the Congregation
## (Numbers 9:15-10:10)

### The cloud signals (Num. 9:15-23):

From the day the tabernacle was set up, the cloud that represented God's presence hovered above it. It looked like a cloud by day, but from evening until morning it glowed like fire. This was the same cloud that had been leading the Israelites since they left the land of Egypt (Exod. 13:21-22).

When the cloud would lift from above the tent, the whole camp would move forward in their journey. When the cloud stopped, the people encamped. At the Lord's command the Israelites set out, and at His command they encamped. As long as the cloud stayed over the tabernacle, they remained in camp. Sometimes the cloud was over the tabernacle for a few days; sometimes it stayed only from evening till morning, and when it lifted in the morning, they set out. Whether it lifted by day or by night, they set out at God's signal. Whether it stayed in place for two days, a month, or a year, the Israelites would remain in camp, but then when it lifted, they obeyed the Lord's command and traveled again.

*Notice how many ways God was demonstrating His presence among His people. The tabernacle itself was a symbol of God's dwelling place among them; and this cloud that was constantly above the tabernacle should have reminded the people that Jehovah was indeed nearby. Remember this as we move forward and hear the people murmur again, wondering if God is still among them.*

## Silver trumpets for signals (Num. 10:1-10):

Jehovah told Moses:

Make two trumpets of beaten silver to use for summoning the congregation and for signaling the camps to move out. When both trumpets are blown, the whole congregation shall assemble at the tent of meeting. If only one is blown, then the leaders, the heads of the clans of Israel, shall assemble.

When it is time to move, blow an alarm for the camps on the east to set out. When they have moved out, blow the alarm a second time and the camps on the south shall move out. Continue blowing the signals until every group has moved out.

Blow an alarm *(a long blast on the trumpet)* to signal the camps to move out, but let it not be an alarm that calls them to assemble *(short, sharp blasts).* The priests are the ones who shall blow the trumpets. This shall be a perpetual statute throughout your generations.

When you go to war in your own land against an enemy who attacks you, sound an alarm with the trumpets, so that you may be remembered before the Lord your God, and be saved from your enemy. *(This promise was used by the Israelites on several special occasions, and the Lord honored His promise. See Numbers 31:6; 2 Chronicles 13:12, 14-17).*

The same trumpets are to be used during your feasts times and new moon festivals. You shall sound them over the special sacrifices that are to be made during those times of rejoicing. They shall be a reminder of you before your God. I am the Lord your God.

*Do you see that the expression, "I am the Lord your God," is used many times in this section? It is an expression of God's authority, and a summary of all that was involved in the covenant between God and the people. He was their God, and they were His people. They had promised to obey Him, therefore He was the One with the right to command.*

# Blessings and Curses

### (Leviticus 26:1-46)

*While they were still at Mount Sinai, God told the Israelites there were two paths set before them. If they were faithful, then they would be highly blessed. If, however, they were unfaithful to Jehovah, then they would be cursed just as surely. The choice was theirs — in every generation.*

## If you are faithful (Lev. 26:1-13):

The Lord said, "Do not make idols or set up any kind of image for you to worship. I am the Lord your God. Observe my Sabbaths and show reverence for my sanctuary. I am the Lord." Then the Lord told them what He would do for them if they would only follow His decrees and keep His commands.

If you obey, I will:

- Send you rain at its proper times; the ground will yield its crops and the trees their fruit.
- The threshing of your grains will continue until time to harvest your grapes, and that harvest will last till time for new planting.

- You will eat all the food you want, and you will live safely in your land.

If you obey, I will:
- Grant you peace in your land, and no one will make you afraid.
- I will remove savage beasts from your land, and the sword will not pass through your country.
- You will chase your enemies, and *they* will fall by *your* sword. Five of you will chase a hundred, and a hundred of you will chase ten thousand, and your enemies will be destroyed before you.

If you obey, I will:
- Look on you with favor, and I will not abhor you.
- I will make your number grow in the land, and I will keep my covenant with you.
- You will still be eating last year's harvest when you have to move it out to make room for the new.
- I will put my dwelling place among you, and I will walk among you, and I will be your God, and you will be my people.
- I am the God who brought you out of Egypt so that you would no longer be slaves. I broke the bars of your yoke and made it so that you could walk with your heads held high.

## But if you are unfaithful (Lev. 26:14-39):

The Lord said, "If you will not listen to me and carry out all these commands, and if you reject my laws and so violate my covenant, then you will be punished severely."

If you will not listen to me:
- I will bring upon you sudden terror, wasting diseases and fever, that will destroy your health.
- You will plant seed in vain because your enemies will eat the harvest.
- I will set my face against you so that you will be defeated by your enemies.
- Those who hate you will rule over you, and you will live in such terror you will flee even when no one is chasing you.

If after all this, you still will not listen, I will make your punishment seven times worse:
- I will break down your stubborn pride by sending severe drought to the land.
- The sky above you will be like iron and the ground beneath like bronze.
- Your strength will be spent in vain, because crops will not grow, nor will the trees bear fruit.

If you still remain hostile and refuse to listen, I will multiply your afflictions seven times more:
- I will send wild animals against you that will rob you of your children and destroy your cattle.
- You will be so few in number your roads will be deserted.

If in spite of all this, you still do not accept my correction, and remain hostile toward me, then I will be hostile toward you, and I will increase the affliction seven times more:
- I will bring the sword upon you to avenge the breaking of my covenant.
- When you withdraw into your cities, I will send a plague among you, and you will be given into the hands of your enemies.
- There will be so little bread ten women will be able to bake their bread in one oven, and they will dole it out by weight.
- You will eat, but you will never be satisfied.

If you still remain hostile, I will punish you in my anger seven times worse:
- You will eat the flesh of your sons and daughters.
- I will destroy your high places, cut down your incense altars, and pile your dead bodies on the worthless bodies of your idols.
- I will abhor you and will turn your cities into ruins, and I will destroy your sanctuaries.
- I will take no pleasure in your sacrifices.
- I will make your land so wasted, even your enemies will be appalled.
- I will scatter you among the nations and will draw out my sword and pursue you.
- Then while you are in exile and your cities lie in ruins, the land will enjoy its sabbath years that it did not have while you lived in it. (See 2 Chronicles 36:21 and its context.)

**Places and events since leaving Egypt:**

**Rameses: Starting point**
**Succoth**
**Etham**
**Red Sea: Crossed on dry land**
**Marah: Bitter waters**
**Elim: Natural oasis**
**Wilderness of Sin:**
- **Quail came**
- **Manna began**

**Rephidim:**
- **Water from a rock**
- **Battle with the Amalekites**

**Mount Sinai:**
- **God makes a covenant with Israel**
- **Ten commandments spoken**
- **Moses gone 40 days**
- **Golden calf**
- **Moses gone 40 days again**
- **Tabernacle built and set up**
- **Priests consecrated**
- **Passover observed**
- **Census of the soldiers**
- **Organization of the tribes**
- **Levites taken for first-born**
- **Passover for those unclean**
- **Signal to travel again**

As for those who are left in the land at that time:
- I will make you so fearful under your enemies that the sound of a wind-blown leaf will put you to flight.
- You will run as if fleeing from a sword, and will fall, even though there is no one pursuing.
- So you will not be able to stand before your enemies.
- You will perish in the land of your enemies — because of your sins and because of the sins of your fathers.

## But if you confess your sins (Lev. 26:40-46):

The Lord continued, "But if they will confess their sins and the sins of their fathers, the things which made me hostile against them, and made me send them into another land:"
- Then I will remember my covenant with Abraham, Isaac, and Jacob.
- For the land will enjoy its sabbaths while they are gone, and they will pay for their sins because they rejected my laws and hated my decrees.
- Yet in spite of all this, when they are in the land of their enemies, I will not reject them entirely.
- I will not break my covenant with them. I am the Lord their God.
- For their sakes I will remember the covenant I made with their ancestors when I brought them out of Egypt in the sight of all the nations to be their God.

## Numbered and Organized

These are the laws and regulations which the Lord established between Himself and the Israelites on Mount Sinai.

*The rest of their history could have been so very different if they had only heeded the warnings given. Unfortunately, they ignored the evidence before them, and too often walked in their own heedless paths. Let us learn lessons from their mistakes. The choice before us is as clear-cut, even though the specific promises that were made to them were more physical in nature, while ours are more spiritual.*

### Time to leave Mount Sinai (Num. 10:11-13):

*In the second year, on the twentieth day of second month, the cloud lifted from over the tabernacle. It was time to leave Sinai. They had been there nearly a full year. Take time to think of all that has happened during that year. They had been slaves in Egypt until the night of that last plague, when God forced Pharaoh and the Egyptians to order the people from their land. Now they are a distinct nation with a law of their own. They are well organized as a separate people. The descendants of Abraham are a nation. That promise has been fulfilled.*

*Some chapters in the Bible, such as Genesis 5, cover many, many years as the text gives only a list of generations. But this is an occasion when many chapters cover only one year. Take time to count how many chapters there are between Exodus 12, when the people left Egypt, until Numbers 10, when they leave Mount Sinai. But think what an important year it has been! This is the year in which they have received the law that will be in effect until Christ nails it to the cross.*

# *From Sinai to Kadesh*
## *(Numbers 10:11-14:45)*



## The Journey Resumes

### The Israelites leave Mount Sinai (Num. 10:11-36):

On the twentieth day of the second month of the second year, the cloud lifted from over the tabernacle and Israel set forth on their journey from Mount Sinai. The tribe of Judah under the leadership of Nahshon set out first as the Lord had commanded (2:3-9). They were followed by the tribes of Issachar and Zebulun — the rest of the camp of Judah.

Meanwhile, the tabernacle had been taken down, and the Gershonites and Merarites moved out, carrying the disassembled tabernacle. Following them was the camp of Reuben *(the tribes of Reuben, Simeon, and Gad)*. Next came the Kohathites bearing the furniture of the sanctuary. Notice that the other two clans of the Levites went ahead of the Kohathites so they could set up the tabernacle and have it ready before the Kohathites arrived with the furniture. Then came the camp of Ephraim *(the tribes of Ephraim, Manasseh, and Benjamin)*, and last the camp of Dan *(Dan, Asher, and Naphtali)*.

As Israel was preparing to leave, Moses spoke to Hobab his brother-in-law, saying, "We are going to the place which the Lord said He would give us. Come with us, and we will do you good, because the Lord has spoken of the good plans He has for us."

Hobab answered, "No, I will not go; instead I will return to my own land and to my own kindred."

Moses did not give up that easily. He said, "Don't leave us, please, because you know where we can best pitch our tents. You can be our eyes. If you go with us, then whatever blessings the Lord gives us, you will share."

The camp moved out and traveled for three days, the ark of the covenant going before them. When the ark would set forward to lead them, Moses would say:

Rise up, O Lord, and let your enemies be scattered,
and let those who hate you flee before you.

Then when the ark stopped its journey, he would say:

Return, O Lord,
unto the ten thousands of the thousands of Israel.

*Though Hobab's answer is not given, it is evident that he did as Moses suggested because his descendants, the Kenites, are found later, living among the Israelites (Judges 1:16; 4:11).*

## Taberah (Num. 11:1-3):

After only three days' journey from Mount Sinai, the Israelites began complaining as if they were undergoing adversity. When the Lord heard it, His anger was aroused, and the fire of Jehovah burned among the people and devoured them in the farthest corners of the camp. The people cried to Moses, and Moses prayed to the Lord, and the fire died down. Therefore the name of the place was called Taberah *(Burning)*, because the fire of the Lord burned among them.

*There is no mention of the people murmuring while they were building their tabernacle, or doing all the other jobs they did after Moses returned from Mount Sinai. Yet here they are murmuring again almost immediately after starting their travels again. Think of their circumstances. These people had been raised as slaves, used to very hard work. Therefore they understood hard work and did it without complaint. But they cannot accept the difficult travel required without losing their faith in God who will provide for them. As we study the examples from the Bible, often we can understand why someone acted as he did in a situation — but that does not excuse his action. Let us learn the lessons.*

**Traveling order:**

**Camp of Judah:**
- **Judah**
- **Issachar**
- **Zebulun**

**Gershonites & Merarites**
**(Carrying the tabernacle)**

**Camp of Reuben:**
- **Reuben**
- **Simeon**
- **Gad**

**Kohathites**
**(Carrying the furniture)**

**Camp of Ephraim:**
- **Ephraim**
- **Manasseh**
- **Benjamin**

**Camp of Dan:**
- **Dan**
- **Asher**
- **Naphtali**

## Kibroth-hattaavah (Num. 11:4-34):

There were no bounds to the lusting of the rabble among them. The people wept and whined: "Who will give us some meat *(flesh)* to eat? Oh, we remember the fish we ate in Egypt, and they cost nothing! There were cucumbers, and melons, and leeks, and onions, and garlic. But now our soul is dried up; there is not a thing to be had but this manna."

Remember that the manna looked like coriander seed: small, pearl-like flakes of white. The people gathered it, and ground it between millstones, or beat it with the mortar, and boiled it, or made baked cakes of it. The taste of it was like wafers made with honey and mixed with oil (cf. Exod. 16:31). When the dew fell at night the manna came with it. The manna was a direct gift from God, and the people were complaining about it. Moses heard the sound of the people weeping and moaning throughout the camp and he was troubled. Each man was sitting in the doorway of his tent weeping. God heard it, too, and His anger was greatly kindled.

Moses asked God, "Why have you treated me like this? What have I done to displease you that you have put this load on me, to have to deal with all this people? Am I their father? Or am I their mother, that you should tell me, 'Carry them in your arms,' as a nursing father *(a foster-father, or a nurse)* carries a suckling, into the land you swore to give to our fathers? Where could I get enough meat to give to all these people? That is what they are crying to me about. I am not able to carry this load; it is too heavy for me. If you are going to deal with me this way, then kill me with no further ado, if I have found favor in your sight."

The Lord responded immediately to Moses' complaint. He saw that Moses needed help. He said, "Gather to me seventy men of the elders of Israel, ones whom you know to be leaders among the people, and bring them to the tent of meeting. I will come down and talk with you there, and I will take of the Spirit which is upon you, and I will put it upon them. Then they will help you bear the burden of the people so you will not have to carry it alone."

God continued: "Tell the people to consecrate themselves for tomorrow — because they will eat flesh. They have wept, saying, 'Oh, that someone would give us meat to eat! We had it good in Egypt.' Therefore I will give you flesh, and you will eat it. You won't eat it just one day, or two days, or five days, or ten days, or even twenty days, but for a whole month — till it comes out your nose, and it will be loathsome to you. You have rejected me though I am among you, and you have wept saying, 'Why did we leave Egypt?'"

Moses answered, "This crowd of people numbers 600,000 foot soldiers, and you have said, 'I will give them enough meat they will eat it for a whole month.' Do you mean to slaughter the herds and flocks? Or do you intend for all the fish in the sea to be gathered for them to have enough?"

The Lord responded, "Has my hand grown weak? Is it too short to reach you, Moses? You wait and see whether my word comes to pass or not."

Moses went out and told the people what God had said. He selected seventy of the elders of the people and had them stand before the tabernacle. Then the Lord came down in the cloud and spoke to Moses. He took of the Spirit that was upon Moses, and He placed it upon the seventy elders. When the Spirit came upon them, they prophesied as a sign they had the Spirit, but they did not continue to do so.

There were two additional elders, Eldad and Medad, who had been written among the elders *(perhaps on a list of suggested elders)*, who were not of the group who had gone out to the Tent, but when the Spirit came, He came upon them also, and they prophesied. A young man came running to tell Moses about this amazing event, and Joshua, Moses' assistant, said, "My lord Moses, tell them to stop!"

Moses asked Joshua, "Are you jealous for my sake? I wish that all the Lord's people were prophets, that He would put His Spirit upon them all!" After this Moses and the elders went back into the camp.

The Lord set about fulfilling His promise to feed Israel with meat. He caused a wind to blow an immense quantity of quails from the sea to fall all around the camp. Within a radius of a day's journey, the quail were piled as much as two cubits deep *(36 inches)*. The people enthusiastically rushed out to gather the quail. That day and night, and the next day as well, they gathered the quail, and the least amount gathered was ten homers full *(more than ten 55-gallon barrels full)*. The people spread the quails out *(to preserve them by drying the meat)* all around the camp.

When they ate the meat, while it was between their teeth, before they even swallowed it, Jehovah's anger was kindled, and He struck the people with a very great plague. So many people died, they called the place

Kibroth-hattaavah *(graves of lust, or the graves of greediness),* because there they buried the people who lusted.

Traveling on, the people came next to Hazeroth.

*The quantity of quail goes far beyond what could normally be found, so the power of God was abundantly demonstrated by this event. His mercy was richly bestowed upon the people. But when they were blind to the significance of the miracle, and oblivious to the mercy of God, He struck them with judgment. Instead of marveling at the power of their God, and instead of being deeply moved by His gracious mercy, all they thought about was their hunger for a different taste in their food. This story certainly contains a warning for our blind and cynical world. We must be grateful, and we must express our gratitude for God's blessings.*

*As the story begins, the expression, "the rabble who were among them," is found. Some translations word the expression: "the mixed multitude that was among them." This was the group specifically mentioned as "lusting" for the meat. It seems that whoever they were, they influenced the whole company to join in the cry against God as they wept for meat and the variety of foods found in Egypt. It may be referring to the more wicked among them, those less willing to rely upon God, or possibly even to the non-Israelite element of the community (see Exod. 12:38). Whoever they were, they definitely were not willing to rely upon God, and their influence caused great grief. This is a lesson we need also: even if there is a wicked element among us who begins to complain against God in some way, I must not join with the company in their whining.*

*Notice that God does not scold Moses for saying the burden is too heavy. Judges were selected to help Moses soon after they arrived at Mount Sinai. That suggestion was made first by Jethro and was carried out with God's approval (Exod. 18:13-26). Whether those judges were temporary, or whether these are additional elders is not certain, but Moses needs more help, and God is quick to respond by placing His Spirit upon men who can help him bear the burden. It was an enormous task that Moses had been given, and God is demonstrating His mercy for Moses as He responds quickly when Moses feels the need. Eldad and Medad received the Spirit in addition to the seventy men who had gathered at the tabernacle. Therefore Moses has 72 new helpers who are guided by Jehovah.*

## Hazeroth (Num. 11:35-12:15):

After the people arrived at Hazeroth, Miriam and Aaron criticized Moses because of the Cushite woman he had married. They said, "Is Moses the only one to whom God has spoken? Hasn't He spoken to us as well?" The Lord heard what they said. Moses did not try to defend himself because he was very meek, more meek *(humble)* than any man on earth.

Jehovah wasted no time in dealing with Miriam and Aaron. He spoke suddenly to the three and said, "Come out, all three of you, to the tent of meeting." Jehovah came down in a pillar of cloud and stood at the door of the tent and called to Aaron and Miriam. They stepped forward, and the Lord said, "Listen to me: If there be a prophet among you, I, Jehovah, will reveal my will to him in a vision, or I will speak to him in a dream. My servant Moses is different. He is faithful in all his service. With him I speak face to face, openly, not in cryptic speeches, and from time to time he even gazes upon the form of Jehovah. Why, then, were you not afraid to criticize my servant Moses?"

The anger of Jehovah was aroused, and He departed. When the cloud lifted, there stood Miriam — left a leper, white as snow! Horrified, Aaron looked at Miriam, beholding her leprosy. He cried to Moses, "Oh, my lord, please don't hold our sin against us. We have behaved foolishly and have sinned. Please don't let her be like a child born prematurely, with its body only half-formed."

Moses instantly interceded with God for his sister: "Heal her, O God, I beg of you."

Jehovah answered, "If her father had only spit in her face *(as an expression of rebuke)*, should she not be ashamed for a week? Let her be shut without the camp for seven days; then she may be brought in again." So Miriam remained outside the camp for a week, and Israel did not travel until she was brought in again.

After the week was complete, Israel moved on from Hazeroth to the wilderness of Paran.

*No details are given regarding this Cushite woman; the text merely includes the parenthetical statement that Moses had married a Cushite woman. Some have sought to identify her as Zipporah, but it was a little late for Miriam and Aaron to be criticizing Moses on that score, because he had been married to her for many years. Also, Zipporah is nowhere else referred to as a Cushite; she was a Midianite (Exod. 2:16-21). Cush is reckoned as a son of Ham (Gen. 10:6), whereas Midian was a son of Abraham by Keturah (Gen. 25:2). More than likely Moses had recently married a Cushite woman about whom nothing else is revealed. The most logical guess about where this woman came from is that she was one of the mixed multitude that went up from Egypt with Israel (Exod. 12:38; Num 11:4). This mixed multitude was not Israelite, but went out of Egypt with Israel and gradually became a part of Israel. We read nothing further of this mixed multitude after the events of Numbers 11. It is not surprising that there would be Cushites as well as other races found among these people.*

*Cush was the name of the ancient empire south of Egypt, the empire later called Ethiopia. Cush, the man, however, begat Nimrod, who established cities such as Babel, Erech, Accad, Calneh, and Nineveh which were located on the shores of, or near, the Tigris and Euphrates rivers (Gen. 10:8, 10-12). The Cushite descendants of Ham, therefore, settled in various places across the Fertile Crescent, as well as in the area south of Egypt.*

*It is obvious that Moses' marriage was not the real point of contention in the complaint of Miriam and Aaron. The real issue was their jealousy of Moses: "Has the Lord spoken only to Moses... Has He not spoken to us also?"*

*Though the scripture does not specifically say that God healed Miriam, it is strongly implied that she was. At least the disease was arrested; otherwise she could not have come back into the camp (Lev. 13:46). Since Moses interceded on her behalf, God probably did as he asked, but He demanded that Miriam wait without the camp for seven days. At the end of that time, according to the law, she would be inspected by the priest to see if she were clean, and if so, she could return to her own dwelling (Lev. 13:1-8).*

***Map assignment:*** *Label your maps.*

- *Taberah, Kibroth-hattaavah, Hazeroth.*

  *The exact location of Taberah, Kibroth-hattaavah, and Hazeroth are unknown. Remember that this is a desert region, and the people were camped at these places for only a short time. They were not cities for the archeologists to find; they were mere campsites. Their approximate location can be estimated because the Israelites were traveling between Mount Sinai and Kadesh-barnea.*

- *Kadesh-barnea and the Wilderness of Paran.*

  *The locations of Kadesh-barnea and the wilderness of Paran are known, even though the boundaries of the wilderness of Paran are indefinite. The wilderness of Paran, according to the Macmillan Bible Atlas, was the entire central part of the Sinaitic peninsula. When the text says, "And the children of Israel set forward according to their journeys out of the wilderness of Sinai; and the cloud abode in the wilderness of Paran" (Num. 10:12), the writer anticipates the whole journey from Mount Sinai to Kadesh. The wilderness of Sinai was the smaller wilderness surrounding Mount Sinai. (See Macmillan Bible Atlas p. 14, Map #6.)*

*Kadesh was located in the northwestern edge of the wilderness of Paran. It is early identified with En-mishpat (spring or well of judgment, Gen. 14:7). The full name is not used until Numbers 32:8. The hyphenated name Kadesh-barnea makes some scholars believe that the city was originally called Barnea and that it was called Kadesh (holy or sanctified) because the Lord sanctified Himself (yikadesh) by bringing a judgment upon Israel when they strove with Him (Num. 20:12-13; see Keil and Delitzsch on Num. 20:14-21). At Kadesh-barnea, the people were only about fifty miles south of the fertile land they were to inherit.*

- *The wilderness of Zin adjoined the wilderness of Paran about where Kadesh was. Occasionally, therefore, the wilderness of Zin is equated with Kadesh (Num. 20:1; 27:14; 33:36).*

# The Sin at Kadesh-barnea
## (Numbers 12:16-14:45)

### Twelve spies are sent (Num. 12:16-13:25):

The Lord commanded Moses, saying, "Send some men to explore the land of Canaan which I am giving to the Israelites. Send a prince from each tribe." At this point, God was ready to fulfill His promise to Abraham (Gen. 12:7) and to allow the people to move forward and take the land before them.

So Moses chose the twelve men, one from each tribe, and sent them on their mission. Among the men chosen were Caleb the son of Jephunneh, of the tribe of Judah, and Hoshea the son of Nun, of the tribe of Ephraim. Moses renamed Hoshea *(Help)* Joshua *(Jehovah —"Yah" — is help)*. This is the same Joshua who has been his assistant from the first.

Moses instructed the spies saying, "Go up into the South *(the Negeb)* and into the hill-country *(the spine of mountains which runs all the way through Canaan north to south)*. Observe the land, what kind of land is it? Find out about the people: are they strong or weak? how many are they? Report on the cities they dwell in: are they mere villages or fortresses? We want to know if the land is good or bad, whether it is forested or bare. Be courageous and bring us some of the fruit of the land." Now it was the time of year for the first ripe grapes *(about July or August; they had left Sinai in May)*.

The men went up and spied out the land from the Wilderness of Zin unto Rehob, in the area of Hamath *(from the southern edge of the land to about Mount Hermon in the north)*. Going up from the Negeb, they came to Hebron where they found Ahiman, Sheshai, and Talmai, the children *(descendants)* of Anak.

The spies also went into the valley of Eshcol. There they found grapes growing and cut off a branch with a cluster on it and carried it back, hung from a pole carried by two men. They also brought back pomegranates and figs. They called the valley Eshcol *(Cluster)* because of the cluster of grapes which they cut down and took back with them. At the end of forty days they returned to camp.

*According to Deuteronomy, the request for the spies to be sent to look over the land came first from the people, and Moses said, "The thing pleased me well" (Deut. 1:22-23). God also approved and gave the command recorded in Numbers 13:2. So, as we combine the passages, the people suggested that the spies be sent, Moses approved, and God gave command as to exactly how it was to be accomplished.*

*At one time Hebron was called Kiriath-arba, that is, the City of Arba. Joshua 14:15 calls Arba, "the greatest man among the Anakim." Anak refers to a man, the ancestor of a tribe of giants. His descendants are called Anakim (Josh. 14:15), and the children of Anak (Num. 13:22). They are also referred to as Nephilim (Num. 13:33). The word Nephilim did not necessarily mean giant, but a tyrant, a bully (see our notes on Genesis 6:4), but by this point in history, it may have come to mean a giant by association and usage (Num. 13:33). Therefore, when the text says the spies found these three descendants of Anak at Hebron, it is saying they found a city in the control of giants.*

*There is evidence that the spies divided up in their survey of the land. It would certainly have made them less conspicuous. When Caleb came to Joshua after the invasion of Canaan, he asked to inherit the city of Hebron with these words: "Moses swore on that day, saying, 'Surely the land over which you have walked will be your inheritance, and your children's forever, because you have completely followed after the Lord'" (Josh. 14:9). This promise made by Moses was that Caleb would have the land he had walked over as a spy. If he had gone with the other spies over all the rest of Canaan, there would have been no reason why Moses should isolate the area around Hebron for Caleb; but if Caleb had been assigned that area to spy out, then it is logical that Moses should say that section would belong to Caleb.*

## The spies make their report (Num. 13:26-33):

When the spies returned to Moses to make their report, they said, "We came to the land where you sent us, and surely it does flow with milk and honey, and here is the fruit of it *(showing the grapes, pomegranates, and figs which they had brought)*. But the people who dwell in the land are strong, and their cities are fortified and very great. What's more, we saw the children of Anak *(giants)* there. Amalek dwells in the land of the Negeb; the Hittite, the Jebusite, and the Amorite dwell in the mountains; and the Canaanites dwell by the sea and along the banks of the Jordan."

The people began to be agitated, and Caleb attempted to calm them by saying, "Let's go up and take the land right now, because we are well able to overcome it."

But Caleb's fellow spies said, "We are not able to go up against this people because they are stronger than we."

The spies *(except for Joshua and Caleb)* thus brought back a negative, discouraging report, saying, "The land which we have spied out is a land which devours its inhabitants. All the people we saw are big people, even giants, the sons of Anak. We looked like grasshoppers to them, and we felt like grasshoppers, too."

## Reaction of the people and their punishment (Num. 14:1-38):

The courage of Israel evaporated. They wailed and cried all that night. The whole community of Israel murmured against Moses and Aaron, saying, "We wish we had died in Egypt! Would that we had died in the wilderness! Why did Jehovah bring us here to let us die by the sword? Our wives and children will be easy prey for anyone. Would it not be better for us to return to Egypt?" They even began to say, "We should choose a leader and go back to Egypt."

Speechless with anguish, Moses and Aaron fell on their faces before the people. Joshua and Caleb ripped their clothes and pleaded with their brethren: "This land we passed through is a fantastic land. If the Lord is pleased with us, He will bring us into this land and He will give it to us, a land flowing with milk and honey. Only don't rebel against the Lord, and don't be afraid of the people. They are going to be like food, like prey, for us to eat. They have no one to defend them, while we have Jehovah. There is no reason to fear." The people remained unmoved by the passionate pleas of Joshua and Caleb. The congregation was so angry they were ready to stone them.

Suddenly all proceedings were interrupted by the appearance of the glory of Jehovah at the tent of meeting before the eyes of all Israel. Jehovah said to Moses: "How long will these people despise me? How long will they rebuff me and refuse to believe in me in spite of all the miracles I have done among them? I will strike them with the plague; I will disinherit them, and I will make of you a nation greater and mightier than they."

Instantly Moses began to plead:

Then the Egyptians will hear the news, because you took this people by your might from among them, and they will tell it to everyone in this land as well. They know that you, Jehovah, are in the midst of this people. They know that your cloud stands over them. They know about the pillar of cloud by day and the pillar of fire by night. If you kill this people to the last man, then the nations which have heard of your fame will start saying, "It was because Jehovah was not able to bring the people into the land He swore He would give them. That's why He has killed them all in the wilderness."

I pray that you will exercise the power you spoke about when you said, "Jehovah is slow to anger, and running over with mercy, forgiving iniquity, but He will not clear the guilty, but will visit the iniquity of the fathers upon the children, even to the third and fourth generation." Pardon, I beg of you, the iniquity of your people in keeping with the magnitude of your mercy, as you have forgiven this people, from Egypt until now.

The Lord answered:

I have pardoned as you have asked, but indeed, as I live, all the earth will be filled with the glory of the Lord. Because these men have seen my glory, and have seen the miracles I performed in Egypt and in the wilderness, and yet have tempted me these ten times, and have refused to listen to my voice, therefore, as surely as I live, and as surely as all the earth shall be filled with my glory, these men will not see the land which I swore to their fathers to give them. Indeed, these who have despised me will not see the land, but my servant Caleb, because he had a different attitude, and has followed me completely, I will bring him into the land into which he went, and his descendants will possess it. The Amalekites and the Canaanites live in the valleys here, so tomorrow, turn around and go into the wilderness in the direction of the Red Sea *(that is, back into the wilderness of Paran in the direction of the Red Sea).*

Jehovah spoke further to Moses and Aaron, "How long shall I put up with this wicked community that murmurs against me? I have heard their complaints. Tell them this:

I am going to do to you as you have said. You said you would prefer to die in this wilderness. Very well, your dead bodies will fall in this wilderness, and all that were numbered of you (Num. 1:45), the total of those twenty and older, you who have murmured against me, you will surely not come into the land that I had sworn to give you. The only exceptions are Caleb and Joshua. But your children, the ones whom you said would be easy prey, I will bring them in, and they will know the land you have rejected.

**You Shall Be My People**

> But as for you, your dead bodies will fall in the wilderness. Your children will be shepherds *(nomads)* in the wilderness for forty years. They will have to put up with the consequences of your wickedness until your corpses all lie in the wilderness. According to the number of days that you took to spy out the land, that is, forty days, for every day a year, you will bear your iniquity, for forty years, and you will suffer the postponement of the fulfilling of my promise.
>
> I, Jehovah, have spoken, and this is what I am going to do to this wicked people. In this wilderness they shall be destroyed, and there they shall die.

The men whom Moses had sent into the land, those who came back with an evil report and caused the whole congregation to grumble, died of a plague before the Lord, but Joshua and Caleb were spared.

*This is the second occasion when God was so angry with the people He threatened to wipe them all out and start over with a new nation through Moses. What had happened on the other occasion to make the Lord so angry? What arguments did Moses make at that time as he interceded? (See Exodus 32.)*

*Think of all the ways God has shown His presence and His providence for the people. Yet here they show such a lack of faith in Him.*

**Memorize the route**
**From Sinai to Kadesh:**

**Taberah:**
- **Fire broke out**

**Kibroth-hattaavah:**
- **The people lusted for meat**
- **God sent quail**
- **Many died of a plague**

**Hazeroth:**
- **Aaron and Miriam complained**

**Kadesh-barnea:**
- **12 spies sent into the land**
- **They brought a bad report**
- **People grieved**
- **God declared they would all die**

*The ones who were sentenced to die in the wilderness were the men of war. They were the ones counted in both censuses (Num. 1:45; 26:2). If there were any doubt, Moses specifically says that it was the men of war in Deuteronomy 2:14. Why would God choose this particular punishment? There were likely reasons in the mind of God that we cannot know, but one point seems clear. These men had been raised as slaves, and they could not adjust to being warriors. It took the death of one generation and the growth of a new one before they could have the courage to fight for a land.*

## The people change their minds — and are defeated (Num. 14:39-45):

When Moses told Israel what God had said, they were very sad and mourned greatly. They rose up early in the morning and said to Moses, "Look, we are here, and we will go up to the place that Jehovah has promised. We realize that we have sinned."

Moses answered, "Why will you now go against what Jehovah has said? You cannot do any good. Don't go up to battle because Jehovah will not be with you, and you will be badly defeated. You will find the Amalekite and the Canaanite waiting for you, and you will fall by the sword. You would not follow Jehovah, so He will not go with you."

Nevertheless, the Israelites insisted on going to fight. Neither the ark of the covenant nor Moses left the camp however. The Amalekites and the Canaanites came down and attacked the Israelites and beat them as far as Hormah.

*There are some sins that are so far-reaching in their consequences that just saying "I am sorry" will not repair the damage. God can forgive a person — while at the same time requiring him to suffer the consequences of his actions. That is what has happened on this occasion, just as it has happened many, many times in the lives of individuals through the centuries.*

*In Deuteronomy 1:43-44, Moses said the Amorites "chased the Israelites like bees," a vivid description of the ignominious defeat of Israel. Moses also said they "beat you down in Seir, even unto Hormah" (Deut. 1:44). Ordinarily, Seir is associated with Mount Seir, the home of the Edomites. It was located on the east side of the Arabah, while Kadesh, where the Israelites were camped, was on the west side. In Deuteronomy 1:44, Seir refers to territory Edom had come to control, not just Mount Seir proper.*

*The mention of Hormah raises a question. Was this Hormah the city formerly known as Zephath that is mentioned in Judges 1:17, or one of the other Hormahs mentioned in scriptures? The probability is that it was not. More than likely, Hormah was the name given to the site where Israel's army was devastated in their effort to invade the land of Canaan. Their invasion route on this occasion was through the eastern Negeb to the beginning of the hill-country. They were thoroughly beaten at a place which was called Hormah (Destruction).*

*The word Hormah is from the Hebrew word "herem." The naming of this place Hormah was definitely related to the meaning of herem. Sometimes it meant a defeat that was utter and complete. The word herem is most often translated "utterly destroyed." There were several related flavors of meaning. Sometimes it had the idea of setting something aside for the exclusive use of God. Thus the city of Jericho was "devoted" to God, "even it and all that is therein, to Jehovah... all the silver, and gold, and vessels of brass and iron, are holy unto Jehovah: they shall come into the treasury of Jehovah" (Josh. 6:17, 19).*

*Sometimes herem had the idea of total annihilation. Thus "Israel vowed a vow unto Jehovah and said, 'If thou wilt indeed deliver this people into my hand, then I will utterly destroy (devote or "herem") their cities.' And Jehovah hearkened to the voice of Israel, and delivered up the Canaanites; and they utterly destroyed (devoted, herem) them and their cities: and the name of the place was called Hormah" (Num. 21:3; cf. 1 Sam. 15:3). In these circumstances, every living thing was killed, and no booty or spoil was taken. Even in these circumstances there was something of the idea of an offering to God involved, as is evident in Numbers 21:3. The idea was that if the Lord would give the Israelites victory, they would take nothing for themselves. There are numerous parallels in the history of other nations where, before a battle, the people would vow total annihilation of the opposing force, even including their goods.*

*This battle the Israelites fought was one in which no participant would ever boast of having had a part in it. In that sense, the term "destruction" would fit, even if a sizable number of soldiers returned to camp. It was complete defeat. It may be that the invading force of Israelites was completely annihilated, or so nearly annihilated, that the term Hormah was appropriate.*

*It is preferable, therefore, to think that Hormah was not the name of just one city, but that it was the name of the place where Israel's disobedient army was routed (Num. 14:45), the name of the area where Canaanite cities were annihilated (Num. 21:3), and the name of a city which was destroyed (Judg. 1:17).*

# *Wandering In the Wilderness*
## *(Numbers 15:32-36; 16:1-22:1)*

## Another Distinct Period of Bible History

**Creation Stories**
**The Flood**
**Scattering of People**
**The Patriarchs**
**The Exodus**

***Wandering**
***Korah, Dathan, Abiram**
***To the Plains of Moab**

**Conquest of Land**
**Judges**
**United Kingdom**
**Divided Kingdom**
**Judah Alone**
**Captivity**
**Return**
**Years of Silence**
**Life of Christ**
**Early Church**
**Letters to Christians**

*Look in the left column at our outline of Bible history again. In the first book of our series, we studied the stories of Genesis, and in that study we covered the first four headings of the outline: the Creation Stories, the Flood, the Scattering of the People, and the Patriarchs. In this book, we began with the book of Exodus and learned how God forced the Egyptians to release His people from slavery. We followed them to Mount Sinai and saw God make a covenant with them. He chose them to be His special people, if they would only obey Him and keep His commandments. Moses went into the mountain to receive the complete law, including the instructions for building the tabernacle and for setting up the worship. By the time the Israelites finished the commanded work, they were a separate nation, completely organized with a law of their own. God's promise to Abraham concerning the nation to come through him had been fulfilled — the nation now existed (Gen. 12:2). The rest of the Bible continues to follow the history of that nation.*

*The people traveled north from Mount Sinai and camped at Kadesh-barnea, only about fifty miles south of the land they were to inherit. God was ready to fulfill His second main promise to Abraham (Gen. 12:7): He was ready to give the land of Canaan to this nation of Abraham's descendants. It should have been a time of joy and expectation, but the spies brought back such a bad report, the people lost their courage (and faith) and refused to move forward. God has set the punishment: they must stay in the wilderness a year for every day the spies were gone, a total of forty years. Every soldier will die (the men 20 years old and above, the ones counted in the census at Mount Sinai).*

*Therefore, we move into the period we call "Wandering in the Wilderness." It has been about a year and a half since they left Egypt, and many chapters of the Bible tell about that period of time. The period of wandering is covered very quickly in the Bible text. For the next 38 years (see Deut. 1:46; 2:14) they merely wait for a generation to die. During these years, they live as shepherds in a dry land. That was part of their punishment (Num. 14:13).During the last year of that forty years, they begin to travel again as the Lord leads them around the Dead Sea to enter Canaan from a different side.*

### A sabbath-breaker is put to death (Num. 15:32-36):

While the children of Israel were in the wilderness, they found a man gathering sticks on the sabbath day. Those who found him brought him before Moses, Aaron, and the whole congregation. He was placed in custody until they could find out from the Lord what should be done with him.

Jehovah answered, "The man shall surely be put to death. Have all the congregation gather together and stone him to death." God meant it when He said they would be His people *if they obeyed* His commands. So the assembly did as the Lord said.

*God will not continue to deal with every sabbath-breaker in this way. This case was one more example to prove He wanted obedience from His people.*

### Tassels on their garments (Num. 15:37-41):

The Lord told Moses to instruct the people:

> Make tassels on the corners of your garments throughout your generations. Put a tassel of a blue cord on each corner, so that you may look at it and remember to do all the commandments of the Lord. Do it so that you will not follow after your own heart and your own eyes, and play the harlot; in order that you will remember to do all my commandments , and to be holy to your God. I am the Lord your God who brought you out from the land of Egypt to be your God. I am the Lord your God.

*We have taken note of the many ways God has reminded His people that He is among them. This commandment is one that the people were to obey to remind themselves that they were in the presence of Jehovah, that they had a covenant with Him. The point of God's presence is the same — but the emphasis in this commandment puts the charge upon the heart of each individual rather than upon the congregation as a whole.*

## Korah, Dathan, and Abiram
### (Numbers 16:1-17:13)

*Most of the activities of the thirty-eight years following the sin at Kadesh-barnea are not recorded. There is no date given for the rebellion led by Korah to show whether it was early or late in the period. The people's reference to this event at the waters of Meribah (Num. 20:3) indicates that it probably took place late in the wandering. At first the leaders of the rebellion were Korah, Dathan, Abiram, and On, but On is not mentioned again, so he must have backed off in his opposition after the rebellion began. There are three parts to this story:*

- *The rebellion and death of Korah and his companions, including the 250 princes who intended to offer incense.*
- *The murmuring of the people the next day and the death of 14,700 of them.*
- *The story of Aaron's rod that budded.*

## The rebellion and punishment of Korah and his companions (Num. 16:1-40):

Korah, of the tribe of Levi, and Dathan, Abiram, and On, of the tribe of Reuben, gathered together with 250 prominent men of the community of Israel. They came against Moses and Aaron, saying, "You two have had the leadership of this people long enough. Since the whole congregation is holy, everyone of them, and the Lord is among them, why do you lift yourselves above the assembly of the Lord?"

When Moses heard these outrageous words, he fell on his face. Then he spoke to Korah and to all his companions, saying, "In the morning the Lord will show whom He has chosen for Himself to be His priests, and who is holy. Do this, Korah and all your companions: get censers and put fire in them, and the man that Jehovah chooses will be the one who is holy. You grasp at too much, you sons of Levi. Did it seem to be a small thing to you that the God of Israel picked you out of all Israel to perform the special work you do in His service in connection with the tabernacle? Must you have the priesthood also? It is Jehovah that you and your crowd have gathered against. Your complaint is not against Aaron because he did not seize the priesthood for himself."

At some point in the proceedings, Dathan and Abiram left, and, when Moses sent for them, they said, "We are not coming. Didn't you do enough when you brought us out of a land flowing with milk and honey to kill us in this wilderness? Do you have to make yourself a king over us as well? Moreover, you have not brought us into a land flowing with milk and honey, nor have you given us an inheritance of fields and vineyards. What will you do, put out the eyes of these men? We are not coming!"

Moses was very angry and he said to the Lord, "Pay no attention to their offering. I have not taken even one donkey from them, nor have I abused them in any way."

Then Moses said to Korah and to his company, "You and all your company be here tomorrow before the Lord, you, and they, and Aaron. Let every man have his own censer, the 250 princes, you, and Aaron."

The next day Korah assembled all the congregation against Moses and Aaron. Korah and the princes had brought their censers with hot coals and incense and stood at the door of the tent of meeting.

The glory of Jehovah appeared to all the congregation of Israel. And He said to Moses and Aaron, "Separate yourselves from these people, that I may consume them instantly."

Moses and Aaron fell upon their faces before the Lord and said, "O God, the God of the spirits of all men, shall one man sin, and cause you to be angry with all the congregation?"

The Lord responded: "Speak to the congregation and tell them to get back from the tents of Korah, Dathan, and Abiram."

As God said, Moses went to the tents of Dathan and Abiram with the elders of Israel following him. He told the assembly of the people: "Let me beg of you, that you all get away from the tents of these wicked men, and don't touch any of their things lest you be devoured in their sin." Everyone moved away quickly from the tents of Korah, Dathan, and Abiram.

Then Moses said, "Let me tell you how you may know that I am following the Lord's instructions, that I have not devised these things on my own. If these men die as men commonly die, or if events happen to them as they do to other men, then Jehovah has not sent me. But if the Lord brings about an entirely new thing, so that the ground splits open like a mouth and swallows these people, and they go alive into Sheol *(the realm of the dead)*, then you will perceive that these men have despised *(spurned)* the Lord."

When Moses had said these words, the ground opened up beneath Korah, Dathan, and Abiram, and swallowed them, along with their households, and all Korah's men. All of the rebels went down alive into the realm of the dead, and the earth closed back together; thus they perished from among the Israelites. The people were terrified and fled when they heard the screams of those who were destroyed.

Fire also came forth from the Lord and burned up the 250 men who had offered incense. Jehovah said to Moses, "Tell Eleazar, the son of Aaron, to take the censers out of the smoldering remains and scatter the coals. The censers of these men whose sins have cost them their lives are holy. Let the censers be beaten into plates for a covering for the altar. They offered them before the Lord, therefore they are holy. Let them be a reminder to the children of Israel."

So Eleazar took the bronze censers and made them into a covering for the altar. It was to be a memorial to the children of Israel so that no one who was not of Aaron's descendants would come before Jehovah to burn incense, so that they would not suffer the fate of Korah and his companions.

*Because Korah was able to influence the whole congregation to assemble "against them" (Moses and Aaron), God was moved to anger against the whole congregation and not just the rebels (16:19).*

*Under ordinary circumstances, Korah would not have been living next door to Dathan and Abiram, because they were of the tribe of Reuben, whereas Korah was a Levite of the family of Kohathites. Both the tribe of Reuben and the Kohathites encamped on the south side of the tabernacle (2:10; 3:29), but the Levites had their own encampment separate from Reuben. Korah appears to have moved his tent near the tents of his confederates (16:24, 27). Also, no family is mentioned in connection with Korah. Only with Dathan and Abiram are families (wives and children) mentioned (16:27, 32). We learn later that the sons of Korah did not die with their father (26:9-11), so with Korah, it was the men who followed him, whether his servants or adherents, who died.*

## The plague against the congregation (Num. 16:41-50):

As the congregation watched the horror of the three men and their possessions being swallowed by the earth, they fled in terror, saying, "The earth may swallow us up!" (16:34). But the very next day, all the congregation grumbled against Moses and Aaron, saying, "You have killed the people of Jehovah."

When they gathered against Moses and Aaron, they saw the glory of the Lord appear at the tent of meeting. Moses and Aaron came to the front of the tent, and the Lord said, "Get out of this assembly, so that I may wipe them out immediately."

Moses and Aaron fell on their faces before the Lord, but God did not wait for Moses' prayer of intercession this time. The plague began! Moses told Aaron, "Take your censer, and put fire in it from the altar, and lay incense upon it. Carry it quickly to the congregation because wrath is gone out from the Lord; the plague has begun."

Aaron hurried and did as Moses told him. Taking his censer, he ran into the midst of the people where the plague was sweeping through them. He put the incense upon the coals to make atonement for the people, and he took his stand between the living and the dead. The plague stopped, but 14,700 were already dead, not counting those who had died in connection with Korah the day before. Then Aaron returned to Moses at the doorway of the tent of meeting.

*This is one of the most chilling stories in the whole Bible. Think about what was happening! God had threatened to destroy the whole multitude before, but this time He actually started the process. From the wording, it seems that God started at the front of the crowd, and killed each one as He came to him. Imagine being the one next in line when the plague was stopped!*

*But think how inexcusable the grumbling of the people was. Not only had they seen all the ways God had blessed them through the years, they had seen the results of rebellion only the day before. They had stood and watched as the earth opened its mouth and swallowed the households of Korah, Dathan, and Abiram.*

*They had seen the 250 who tried to offer incense destroyed. But instead of learning the lesson of submission to the Lord and to His appointed leaders, they complained and blamed Moses and Aaron for the death of those rebels. No wonder God determined to destroy them all.*

## Aaron's rod that budded (Num. 17:1-18:7):

Jehovah told Moses, "Tell the children of Israel to take a rod *(a wooden walking stick)*, one for the prince of each tribe, twelve rods, and write each man's name on his rod. Write Aaron's name on the rod of Levi. Lay them up in the tent of meeting before the testimony where I meet with you. Then I am going to cause the rod of the man I shall choose to bud. Thus I will put an end to the bickering of the children of Israel over this matter." Moses told the children of Israel what God had said, and he laid the rods before the Lord in the tent where the ark was.

In the morning, when Moses went into the tent, the rod of Aaron, for the house of Levi, had budded and produced blossoms and had borne ripe almonds. Moses brought the rods out and showed them to the children of Israel, and every man took the rod which belonged to him.

Then the Lord said to Moses, "Put the rod of Aaron before the testimony to be kept for a reminder for these rebellious people, so that you can put an end to their murmurings before they die."

The children of Israel were very impressed with this display, and they said, "We are going to die! Everyone who comes close to the tabernacle of the Lord dies. Are we all going to die?"

In direct answer to the question the people have raised, God repeats His instructions to Aaron about who was to approach the tabernacle. He said:

> Aaron, you and your sons and your father's household shall bear the guilt in connection with the sanctuary, by way of your priesthood *(as mediators)*. But bring your brothers, the tribe of Levi, that they may be joined with you to serve you, while you and your sons are serving before the tent of the testimony. They shall attend to your obligations and the obligation of all the tent, but they shall not come near the furnishings of the sanctuary and the altar, lest both they and you die. They shall serve with you, but no outsider may come near you, that there may no longer be wrath upon the sons of Israel. Behold, I Myself have taken your fellow Levites from among the sons of Israel. They are a gift to you, dedicated to the Lord, to perform the service for the tent of meeting. But you and your sons with you shall attend to your priesthood for everything concerning the altar and inside the veil. You are to perform that service. I am giving you the priesthood as a bestowed gift, but the outsider who comes near shall be put to death.

God continues His instructions concerning the duties and privileges of the Levites in the remainder of Numbers 18. Look back to the chapter on "Rules for the Sacrifices" under the section on portions for the priests and Levites for a look at the rules given in Numbers 18.

*The Hebrew writer indicates that Aaron's rod was kept inside the ark of the covenant (Heb. 9:4). Here we find that instead of literally being kept inside the ark itself, the rod was placed before the testimony. In other words, the rod was habitually placed in a position near the ark, in the presence of God.*

*This fear of Israel at this time was not a reverential fear based on love for God and faith in Him, but a terror of the consequences of sin. But perhaps it would serve in some measure to preserve the people from God's wrath. Both kinds of fear play a part in God's plan for mankind.*

# To the Plains of Moab
## (Numbers 20:1-22:1)

### Miriam dies (Num. 20:1):

The children of Israel came into the Wilderness of Zin in the first month *(of the fortieth year, 33:38)*. While the people resided at Kadesh, Miriam died and was buried.

***Chronology note:*** *It is the first month of a new year, and though 20:1 does not specify which year it is, it becomes obvious as the story proceeds that it is the first of the fortieth year of their wandering. They will be entering the land one year from this point.*

***Map assignment:*** *Remember that the wilderness of Zin joined the wilderness of Paran about where Kadesh was located. Therefore the names Zin, Paran, and Kadesh are closely related. Be sure your map is labeled.*

### The waters of Meribah (Num. 20:2-13):

Once again Israel found themselves without water, and the people gathered against Moses and Aaron. They fussed at Moses, saying, "We wish we had died when our brothers died before the Lord *(presumably as part of the rebellion led by Korah, Dathan, and Abiram)*. Why have you brought us into this wilderness to die, we and our livestock? For that matter, why did you bring us out of Egypt to this awful place? It is no place to plant seed, or to grow figs or vines or pomegranates. Neither is there any water to drink."

Moses and Aaron left the people to go to the door of the tent of meeting. They fell on their faces, and the glory of the Lord appeared to them. The Lord told Moses, "Take the rod, and gather the people together, you and Aaron. Speak to the rock in their view so that it will give forth water, and thus you will provide for them and their livestock from the rock."

So Moses took the rod that had been laid up before the Lord (17:10), just as He had commanded them. Then he and Aaron gathered the people together before the rock, and Moses said, "Listen now, you rebels: shall we bring water for you from this rock?" Moses lifted the rod in his hand and struck the rock twice. Water came forth abundantly, so that Israel had plenty for themselves and for their livestock.

The Lord, however, was displeased with Moses and Aaron, and He said, "Because you did not show your reliance upon me and did not honor me in the sight of the children of Israel, you will not be allowed to enter into the promised land."

The waters were called Meribah *(strife or quarreling)* because the children of Israel fussed and complained and strove with the Lord. But He upheld His great name and character, because He showed both His mercy, in giving the water which was needed so badly, and His righteousness, by not allowing even Moses to escape the results of transgression.

*There was more than one thing wrong with what Moses and Aaron did on this occasion. Of course, Moses struck the rock instead of speaking to it as God had commanded. In addition, Moses and Aaron did not give God the glory in what they said. Notice that Moses said, "Shall we bring forth water from this rock?" Thus they failed to give glory to the Lord either by their actions or by their speech. God demanded that they pay the consequences for their sin. Neither of them could go into the land of Canaan. Though Moses is the one who actually struck the rock, and spoke the words that were displeasing, God held both men responsible for the sin.*

*One point we should emphasize, however, is that although Moses was required to pay a severe consequence for his sin, it is evident from the New Testament that Moses was forgiven and went to heaven when he died. Moses was one of the two who met with Jesus on the mount of transfiguration (Matt. 17:3). Satan strove with the archangel Michael over the body of Moses, but he could not have it (Jude 8-9). We are given no specific information about Aaron's final destiny.*

*This is one more example that shows that a mere "I'm sorry" did not remove the consequences for the sin committed. God forgave, but He demanded that the consequences be endured.*

*Notice that the rod God commanded them to use this time is the rod that had been laid up before Jehovah —that is, the rod that budded and grew almonds overnight (Num. 17:1-13). Was this the same rod that had been used for all the other miracles that had been performed since Moses was first commanded to go to Egypt to deliver the Israelites (see Exod. 4:17)? Since this was the rod used for this miracle, there is a strong probability that it is the same rod we have been observing in the story all along. —but there is no way to know for sure. In chapter 17, Aaron's name was written upon the rod for the tribe of Levi. The rod for each tribe was brought from the head or prince of each tribe, with Aaron acting as the head of the tribe of Levi. So it is a logical assumption that his name was written (as the representative of the tribe of Levi) on the rod he had used from the first.*

## Moses asks permission to cross Edom's territory (Num. 20:14-21):

From Kadesh, Moses sent messengers to the king of Edom, saying, "This is what your brother Israel would like to say: 'You know all the trials and suffering that have befallen us. Our fathers went down into Egypt where we remained for a long time, and the Egyptians oppressed us and our forefathers. But when we cried unto Jehovah, He heard and sent an angel and brought us out of Egypt. Now we are in Kadesh, a city on the edge of your territory. Please let us pass through your country. We will not go through your fields or vineyards; neither will we drink water from your wells. We will follow the king's highway. We will not stray from it until we have passed through your borders.'"

But the Edomites said, "Do not try to go through our land or we will come out against you with the sword."

The Israelites said, "We will stay on the highway, and if we or our livestock drink of your water, we will pay you whatever it costs; just let us pass through."

The Edomites, however, would not hear of it. They came out with a large force to block their passage. Though the temptation was strong to fight Edom, God said, "Be careful not to fight the Edomites for their land, because I have given Mount Seir to them for their possession" (Deut. 2:1-8). So the Israelites turned away from the route they had hoped to follow.

*The Israelites were asking permission to move east across the heart of Edom's territory where they would join the major trade route of the area, the King's Highway, and then travel north along it. But Edom refuses, so they have to go down into the rugged valley of the Arabah and travel north through it to the Dead Sea. They were in the edge of Edom's territory even there, but not on the easier route they had requested.*

*Who were the Edomites? Why would God be concerned about them? Look back to Genesis 36 for the answer.*

***Map assignment:***

- *Label Edom's territory.*
- *Draw in the King's Highway and label it.*
- *Find and label the deep ravine of the Arabah.*

## Death of Aaron (Num. 20:22-29):

Israel traveled east from Kadesh toward the Arabah. Their course took them to Mount Hor. There the Lord spoke to Moses and Aaron, saying, "Aaron is about to die because he shall not enter into the land which I have given to Israel, because you *(the word is plural in the original)* rebelled against my word at the waters of Meribah. Take Aaron and Eleazar his son, and bring them up Mount Hor. Remove Aaron's garments and put them upon Eleazar his son. Aaron will die there on the mountain."

Moses did as Jehovah commanded and took Aaron and his son Eleazar into the mount in the sight of all the people. He transferred the garments of the high priest to Eleazar. Aaron died there on the mountain top, and Moses and Eleazar returned to the congregation. The people saw that Aaron had died and that the priesthood had passed to his son. They mourned for Aaron for thirty days.

***Map assignment:*** *Authorities are not certain of the location of Mount Hor, but recent maps show it a few miles northeast of Kadesh.*

## Battle with King Arad (Num. 21:1-3):

The Canaanite king of Arad in the Negev heard that the Israelites were coming by the way of Atharim *(this term may refer to the route followed by the spies more than thirty-eight years earlier, because Atharim means spies)*. He went out and fought against Israel and took some of them captive. So Israel vowed unto the Lord, saying, "If you will, in fact, deliver this people into our hands, then we will devote their cities to you."

Jehovah answered their prayer and delivered the Canaanites into their hand, and they utterly destroyed *(devoted)* them and their cities. The name of the place was therefore called Hormah *(destruction, devotion, banning)*.

*The Israelites did not stay to claim this territory for themselves. They are not yet ready to claim land and settle in it. There is no question about whether the king of Arad came out and took captives at this time, or that the people made a vow to God concerning the cities, but there is a question about whether the Israelites retaliated now or after they went into the land. The people are into their last year of wandering, and they will soon be conquering more kings, so it fits for this battle to take place here where it is told. If so, this is the first of many times when Israel will destroy a city and its environs in the land of Canaan under the leadership of Joshua.*

*The king of Arad is listed by Joshua as one of the kings defeated in their taking of the land (Josh. 12:14).The strong implication in that list is that it was Joshua's army that defeated him. There are different possibilities that would explain the seeming difference:*

- *Many times a king and his army was defeated, but there was a city left standing. A new king might be selected and the battle had to be fought again for possession.*
    - *In this case, it says Israel "completely destroyed" these Canaanites and their cities. Israel may have destroyed the king of Arad and his territory in Numbers 21:1-3, and yet left survivors who selected a new king to be destroyed by Joshua.*
- *Or, the destruction referred to in Numbers may actually have taken place a little later, after Israel went into the land of Canaan.*
- *In either case, the destruction was a result of the king's actions against Israel and their vow of retaliation with God's help.*

*This is the same area, or very near the area, where Israel was defeated in Numbers 14 after they tried to fight when God had said they must wander. At that time, the name Hormah was used because of the destruction of the Israelite army. Now the name is given as a result of the destruction of the Canaanites.*

## Plague of the fiery serpents (Num. 21:4-9):

The people traveled from Mount Hor by the way to the Red Sea to go around Edom.

*Numbers 21:4 is a summary of the way the people had to go after Edom refused their request to go by way of the King's Highway. Some have thought that they went as far south as the Red Sea (the tip of the Gulf of Aqaba), but that seems unlikely because they were at the northern end of the wilderness at Kadesh-barnea and at the places that have been mentioned since they left there (Mount Hor and Arad). More likely the road they were traveling in the depths of the Arabah was called "the way to the Red Sea," because it was the road that traversed the 110 miles from the southern tip of the Dead Sea to the northern tip of the Gulf of Aqaba. There was no reason for the Israelites to go as far south as Aqaba to get onto the road in the valley.*

*Notice it says they were "going around Edom." It seems that Edom claimed this territory at this point of history, but it was on their outer border. The valley was a rugged one, and the Edomites would have claimed it in order to hold control of the road through it, not as a home for their people..*

The spirits of the people were very depressed because of the difficulties of the way. They complained and criticized God and Moses: "Why have you brought us out of Egypt to die in the wilderness? There is no bread, and there is no water, and our souls abhor this vile bread" *(the miraculous manna!)*. Jehovah responded by sending fiery *(burning)* serpents which bit the people, and many of them died.

The people cried out to Moses and said, "We have sinned because we have criticized the Lord and you. Intercede with the Lord, that He will take the snakes away."

Moses prayed for the people, and the Lord said, "Make a fiery serpent and set it upon a pole. Then, when one is bitten, he may look upon the serpent which you have made and live." So Moses made a bronze snake and put it upon a pole, just as God had said, and gave Israel relief.

*The serpents were fiery either because their bite was burning and painful, or because their appearance was fiery, or both.*

*Many years later, in the days of King Hezekiah of the kingdom of Judah, the wicked people of his day were offering incense to this brass serpent which Moses made on this occasion. As Hezekiah was trying to destroy the idolatry of his day, he broke in pieces this serpent and he called it "Nehushtan," which sounds like the Hebrew words for "bronze" and "snake," and for "unclean thing." (See 2 Kings 18:4.)*

## Journey to Mount Pisgah (Num. 21:10-20):

*The route of the Israelites from Kadesh to Mount Pisgah is one of the most disputed points of geography in the Old Testament. The point is not all that important, except for one thing: As a teacher of the Bible, you must be careful not to teach some of the modernistic ideas found in some (if not most) Bible atlases. Do not describe a route that denies plain teaching of the scriptures.*

*One of the most common ideas in the atlases is that there are two different routes given: They say that the route given in Numbers 20 and 21 is an earlier route followed by several tribes, and the list of camps in Numbers 33 is a later route taken by a different group. Thus the migration of Israel was not one migration of the twelve tribes of Israel led by Moses, as the Bible says, but a piecemeal movement of groups of tribes at different times. The theory is simply not true. The route given here in chapter 21 is a list of the camping places through the Arabah, into the valley of the Zered, and around to the plains of Moab. In chapter 33, Moses lists all the camping places from Egypt to the plains of Moab. That means it includes some that we have already talked about where particular events are told, plus many places where no stories are told. There is no conflict in the passages.*

*Look at the route so far since this last year began:*
- *The children of Israel were in the Wilderness of Zin as the year began (Num. 20:1).*
  - *Miriam died there.*
- *They moved northeast from Kadesh to Mount Hor (20:22; 33:37).*
  - *Aaron died there (20:23-29; 33:38-39).*
- *Israel followed the way of the Atharim.*
  - *They came into conflict with the king of Arad (21:1-3; 33:40).*
- *Then they traveled from Mount Hor by the way of the Red Sea (that is, they traveled on the road which ran north and south between the Red Sea and the Dead Sea).*
  - *The people complained, and suffered the plague of the fiery serpents (21:4-9).*

*Different locations are given for the places mentioned such as Oboth. The most sensible route for avoiding Edomite territory would be to go up the Arabah to the valley of the Zered River. This is the route shown in <u>Baker's Bible Atlas</u>, and it is the route that we will assume is correct as we finish our narrative of the Israelite journey to the Plains of Moab.*

***Map assignment:***
- *Draw a circle around Kadesh-barnea and the wilderness immediately surrounding it to indicate their years of wandering.*
- *Label their route from Kadesh to the edge of Sihon's kingdom.*
- *Label the four rivers that flow into the Dead Sea or the Jordan from the east. Their names will help you in locating the various places spoken of during the rest of Old Testament history.*
  - *Starting from the south, the rivers are: the Zered, the Arnon, the Jabbok, and the Yarmuk.*

The Israelites continued their travels and encamped at Oboth and then Iyeabarim. They moved eastward up the valley of the Zered. Skirting Moab on the east, they turned north until they came to the Arnon River on the border between Moab and the Amorites. They camped at a place they called Beer *("well")*, because the Lord told Moses to assemble the people so that He could give them water. In celebration, the people sang a song:

Spring up, O well! Sing to it!
The well, which the leaders sank,
Which the nobles of the people dug,
With the scepter and with their staffs.

As they moved from the wilderness, they encamped at Mattanah, Nahaliel, Bamoth, to a valley in Moab, and on to the top of Mount Pisgah which overlooks the desert.

***Map assignment:***

- *Notice on your map that, as the Israelites passed by the east side of Moab, and turned west at the Arnon River toward the territory of the Amorites, they were passing between the territories of Moab and Ammon. God told Moses and the Israelites that they could not have the land of Moab (Deut. 2:9) or the land of Ammon (2:19).*
  - *Why would God not want them to have the lands belonging to Moab and Ammon? Who were the Moabites and the Ammonites? Who was their forefather? Look back to Genesis 19:30-38 for the answers.*
- *The Ammonites lived northeast of the Moabites on the edge of the desert at this time. They had earlier owned the land immediately north of the Moabites and east of the Jordan River, but they had been driven out by the Amorites before the Israelites came into the area. This fact will play a part in the story of Jephthah in the days of the judges (Judg. 11).*
  - *Do not confuse the names of the Ammonites and the Amorites. They were very different people. We will discuss the Amorites more in a moment.*
- *Label the territories of the Moabites, the Ammonites, and the Amorites under the control of King Sihon.*

## Israel defeats Sihon, king of the Amorites (Num. 21:21-32; Deut. 2:26-31):

When the Israelites arrived at Mount Pisgah, they asked Sihon, king of the Amorites, to let them pass through his land peaceably. Just as they had asked Edom, they asked Sihon, "Let us pass through your country. We will not turn aside into any field or vineyard, or drink water from any well. We will travel along the king's highway until we have passed through your territory."

Sihon would not consider such a thing and he came out to a place called Jahaz to fight against Israel. But there was one difference between Edom and the Amorites — the Amorites were no kin to the Israelites. Instead, they were the strongest of the Canaanite tribes.

God told Moses that He would deliver Sihon into Israel's hands, so they struck him with a sword *(killed him)*, and defeated his whole army. They took his capital city of Heshbon and all the rest of his territory. The Israelites moved into the cities and dwelt there. Sihon's kingdom reached from the Arnon River on the south, to the Jabbok River on the north, west to the Jordan River, and east to the land of the Ammonites.

As Moses describes the battle in the book of Deuteronomy, he says that the Lord delivered the Amorites into their hands. They struck Sihon down, with his sons, and his whole army. They took all his towns and completely destroyed them, leaving no survivors, but they kept the livestock and plunder for themselves. Not one city was too strong for them to take. Therefore they wrote a proverb in celebration of their victory:

Come to Heshbon! Let it be built!
So let the city of Sihon be established.
For a fire went forth from Heshbon,
A flame from the town of Sihon;
It devoured Ar of Moab,
The dominant heights of the Arnon.
Woe to you, O Moab!
You are ruined, O people of Chemosh!
He has given his sons as fugitives,
And his daughters into captivity,

To an Amorite king, Sihon.
But we have cast them down,
Heshbon is ruined as far as Dibon,
Then we have laid waste even to Nophah,
Which reaches to Medeba.

***Map assignment:***
- *Find all four boundaries of Sihon's kingdom.*
- *Heshbon was located about halfway between the Arnon and the Jabbok. Medeba was due south of Heshbon a few miles; Dibon was just a little north of the Arnon, not far from Aroer; and Jazer was about ten miles north of Heshbon.*

## Israel defeats Og, king of Bashan (Num. 21:33-35; Deut. 3:1-11):

Og the king of Bashan, having heard of the defeat of Sihon, decided to come out and attack the Israelites. He dwelt in Ashtaroth and Edrei (see Josh. 13:12; Deut. 1:4). He brought his whole army out to meet Israel at Edrei.

The Lord said to Moses, "Do not be afraid of him because I have delivered him into your hand, and you will defeat him as you did Sihon, king of the Amorites."

So the Israelites defeated Og and his sons and all his people until there was none left. They took all his cities; there was not one among the sixty too strong for them to take, even though they were well fortified with high walls and strong gates. In addition to the fortified cities, there were many un-walled villages that they took also. They completely destroyed the cities and the people, just as they had destroyed the cities of Sihon's kingdom. But, again, they kept the plunder and the livestock for themselves. To add to the victory was the knowledge that Og was a giant who slept in a iron bedstead thirteen and one-half feet long.

When the battles with Sihon and Og were over, the Israelites controlled all the land from the Arnon River north to Mount Hermon, except for a small buffer zone between the two kingdoms called Gilead. Even that section was soon conquered by men from the tribe of Manasseh (Num. 32:39). After the battles, the Israelites moved forward and camped on the plains of Moab, overlooking the Jordan Valley.

***Map assignment:***
- *Label Og's kingdom of Bashan.*
- *Label Gilead as the buffer zone between Sihon's kingdom and Og's kingdom.*
- *Label Mount Hermon.*
- *Notice how large the area was that they have now conquered. See the boundaries.*
  - *This territory on the eastern side of the Jordan was not part of the original promise to Abraham, yet it is the first part they possess.*
  - *Only the land on the western side of the Jordan was part of Canaan proper, not Trans-Jordan.*
- *Label the Plains of Moab.*
- *Finish drawing your line to label the route of the Israelites to the Plains of Moab.*

*The spies were afraid of giants and fortified cities back there at Kadesh-barnea (Num. 13:26-33). By now this new generation has conquered many fortified cities —and even taking them from a giant.*

# *On the Plains of Moab*
## *(Numbers 22-36)*



## The Story of Balaam
### (Numbers 22:2-25:18; 31:1-54)

*There is more to the story of Balaam than just his effort to curse the Israelites. Several of the events that followed were a direct result of his coming.*

***Map assignment:***
- *The children of Israel are encamped on the Plains of Moab, across the Jordan River from Jericho.*
- *Label the Jordan River and Jericho on your map.*
- *Notice how near the people are to the borders of Moab.*

### Balak calls for Balaam (Num 22:1-14):

Balak, the king of Moab, saw what Israel had done to the Amorites, and he was very afraid because of their multitude and their strength. So the Moabites contacted the elders of Midian and said, "This multitude will eat up everything around us like an ox eats the grass of the field."

Then Balak sent messengers to a soothsayer, or diviner (Josh. 13:22), named Balaam, the son of Beor, who lived at Pethor by the Euphrates River. The elders of Moab and the elders of Midian took suitable payments for charms and curses to be placed and went to Balaam to tell him what Balak had said. Balak had much confidence in Balaam because, as he said, "I know that he whom you bless is blessed, and he whom you curse is cursed."

The elders of Moab and of Midian arrived at Balaam's house and gave him the message from Balak: "A certain people have come out of Egypt. They cover the face of the earth, and they are here next to my country. Therefore, I beg of you, come and put a curse upon this people. They are too powerful for me to drive out. Maybe in this way I can get rid of them."

Balaam said, "Spend the night here, and I will let you know something as the Lord speaks to me." So the princes remained with him.

God came to Balaam and said, "Who are these men?"

Balaam said, "Balak, the king of Moab, has sent these men to ask me to come place a curse upon a people who came out of Egypt and have moved in on his borders. He has asked me to curse them so that he can fight them and drive them out."

God replied, "Do not go with these men. You will not curse these people because they are blessed."

The next morning Balaam told the princes of Balak, "Go back to your land because Jehovah refuses to let me go with you."

The princes of Moab went back home and told Balak, "Balaam refused to come."

***Map assignment:***

- *There is collaboration between Moab and Midian throughout this whole story. We have been meeting Midianites since Moses first fled into the desert of Sinai (Exod. 2:15). But the Midianites were nomads from the desert, and since they were joined with Moab in this story, this group of them was obviously living nearby where they, too, were worried about the Israelites.*
  - *Therefore, label the area to the southeast of Moab as territory belonging to this group of Midianites at this moment.*
  - *See how far it is between this group of Midianites and the group living near Mount Sinai.*
- *Balaam was from Pethor near the Euphrates River. The map in this book does not include enough territory to see the Euphrates. The exact location of Pethor is uncertain.*
  - *Put an arrow at the top of your map, pointing off to the northeast to indicate where Balaam came from.*

*No information is given about Balaam before he is introduced here. Joshua calls him a "sooth-sayer" (Josh. 13:22), that is, one whose methods, ordinarily, would have been to go and "read the clouds," or to look for omens. Yet he obviously had some knowledge of Jehovah, because he speaks of Jehovah as his God (Num. 22:18). He knew enough to know that if God said do not go, then he should not go. If he had been only a false prophet, then he would have been accustomed to manipulating the omens and signs to fit his desires. Whether he was a true prophet, or merely a soothsayer with a reputation for being right, God really did give him a message on this occasion, saying: "I do not want you to go; I do not want these people cursed."*

*Balaam has done the right thing so far. The visitors made their request; he told them to wait until he had an answer from God; he received his answer from God; and he told the men he could not go with them because God had said no. There is no sin yet.*

## Balak tries again — and Balaam goes (Num. 22:15-40):

Balak sent more princes, of greater nobility, and they came to Balaam, saying, "Balak has sent us to tell you to let nothing keep you from coming to him. He says, 'I will promote you to great honor, and you can just name your price. Please come, therefore, and curse this people for me.'"

Balaam answered Balak's servants, "If Balak were to give me his house full of silver and gold, I cannot go beyond the word of Jehovah, my God, in anything either small or great. Therefore, please spend the night with me again, and I will find out what else the Lord will speak to me."

Once again God came to Balaam during the night and said, "If these men have come for you, get up and go with them, but you will do only what I tell you."

Balaam arose the next morning and went with the princes of Balak. But God was angry at Balaam because he went with the princes, so the angel of God came as an adversary to him. Balaam was riding his donkey, and two servants were with him. Suddenly the donkey saw the angel standing in the way with a drawn sword, and she turned out into the field. Since Balaam could not see the angel, he thought the donkey was being contrary, and he struck her with his stick to drive her back onto the path.

A little later the angel of Jehovah stood in a narrow path between two vineyards, with a wall on either side. This time when the donkey saw the angel, she tried to go around him and crushed Balaam's foot against the wall. Balaam hit her again.

The angel moved farther along the road and stood in a place where there was no room to move left or right. This time, when the donkey saw the angel, she lay down under Balaam. By now Balaam was very angry, and he struck his donkey a third time with his stick.

Just then, Jehovah gave the donkey the power of speech, and she said to Balaam, "What have I done to you to deserve being hit these three times?"

Balaam answered, "It is because you made a mockery of me! I wish I had a sword with me. If I had, I would already have killed you."

The donkey said, "Am I not your donkey that you have ridden all your life until now? Did you ever know me to act this way?"

Balaam answered, "No."

Then the Lord enabled Balaam to see the angel standing in the way with his sword in his hand. Balaam bowed all the way to the ground. The angel asked, "Why have you hit the donkey three times? I have come to be your adversary because your behavior is rebellious before me. But the donkey saw me and turned aside from me these three times. If she had not turned aside, I would surely have killed you just now, and let her live."

Balaam said, "I have sinned because I did not know you stood in the way before me. If what I am doing displeases you, I will go back."

The angel of Jehovah answered, "Go with the men, but be careful to speak only the word I give you." After this, Balaam continued his journey with the princes of Balak.

When Balak heard that Balaam had come, he went out to meet him at the Arnon River, at the very edge of his border. He greeted Balaam, saying, "Didn't I give you an urgent call to come? Why didn't you come to me? Am I unable to reward you suitably?"

Balaam replied, "Look, I have come now! Do I have power to make up what I say? What God puts into my mouth is what I will say."

Balak took Balaam with him to Kiriath-huzoth where he sacrificed cattle and sheep and gave portions to Balaam and to the princes with him.

*Balaam did the right thing when he asked God for permission to go when the men first came to him. His sin began when he went to ask God a second time, because by then he already knew God's answer. By the time the donkey spoke to him, it was obvious that God was displeased, because He had sent His angel to destroy Balaam, or at least to warn him. But why would God be angry after He told Balaam to go? God had already expressed His will: He did not want Balaam to curse His people! But it was evident that Balaam wanted to go in spite of God's instructions. Therefore God let Balaam be a free moral agent by letting him go try for that money and honor, but He kept Balaam from harming His people.*

*Notice Balaam's confession. He apologized, because "I did not know you were standing in the way against me..." The only sin he recognized was that he had beaten his animal unfairly. That was only a minor action. His sin was in going with the men in spite of God's expressed will. Though God has said, "Go," He has demonstrated both in words and in actions that it is not His will that Balaam do so. Balaam never admitted sin on that account. We, as individuals like Balaam, must learn the lesson that we must obey God —even when we do not like God's instructions. And, as teachers, we must see that this is the lesson we teach our students from the story of Balaam. Could there be a more important lesson for our children to learn? It is a lesson that will affect every decision of their lives.*

*Balaam warns Balak that he can only speak what God gives him to say, but Balak has no doubt of the outcome. He was sure Balaam would see the need to curse the people when he saw them.*

## Balaam tries to curse the people (Num. 22:41-23:12):

The next morning, Balak took Balaam to Bamoth-baal, a place of worship sacred to Baal. From there Balaam could see a portion of the camp of Israel. Balaam told Balak, "Build seven altars here for me, and sacrifice seven bullocks and seven rams. Then you stand here by your burnt offering, and I will go. Perhaps the Lord will meet me, and whatever He shows me, I will tell you." And Balaam went to a bare height.

God did meet Balaam, and He said, "Return to Balak and tell him what I give you to say."

So Balaam returned to Balak who was still standing with his princes by the burnt offering. Balaam proceeded to give Balak the Lord's message:

From Aram Balak has brought me;
The king of Moab has called for me saying,
"Come, curse Jacob for me and threaten Israel."
But how shall I curse one whom God has not cursed?
How shall I threaten one whom Jehovah has not threatened?
Here from the top of the rock, I look upon him.
Behold, a people who dwells apart!
It is a people which shall not be reckoned among the nations.
Who can count the dust of Jacob,
Or number the fourth part of Israel?
Let me die the death of the righteous,
And let my final end be like his.

No doubt the amazement on Balak's face grew as he heard these words that were blessing Israel. He said, "What have you done to me? I brought you to curse my enemies, and all you have done is bless them!"

Balaam answered, "Don't I have to say what Jehovah puts into my mouth?"

## Balaam tries again (Num. 23:13-26):

Balak said, "If you will, come with me to another place from which you can see Israel; you will not be able to see the whole camp, but just a part of them. Curse them for me there."

Balak took the soothsayer to the top of Pisgah and built seven altars and offered a bullock and a ram upon each altar. Once again, Balaam told Balak, "Stand here by your burnt offering while I meet Jehovah." *(The original is uncertain here, so there is some question about whether he was by now trying to find some message besides that from Jehovah.)* But once again, Jehovah put a message into Balaam's mouth and told him to go back and tell Balak.

When Balaam returned, Balak was standing by his burnt offering, and the king said, "What has Jehovah said?"

Balaam answered:

Listen carefully, Balak, and hear what the Lord says.
God is not a man that He should lie or change His mind.
Has He promised to do something and then not done it?
I have been told to bless, and He has blessed,
So I cannot reverse it.
God does not see iniquity in Jacob,
Nor perverseness in Israel.
The Lord his God is with him,
And the shout of the king is among them.
God brings them forth out of Egypt.
He has the strength of the wild ox.
Surely there can be no enchantment against Jacob,
No divination against Israel.
Now shall it be said of Jacob and of Israel,
"What hath God wrought!"
Behold, the people rise up as a lioness,
And as a lion does he lift himself up.
He shall not lie down until he eats of the prey,
And drinks the blood of the slain.

Balak could scarcely contain himself. "Neither curse them, nor bless them!"
But Balaam replied, "Did I not tell you that whatever the Lord speaks, that I must do?"

*Notice that Balaam says, by the inspiration of God, that "God does not see iniquity in Jacob, nor perverseness in Israel." As Balaam tried to find a way to help Balak, he remembered this statement and sought a way to make God find iniquity and perverseness in Israel. Watch for it.*

## Balaam tries once more (Num. 23:27-24:9):

Balak said, "Come, I will take you to still another place. Perhaps it will please God for you to curse them from that place." He took Balaam to the top of Peor which brought him nearer the Israelite camp, so that he could see the separate tribal encampments of Israel.

Balaam said, "Build seven altars for me here and offer on each one a bullock and a ram." Again Balak did as Balaam said.

This time, Balaam, seeing that it pleased the Lord to bless Israel, did not go to seek omens or enchantments as he had done the other times. Instead he faced the wilderness *(steppes, plains)* of Moab where Israel was encamped, and when he looked, he saw the nation of Israel dwelling according to their tribes, and the Spirit of God came upon him. Once again Balaam spoke the message God gave him:

This is what Balaam the son of Beor says.
This is the man whose eye is opened,
The one who hears God's word,
And sees a vision of the Almighty;
He fell down, and his eyes were opened.

He says:
How beautiful are your tents, O Jacob.
Like valleys they are spread out,
Like gardens by the riverside,
Like aloe trees which the Lord has planted,
Like cedar trees beside the waters.
Water shall flow from his buckets,
And his seed shall be by many waters.
His king will be higher than Agag,
And his kingdom will be exalted.
God has brought him out of Egypt.
He is as strong as the buffalo.
He will devour the nations which are his adversaries.
He crouches as a lion seeking his prey.
Who will dare rouse him up?
Blessed is everyone that blesses you, O Israel,
And cursed be everyone who would curse you.

*Again, these are expressions denoting great blessings: strong trees, planted by the waters; strong kings, greater than Agag (the title for kings of the Amalekites); strong animals, able to devour their adversaries. Blessings to others depend upon the way they treat Israel.*

## Balaam's message to the enemies of Israel (Num. 24:10-25):

By now Balak was truly incensed at Balaam. He struck a fist into his hand and said, "I called you to curse my enemies, and all you have done is bless them these three times. Now flee for your life back to your own place. I had plans to promote you to great honor, but Jehovah has kept you from getting it."

Balaam said, "Didn't I tell your messengers that if Balak were to give me his house full of silver and gold, I could not go beyond the word of Jehovah? Whatever the Lord said, that is what I had to say. Now, as you say, I will go to my people, but before I do, let me tell you what this people will be to your people in later times." So Balaam spoke again:

Balaam, the son of Beor,
The one whose eye was closed,
The one who heard the word of God,
And knows what the Most High has revealed,
Says:
I see him, but not now; I look upon him, but not soon.
There will be a star to come out of Jacob,
A scepter will rise out of Israel,
And will smite through the corners of Moab,
And break down all the sons of confusion.
Edom will become a possession,
While Israel gains power.
And out of Jacob one will have the rule,
And will destroy the remnant of Edom in every city.

Balaam looked upon Amalek, upon the Kenites, and others of Israel's enemies and continued his discourse:

Amalek was the first of the nations to attack Israel,
But his later end will be destruction.

To the Kenite:
Your place of residence is strong,
And your nest is set among the rocks.
Nevertheless Kain shall be wasted,
Until Asshur shall carry you away captive.

Alas, who shall live when God does this?
But ships shall come from the coast of Kittim,
And they shall afflict Assur,
and shall afflict Eber;
And he shall also come to destruction.

Balaam arose and went on his way, while Balak returned to his home.

*The fourth vision of Balaam was about the future, the days after Balaam, "the latter days," "not soon" (Num. 24:14, 17). The one who would smite Moab and Edom and who would have dominion over the region could be a reference to David, who conquered all the nations around him (2 Sam. 8:2,13-14). More likely, it is a double reference, including the Messiah in its application.*

*It is a vision of a succession of empires. One will rise to power, only to be destroyed by another. So the local tribes will fall under the dominion of Israel, until the strong power of Asshur comes to destroy. But then Asshur will, in its turn, fall to a power from the west, before that power too comes to destruction.*

*In Balaam's prophecy the specific agents of destruction are somewhat vague. This omission seems a little strange, until we remember that all through this fourth prophecy, there is a "star of Jacob" who will bear the scepter, who will "have dominion." Then the most sensible interpretation is that this whole fourth speech is a Messianic prophecy which tells how the Messiah and His kingdom will triumph over the kingdoms of men (Psalm 2). In this interpretation, the passage fits into one of the main themes throughout the whole Bible. Remember that God made His plans in eternity (Eph. 3:11), and all of history was looking to the day when the Messiah would come and set up the kingdom that was begun after His resurrection and ascension back to heaven — on the day of Pentecost (Mark 16:19; Acts 1:9-11; 2:30, 34-36; Rev. 4-5).*

## The sin of Baal-Peor (Num. 25:1-18):

While Israel continued in the Plains of Moab, the people began to behave like harlots with the daughters of Moab. The Midianites (25:6) and Moabites worked together to seduce the Israelites into idolatry. The women of these two nations enticed the people of Israel to make sacrifices to their gods and to engage in ritual fornication. So the Israelites joined themselves to the Baal of Peor.

The anger of Jehovah was aroused against Israel, and He said, "Take the ring-leaders of the people and hang them before the Lord, so that the fierce wrath of the Lord may be turned away."

Moses told the judges of Israel, "Everyone of you put to death whatever man is your responsibility to judge, if you find that he has joined himself to Baal-peor."

## On the Plains of Moab

While Moses and the children of Israel were still weeping over the sin of the people and the execution of the divine wrath, an Israelite man came, in sight of the whole congregation, bringing a Midianite woman to the tent of his family to commit fornication with her. He was Zimri, a prince of the tribe of Simeon, and the woman was Cozbi, the daughter of Zur, one of the princes of Midian.

Phinehas, the son of Eleazar and grandson of Aaron, was so moved with indignation at their audacity, he seized a spear and went into the tent and thrust it through the bodies of both of them while they were engaged in fornication. With this bold act, the plague of the Lord was brought to an end, but 24,000 already lay dead.

The Lord spoke to Moses, saying, "Phinehas has turned my wrath away from the children of Israel because he was very jealous for my cause, so I will not destroy the sons of Israel in my jealousy. Therefore I give him my covenant of peace. It shall be the covenant of an indefinitely long priesthood for him and his seed after him, because he was jealous for his God, and made atonement for the children of Israel."

Jehovah ordered Moses to treat the Midianites as enemies and to strike them because of their part in the matter of Peor. They had certainly treated Israel as an enemy by enticing them to do wrong.

*Remember that the Midianites and the Moabites were working together in this project from the beginning (Num. 22:4, 7).*

*Peor was a mountain near Heshbon. Very often the name of the prominent idol Baal is joined by a hyphen to the name of some place, as it is here. This means that it was the Baal worshiped at that particular city or place —such as the Baal of Peor, thus Baal-peor.*

*Baal was a god of fertility, so worship to Baal always involved fornication. That is one reason it had such an appeal to the people through all their history, and one reason it was so heinous a sin. Not only did it mean they had turned away from Jehovah, it was degrading to their morals.*

*Notice that this time God demanded that the judges seek out and kill the guilty people. God did not take a direct hand in this punishment as He had on other occasions.*

## The Israelites slaughter the Midianites (Num. 31:1-54):

*There are some significant events that are told between the story of the sin of Baal-peor and the avenging of the Midianites, but we are including this part of the story here to make the circumstances clear.*

The Lord said to Moses, "Take full vengeance for the sons of Israel upon the Midianites. Afterward you will be gathered to your ancestors."

Moses commanded the people: "Arm men from among you to go to war against Midian to execute the Lord's vengeance upon them. Select a thousand men from every tribe for the war."As Moses commanded, a force of 12,000 men went to war against Midian, accompanied by Phinehas the son of Eleazar who carried the trumpets of alarm in his hand.

*No better choice could have been made for a priest to accompany the army. Phinehas had shown himself to be a decisive man filled with zeal for God. Such zeal would be an inspiration to the army. Notice that he carried the trumpets of alarm into battle with him. Do you remember that before they left Mount Sinai they were given instructions about silver trumpets that they were take into battle to use to call upon God for help? (See Numbers 10:9.)*

The army of Israel warred against Midian and killed all the adult males, including the five kings of Midian: Evi, Rekem, Zur *(the father of Cozbi),* Hur, and Reba. They also slew Balaam the son of Beor. The children of Israel took captive the women of Midian and their children, their livestock, and all their possessions for spoil. Then they burned all their cities and encampments. They brought the captives and the spoil to Moses and Eleazar the priest and to the congregation of Israel at the Plains of Moab.

Moses and Eleazar and all the princes of the congregation went out to meet the army outside the camp. Moses was very angry at the officers of the host when he saw the captives they had brought back. He said:

> You have saved all the women alive, have you? Do you not remember that these women caused the children of Israel, through Balaam's advice, to transgress against Jehovah in the matter of Peor, and the plague of the Lord was among the congregation? Therefore, kill all the males among the children, and kill every woman who is not a virgin. All the little girls who are still virgins you may keep.
>
> You must camp outside the camp for seven days. Whoever has killed anyone, and whoever has touched a dead body, must purify himself on the third day and on the seventh day, you and your captives. Be sure to purify every garment, and everything made of skin, goats' hair, and of wood.

Eleazar, according to his duties as the presiding high priest, issued more detailed instructions: "This is the commandment the Lord has issued regarding cleanness, as He commanded Moses. The gold, the silver, the brass, the iron, the tin, and the lead — everything that can stand exposure to fire without being destroyed — you must pass through fire, and sprinkle it with the special water for purification (see Num. 19). Then it will be clean. Whatever will not stand the fire must be washed in water. You yourselves will wash your clothes on the seventh day, and you will be clean, after which you may return to camp."

Jehovah commanded Moses: "Count the people and the livestock which were taken, you, and Eleazar, and the heads of the clans. Divide all the living part of the booty into two parts: one part for the men of war, and one part for the congregation. Take a tribute to the Lord from the soldiers' part, consisting of one person and one animal from every 500 and give it to Eleazar the priest, for Jehovah's heave offering. From the congregation's half, take one person and one animal out of every fifty, and give them to the Levites who keep the tabernacle of the Lord." Moses and Eleazar did as the Lord commanded.

The part of the booty that went to the men of war is shown below. The Lord's tribute from this portion was given into the hands of Eleazar.

| Booty for the men of war: | | The Lord's tribute: | |
|---|---|---|---|
| 337,500 sheep | 30,500 donkeys | 675 sheep | 61 donkeys |
| 36,000 oxen | 16,000 people | 72 oxen | 32 people |

The part of the booty that went to the congregation matched the share for the men of war, but their portion taken for the Lord's tribute was higher. This part of the tribute went to the Levites as their share.

| Booty for the congregation: | | The Lord's tribute: | |
|---|---|---|---|
| 337,500 sheep | 30,500 donkeys | 6,750 sheep | 610 donkeys |
| 36,000 oxen | 16,000 people | 720 oxen | 320 people |

When the officers of the army counted their men, they were astonished to find they had not lost a man, though so many of the enemy had been killed. They came to Moses and said, "We have counted the men of war who were under our command, and there is not one missing. We, therefore, the captains of thousands and the captains of hundreds, have brought an offering from what we have taken personally as our booty during the fighting *(because all the men of war had captured spoil for himself)*. Here is our offering of jewels of gold, ankle-chains, bracelets, signet rings, earrings, and necklaces to make expiation for our souls."

So Moses and Eleazar took the offering and brought it into the tent of meeting for a memorial, placing it into the Lord's treasury.

*Balaam left Moab at the end of chapter 24, but he did not go back to his home on the Euphrates. From 31:16 we learn that it was Balaam who advised the Midianites and Moabites to send their women into the Israelite camp to seduce the Israelites to commit fornication and to worship idols. In this way he could cause Israel to be cursed by God, and he thought he could get the money he wanted so badly. It is a fitting end to his story to find that he was killed in the battle of vengeance that was commanded by Jehovah.*

*In the New Testament, false prophets are said to follow "the way of Balaam the son of Beor, who loved the hire of wrong-doing, but he was rebuked for his own transgression: a mute ass spoke with man's voice and stayed the madness of the prophet" (2 Pet. 2:15-16). Jude says that false teachers "went in the way of Cain, and ran riotously in the error of Balaam for hire, and perished in the gainsaying of Korah" (Jude 11). Jesus instructed John to write in His letter to the church at Pergamum, "But I have a few things against thee, because thou hast there some that hold the teaching of Balaam, who taught Balak to cast a stumbling block before the children of Israel, to eat things sacrificed to idols, and to commit fornication" (Rev. 2:14). By his advice, Balaam caused Jehovah to "see iniquity in Israel." In similar ways, for the love of money, false prophets today entice people to turn aside from truth and cause God to see iniquity in their followers.*

*The men of war were humbled by the tremendous blessing God had given them, and felt unworthy of it. In other words, they were made conscious of their sins.*

*Secular history tells of other occasions when not a single man was lost from an attacking force. Tacitus tells of an attack by the Romans against the Armenians in which, "The attack was so energetic that, before the day was one-third gone, the Armenian defenders were swept from the walls, their barricades at the gates flattened, fortifications scaled and taken, every adult male killed — without the loss of one Roman soldier, and with very few wounded" (Annals of Tacitus, XIII, p. 302).*

*The enormous quantity of booty is consistent with what is known of the habits of nomadic tribes who carry their wealth in the jewelry they wear.*

*When booty was "given to the Lord," the money and precious metals were put into the treasury of the tabernacle, and the animals were added to flocks that were kept to provide animals for the sacrifices for the whole congregation. There were daily sacrifices, extra sacrifices on the sabbath days, more on the first day of each month, and special sacrifices on each of the feast days (see Numbers 28-29). Therefore these flocks had to be large in order to produce the animals required to fulfill all the obligations of the law.*

# Other Events on the Plains of Moab

## The second census of Israel (Num. 26:1-65):

The first census was taken before the children of Israel left Mount Sinai (Num. 1:1-3), at the beginning of their second year out of Egypt. Now, nearly at the end of the forty years of wandering, after the plague for the sin of Baal-peor, another census is taken.

God spoke to Moses and Eleazar, saying, "Take a census of all the congregation of the sons of Israel from twenty years old and upward, by their fathers' households, whoever is able to go out to war." This was the same category of men who were counted in the first census. So Moses and Eleazar instructed the tribes, and the commandment was carried out just as God had instructed. The results were:

| | | | |
|---|---|---|---|
| Reuben: | 43,730 | Manasseh: | 52,700 |
| Simeon: | 22,200 | Ephraim: | 32,500 |
| Gad: | 40,500 | Benjamin: | 45,600 |
| Judah: | 76,500 | Dan: | 64,400 |
| Issachar: | 64,300 | Asher: | 53,400 |
| Zebulun: | 60,500 | Naphtali: | 45,400 |

The total number of soldiers was 601,730. The Levites were numbered also, but separately from the other tribes. Of the Levites, there were 23,000 males one month old and older. No inheritance of land was to be given to them because the Lord was their inheritance.

Jehovah said, "Divide the land according to the number of the people. To those tribes with more, give more inheritance. The land shall be divided by lot. They shall receive their land according to the names of the tribes of their fathers, and by the size of their group."

When the count was complete, it was found that there was not a single man left of the men numbered by Moses and Aaron at Mount Sinai except for Joshua and Caleb, for God had said, "They shall surely die in the wilderness" (14:28-35). God makes no mistakes!

*From this census we learn that though Korah died in the rebellion he led, his sons did not (26:11). A comparison of the figures in Numbers 1 and 26 reveals that Reuben, Judah, Zebulun, and Dan had changed their total number only slightly. In the case of the others, however, big changes had taken place. Simeon had lost over half; Issachar was up by 10,000, while Manasseh had grown by 20,000. The overall figure was 601,730 compared to 603,550 thirty-nine years earlier.*

*According to these instructions from God, the land will be divided to the tribes. Those tribes with more men would need more land, and those with fewer would need less land. That is easy to understand. But then it says "the land is to be divided by lot." What does that mean? It is this: the total amount of land for the tribe depended upon the number of men within the tribe, but the exact location of that inheritance was to be decided by lot —not by some means that would show partiality. In the same way, each soldier had a right to have his own portion of land within his tribe's inheritance, but the exact location of his farm was determined by lot —not necessarily by his personal choice.*

## Zelophehad's daughters ask a question (Num. 27:1-11; 36:1-13):

The five daughters of Zelophehad, of the tribe of Manasseh, stood before Moses and Eleazar, and before the princes and all the congregation, and asked an important question. They said, "Our father died in the wilderness. He did not take part in the rebellion of Korah, but died in his own sins, and he had no sons. Why should the name of our father disappear from among his family simply because he had no son? Give us a possession among our father's people."

*That is, Zelophehad died as one of the soldiers condemned to die in the wilderness, but he had not participated in any of the open rebellions against God as Korah had. He was one of the ordinary men of Israel with the right to an inheritance.*

Moses brought the matter before the Lord, and the Lord answered, saying, "The daughters of Zelophehad have spoken correctly. You will surely give the inheritance of their father to them. Furthermore, tell the children of Israel that from henceforth, if a man dies leaving no sons, his inheritance is to go to his daughters. If he has no daughter, then the inheritance will go to his brothers. If he has no brothers, then it will go to his father's brothers. And if his father has no brothers, then the inheritance will go to the one who is closest kin to him. Let this be a law among you."

This answered the question for the moment, but after a time, the family heads of the tribe of Manasseh, came to Moses with a related question. They said, "When the Lord commanded to give the land as an inheritance to the Israelites by lot, He said to give the inheritance of our brother Zelophehad to his daughters. But what if they marry men from other Israelite tribes? Then their inheritance will be taken from our ancestral inheritance and will be added to that of the tribe they marry into, and thus part of the inheritance allotted to us will be taken away. When the Year of Jubilee comes, their inheritance will be counted as part of the tribe they married into, and will be lost to us."

God gave His answer to the question by saying: "What the tribe of Manasseh is saying is correct. Therefore, this is what the Lord commands for Zelophehad's daughters: They may marry anyone they please, as long as they marry within the tribal clan of their father. No inheritance of Israel is to pass from one tribe to another. Every daughter who inherits land in any Israelite tribe must marry someone from her father's own tribe, so that every Israelite will possess the inheritance of his fathers. Each tribe is to keep the land it inherits, and the land is not to pass from one tribe to another."

So Zelophehad's daughters did as the Lord had commanded. All five daughters — Mahlah, Tirzah, Hoglah, Milcah, and Noah — married within their own tribe. They married cousins on their father's side and their inheritance remained within their father's clan and tribe.

*Notice that there were questions such as this one for which the Lord had not already given specific answers in the law. It was not that God had forgotten to take care of these matters, He just chose to wait until the question arose in the minds of the people. Other such questions were how they should deal with a person who blasphemed God (Lev. 24:10-16), or one who was unclean at the proper time to partake of the Passover (Num. 9:6-13), or one who broke the sabbath law (Num. 15:32-36). God answered each question when the proper time came for it to arise in the normal course of living. By the time His full will was revealed, the questions were answered by His law.*

*Since men normally inherited the land, a woman's inheritance was counted as her husband's land, and would be passed to their son as his land. That is why the men of Manasseh were concerned about this question. By marrying within their own tribe, the land would remain in the correct tribe, even though it would pass through the name of the husband, rather than through the name of the wife.*

*The Year of Jubilee is mentioned here in connection with the right of inheritance (36:4). Simply put, the law of the jubilee was that every fifty years all land was to return to its original owners. The people could sell their land — but in reality, they "leased" the land until the Year of Jubilee. In that way, no tribe would lose its inheritance as long as the people were faithful and remained in the land. (See Leviticus 25.)*

## Joshua is named as Moses' successor (Num. 27:12-23):

Jehovah told Moses, "Go up into this mountain of Abarim *(Nebo, or Pisgah)* and look at the land which I have given to the children of Israel. When you have seen it, you will be gathered to your people as your brother Aaron was. You will not enter the promised land because you rebelled against my word in the wilderness of Zin and did not sanctify me before their eyes."

Moses made a request of the Lord, saying, "Let Jehovah, the God of the spirits of all flesh, appoint a man to be leader of the congregation — to go out and come in before them. Do not let the congregation of the Lord to be as a flock without a shepherd."

Jehovah said, "Take Joshua the son of Nun, a man in whom is the Holy Spirit, and lay your hand upon him. Set him before Eleazar and before the whole congregation and give him a charge in the sight of all. You will convey your honor upon him so that all the congregation may obey him. He will stand before Eleazar the priest who will inquire for him by use of the Urim before Jehovah. Everyone will go by his word."

Moses did as the Lord said and appointed Joshua as his successor.

*Moses is told here what is to happen to him, but he does not go into the mountain immediately. Only a few weeks pass from this point until the time of his death, but several more chapters of the Bible are recorded before that time (see Deuteronomy 34).*

*Remember that the Urim and Thummin stayed in the pocket of the breastplate of the high priest, and God communicated with the priest via these items. Very little information is given about the Urim and Thummin otherwise. What God is telling Moses here is that He will communicate with Joshua through the priests, just as He would do with nearly all future leaders, not in the personal way He had communicated with Moses.*

## Reuben and Gad ask for their inheritance (Num. 32:1-42):

The tribes of Reuben and Gad had a very great number of cattle, and when they saw the land of Jazer and the territory of Gilead, they could tell it would be excellent for grazing. They, therefore, went to Moses and Eleazar and the leaders of the congregation and said: "Ataroth and Dibon, Jazer and Heshbon, the land which the Lord conquered before the congregation of Israel, is a land for cattle — and we have cattle. If it suits you to do this favor for us, let us have this land for a possession. Don't take us over the Jordan."

Moses, not understanding the intent of the men from Gad and Reuben, was very upset. He said, "Do you expect your brothers to go to war while you sit here? Why are you discouraging the people from going over into the land which the Lord has given them? This is what your fathers did when I sent them from Kadesh-barnea to scout out the land. When they went up into the valley of Eshcol and saw the land, they discouraged the children of Israel, with the result that they were not able to go into the land which the Lord was planning to give them. The Lord became angry and swore that none of the men from twenty years old and up would see the land He swore to give to Abraham, except for Joshua and Caleb. So He made the people to wander for forty years in the wilderness. Now you come along in your ancestors' place, another generation of sinful men, to add to the Lord's anger against Israel. If you turn away from Him, He will yet again leave the people in the wilderness, and you will cause them to be destroyed."

The men of Reuben and Gad entreated Moses, saying, "We will build corrals for our livestock and cities for our little ones, but we ourselves will go armed and ready before our brethren until we have brought them into their place, and we will not return to our homes until all the children of Israel have their inheritance. We will not inherit with them on the west side of the Jordan because this is the place we want to inherit."

Now Moses understood their request, so he replied, "If you will do as you have said and go fight for your brethren until the Lord has driven out His enemies, and the land is subdued, then you can come back here without guilt toward God or toward Israel, and this land will be your possession. If, however, you do not do as you have said, know that your sins will catch up with you."

Moses spoke to Eleazar the priest and to Joshua, his appointed successor, and to the leaders of the clans of the tribes of Israel, saying, "If the children of Gad and of Reuben pass over with you, armed for battle, and help you until the land is subdued, then you will give them the land of Gilead for an inheritance. If not, then they will receive their possession among you in the land of Canaan."

Once again the men of Gad and of Reuben swore that they would do as they had promised. Therefore Moses allotted to the tribe of Gad, to the tribe of Reuben, and to half the tribe of Manasseh their territory on the east side of the Jordan — Reuben in the south, just north of the Arnon River; Gad in the middle; and Manasseh in the north. The territories once belonging to Sihon and Og were divided between these tribes. They took the territory and rebuilt cities, or fortified them, and gave them new names.

Men from Manasseh were not with the original group of men from Gad and Reuben as they made their first request (32:1-5), but the sons of Machir, the descendants of Manasseh, went to the portion of land between the territories of the two mighty kings Sihon and Og which was called Gilead. They conquered it and dispossessed the Amorites who were living there. So Moses gave the land to that portion of the tribe of Manasseh as their possession from that time forward.

***Map assignment:***

- *All the places these tribes named in their first request belonged to the territory they had taken from Sihon.*
- *As the Israelites entered the area, only a small buffer zone between Sihon's kingdom and Og's kingdom was called Gilead.*
- *We will mark the tribal territories more carefully in our study of the conquest and division of the land in our study of the books of Joshua and Judges.*

*Once history has occurred it is set in concrete and cannot be changed, but we tend to look back on events and think they could not have been changed then either. If the spies had brought back a good report at Kadesh, and the people had moved forward, there would never have been a period of wandering in the wilderness. Now, here at the end of the forty years, Moses thinks these men from Reuben and Gad are trying to discourage the people again, and that the Lord may demand that they wander more years. He thinks they are afraid to take the land of Canaan, but that is not their intent at all, as they hasten to explain.*

*The "half-tribe of Manasseh" is not mentioned in these proceedings before 32:33. Verse 39 says that "the children of Machir" (from the tribe of Manasseh) had gone to Gilead and had taken it. It is not made clear in the text whether, having heard the request the two tribes have made, they went and conquered Gilead now, and asked for it as theirs — or whether they had already conquered it as part of the battles with Sihon and Og, and just now ask for it as their portion. The end result is the same.*

*Some have gotten the mistaken idea from the mention of the "half-tribe of Manasseh" that Manasseh and Ephraim were each only "half-tribes" and not full tribes like the others. That is not true at all. When Jacob told Joseph that his sons would inherit as tribes, he said that they would be like Reuben and Simeon — that is, full tribes (Gen. 48:5). Instead of Joseph's inheritance being that of one tribe like all the other sons, he received the birthright, giving him two complete shares of the inheritance (see 1 Chron. 5:1-2). As further proof, one half of the tribe of Manasseh received its inheritance on the east side of the Jordan and the other half received its share on the west side — and two halves definitely make one complete whole!*

## The encampments of Israel from Rameses to the Plains of Moab (Num. 33:1-56):

*Moses kept a record of all the camping places where the Israelites stayed during their entire forty years, and it is recorded in chapter 33. There are some difficult questions that arise because this list includes many more names than have been included in the narrative so far. Most of the places cannot be definitely located because they were camping places, not cities. God had deliberately led them away from settled communities during this time, and they were in a wilderness, so there were places that had never been named until the Israelites gave them names — such as Taberah. Look at the places named, but do not worry too much about the difficult questions that arise. Though we cannot pinpoint every place, we can tell the general direction they were moving. For our purposes, we will remember only the places where specific events took place. We have already included text boxes to show the route from Egypt to Mount Sinai, and from Sinai to Kadesh-barnea, so we emphasize the later places here.*

**Places and Events From Kadesh to the Plains of Moab:**

**Years of Wandering:**
- **Rebellion of Korah, Dathan, Abiram**

**Kadesh to the Plains of Moab:**
- **Kadesh: Miriam dies**
  - **Moses and Aaron sin**
- **Mount Hor: Aaron dies**
  - **King Arad attacks**
- **Through the Arabah:**
  - **Avoiding Edom**
  - **Fiery Serpents**
- **To the Plains of Moab:**
  - **Avoiding Moab and Ammon**
  - **Battle with Sihon**
  - **Battle with Og**

**Plains of Moab:**
- **Balak and Balaam**
- **Sin of Baal-peor**
- **Second Census**
- **Joshua named successor**
- **Inheritance for two and a half tribes**
- **Speeches of Deuteronomy**
- **Death of Moses**

The Israelites set out from Rameses in Egypt on the fifteenth day of the first month, the day after the Passover. They left in victory, while the Egyptians were burying their firstborn who had been struck down by the Lord, for God had brought severe judgment upon the Egyptians and their gods.

The Israelites camped at Succoth and at Etham, and then "turned back" and camped at Pi-Hahiroth *(making Pharaoh and his officials think they were lost in the land — Exod. 14:1-3)*. Then they crossed the Red Sea into the wilderness and went south three days' journey without finding water, until they came to Marah. From there they camped at Elim, on to the Desert of Sin, and on to Dophkah *(Rephidim)*, before arriving at Mount Sinai. After their time in the Desert of Sinai, they traveled up the eastern side of the peninsula, stopping at Kibroth-hattaavah, at Hazeroth, and on to Rithmah.

*This is one of the difficult spots. Where was Rithmah, and why is it listed next instead of Kadesh-barnea? So far, the list here pretty well matches the account in the narrative (with a few additional names where they must have stopped for only short periods). But in Numbers 33, after Hazeroth, nineteen places are mentioned before Kadesh (v. 36), including Ezion-geber at the head of the Gulf of Aqaba. Then Kadesh is listed, followed by Mount Hor. It is very unlikely that there would have been nineteen encampments from Hazeroth to Kadesh on that first trip north. Neither is it likely that they would have gone north, circled back to Ezion-geber, and immediately back to Kadesh all on the same journey north (see v. 36).*

*It was only eleven days' journey from Mount Horeb (Sinai) to Kadesh-barnea (Deut. 1:2). This expression denotes distance, not the exact number of days they traveled — because the story indicates they took more days than that to make the trip (see Num. 10:33; 12:14-15). But, though they took more than eleven days, they did not need all the camping places named. Not counting time they remained in any particular camp, their traveling time would have had to be divided between 18 encampments if all nineteen places listed between Hazeroth in verse 18 and Kadesh in verse 36 were all on that first trip north. Then if all the places named in verses 18-36 were on that first trip, there is no list of the places they encamped during the years of wandering.*

*Almost certainly, Rithmah was a place near enough to Kadesh for its name to be substituted for Kadesh in the list in Numbers 33:19. Then the list of places after Rithmah are encampments during the thirty-eight years of wandering in the wilderness — including a stop at Ezion-geber. There are still questions that remain, but this is the most plausible explanation for the seeming conflict between the account of travel in Numbers 12 and the one in Numbers 33.*

Numbers 33:36 tells of the same arrival at Kadesh that is described in Numbers 20:1, that is, at the beginning of the fortieth year in the wilderness. From Kadesh, they went to Mount Hor where Aaron died. It was the first day of the fifth month of the fortieth year after they came out of Egypt. They were then attacked by King Arad of the Canaanites.

After that they camped at Zalmonah, Punon, and Oboth — seemingly places located on the edge of, or down in the ravine of the Arabah. They turned east along the Zered River and camped at Iye Abarim on the border of Moab, finally coming to the plains of Moab, across the Jordan from Jericho, where we left them encamped in our narrative.

On the plains of Moab, the Lord told Moses to tell the Israelites:

> When you cross the Jordan into Canaan, drive out all the inhabitants of the land. Destroy all their carved statutes, and the images they have cast in the fire. Demolish their shrines of worship. Take possession of the land and live in it, because I am giving it to you as your own possession.
>
> You will inherit the land by lot according to your clans. Those tribes who have more people will receive a larger area, but within that area, each clan will receive its portion by lot.
>
> If, however, you do not drive out the people of the land, they will become as pieces of trash in your eyes and as thorns in your sides. They will become a serious problem to you, and, eventually, I will do to you as I plan to do to them.

## Borders of the land (Num. 34:1-15):

The Lord set forth the borders of the land the Israelites were to inherit as follows:

- The eastern end of their southern border would run from the south end of the Dead Sea toward the desert.

- From the territory of Edom it would run west through Kadesh-barnea and follow the brook of Egypt out to the Great Sea.
- The Great Sea *(the Mediterranean)* would be their western border.
- The northern border began at Mount Hor on the coast north of Byblos *(considerably north of Tyre and Sidon).*
  - From there the border went eastward to Lebo-Hamath. *(The word "Lebo" is translated commonly as "the entrance of Hamath." Lebo was a city-kingdom in ancient times.)*
  - The northern border extended to Zedad, Ziphron, Hazar-Enon.
- Then the border went south and came back to the sea of Chinnereth *(Sea of Galilee).*
- From there it went down the Jordan to the north end of the Salt Sea *(Dead Sea).*

Moses commanded the children of Israel, saying, "This is the land you are to inherit by lot among nine of the tribes, and the half tribe of Manasseh, because the tribe of Reuben, the tribe of Gad, and the other half of the tribe of Manasseh have received their inheritance on the east side of the Jordan."

*Obviously, the land of Canaan itself did not include the land on the east side of the Jordan. If it had, Moses would not have been upset when Reuben, Gad, and part of Manasseh asked for their inheritance there. And, it would have been included within the borders described for the land in this passage. Map #50 in the Macmillan Bible Atlas is very helpful on this point.*

*Though the Israelites inherited all the land God intended to give them in the days of Joshua, it is not until the days of David and Solomon that they control as far north as this description gives. It was God's plan that they continue to spread their borders as they became strong enough to hold the land (see Deut. 19:8-9).*

***Map assignment:***
- *Be sure you have labeled all the places where we have stories told from Rameses to the Plains of Moab.*
- *Find all the places used in the descriptions of the borders of the land God is giving them.*

***Chronology note:***
- *The years of aimless wandering totaled thirty-eight and one-half years (see Deut. 2:14 and Num. 33:38).*
- *Approximately seven months passed after Aaron's death until the children of Israel crossed the Jordan and encamped at Gilgal (Deut. 1:3; Josh. 4:19).*
  - *During those seven months, they were traveling, preparing to enter the land from the east.*
- *The time spent traveling from Egypt to Mount Sinai, and the time at Mount Sinai, totaled one year and one month (Num. 9-10). That year was counted as one of the forty years of wandering in the wilderness, even though the sentence to wander did not come until after that year was past (Num. 14).*
  - *Why was it counted as one of the forty?*
    - *Until Kadesh, the children of Israel were on their way to Canaan.*
    - *When they refused to go into the land, it made that year a year of vain traveling.*
  - *It, too, had been a time filled with murmurings and rebellions.*
  - *Therefore it was counted because it was one of forty years that Israel spent in the wilderness rather than in the land God promised.*

## Men are appointed to be in charge of dividing the land (Num. 34:16-29):

God spoke to Moses, telling him the names of a prince from every tribe who should help Eleazar and Joshua apportion the land for inheritance. God was very specific in every detail about how the land was to be conquered and divided.

## The cities of the Levites (Num. 35:1-8):

While they were still in the Plains of Moab, across from Jericho, the Lord told Moses: "Command the children of Israel to give cities with their surrounding lands to the Levites for an inheritance. The Levites will live in the cities, and the surrounding fields will be for their livestock. Measure 1,000 cubits *(1,500 feet)* out from the walls of the city north, south, east, and west. Measure 2,000 cubits *(3,000 feet)* on each of four sides. This outlying land will be for pasture."

The Lord continued, "You will give the Levites six cities that will be used as cities of refuge, plus forty-two more cities. Take the cities from the children of Israel according to the number of cities within their possessions. From those that have many, take more. From those that have few, take less."

*These verses are too uncertain in meaning for anyone to be positive about how these measurements were to be made. Look at some possible explanations:*

- *In verse four, the people were told to measure out 1,500 feet from the walls on each side, with the city in the middle. These dimensions obviously do not include the size of the city itself.*
- *Verse 5: It may be that the measurements of 3,000 feet on each of four sides also did not include the size of the city itself.*
- *Some have suggested that the first instructions may apply to existing cities, and that the second dimensions are given for new city locations.*
- *Whatever the meaning of these instructions for measuring the land, it is clear that the Levites were given a portion of land around their cities which was to be for their fields and pastures.*

*Remember that the Levites were not to receive a specific portion of land the way the rest of the tribes were to inherit. Their income was from the sacrifices to the Lord, from the tithes, and from other such sources. (See the description in Numbers 18 of the portions belonging to the priests and Levites from the tithes and offerings. Also, look into our companion book on the law for a fuller discussion of the inheritance of the Levites.) But they had to have places to live, and places to care for their cattle and possessions. One of their tasks was to teach the people the law, so by giving them cities scattered over the land, not only was God providing for His special tribe, He was also seeing to it that the Levites would be distributed up and down the land so that they could keep the law of the Lord alive in the hearts of the people if they, in turn, would only fulfill their obligations.*

## Instructions regarding the cities of refuge (Num. 35:9-34):

Jehovah told Moses to give the Israelites the following instructions:

- When you cross over the Jordan into the land of Canaan, set aside cities of refuge so that one who kills another accidentally will have a place to flee so that he will not be killed until he can stand before the people for judgment.
  - Set aside six cities, three in Trans-Jordan and three in the land of Canaan.
  - These will be for the Israelites as well as for the stranger and the visitor.

- If, on the other hand, someone deliberately strikes another with a weapon of iron, stone, or wood in his hand, so that the person dies, he is a murderer. He is to be put to death by the avenger of blood.
- If a man kills another because of hatred or jealousy, he shall surely be put to death by the avenger of blood. He is a murderer.
- But if one kills another, and there is no apparent motive, and the killing appears to have been accidental, then the one who has killed will be delivered from the avenger of blood.
    - Upon investigation, if the manslayer is found innocent by the community, he shall be restored to the city of refuge to which he has fled.
        - He must remain there until the death of the high priest.
        - If he should leave before then, and is slain by the avenger of blood, the avenger of blood shall not be guilty because the victim should have remained in the city of refuge until the high priest died.
- These commandments are to be regarded as laws and statutes among you.
    - When one kills another, the murderer shall be executed upon the testimony of more than one witness.
    - No fine is to be paid in exchange for the life of the murderer, nor can a fine be paid to release one confined to a city of refuge.
- By following these instructions you will keep the land pure.
    - Blood pollutes a land, and no righting of the wrong can be accomplished except by execution of the guilty.
    - You are not to defile the land I am giving you because I, Jehovah, dwell among you.

*The term "avenger" comes from the Hebrew word "gaal" which means "to redeem." It most likely refers to the same "nearest of kin" who had the right to redeem the property of a dead relative (see Lev. 25:25; Num. 27:8-11). If the matter were not handled promptly, there were occasions when the whole family of the slain one would rise up demanding the execution of the murderer (see 2 Sam. 14:7, 11). Look into our companion book on the law of Moses under "thou shalt not kill" for a further analysis on the rules for the cities of refuge.*

## Three cities of refuge in Trans-Jordan (Deut. 4:41-43):

Since the land on the east side of the Jordan is already conquered, and it has been divided among the families of the tribes of Reuben, Gad, and half of the tribe of Manasseh, it was time for them to go ahead and set aside three cities of refuge on this side of the river. Moses set aside Bezer in Reuben's territory, Ramoth in Gilead for Gad, and Golan in Bashan for Manasseh.

**Map assignment:**

- Find and label Bezer, Ramoth, and Golan on your map.
    - Underline them as cities specially set apart as cities of refuge.
- Very soon in their history, all the area the Israelites controlled on the eastern side was called Gilead.
    - Israelite cities on the eastern side were usually identified by the city's name, followed by a hyphen and the name Gilead, such as: Ramoth-gilead. This identified it as the Ramoth on the east side of the Jordan, rather than one on the west.

# *Moses' Speeches on the Plains of Moab*

## *(The Book of Deuteronomy)*



*It is somewhat arbitrary to make a new chapter at this point, because the Israelites are still encamped on the plains of Moab, but the subject matter of the book of Deuteronomy is so distinct it needs special attention.*

*When the book of Deuteronomy opens, it is the first day of the eleventh month of the fortieth year since the Israelites left Egypt. This means it is nearly time to enter the land. They are still encamped in the plains of Moab, just across the Jordan from Jericho. Moses has already been told that he is to go to the top of Mount Nebo (Pisgah), view the promised land, and then die. It is only one month before his death. He knows how many times he has pleaded with God to spare these people, and now he knows he will not be there to plead for them again. The book of Deuteronomy is a series of speeches that this very old man makes to this new generation of Israelites.*

*Remember that the old generation who rebelled at Kadesh-barnea has already died, and the new census has been taken (Num. 26). Of the men who were above twenty years old when they left Egypt, only Joshua, Caleb, and Moses are still living — and Moses is facing death in a few weeks. Even though this is a new generation that needs to be reminded to be faithful, there are many who were plenty old enough at Mount Sinai (nineteen and below) to be able to remember slavery, the plagues, and all the great events that have happened during these whole forty years.*

*Moses pleads with this new generation to be faithful to God: in the immediate future and throughout all the generations to come. It is a beautiful, poignant book as we look into the heart of Moses, and then as we see God Himself telling Moses that the people will not remain faithful in spite of all the warnings.*

*As Moses reviews the events of their history, take time to review them in your own mind too. Be sure you remember each episode that is described. Be sure you understand the exact point Moses is making each time he mentions one of these events. The book seems needlessly repetitive until you understand why an occurrence is mentioned again. The points Moses is making are so rich they will enhance your own service to Jehovah as you see how obedience and blessings fit together so closely.*

*Do not bog down in the details of the book of Deuteronomy. Use it as Moses intended: it was to be a reminder of the things that had taken place over these last forty years, a reminder of the lessons they should have learned from their experiences, and a reminder that they must remain faithful to Jehovah if they hoped to receive His blessings. We have given relatively short summaries of the speeches. As you study them, look more closely at the full speech in the Bible text, but do not forget that it was a speech —and understand the underlying message of each speech.*

*Notice how often Moses warns the people that things will go well with them in the land, that God will bless them greatly, so long as they are faithful —but that God will remove them from the land if they turn from Him and begin to serve idols. It is heartbreaking to remember their history through the rest of the Old Testament as we see the Israelites forget these warnings —and to see them finally lose their land because of their wickedness. Their history could have been so different. Let us learn the lessons they failed to learn.*

*The sections of Deuteronomy are discernible by virtue of the subject matter discussed in each, and by the formulas by which new sections are begun. These formulas are found in 1:1; 4:44; 5:1; 12:1; 27:1; 29:1; 31:1. In each case, an introductory expression is used, such as, "These are the words," or, "These are the statutes." As is often the case in the study of any subject, students divide the book differently. Do not be disturbed by such differences in divisions of the book. Concentrate on its message.*

## Moses' First Speech: Do Not Be Afraid; Remain Faithful

### (Deuteronomy 1:1-4:40)

These are the words Moses spoke to Israel in the plains of Moab, in the fortieth year, the eleventh month, and the first day of the month after Israel left Egypt:

> The Lord our God spoke to us in Horeb *(Sinai)* and said, "You have stayed at this mountain long enough. Get up to the hill-country of the Amorites and take possession of the land which the Lord swore to your ancestors to give to their descendants."
>
> At that time I found that I could not deal with your problems alone, so I took leaders from among you and made them judges over you. I charged them to judge fairly and honestly without fear or favor. Any cause too hard for them was brought to me.
>
> We journeyed from Horeb, through that great and terrible wilderness which you saw, to Kadesh-barnea. I said, "You have come to the hill-country of the Amorites. Go up now and take possession of the land God has promised."
>
> You approached me and said, "Let us send men before us to explore the land and bring back a report." I thought it was a good idea and sent twelve men into the land. They took of the fruit of the land and came back, saying, "It is a good land which the Lord our God gives us."
>
> But you would not go up; you rebelled against the Lord's commandment. You murmured and complained. You said, "The Lord hates us and has brought us here to die. Where will we go?"
>
> I told you not to be afraid. I said, "The Lord will fight for you. He will help you just as He has done all along."

But the Lord heard your words and He was angry. He said, "Not one of these men will see the good land I have sworn to give, except Caleb and Joshua." Also the Lord was angry with me because of you and said, "You also will not go in. Instead, Joshua, your assistant, will take the people in." *(This particular episode happened possibly several years after the matter of the spies at Kadesh-barnea.)* "Moreover, your little ones whom you said would be a prey, and your children who do not know good from evil, they will go into the land, but as for you, turn around and journey into the wilderness."

Then you decided that you would fight. So you confessed you had sinned, and you took up your weapons. I warned you not to go, that it was too late, but you wouldn't listen. Therefore you were badly beaten.

We turned around and traveled in the vicinity of Mount Seir for a long time, until God said, "You have stayed here long enough; turn north. Command the people that as they pass through the possession of Esau, they are to be careful, because I will not give you one square foot of the Edomites' land. I have given Mount Seir to the Edomites for an inheritance. You can buy the things you need because the Lord has blessed you through these forty years so that you have lacked nothing." So we passed by our brethren, the children of Esau, traveling the way of the Arabah, on the road from Elath and Ezion-geber.

The Lord likewise told us not to take the land of Moab because He had given them their land. Giants formerly dwelt in their land. The Moabites called them Emim. The Horites were found in Mount Seir before the Edomites destroyed them.

Jehovah said, "Now, get up, and cross over the Zered." We did so. It had been thirty-eight years since we came to Kadesh-barnea until we crossed the Zered. All that generation of the men of war were dead. The hand of the Lord had been against them to cause them to be destroyed.

When all the men of war were gone, the Lord said, "You are to pass over the Arnon, and when you come near the children of Ammon, do not fight with them to take their land, because I have given it to them for a place to live." That land is also a land of giants, whom the Ammonites call the Zamzummim, a great and numerous people, but the Lord destroyed them from before the Ammonites, as He did for the Edomites. Likewise, the Avvim, who dwelt in settlements as far as Gaza, were destroyed by the Caphtorim *(Philistines)*, who came from Caphtor.

*The point Moses is making about the giants is that Israel had been afraid of giants, but if the Lord could give land with giants to the Edomites, Moabites, Ammonites, and Philistines, He could certainly deliver giants into the hands of His chosen people. Therefore they should not be afraid to take their land.*

Moses continues:

"Get up now and continue your journey," God said. "Look, I have given you the land of Sihon, king of the Amorites. Fight him and take his land. Today I will begin to put the fear of you upon the nations that are under the sky."

I sent messengers to Sihon, seeking permission to pass through his land. I offered to pay for what we ate and drank and for any damage we might do. But he refused and brought his army against us, and the Lord delivered him into our hands. We slew him, and his sons, and all his people. We took only the livestock alive to go with the booty we took from the cities. From Aroer on the Arnon River throughout Gilead, there was not one city that was too high for us to take.

Then we moved on toward Bashan. Og and all his forces came out against us to battle at Edrei. Jehovah told me, "Do not be afraid. I have given him into your hand, and you will do to him as you have done to Sihon." The Lord gave him into our hands, and we destroyed his forces until there was none left. We took sixty cities in the region of Argob in Bashan, and every one of these was strongly fortified. We utterly destroyed the cities, except for the booty and the livestock.

Thus we took all the land from the Arnon River north to Mount Hermon. By the way, Og was the only one of the giants left in that area. His bed frame was made of iron and was thirteen and a half feet long and six feet wide. It is located today in Rabbah of the children of Ammon.

*The spies had been afraid of walled cities, but God has already helped them take such cities —even from a giant! The message was, "Do not be afraid to take other cities."*

Of this land, I gave to the tribes of Reuben and Gad the territory from the Arnon north, including half of Gilead. The other half of Gilead, plus the area of Argob, that is, Bashan, I gave to half the tribe of Manasseh. This land was called the Land of Giants.

I told the men of Reuben, Gad, and the half tribe of Manasseh, "You are to go across the Jordan with your brethren, armed for war. Your wives and your little ones, and your livestock, will remain in the cities I have given you, until the Lord has given rest to your brethren."

I also told Joshua, "You have seen with your own eyes what Jehovah has done to these two kings; so will He do to these nations where you are going. Do not fear them because Jehovah will fight for you."

I begged Jehovah at that time, saying, "O Lord Jehovah, you have begun to show me your greatness and your strong hand. What god is there in heaven or earth who can do the mighty things you have done? Please let me cross the Jordan so that I can see that good land." But Jehovah was angry with me because of you, and He said, "Do not speak to me any more of this matter. Get up to the top of Pisgah and look up and down the land, but you will not cross this Jordan. Instead, charge Joshua with this responsibility, and encourage him, because he is the one who will lead the people over to inherit their land."

And now, O Israel, pay careful attention to the laws I have given you, so that you can live and possess the land which Jehovah your God is giving you. Do not add to the word I have commanded, neither shall you subtract from it, so that you may do exactly what God has said.

You know what happened in the matter of Baal-peor. The Lord destroyed those who followed Baal-peor, but those of you who remained faithful to the Lord are alive today.

I have taught you all the commandments and statutes so that you can live by them in this land you are going to take for your own. Therefore be sure and keep these commandments, because they are the source of your wisdom and the means of your understanding in the sight of all people. They will hear of your laws and they will say, "Surely this people is a wise and understanding people." What other nation has a God so accessible to them as Jehovah is to us whenever we call upon Him? And what great nation has statutes and laws as righteous as all these commandments which I set before you today?

You must, however, be very careful not to forget the things you have seen, lest they depart from your heart all the days of your life. Teach them carefully to your children and to your grandchildren.

Do you remember the day you stood before the Lord to hear His voice at Horeb? The mountain burned with fire which ascended into heaven, and Jehovah told me to assemble all the people before Him, so that you might learn to fear Him all the days you live upon the earth, and so that you might teach your children. He made known to you His covenant, even the ten commandments, and wrote them upon two tables of stone.

Remember that you saw no kind of form at all when the Lord spoke to you. Therefore, see that you never make any kind of image whatever, man or beast. Beware lest you lift up your eyes to heaven and see the sun and the moon and the stars, and be drawn away and worship them. It was Jehovah who brought you up out of Egypt to give you this land. The Lord became angry with me because of you and what you provoked me to do, so I will not be going over the Jordan, but you will. Be careful lest you forget the agreement you made with God and make yourselves a graven image. Jehovah your God is a consuming fire.

When time has passed, and you have been in the land a long time, and you make a graven image of anything and do evil in the sight of Jehovah, then I call heaven and earth to witness against you that you will soon perish from the land you are about to enter. Jehovah will scatter you among the nations, you will be left few in number, and you will serve gods that are mere works of men's hands.

Wherever you are, if you seek God, you will find Him — if you seek Him with all your heart and soul. When you are in deep trouble in later times, if you will turn back to God and pay attention to His voice, He is a merciful God. He will not destroy you or forget the covenant which He swore to your ancestors.

Ask of the days that have gone before: has ever such an amazing thing been done? Has any people heard the voice of God speaking from the midst of the fire and lived? Has God ever before ventured to take for Himself a nation from within the midst of another nation?

These things were shown to you so that you might believe that Jehovah really is God. There is no one like Him. He has made you hear His voice out of heaven, and upon the earth He made you see His great fire, and you heard His words out of the midst of the fire. And, because He loved your ancestors, He has chosen you and brought you out of Egypt and will drive out nations greater than you to give you their land for an inheritance. Be aware then this day and remember that Jehovah is God in heaven above and upon the earth beneath. There is none other. You are to keep His statutes and commandments which I command you so that you can keep the land which Jehovah is giving you for a very long time.

# Moses' Second Speech: Beware Lest You Forget to Obey the Lord
## (Deuteronomy 4:44-11:32)

*This is one of the places where we could divide the book in more than one way. In 4:44, the heading begins by saying, "This is the law which Moses set before the children of Israel," that is, before this new generation. The thought continues all the way through 26:19. Chapters 5-11 deal with the law more generally, and chapters 12-26 deal with many specific commandments and statutes. But a distinct theme is emphasized in chapters 5-11: "Beware lest you forget to obey the Lord." Therefore, we are giving this section a major heading, and then we will deal with the more specific laws under the next heading.*

### Beware lest you forget to obey (Deut. 4:44-11:32):

This is the law Moses set before the Israelites when they came out of Egypt and were encamped in the valley near Beth Peor, east of the Jordan, in the land of Sihon, king of the Amorites. The Israelites had already taken the land of Sihon and the land of Og, the two Amorite kings east of the Jordan. This land reached all the way from Aroer on the rim of the Arnon Gorge, to Mount Hermon, and it included all the Arabah *(ravine of the Jordan valley)* east of the river as far south as the Dead Sea.

Moses called all the Israelites together and he said:

Hear, O Israel, the statutes and commandments which I tell you today, so that you can do them. Jehovah made a covenant with us in Horeb. He did not make this covenant with our ancestors, but with us, all of us who are here alive today. Jehovah spoke with you face to face out of the midst of the fire. When you were afraid, I stood between Jehovah and you so that I might show you the word of God.

These words are the ones Jehovah spoke to you from the mount. He also wrote them upon tables of stone and gave them to me. He said:

I am the Lord your God who brought you out of the land of Egypt, out of the house of slavery.

- You shall have no other gods before me.
- You shall not make for yourselves any idol, or any likeness of anything in heaven, or on earth, or in the water. Neither shall you worship them or serve them, for I am a jealous God.
- You shall not take the name of the Lord your God in vain.
- Observe the sabbath day to keep it holy. Do your work in six days, but the seventh day is a sabbath unto the Lord. You and all your family, your servants, and your animals shall rest. Remember that you were slaves in Egypt, and the Lord your God brought you out by a mighty arm; therefore He commanded you to observe the sabbath day.
- Honor your father and your mother, so that it may go well with you in the land which God gives you.
- You shall not murder.
- You shall not commit adultery.
- You shall not steal.
- You shall not bear false witness.
- You shall not covet anything that is your neighbor's.

When you heard the voice of God, you came to me in fear and said, "We have heard the voice of God. Now then, why should we die? You go and hear all that Jehovah says, and come tell us, and we will hear and do it."

Jehovah heard you and He said, "Oh, I wish they would always reverence me in this way so they might always keep my commandments. But you stay here by me, and I will tell you all the commandments they are to obey in order that they may remain in the land and keep it."

You will, therefore, be very careful to do exactly what Jehovah has told you, not turning to the right or to the left. Walk in the way Jehovah has commanded you so that things will go well with you, and so that you may lengthen the days you remain in the land.

The Lord wants you to fear Him so that you will obey His commandments all your life, and your sons, and grandsons after you. In this way things will go well for you, and you may increase greatly in the land Jehovah is giving you, a land flowing with milk and honey.

## Moses' Speeches

Listen, O Israel, Jehovah our God is one Jehovah. Love the Lord your God with all your heart, with all your soul, and with all your might. Keep His words ever in your heart, and teach them diligently to your children. Talk of them when you sit in your house, when you walk by the way, when you lie down, and when you rise up. Write them in every prominent place before you.

When the Lord brings you into the land He swore to give to Abraham, Isaac, and Jacob, you will move into cities and houses you have not built. You will enjoy cisterns you have not hewn out, and vineyards and olive yards you did not plant. When you are living in the lap of luxury, be careful lest you forget Jehovah who brought you out of the slavery of Egypt. Be careful to worship Jehovah your God, and Him only shall you serve. Do not go off after other gods, because Jehovah is a jealous God, and His anger will be kindled against you, and He will wipe you off the face of the earth.

Do not try to see if the Lord will do as He has said — He will! Diligently keep His commandments. Do that which is right and good in the sight of Jehovah so that you can insure a long stay in the land you are about to receive.

When your son asks you in time to come, "What is the meaning of all these commandments and laws?" tell him, "We were slaves in Egypt, and Jehovah our God brought us out with a wondrous display of power. He brought us into this land, and He said for us to obey these commandments for our good always, so that He will keep us alive as He does right now. It will be righteousness to us if we do these things Jehovah our God has commanded."

When Jehovah brings you into the land, and drives out the present inhabitants — the Hittites, Gergashites, Amorites, Canaanites, Perizzites, Hivites, and Jebusites — you must completely wipe out the inhabitants. Show them no mercy; make no treaties with them, and do not intermarry with them. Intermarriage will cause you to follow after their idols. Then the Lord will quickly destroy you from the land. Completely destroy their idols, their altars, and cut down their Asherah poles.

*The seven "nations" named in 7:1 were seven tribes of Canaanites who lived in various parts of the land. All of these tribes were descendants of Ham through his son Canaan (Gen. 10:15-19). The name Canaanite is used most often in a collective sense to include all these tribes. Thus the land was named Canaan as the home of the Canaanite tribes. But it must also have been used to apply to one particular tribe since it is listed here and elsewhere as one of the "nations" they would find.*

*The Amorites were the largest and strongest of the tribes in the land at this time. They had moved out of the desert into the fertile land in the era immediately before God's first call to Abraham (c. 2000 B.C.). Their name is often used collectively to include all the tribes just as Canaanite is used.*

*The Hittites established an early kingdom along the Halys River in the territory that was called Asia Minor by New Testament days. There had been trade and contact between the Hittite kingdom and the peoples of the Fertile Crescent from the earliest days. Groups of Hittites migrated throughout the area. Joshua's army will find them firmly entrenched in the central hill country.*

*The Hivites, Gergashites, Perizzites, and Jebusites were smaller, less powerful tribes.*

*Asherah poles, or the plural form "Asherim," were the female counterpart to the god Baal. These were usually carved from tree stumps that had been cut to the desired height. As the female counterpart to the fertility gods, worship of them corrupted the morals of the worshipers.*

Moses continued:

You see, you are a holy people. The Lord has chosen you to be His special people. He did not choose you because you were a great nation, with a great number, because you were not — you were the fewest of people! He chose you because He loved you, and because of the oath He swore to your ancestors. Remember, therefore, with whom you are dealing. He is merciful to a thousand generations of those who love Him and keep His commandments, but He will not hesitate to punish those who disobey. Therefore you shall keep the commandments which I am commanding you today.

As time passes, if you obey these commandments, the Lord will continue His mercy upon you which He swore to your ancestors. He will bless your families, your fields, and your flocks. There will be no barren among you, and Jehovah will take away all sickness, and will suffer none of the diseases of Egypt to be upon you. He will drive out all of your enemies. You shall not pity them, neither serve their gods. That would be a pitfall to you.

Do not be afraid. Remember what God did to Pharaoh and to all Egypt. Remember what you have seen in the wilderness. So will He do to those whom you might be tempted to fear in the land. He will send a hornet to search out and destroy those who try to hide from you. Jehovah your God is in your midst, and He is a great God and awesome.

Jehovah will cast out the nations from before you gradually, little by little, so that the wild animals will not take over the land. But He will consume them until they are no more. He will deliver them before you, and will throw them into confusion until they are destroyed. He will deliver their kings into your hands so that you will make their name perish from under heaven. No man will be able to stand before you until you have destroyed them.

Burn their graven images. Do not desire even the gold and silver on their idols, lest you find it a pitfall. Do not bring such an abomination into your home.

Be careful to do all the instructions I give you today so that you may live and prosper, and so that you may be able to have and to keep the land which Jehovah promised to your fathers. Remember the experiences of these forty years, how God placed you in different situations to see whether you would obey Him or not. He humbled you and allowed you to get hungry and then fed you with manna which neither you nor your ancestors ever heard of, so that He might teach you that man's life does not depend upon having something to eat. He lives when he follows every word Jehovah speaks. Jehovah has cared for you these forty years. Even though there were times of difficulty when you were disciplined as a father trains his son, your clothes did not grow old, neither did your feet swell.

Keep the commandments of Jehovah your God. When you have come into this wonderful land — a land of brooks of water, of artesian wells and springs flowing out of its valleys and hills, a land of wheat and barley, of grape vines, fig-trees, and pomegranates, a land of olive-trees and honey, a land which will abundantly supply all your needs — remember to bless Jehovah your God for all the good He has done you.

Beware lest you forget Jehovah your God. If you are not careful, you will get into the land, and you will occupy your houses, and vineyards, and fields, and everything will be so good you will forget Jehovah and will neglect to keep His commandments. You will begin to say, "I have gotten all of these things by myself," and you will forget the mighty God who brought you through the terrible wilderness, who gave you water from the flinty rock and manna from heaven.

I tell you now that if you forget God, and walk after other gods to serve them and worship them, you will perish. As the nations presently in the land are about to perish, so you will perish because you would not pay attention to Jehovah your God.

Listen to me, O Israel! You are about to cross over the Jordan today to cast out nations greater and mightier than you, whose cities are fortified to the skies, whose people are giants, of whom you have heard it said, "Who can stand up to the sons of Anak?" Well, your God is a raging fire that will utterly destroy everything before you, so that no one can resist you.

When you have conquered the land, do not say, "It is for my righteousness that Jehovah has brought me into this land." It is not for your righteousness, but because of the wickedness of the nations before you. You are receiving this great blessing because of the word Jehovah spoke to Abraham, to Isaac, and to Jacob.

No, it is not for your righteousness, because you are a hard-headed people — and always have been. Even at Horeb you provoked Jehovah to wrath. At the end of the forty days when I was in the mountain, and Jehovah gave me the tables of the covenant which He had made with you, the Lord said, "Get up quickly, and go down to the people, because those people you brought up from Egypt have already strayed." At that very time, Jehovah decided to wipe you out, but I pleaded for you. When I came down from the mount, I saw the golden calf you had made, so I took the two tables and broke them before your eyes.

Once again I went before Jehovah for forty days and forty nights. Jehovah was angry with you. He was very angry with Aaron and was inclined to destroy him, so I prayed for him, too. I pleaded with God to remember His great reputation and how it would appear to the Egyptians if He destroyed the nation He had brought out of their land. They would say, "It was because He was not able to bring them into the land which He promised, and because He despised them. He just took them out into the wilderness as a cruel joke, to slay them."

The Lord heard me and He said, "Hew two tables of stones and come up here before me." And Jehovah wrote upon the tables as He wrote on the first ones, the ten commandments. Then I came down, and we departed. But at Taberah, and at Massah, and at Kibroth-hattaavah, you provoked His anger. When we got to Kadesh-barnea, and Jehovah told you to go up and take the land He had promised, you would not do it. You refused and would not listen to Him. You have been rebellious ever since I have known you.

Listen, O Israel. This is what Jehovah wants of you: to fear Him, to walk in His ways, and to serve Him with all your being, and to keep His commandments which I am commanding you today for your good. Look at Jehovah: He owns heaven and the heaven of heavens and the whole earth. Why should He bother with you at all? It is because He took delight in your ancestors to love them, and He chose their descendants, even you, out of all the peoples.

Prepare your hearts to be as they should be, and be no longer stiff-necked. Jehovah your God is God of gods, and Lord of lords, the great God, who pays no attention to a person's social status, and who takes no bribes. He looks after the fatherless and the widows and loves the sojourner. You need to love sojourners also, because you were sojourners in Egypt.

Fear the Lord, and serve Him. He is the only thing you have that is worthy of praise. He has done awesome things for you. Your ancestors went down into Egypt with seventy people; now Jehovah has made you as the stars of heaven in number.

Therefore, love the Lord your God, and keep His commandments. I am not speaking with your children that have not known, and who have not seen the chastisements of the Lord, and all the great deeds of God which He has done. I am speaking to you; your eyes have seen all the great work of Jehovah which He did.

Keep the commandments of the Lord so that you may be able to take possession of the land you are entering. This land is not like the land of Egypt from which you came. There you sowed your seed and then had to irrigate carefully, or the seed would not grow. This land is a land of hills and valleys. It drinks water from the rain of heaven, a land which Jehovah especially protects.

Moreover, Jehovah says, "If you pay attention to me to do my commandments, I will give you the early rain to bring your seed up, and the later rain to help your crops to make. You will have plenty of grain, new wine, and olive oil." But, if you do not obey the Lord, He will be angry and will shut up the skies, and there will be no crops. You will quickly perish from the good land which Jehovah gives you.

Therefore, do your utmost to remember these things. Impress these words upon your heart. Keep them before you at all times. Teach them constantly to your children, so that you may stay in this land for a very long time. If you will do as I have said, Jehovah will drive out your enemies, and you will possess the land, and no one will be able to bother you.

Today I set before you a blessing and a curse. The blessing will be if you pay attention to Jehovah; the curse, if you refuse to listen and turn away to other gods. When you get into the land where Jehovah is taking you, set the blessing upon Mount Gerizim, and the curse upon Mount Ebal, so that they may be before you. *(There will be a fuller explanation of how they were to set the blessings and curses upon the mountains when we get to chapter 27.)*

# The Law Which Moses Set Before Israel
## (Deuteronomy 4:44-26:19)

*Having looked at the theme Moses develops in chapters 5-11, in which he urges the people to beware lest they forget to obey God, we come back to the whole section that begins in 4:44 and continues through 26:19. Moses gives a cross-section of the whole law as he reminds this new generation to be faithful. Most of these laws deal with how the people were to live together and treat one another in the land, but even those were always because of their unique relationship to God. As we summarize the laws Moses felt needed to be emphasized before they enter the land, we stress the lessons he taught them about their relationship to God and about the importance of their keeping the law. Our companion book, Jehovah's Covenant With Israel, includes all these laws classified under the appropriate subjects.*

### Laws Moses emphasized here:

Moses said, "These are the decrees and laws you must be careful to obey in the land Jehovah is giving you:"

1. **The Ten Commandments (5:6-21):** Moses repeats the ten commandments as he begins reminding this generation of the laws Jehovah had given them. There are a very few points made here that are not included in the original list in Exodus 20.

   For example, one fact included here is the reason *why* God commanded Israel to observe a sabbath day. They had been slaves, with no right to take a day of rest. Therefore, the day God gave for rest was to be remembered as a blessing — the direct result of being freed from slavery. In Exodus 20, God tells that He chose the seventh day as the day of rest because He created the heavens and the earth and all that is in them in six days, and rested on the seventh day.

2. **Destroy the people and their idols that you find in the land (7:1-16):** This was a strong reminder to the people to get rid of all the idols they find in the land. They were to destroy all the people and all signs of their idols, lest they be tempted to turn aside to follow them.

3. **Offer sacrifices in the place God specifies (12:1-32):** Destroy all the worship places on every hill where the people of the land have been worshiping their idols. Break down their altars, smash their sacred stones, and burn their Asherah poles. Wipe out their names from those places. You must not worship the Lord your God in their way. Instead of worshiping Him on whatever hill is near you, you must go to the place where He chooses to put His name. Take your sacrifices, your firstfruits, and your vows there to offer them to the Lord and to eat before Him and to rejoice in the blessings He has given you. *(Remember this prohibition against offering sacrifices on the "high places" when you come to the stories of the divided kingdom. A place might start out as a place to worship Jehovah, but it would soon deteriorate into a place of idolatry.)*

   If you want to kill an animal to eat, not as a sacrifice to the Lord, then you may kill it and eat it in your own territory, just as you would kill a wild deer or gazelle. But if it is an animal you have vowed to give to the Lord, then it must be taken to the tabernacle and offered there.

4. **Put to death those who turn to idols (13:1-18):** If a prophet comes to you and tries to tell you a false god has given a message, do not listen to him even if his prophecy comes true. That prophet must be put to death. If your dearest relative — your brother, your child, your wife, or your dearest friend — suggests that you turn to idols, do not yield to him. That one must be put to death. Show him no mercy. If that one is put to death, then others will hear of it and will be afraid to turn away from God. If a city turns to idols, then that city must be destroyed. Kill the people and slaughter all the livestock. Even the spoil of the city is to be piled in the middle of the city and burned completely. The city is to remain a ruin forever; it must never be rebuilt.

5. **You are a holy people, so do not pollute yourselves (14:1-21):** God has chosen you as His holy people out of all the peoples of the earth. Therefore He expects you to be different. Do not mar yourselves by cutting yourselves or shaving your heads. Do not pollute yourselves by eating animals that God has decreed as unclean — whether it is a wild animal or one you have raised, fish, birds, or insects. Do not eat anything you find dead. You are to be clean, holy, before the Lord.

6. **Give your tithes to the Lord (14:22-29):** Set aside for God a tenth of all that your fields produce each year. Take your tithes and your firstborn to the place God has chosen and eat them there before the Lord. But if your home is distant from the place where God has put His name, and you cannot carry your tithe because of the distance, then you may sell the produce and take the money. Use the money to buy produce when you arrive at the chosen place and eat it before the Lord.

   At the end of every three years, bring all your tithes for that year and store them up in your towns. Then the food can be eaten by the Levites who have no inheritance of their own, and it can be shared with the foreigners living in your midst, with the widows, and with the fatherless. They can be filled, and God will bless you in all the work of your hands.

7. **The seventh year (15:1-18):** At the end of every seven years, cancel all debts to fellow Israelites. You may collect debts from foreigners, but cancel all those to your brethren. This is God's way of preventing

poverty among you. God is giving you this land and He will richly bless you in it, if you obey Him fully. If you serve Him, then you will lend to many nations and will borrow from none.

If there is someone in your midst who is poor and needs your help, loan to him freely. Beware lest you refuse because you see the seventh year, the year of canceling debts, approaching. If you refuse to help, and that poor one cries to God, you will be held guilty of sin. But if you give to him generously, God will bless you greatly in everything you do. There will always be poor among you, so open your hearts and give freely.

If a fellow Hebrew has sold himself to you as a slave, he is to serve you six years, and you are to let him go free in the seventh year, unless the slave himself asks permission to stay. And when he leaves, supply him liberally from your flocks, your threshing floor, and your winepress. Remember that you were slaves in Egypt and the Lord redeemed you. This is why I give you this commandment today. Do not consider it a hardship to let your slave go free, because he has been of greater value to you than a hired hand would have been. The Lord will bless you greatly in everything you do.

8. **Set apart the firstborn (15:19-23):** Set apart for the Lord every firstborn male from all your animals. Eat it before the Lord in the place where He chooses to put His name. If the animal should have a defect of some kind, eat it in your home town, rather than taking it as a sacrifice to God. Eat the flesh of the animal, but you must not eat the blood. Pour it out on the ground like water.

9. **Observe the feast days (16:1-17):** Observe the Passover in the month Abib, according to all the rules and regulations that God has commanded. This feast is to remind you of the night God brought you out of the land of Egypt. Eat unleavened bread for seven days as a reminder that you left Egypt in haste.

   Count seven weeks from the time you begin to put the sickle to the standing grain, and then celebrate the Feast of Weeks by giving a freewill offering to the Lord. Rejoice before the Lord in the place where He puts His name. Remember you were slaves, and follow all these decrees carefully.

   Celebrate the Feast of Tabernacles for seven days at the end of your harvest. Rejoice, for the Lord will bless you in all your harvest, and in all the work of your hands, so that your joy may be complete.

   Three times a year all your men must appear before the Lord to keep the appointed feasts. Do not come empty-handed. Bring a gift in proportion to the way the Lord has blessed you.

10. **Appoint judges in every town (16:18-20):** Appoint judges and officials for every tribe and in every town, and they shall judge fairly. They must not take bribes, show partiality, or pervert judgment in any way. Follow justice, and justice alone, so that you may live long and prosper in the land.

11. **Stone the one who turns to idols (16:21-17:7):** Do not set up any idol beside an altar to Jehovah, for the Lord hates these. Do not offer a defective animal to the Lord, because that would be detestable.

    If a man or woman living among you turns aside to idols, and you learn of it, investigate very carefully to see if it is true. On the testimony of two or three witnesses, stone that person to death. The hands of the witnesses must be the first in putting him to death, and then the hands of all the people. You must purge the evil from among you.

12. **Bring difficult cases to the priest (17:8-13):** If a case comes to court that is too difficult to judge, bring the matter to the priests. Let them give a verdict; then you must abide by their decision. Act according to the law they teach you and according to the verdicts they give. The man who shows contempt for the

judge, or for the priest, must be put to death. You must purge the evil from Israel. All the people will hear and be afraid, and they will not be contemptuous again.

13. **Instructions for kings (17:14-20):** When you come into the land, and you say, "I will set a king over me like the other nations," then you will set up the one God chooses, an Israelite, not a foreigner. Your king is not to multiply horses, or cause the people to return to Egypt. You are not to go back there. Neither is the king to multiply wives for himself, lest they turn his heart away. Neither shall he greatly multiply for himself silver and gold. When he sits upon his throne, he shall have a copy of this law written in a book, copied from that book which is with the priests, the Levites. He is to read the law all his days so that he may learn to fear Jehovah, to do God's will, so that he may prolong the days of his kingdom, he and his children. (*Remember this passage when you get to the story of Solomon.)*

14. **Offerings for the priests and Levites (18:1-8):** The priests and Levites among you are not to receive an inheritance like the other tribes. Instead, they are to live on the offerings that are made to the Lord. Be sure they are given their proper portions of the sacrifices, the firstfruits of your harvests, and the firstfruits from the shearing of your animals. The Lord has chosen the Levites out of all the tribes to minister before Him.

    If a Levite moves from the town where he is living, and comes to serve in the place where God will put His name, then he may fully share in the work and in the offerings for the Levites, even if he has received money from the sale of his family possessions.

15. **Do not engage in detestable practices (18:9-13):** When you enter the land, do not copy the detestable practices of the nations before you. Let no one be found who sacrifices his son or daughter in the fire, who practices any kind of sorcery or witchcraft, or any of the other detestable practices for which the Lord is driving out these nations. You must be blameless before the Lord.

16. **God will raise up a prophet (18:14-22):** The nations around you listen to those who practice divination, but Jehovah will not permit you to do so. Instead, He will raise up a prophet from among your own brethren. He is the one you must hear. You asked that God never speak aloud to you again, so God will raise up a prophet, put His words into his mouth, and that prophet will tell you God's message. God will hold everyone responsible for heeding the message of the prophet.

    But any prophet who presumes to speak when the Lord has not given him a message, or one who speaks in the name of another god, must be put to death. If you are wondering whether the prophet is speaking the truth or not, see if his prophecy comes true. If it does not, then do not be afraid of him. He has spoken presumptuously.

*This passage is applied by the inspired writers of the New Testament to the Messiah (Acts 3:22), the prophet like unto Moses whom God would raise up. Jesus came as the ultimate prophet from God. He was like Moses in that He was a lawgiver and a mediator. But this passage also applies to all the other prophets who arose to speak to the people at the direct command of God. There were many such prophets through the years, and the people were to give heed to them just as surely as if God had been speaking that message aloud. This is the primary emphasis in the passage here, although it certainly applied to Jesus in its ultimate fulfillment.*

17. **Cities of refuge (19:1-13):** When you enter the land, set aside the cities of refuge that have been commanded for the one who kills his neighbor accidently. Build roads to the cities to make it convenient for the manslayer to reach, so that the avenger of blood will not overtake him and kill him. If the Lord increases your borders, then set aside three more cities.

    But if a man hates his neighbor and kills him deliberately, then the elders of his town are to send for him, and he is to be tried for murder. Show him no pity. You must purge the land of the guilt of shedding innocent blood.

18. **Boundary markers (19:14):** Do not move your neighbor's boundary stone that marks his inheritance.

19. **Witnesses (19:15-21):** Every accusation of crime must be proven by the mouth of two or three witnesses. One witness is never enough to convict a man.

    If the witness is proven to be false, then the accused man and the witness are to be brought before the priest. After careful investigation, if the witness is false, then do to him as he intended to do to the accused. You must purge the evil from among you. Show him no pity: life for life, eye for eye, tooth for tooth, hand for hand, foot for foot.

20. **Rules for going to war (20:1-20):** When you go to war against an army larger and stronger than yours, do not be afraid of them, for the Lord your God, who brought you up out of Egypt, will be with you. The priest shall address the army, saying, "You are going into battle today against your enemies, but do not fear them, for Jehovah is the one who goes with you to fight for you and to give you victory."

    If a soldier has built a new house, he is to go home, lest he die in battle and someone else gets to live in the house. If he has planted a vineyard, and has not yet begun to enjoy the fruit of it, let him go home. If a man is pledged to a woman, but has not married her, let him go home lest he die and someone else marries her. If anyone is afraid, let him go home, so that his brethren will not become frightened also.

    When you approach a city to fight against it, make an offer of peace. If they accept, then all the people inside shall be subject to forced labor for you. If they refuse and engage in battle, lay siege to the city. When the Lord delivers the city into your hands, kill all the men, but the women, children, livestock, and goods may be your plunder. This is how you are to treat all cities that are a distance away from you and do not belong to the nations nearby.

    But, in the cities of the nations Jehovah is giving you as an inheritance, do not leave alive anything that breathes. Completely destroy them — the Hittites, the Amorites, the Canaanites, the Perizzites, the Hivites, and the Jebusites. If you leave them, they will teach you to follow all their detestable things they do in worshiping their idols, and you will sin against Jehovah.

    When you lay siege to a city, do not destroy the fruit trees, because you can eat the fruit from them. However, you may cut trees you know are not fruit-bearing in order to build the siege works needed.

21. **An unsolved murder (21:1-9):** If a man is found murdered in a field, and the murderer is unknown, then the elders and judges from the nearby towns are to go out and measure to see which is the nearest to the body. Then the elders of that town are to take a heifer that has never been worked to a valley that has never been plowed, and there they are to break its neck. The priests are to step forward and pronounce a blessing, while the elders of the city wash their hands over the animal, and declare their innocence, and pray that God accept their atonement for the blood that has been shed. Thus you will purge yourselves from the guilt of shedding innocent blood, because you have done right in the eyes of the Lord.

22. **Marrying a captive woman (21:10-14):** When you take captives from a city you have defeated, and you see a beautiful woman among the captives, and want to marry her, you may take her for your wife. But before you do so, you must bring her to your home, shave her head, trim her nails, and put aside the clothes she was wearing when she was captured. She is to stay in your house and mourn for her parents a full month, and then you may take her for your wife. If you are not pleased with her, you must let her go free wherever she chooses. You may not sell her or treat her as a slave, because you have dishonored her.

23. **The right of the firstborn (21:15-17):** If a man has two wives, and he loves one more than the other, but his firstborn is the son of the lesser loved wife, that son is to receive the double portion of the inheritance *(the birthright)*. The father cannot choose to give it to the firstborn son of the beloved wife.

24. **A rebellious son (21:18-21):** A rebellious, disobedient son is to be stoned to death. You must purge the evil from among you. All Israel will hear and be afraid.

25. **Bury the criminal (21:22-23):** Do not leave the body of a criminal on a tree overnight. Bury it the same day, because anyone hung on a tree is under the curse of Jehovah. Do not desecrate the land God is giving you.

26. **Be considerate of your neighbor's possessions (22:1-4):** If you find an article or an animal that has been lost, return it to its owner. Do not ignore it. If you do not know the owner, take the item home with you until you can find the owner and return it to him. If you find your neighbor's animal fallen on the road, help it to its feet. Do not ignore it.

27. **Inappropriate conduct (22:5, 9, 10, 11):** A woman must not wear man's clothing, nor a man woman's clothing. Jehovah detests those who do so. Do not plant two kinds of seed in your vineyard, or both your crops and your vineyard will be defiled. Do not plow an ox and a donkey yoked together. Do not wear clothes of wool and linen woven together.

28. **Show consideration (22:6-8):** If you find a bird's nest, you may take the young, but you must not take the mother. Let it go free so that it may be well with you in the land. When you build a house, put a bannister around the roof so that you will not be responsible for someone falling from the roof and suffering an injury.

29. **Tassels (22:12):** Make tassels on the four corners of the cloak you are wearing.

30. **Accusation of unchastity (22:13-21):** If, when a man takes a wife, he charges that she is not a virgin, then take the matter before the elders of the city. The young woman's parents must bring forth the tokens of her virginity. If the charges of the husband are thus demonstrated to be untrue, then the husband must be chastised and fined a hundred shekels of silver to be given to the young woman's father. The husband who falsely accused his wife must never divorce his wife.

    On the other hand, if the accusation is true, then the young woman must be brought before the door of her father's house and stoned to death by the men of her city. In this way evil will be kept from your midst.

31. **Rules regarding adultery (22:22-30):** If a man is found in bed with a married woman, both of them are to be put to death. In this way evil will be expelled from your midst.

    If a man goes to bed with a betrothed maiden in the city, and they be found, both shall be brought to the gate of the city and stoned to death: the maiden because she did not cry out for help, and the man because he has been intimate with another man's wife.

    If, however, a man finds a betrothed maiden in the country, and he takes her by force, then the man shall be put to death, but nothing shall be done to the maiden, because she cried out, and there was none to save her. The crime of rape must be treated as if it were murder.

    If a man meets a young woman and he takes her, and goes to bed with her, and they be found, then he is to pay the woman's father fifty shekels of silver, and she will be his wife. He cannot divorce her as long as he lives.

    A man shall not take his father's wife, thus being intimate with one with whom his father has been intimate.

32. **Rules regarding who can be a part of the assembly of Israel (23:1-8):** One who has been mutilated sexually cannot be a part of the assembly of Israel. One of illegitimate birth cannot be a part of the assembly.

    Neither an Ammonite, nor a Moabite can be a part of the assembly, even to the tenth generation, because they did not meet you with bread and water when you came up out of Egypt, and because they hired Balaam the son of Beor to curse you, though God would not allow him to curse you. Never seek their peace or their prosperity.

    Do not abhor an Edomite, because he is your brother. Do not abhor an Egyptian, because you were a visitor in his land. Their descendants of the third generation may enter into the assembly of Jehovah.

33. **Cleanness in the camp (23:9-14):** Your army camps must be kept clean, because the Lord your God moves about in your camp to protect you and to deliver you from your enemies. Therefore your camp is to be clean so that He will not see anything indecent among you and turn away from you. So if a man has a nightly emission, he must go outside the camp and stay until evening, when he is to wash himself and return to his tent. Appoint a place outside the camp for the purpose of elimination. As part of the soldier's equipment, he is to have a paddle to dig a hole. Then after he has relieved himself, he is to cover the hole and return to camp.

34. **A runaway slave (23:15-16):** If a slave flees from his master and comes to you for refuge, do not return him to his master. He may live wherever he chooses. Do not oppress him.

35. **Temple prostitutes (23:17-18):** No Israelite man or woman is to serve as a temple prostitute *(as was the habit of the worshipers of the fertility gods)*. Neither shall you bring the earnings of a prostitute to the temple to pay a vow to Jehovah, because Jehovah detests both kinds of prostitution *(harlot or sodomite)*.

36. **Interest on loans (23:19-20):** Do not charge a fellow Israelite interest on a loan. You may charge a foreigner interest, but not an Israelite, so that God may bless you in everything you do in the land.

37. **Vows (23:21-23):** If you make a vow to the Lord, be prompt in paying it, for the Lord will demand payment, and you will be guilty of sin if you do not do so. It is not necessary to make vows, but if you do, you must do whatever your lips have vowed, because you made that vow of your own free will.

38. **Your rights in your neighbor's field (23:24-25):** If you are passing through your neighbor's vineyard, you may eat all the grapes you want, but you may not put any into a basket to carry away with you. If you are passing through your neighbor's grainfield, you may pick kernels with your hands and eat them, but you may not cut some for your use.

39. **Re-marrying a woman who is put away (24:1-4):** If a man marries a woman and then divorces her, and she marries again, the first husband may never take her back as his wife — even if the second husband has divorced her or has died. She is counted as defiled, and it would be detestable in the eyes of Jehovah for her husband to take her again. Do not bring sin upon the land the Lord is giving you for an inheritance.

40. **Exempt from war (24:5):** A man is exempt from war for one year after he marries, so that he may stay at home and bring happiness to his wife.

41. **Securities for loans (24:6, 10-13, 17-18):** Do not take millstones as security for a loan, because you would be taking away that man's livelihood. When you make a loan, do not go into the man's house to get what he is offering for a pledge. Let him choose the pledge to give you. If the man is poor, do not sleep with the pledge in your possession. Return his cloak by sunset so that he may sleep in it. Then he will thank you, and God will regard it as a righteous act on your part. Do not deprive the orphan or the stranger of justice. Do not take the cloak of a widow as a pledge. Remember that you were slaves in Egypt, and the Lord your God redeemed you from there. Therefore, God gives you these commandments to show justice and consideration to those in need.

42. **Kidnaping (24:7):** The one guilty of kidnaping must be put to death. Purge the evil from your land.

43. **Leprosy (24:8-9):** Be sure all rules concerning leprosy are followed exactly the way the priests or Levites instruct. Remember how God struck Miriam with leprosy as you made your way through the wilderness.

44. **A hired man (24:14-15):** Do not take advantage of a hired man who is poor, whether he is a fellow Israelite or a stranger. Pay his wages each day before sunset because he may need it. Otherwise he may cry to the Lord against you, and you would be counted as a sinner.

45. **The guilty one dies (24:16):** The father shall not be put to death for the son's crime, nor the child for his father's crime. Only the guilty one is to die.

46. **Leave the last for the poor (24:19-22):** When you harvest your crops, leave the last for the poor. Do not go back for a sheaf that was forgotten. Do not go back over your olive trees or your grape vines a second time. Leave the part that remains for the stranger, the widow, or the fatherless, so that Jehovah may bless you in all the works of your hands. Remember you were slaves in Egypt, so I command you to show kindness to the poor.

47. **Beating for the guilty (25:1-3):** If two men have a dispute, and take it to court, and the judge determines one man is guilty and should be beaten, then it is to be done immediately. The guilty man is to lie down, and he is to be beaten in the sight of the judge the number of lashes his crime deserves. But he must never be given more than forty lashes, lest he be degraded in your eyes.

48. **Ox (25:4):** Do not muzzle an ox while it is treading out the grain.

49. **Duty of a brother to a widow (25:5-10):** If a man dies without an heir, his widow must not marry outside the family. Her husband's brother is to take her as his wife, and fulfill the duty of a brother-in-law to her. The first son she bears will carry the name of the dead brother so that his name will not be blotted out from Israel.

    If a man will not marry his brother's wife, she is to go to the elders of the city and tell that he refuses to allow his brother's name to be carried on in Israel. The elders are to question the man, and if he still refuses to marry her, then his brother's widow is to go up to him in the presence of the elders, take off one of his sandals, spit in his face, and say, "This is what is done to the man who will not build up his brother's family line." From then on, that man's line will be known as "The Family of the Unsandaled."

50. **A woman who seizes the private parts of a man (25:11-12):** If two men are fighting, and the wife of one tries to rescue her husband by seizing the private parts of the other man, she is to have her hand cut off. Show her no pity.

51. **Accurate weights and measures (25:13-16):** Do not have differing weights or measures — one large and one small. You must have accurate and honest weights and measures in all your affairs, so that you may live long in the land Jehovah is giving you. For Jehovah hates the one who deals dishonestly.

52. **Remember the Amalekites (25:17-19):** Remember how the Amalekites attacked you soon after you came out of Egypt, when you were weary, and they showed no fear of Jehovah. When the Lord has given you rest from all your enemies in the land He is giving you, you shall blot out the memory of Amalek from under heaven. Do not forget.

53. **Firstfruits and tithes as thanksgiving offerings to God (26:1-15):** When you enter the land and have settled in it, take some of your firstfruits to the place where Jehovah puts His name. There before the priests, say, "I declare that I have indeed come to the land God promised to our forefathers. My father was a wandering Syrian and he went to Egypt with only a few people. But they lived there and became a great nation, powerful and numerous. The Egyptians mistreated us, putting us to hard labor, and we cried out to the Lord our God. He heard our prayers and came to our rescue. He brought us out of Egypt with a mighty hand and with great signs and wonders. He brought us into this land that is flowing with milk and honey. And now I bring of the firstfruits of the land that you, O Lord, have given me." Worship the Lord there with your firstfruits, and rejoice in all the good things Jehovah has given to you and to your family.

    In the third year when you have set aside your tithes for the Levites, the stranger, the fatherless, and the widow among you, then rejoice before the Lord. Say, "I have brought all the devoted things out of my house and have given them to the Levites and to the poor. I have not turned aside from your commandments, nor have I forgotten any of them. Please look down from heaven, your dwelling place, and bless your people Israel and the land you have given to us in fulfillment of the promise you made to our forefathers."

### Mutual vows between Jehovah and Israel (Deut. 26:16-19):

Moses said,

Today Jehovah lays upon you the responsibility to keep His commandments. You will therefore keep His commandments with all your heart. Today you have vowed that Jehovah will be your God, and that you will walk in His ways and keep His word. Likewise, Jehovah has vowed that you will be His special people, His treasured possession, as He promised you, so that you can keep His commandments, and so that He might raise you above all the nations He has made, in your praise, in name, and in honor. His plan is that you shall be a holy people unto the Lord your God.

## The Blessings and the Curses Are Set Before You

**(Deuteronomy 27:1-28:68)**

### The curses to be read at Mount Ebal and Mount Gerizim (Deut. 27:1-26):

Moses and the elders of Israel commanded the people to keep all the commandments of the Lord. Moses said, "When you pass over the Jordan, set up great stones and cover them with plaster and write upon them all the words of this law. Set up these stones on Mount Ebal. Build there an altar of unhewn stones and sacrifice peace offerings and eat them there and rejoice before the Lord."

Moses and the priests, the Levites, spoke to Israel, saying, "Be silent, and listen, O Israel. Today you have become the people of Jehovah your God. You must obey the voice of Jehovah and do His will."

Moses gave these instructions for the ceremonies that were to be held at Mount Ebal and Mount Gerizim when they set up the great stones:

These tribes stall stand upon Mount Gerizim to bless the people: Simeon, Levi, Judah, Issachar, Joseph, and Benjamin. And these tribes shall stand upon Mount Ebal for the curses: Reuben, Gad, Asher, Zebulun, Dan, and Naphtali. With all the people in place, the Levites shall say to all the men of Israel with a loud voice:

"Cursed be the man who makes an idol and sets it up in secret."
And all the people shall answer, "Amen."
"Cursed be he who fails to respect his father or his mother."
And all the people shall answer, "Amen."
"Cursed be the one who removes his neighbor's landmark."
And all the people shall say, "Amen."
"Cursed be the one who leads the blind off his path."
And all the people shall say, "Amen."
"Cursed be the one who robs the weak and defenseless of the justice which is due to them."
And all the people shall say, "Amen."

"Cursed be the one who lies with his father's wife."
And all the people shall say, "Amen."
"Cursed will be the one who lies with any kind of animal."
And all the people shall say, "Amen."
"Cursed be the one who lies with his sister or his step-sister."
And all the people shall say, "Amen."
"Cursed be the one who lies with his mother-in-law."
And all the people shall say, "Amen."
"Cursed be the one who strikes his neighbor in secret."
And all the people shall say, "Amen."
"Cursed be the one who takes a bribe to kill an innocent person."
And all the people shall say, "Amen."
"Cursed be the one who does not uphold all the words of this law to do them."
And all the people shall say, "Amen."

## The potential blessing — If you are faithful (Deut. 28:1-14):

After describing how the ceremonies were to be conducted on the mountains of Ebal and Gerizim, Moses continued talking to the people on the theme of the blessings and curses that lay before them. While they were still at Mount Sinai, he had told the earlier generation *(that is, God said through Moses)*, the group that was now dead, the same thing (Lev. 26). Here, he said:

"If you will diligently obey the Lord your God, being careful to do all His commandments which I command you this day:"

- God will set you high above all the nations of the earth.
- All these blessings will come upon you and overtake you:
  - You will be blessed in the city;
  - You will be blessed in the country.

- Blessed shall be:
  - The offspring of your body,
  - The produce of your ground,
  - The offspring of your beasts,
  - The increase of your herd,
  - And the young of your flock.
- Blessed shall be:
  - Your basket,
  - And your kneading bowl.
- Blessed shall you be:
  - When you come in,
  - And when you go out.

- Your enemies will be defeated:
  - They will come at you in one direction,
  - And flee before you in seven directions.

- The Lord will command the blessing upon you:
  - In your barns,
  - And in all that you put your hand to.
- He will bless you in the land which the Lord your God gives you.

- The Lord will establish you as a holy people to Himself, as He swore to you:
  - *If* you keep His commandments,
  - And walk in His ways.
- So all the peoples of the earth will see that you are called by the name of the Lord:
  - And they will be afraid of you.

- The Lord will make you abound:
  - In prosperity,
  - In the offspring of your body,
  - In the offspring of your cattle,
  - In the produce of your ground — in the land God is giving you.
- The Lord will open up His storehouse, the heavens:
  - To give rain to your land in its season,
  - To bless the work of your hand.
- You shall lend to many nations,
  - But you shall borrow from none.
- The Lord shall make you the head, not the tail.
  - You will be above, not underneath.

- All of these blessings will come upon you *if:*
  - You will listen to the commandments of the Lord which I charge you today, to obey them carefully.
  - Do not turn aside from any of the words which I command you — to the right or to the left.
  - Do not go after other gods to serve them.

## The potential curses — If you disobey (Deut. 28:15-68):

"But if, in the passing of time, you refuse to listen to Jehovah, then all these curses will come upon you and overtake you."

- You will be cursed:
  - In the city, or in the country;
  - When you come in, when you go out.
- Cursed shall be:
  - Your basket and your kneading trough.
  - The offspring of your body,
  - The produce of your ground,
  - The increase of your herd,
  - The young of your flocks.

- The Lord will send:
  - Curses, confusion, and rebuke in all you do,

    - Until you are destroyed, and you perish quickly,
  - Because of your evil deeds,
    - Because you have forsaken God.
- The Lord will cause:
  - Pestilence to cling to you until He has consumed you from the land.
  - Consumption, fever, inflamation, fiery heat, drought, blight, and mildew to come upon you until you perish.
- The heavens above you shall be as bronze;
  - The earth beneath you as iron.
- The rains shall be as powder and dust — until you are destroyed.

- You will be defeated before your enemies:
  - You will go out one way against them,
    - But you will flee from them seven ways.
  - You will be an example of terror to all the kingdoms of the earth.
  - Your carcasses will be food to all the birds and to all the beasts,
    - And there will be no one to frighten them away.

- The Lord will smite you with:
  - Madness, blindness, and bewilderment.
  - You will grope at noon, as a blind man gropes in darkness.
- You shall not prosper:
  - You will be oppressed and robbed — with none to save you.
  - Your shall betroth a wife — but another shall take her.
  - You will build a house — but you will not live in it.
  - You will plant a vineyard — but you will never eat its fruit.
  - Your ox will be slaughtered before your eyes — but you will not eat of it.
  - Your donkey will be taken from you — and never returned.
  - Your sheep will be given to your enemy — and none will save you.
  - Your sons and daughters will be taken captive,
    - You will yearn for them — but there will be nothing you can do.
  - A people you do not know will eat your crops,
    - While you are only oppressed and crushed continually.
  - You will be driven mad by what you see.
  - The Lord will cover you with boils that cannot be healed.

- The Lord will bring you and your king whom you will set over you:
  - To a nation which you nor your fathers have known.
  - There you will serve other gods, made of wood and stone.
  - You shall become a horror, a proverb, and a taunt among all the people where the Lord will drive you.

- You will fail:
  - You will plant much seed, but will harvest little,
    - For the locust will consume it.

- You will plant vineyards, but you will not drink its wine,
  - For the worm will eat the grapes.
- You will have olive trees all over your land, but you will not anoint yourself with oil,
  - For the olives will fall off the trees.
- You will have children, but they will not be yours,
  - For they will go into captivity.
- The insect will possess the increase from your trees and from your ground.

- The alien among you will rise higher and higher,
  - While you sink lower and lower.
  - He will lend to you, but you will not lend to him.
  - He will be the head, you the tail.

- So all these curses will come upon you, will pursue you, and overtake you until you are destroyed:
  - Because you would not obey the Lord your God by keeping His commandments.
- The curses will become a sign and a wonder on you and your descendants forever.
  - Because you did not serve the Lord your God with joy and a glad heart *(no gratitude)*,
    - For the abundance of the blessings you had.
  - Therefore, you shall serve your enemies:
    - In hunger, in thirst, in nakedness, and in the lack of all things.
    - God will put an iron yoke on your neck until He has destroyed you.

- The Lord will bring a nation of fierce countenance from the end of the earth, like an eagle swooping down:
  - A nation whose language you do not understand.
  - One that will have no respect for old or young.
- That nation shall:
  - Eat your animals and your produce from the ground, until you are destroyed.
  - Leave you no grain, new wine, oil, cattle, or flocks until you perish.
  - Besiege you in all your cities until your high, fortified walls fall.
    - In the siege:
      - You will eat the offspring of your own body — your sons and daughters.
      - The refined man will be hostile to his family so that he will not share any of the flesh of his children which he is eating.
      - The delicate woman among you, the one who would not soil her foot, shall be hostile to her family and will not share even the afterbirth from her newborn baby.
        - She will eat it in secret, because she has nothing else to eat.

- If you are not careful to observe all the words of this law which are written in this book:
  - If you do not reverence this honored and awesome name:
    - Then the Lord will bring extraordinary plagues upon you and your descendants,
      - Severe, miserable, chronic plagues that cannot be healed.
    - He will bring back all the diseases of Egypt which you feared, and they will cling to you.
    - He will bring upon you new sicknesses and diseases,
      - Until you are destroyed.

- Then you will be left few in number,
  - Whereas you were as the stars of the heavens,
    - Because you did not obey the Lord your God.
- Just as the Lord has delighted over you to prosper you and multiply you,
  - So He will delight over you to make you perish and to destroy you.

- You will be torn from the land where you entering to possess it.
  - The Lord will scatter you among all peoples,
    - From one end of the earth to the other.
    - There you will serve other gods.
  - Among those nations:
    - You will find no rest,
      - There will be no resting place for the sole of your foot.
    - The Lord will give you:
      - A trembling heart, failing eyes, despair of soul.
    - You life will hang in doubt:
      - In the morning you will say, "Would that it were evening!"
      - At evening you will say, "Would that it were morning!"
        - Because of the dread and horror of what you see.
- The Lord will bring you back to Egypt *(bondage)*,
  - The place where you hope never to see again.
  - There you will offer yourself for sale as a slave,
    - But no one will buy you.

*What a chilling picture! And how sad it is to know that it was the curses that eventually came upon the Israelites when they turned their backs upon God. Take time to look closely at the curses described in Deuteronomy 28 and tie it with Leviticus 26 in your mind. As you continue studying the history of Israel, remember that every blessing they received, and every punishment that ever came upon them was predicted. It all depended upon the choices they made about whether they would obey Jehovah. The blessings and curses that are set before us in the new covenant of today are spiritual ones, but they exist just as surely as these predictions existed. They will come to pass just as surely — based upon the choices we make. Let us learn the lessons.*

## A Covenant Is Made on the Plains of Moab
### (Deuteronomy 29:1-30:20)

These are the words of the covenant which Jehovah commanded Moses to make with the children of Israel in the plains of Moab, besides the covenant which He made with them in Horeb.

*This is a renewal of the covenant that Jehovah will be their God and they His chosen people, but notice that it is more specific than the one made at Sinai. This one deals primarily with their keeping the land. If they are faithful, they may keep the land; but if they are unfaithful, they will surely be driven out of it.*

## Moses' Speeches

Moses called the people together and said:

You have seen all that Jehovah did in your sight in the land of Egypt — to Pharaoh and to his servants, all those great signs and wonders — but you still do not understand and apply the lessons you should have learned. The Lord says, "I have led you for forty years in the wilderness. Your clothes have not grown old, nor have your shoes worn out. You have not eaten bread, neither have you drunk wine or strong drink, so that by your dependence upon me you might know that I am Jehovah your God."

When we came into this area, Sihon the king of Heshbon and Og the king of Bashan came out to fight against us, but we defeated them and took their land. We gave that land to Reuben, Gad, and to half of the tribe of Manasseh for an inheritance. Keep, therefore, the words of this agreement and do them, so that you may prosper the same way in all that you do.

All of you stand before Jehovah to enter into this agreement *(this covenant)*: your leaders, your children, your wives, the sojourners among you, even your servants and slaves. God's purpose is to establish you today as His people, so that He may be your God as He swore to our fathers: Abraham, Isaac, and Jacob.

I do not make this covenant just with those who are here today, but with those who will live in days to come. You have seen the abominations, the idols, of the Egyptians and of the nations we have encountered. We do not want this covenant between Israel and Jehovah to last for only one generation. Therefore, beware lest there be a man or woman, a family or tribe, among you who will say that, in spite of the curse that God has placed upon idolatry, "I can get away with my sin." Jehovah will never pardon him; His anger will burn against that one, and every curse that is written in this book will rest upon him. God will blot out his name from beneath the heavens.

When the generations to come — your descendants, and even foreigners who come from distant lands — see that the whole land is brimstone and salt, and parched so that nothing grows on it, not even grass, they will say, "Why has Jehovah done such a thing to this land?"

Then men will answer, "Because they turned their backs on Jehovah their God and they forsook the covenant they made with Him. They served other gods and worshiped them. So the anger of Lord burned against the land, and He brought upon it every curse which is written in this book. Jehovah uprooted them from the land in anger, in great wrath, and He threw them into another land, as it is this day." The secret things belong to Jehovah our God, but the things that are revealed belong to us and to our children forever, so that we may keep all the words of this law.

In days to come, when all these things have come to pass, both the blessings and the curses, and you remember them among all the nations where Jehovah your God has driven you, if you return to Him and will obey His voice with all your heart, then no matter where you are — even to the ends of the earth — Jehovah will gather you together and will bring you back to the land of your ancestors. He will bless you and He will circumcise your hearts so that you will love the Lord your God with all your heart and with all your soul, in order that you may live. Then He will inflict all these curses upon your enemies who hated you, and who persecuted you.

When you obey the Lord, He will bless you once again in whatever work you do. Your families will be fruitful, and so will your livestock and your crops. For the Lord will rejoice again over you for good, just as He rejoiced over your fathers — if you obey the Lord your God to keep His commandments and His statutes which are written in the book of the law, if you turn to the Lord with all your heart and soul.

## You Shall Be My People

The commandment which I lay upon you is not too hard for you, neither is it beyond you. It is not in heaven so that you need to say, "Who will go to heaven and get this commandment and bring it back and tell us so that we may do it?" Neither is it beyond the sea so that someone has to ask, "Who will go over the sea and get this commandment and bring it back and tell us so that we may do it?" The message has been given to us; it is planted in our hearts and in our minds, that we may be able to obey it.

See, I have set before you today the choice of life and good things, or of death and calamity. I have told you to obey the Lord so that you might live and enjoy blessings. But, on the other hand, if you turn away from God, and you will not listen any longer, and turn after other gods, then you will perish. You will not prolong your stay in this land.

I call heaven and earth as witnesses against you this day, that I have set before you life and death, the blessing and the curse. Therefore, choose life for yourself and for your children after you. Choose to love Jehovah, to obey His voice, and to cling closely to Him — for He is your life and the secret to long life.

*Never have any doubt about whether God was just in punishing Israel. It was their choice. He warned them over and over about what would happen if they chose evil. And it came to pass just as He said.*

*As people travel to the lands of the Bible days, many wonder why the land looks so desolate today. They wonder why it was ever called "a land flowing with milk and honey." The answer is plainly given in Deuteronomy 29:22-29. It is because the people did not heed God's word, and He cursed the land. It is no secret: God foresaw the question, and He plainly revealed the answer; it is for us and for our children to know that answer. If you hear someone wondering why, direct them to this passage. If we do not know why the land is barren, we are proclaiming our ignorance of this passage and many more like it.*

*There is one more point we must understand in our day. God predicted the captivity of the people, and He promised that they would be allowed to return to the land if they returned to Him. He promised them blessings upon their return if they would only serve Him. Know that the people did go into captivity —part of them into Assyrian captivity and part of them into Babylonian captivity. But know just as assuredly that God kept the next part of His promise also. Seventy years after the first captives were taken to Babylon, the first group of them returned to Jerusalem —just as God had promised. A second group returned under the leadership of Ezra. Nehemiah came and led the people in rebuilding their walls and their city of Jerusalem. God was with the returned group, but He was not able to bless them the way He would have liked to bless, because they were negligent in their service to Him, just as they had been in all the preceding generations. Look into the books of Ezra, Nehemiah, Haggai, Zechariah, and Malachi to see the condition of the people of that day. God's blessings have always been conditional upon the faithfulness of the people.*

*There is nothing in this prediction of a return —or in any other prediction of a return —that gives hope for the Jews today. God made His promises in the long ago — and then He kept His promises at the appropriate times. The people were the ones who failed to take advantage of the promises. There are no promises left for the Jews as a nation. Only as an individual Jew accepts the new covenant, and turns to God for forgiveness of his sins, can he be saved. He has the same opportunity that every other person on earth has —but there is nothing for him to hope for as a separate nation of people.*

# God Predicts Israel's Rebellion
## (Deuteronomy 31:1-32:47)

### Joshua is officially commissioned as Moses' successor (Deut. 31:1-29):

Moses spoke to Israel again, saying: "I am a hundred and twenty years old, and I can not continue my activities much longer because Jehovah has told me I can not cross over Jordan. Jehovah will go with you and He will destroy all the nations before you. Joshua is to go before you as your leader, as the Lord has spoken. Be strong and courageous because God will deliver your enemies into your hands just as He delivered the kings, Sihon and Og."

Moses called Joshua to him and, before all the nation of Israel, he said, "Be strong and courageous, because you will go into the land which Jehovah has sworn to our ancestors to give us. You will cause the people to inherit it. Jehovah Himself will go before you. He will be with you, and He will not let you down. Do not be afraid, and do not worry."

Moses wrote the law and gave it to the priests to keep. He commanded, "At the end of every seven years, in the appointed time for the release of debts (see Deut. 15:1-2), at the Feast of Tabernacles (see Lev. 23:34; Deut. 16:13), when all Israel comes to appear before Jehovah at the place where He has chosen, you shall read this law in the hearing of all the Israelites. Assemble men, women, children, and all who live among you, so that they may hear and learn what Jehovah would have them to do. Their children, who have not heard this law, must know the law and be able to obey it as long as you live in the land you are about to conquer."

Jehovah spoke to Moses, saying, "The time of your death is near. Call Joshua, and the two of you present yourselves before the tent of meeting so that I may give him a charge."

When Moses and Joshua arrived at the tent of meeting, the Lord appeared in a pillar of cloud that stood over the entrance, and He said to Moses:

> You will now sleep with your fathers, and this people will act as a prostitute seeking after strange gods, and they will forsake me and will break the agreement we have. Then my anger will be kindled against them, and I will abandon them and will hide myself from them.
>
> Therefore, write this song and teach it to the children of Israel. Put it on their tongues so that the song will be a witness for me against them. In this way, when they have everything as they wish, and grow fat, and forsake me, and suffer many calamities, this song will testify for me, because it will not be forgotten by their descendants.

Then Jehovah said to Joshua, "Be strong and courageous because you will bring the children of Israel into the land I have sworn to give them, and I will be with you."

When Moses finished writing the words of the law, he commanded the Levites, saying, "Take this book of the law and put it by the side of the ark of the covenant of Jehovah your God, so that it may be a witness against you. I am familiar with your rebellion. You have been rebellious while I have lived, why should I think you will behave better when I am dead? Gather all the elders of the tribes and your officers to me so that I can tell them these words and call heaven and earth to witness against them. I know that after I am dead, you will become completely rotten, and will turn aside from the way I have commanded you, and calamity will fall upon you."

*What a sad picture! Even after all the warnings they have been given, the Lord knows the people will be unfaithful to Him. Oh, if only they had heeded the warnings and had remained faithful, how different the story could have been! In the same way: Oh, that we today could learn the lessons from their mistakes and remain faithful to the Lord — how blessed we would be!*

## Moses teaches Israel the song of Jehovah (Deut. 31:22, 30; 32:1-47):

Moses wrote the song as Jehovah had commanded and taught it to the children of Israel. The thought of the song was:

Listen, O heavens, to my words, and let the earth hear what I say.
For I will proclaim the reputation of Jehovah;
I will tell you what is so great about our God.
The Rock is perfect in what He does.
He is utterly dependable and never does evil.
His people have dealt corruptly with Him;
They are a perverse and crooked generation.

O foolish people, do you thus repay Jehovah for all His blessings?
Consider the days gone by: ask your father, your elders, and they will tell you:
From among the nations Jehovah chose Israel for His people.
Jacob is His inheritance.
He found him in the wind-swept desert.
He nestled him in His arms, and tenderly cared for him as the eagle hovers over her young.
He spread His wings and carried him on His back.
There was no foreign god with Him.
He made him to suck honey from the rock, butter of the herd, milk of the flock,
with fat of lambs, with the finest of the wheat, and with wine.

But Jeshurun *(a term of endearment: "dear righteous one")* grew fat and sleek,
Then he forsook the God who made him,
He scorned the Rock of his salvation.
They made Him jealous with strange gods.
They sacrificed to demons who were not God,
New gods whom they had not known.
You neglected the Rock who begot you, the God who gave you birth.

Jehovah saw the behavior of His people and abhorred them.
He said:
I will hide my face from them; I will see what becomes of them.
They have moved me to jealousy with that which is no god.
I will provoke them to jealousy with those who are no people.
My anger has been kindled.
It is a raging fire that burns up the earth and sets on fire the foundation of the mountains.
I will heap calamities upon them.
They will waste away with hunger and will die from the teeth of beasts
and from the poison of things that crawl in the dust.

## Moses' Speeches

I said I would scatter them afar.
I would erase their presence from the memory of men if I did not fear the taunts of the enemy,
lest they say, "Our hand is invincible; Jehovah has not done it."

They are a nation with no sense.
Oh that they were wise and understood!
If only they would consider where their course will take them!

Israel would have continued to put their enemies to flight if their Rock had not sold them.
The rock of other peoples is not as our Rock.
Their grapes are grapes of gall.
Their wine is the poison of serpents.

The Lord says:
Vengeance belongs to me. I will repay.
When their foot slips, and the day of their calamity comes, Jehovah will judge His people.
When their power is gone, He will say,
"Where are your gods, the ones you depended upon, the ones to whom you sacrificed?
Let them get up and help you."
See now that I, even I, am He. There is no god with me.
I kill, and I make alive. I wound, and I heal.
None can escape from my hand.
I lift up my hand and say,
"As I live forever, if I sharpen my flashing sword, and unleash my judgments,
I will render vengeance to my enemies.
I will make my arrows drunk with blood,
My sword will devour the flesh of my enemies."

Rejoice, O you nations, with His people.
For He will avenge the blood of His servants,
He will see that the debt is paid for His land and for His people.

So Moses taught the words of this song to all the people, along with Joshua *(alternate spelling, Hoshea)* the son of Nun. When he finished, he said: "Take seriously the words which I have told you today. Be sure to tell your children to do these things as well, to do all the words of this law. It is no trifling matter that I speak of. Your life depends upon it. By this means your days will be prolonged in the land which you are about to take."

# Moses Blesses the Tribes
## (Deuteronomy 32:48-33:29)

### "Go up to this mountain, Moses" (Deut. 32:48-52):

Jehovah spoke to Moses that very day, saying, "Go up into this mountain of Abarim, to Mount Nebo, which is in the land of Moab across from Jericho. View the land of Canaan which I am giving to the children of Israel for a possession. There you will die in the mountain, as Aaron your brother died in Mount Hor. You will see the land, but you will not go into it because you transgressed against me and did not honor me in the midst of the children of Israel at the waters of Meribah at Kadesh in the wilderness of Zin."

### The blessing Moses gave to the tribes (Deut. 33:1-29):

*One more thing is recorded between this final command to climb the mountain and Moses' death. It is the blessing which he gave to each tribe —reminding us of the blessings that Jacob gave to his sons as he prepared to die (Gen. 49). These words of Moses are spoken on the day of his death.*

*Notice that often the twelve tribes are listed the same as the twelve sons of Jacob. The sons were the ancestral fathers of the tribes. Never is there a list of thirteen tribes; if the names of Levi and Joseph are included, then the names of Ephraim and Manasseh are omitted.*

First comes a general blessing to the whole multitude. It is the blessing with which Moses, the man of God, blessed the children of Israel one last time before his death:

Jehovah came from Sinai,
His glory rose from Mount Seir
and shone forth from Mount Paran.
He came from the myriads of His holy ones.
At His right hand was a bolt of lightning.
Surely He loves the nations,
and all the angels are in His hand.
They sit at His feet. They rise up at His words.
Moses appointed us a law,
a possession for the congregation of Jacob.
And He *(Jehovah)* became king in Jeshurun *(the "dear upright one," that is, Israel).*
There the tribes of Israel gathered together.

Then Moses turned to the individual tribes and blessed each in turn, describing particular characteristics or particular blessings each would have, just as Jacob had done.

**To Reuben (33:6):** "Let Reuben live and let his men not be few."

**To Judah (33:7):** "Hear, Jehovah, the cry of Judah, and bring him back to his people *(as from victorious battle)*. With His hands, He fights for Judah. O, be His help against his adversaries."

*Judah would be the leader of the other tribes and would go before them into battle (Judg. 1:1-2). It was also the first tribe to move out when the camp moved (Num. 2:9).*

## Moses' Speeches

**To Levi (33:8-11):** "Your Thummin and your Urim are with your godly man whom you proved at Massah, with whom you strove at the waters of strife, with the man who said of his father, and of his mother, 'I have not considered him,' neither did he pay any attention to his brethren or even to his own children. They observed your word and kept your covenant. They will teach Israel your laws, and will offer incense before you, and whole burnt offerings upon your altar.

"O Jehovah, bless his strength, and accept his work. Strike those who rise up and hate him so that they cannot get up any more."

*Generally Levi had proven to be a tribe faithful to the Lord. The reference in verse 9 seems to be to the activities of the Levites who came to Moses' side at the time of the golden calf, and killed the wicked ones, regardless what their personal relationship with them might be (Exod. 32:25-29).*

**To Benjamin (33:12):** "The beloved of Jehovah will dwell in safety by Him. He shields him all day long, and Benjamin dwells upon His back."

**To Joseph (33:13-17):** "Let the Lord bless his land. Let him enjoy the precious things of heaven and earth, the precious things of the mountains, and the good will of the One who dwelt in the bush *(the burning bush - Exod. 3:2)*. Let the blessing come upon the one who was elevated among his brothers. His dignity is that of the firstling of the herd. His horns are like the horns of the wild buffalo; with them he will gore the nations to the end of the earth. They are the ten thousands of Ephraim and the thousands of Manasseh."

**To Zebulun and Issachar (33:18-19):** "Rejoice, Zebulun, in your activities, and Issachar, in your tents. They will call the peoples to the mountain. There they will offer sacrifices of righteousness. They will suck the abundance of the seas and the hidden treasures of the sand."

**To Gad (33:20-21):** "Blessed is the One who has given Gad the opportunity to expand his territory, in keeping with his war-like nature. He chose the lions' share for himself. He came to the leaders of the people. He executed the righteousness of Jehovah and upheld His ordinances with Israel."

*From the days of Jacob (Gen. 49:19), Gad's war-like nature was prophesied. Gad received the bulk of the land of Gilead and he was more able to preserve his inheritance from the desert tribes than Reuben or the half-tribe of Manasseh were. Probably the reference to their upholding the righteousness of Jehovah refers to their promising to cross Jordan and help their brethren win their inheritance (Num. 32:16-19).*

**To Dan (33:22):** "Dan is a young lion, leaping out of Bashan."

**To Naphtali (33:23):** "O, Naphtali, satisfied with favor, and full of the blessing of Jehovah, possess the sea and the south."

**To Asher (33:24-25):** "Let Asher be blessed above the sons; let him be favored among his brethren. Let him dip his foot in oil. Let him dwell in strength securely."

Then Moses turned back to a general expression in praise of God, saying:

There is no one like Jehovah, O Jeshurun *(dear righteous one)*,

who rides upon the heavens to help you.
The eternal God is your dwelling place,
His everlasting arms are beneath you.
He threw out the enemy before you, and said, "Destroy."
So Israel will dwell in safety in a land of grain and new wine.

Best wishes *(blessed)* to you, O Israel.
Who is like you, a people saved by Jehovah?
He is your shield of defense, the sword of your excellence.
Your enemies will bow down before you,
You will ride upon their heights.

# Moses' Death
## (Deuteronomy 34:1-12)

### Death of Moses (Deut. 34:1-8):

Moses climbed from the plains of Moab up into Mount Nebo, to the top of Pisgah, which is opposite Jericho. Jehovah showed him all the land of Gilead as far as Dan *(probably a Dan in northern Gilead, not the later Laish/Dan).* He showed him Naphtali and Ephraim, and Manasseh, and all Judah stretching to the western sea (*the Mediterranean).* That is, God showed Moses the land that these tribes would inherit, the land of Gilead and Canaan, the land on the east and west sides of the Jordan.

Jehovah said, "This is the land I swore to give to the descendants of Abraham, Isaac, and Jacob. I have let you see it, but you will not go into it."

So Moses, the servant of Jehovah, died there in the land of Moab as Jehovah had said. And Jehovah buried him near Beth-peor, but no man knows where his sepulcher is. Moses was a hundred and twenty years old when he died. He still had good eyesight, and his natural vigor was unabated.

The children of Israel wept for Moses in the plains of Moab for thirty days.

### Epilogue (Deut. 34:9-12):

Joshua was filled with the Spirit of wisdom because Moses had laid his hands upon him, and the children of Israel listened to Joshua, and did as Jehovah commanded Moses.

There has not since arisen a prophet in Israel like Moses, whom Jehovah knew face to face. No one has done the signs and wonders which Jehovah sent him to do in the land of Egypt. No one since has exercised the mighty hand and done the awesome things which Moses did in the eyes of Israel.

*After so long a time of studying intimately the life of this great man, we weep with Israel as we see him make his way up the slopes of Mount Nebo. We watch him as he stands on Mount Nebo, looking up and down the promised land. Oh, the torrent of thoughts that must have rushed through his mind! Oh, the emotions that must have boiled within his heart as he stood surveying the land which would be Israel!*

*Moses was one of the spiritual giants of the Bible. Of Enoch it is said that, "He walked with God, and he was not, for God took him" (Gen. 5:24). Of Elijah it is said that he was taken up in a whirlwind (2 Kings*

*2:11). Moses was not taken to heaven without dying as those men were, but he was set apart in his death by a special act of God: God buried Moses' body.*

*It is obvious that the last chapter was added by someone other than Moses. It is very significant that the comment was made in 34:10 that there has not arisen another prophet like Moses. There was not one in all the Old Testament that could be compared to Moses — a prophet, a mediator, and a law-giver. Yet Moses himself had said, "The Lord thy God will raise up for you a prophet from your midst, of your brethren, like me; to Him you will hearken in all things" (Deut. 18:15). Not until the Lord Jesus Christ did that prophet arise.*

*One very important lesson we should learn from the story of Moses: that is, when a man is offered great opportunities as Moses was offered, then God places a very great responsibility upon him. He expects that one to be very strong. We have never walked up a mountain to commune with Jehovah, and we have never been put into a similar position to Moses' position as mediator between God and a people — but we in America are so very blessed. We have opportunities on every hand to study and learn God's word. Will God not hold us responsible for using those opportunities and growing thereby?*

# *Journey's End*
## *(Joshua 1:1-5:12)*

*Though we enter a new book of the Bible, the thought continues without interruption. The forty years were not quite over when Moses died, so we include the first few chapters of Joshua in this material in order to complete the story of the wandering in the wilderness. The book of Joshua begins after the death of Moses, just prior to Israel's preparations to cross the Jordan. As the book opens, it is only a few days before the children of Israel cross the Jordan to receive the land promised to their fathers.*



## Crossing the Jordan
### (Joshua 1:1-4:24)

### Joshua takes the reins of leadership (Josh. 1:1-9):

Joshua had been appointed and presented to the people as the new leader before Moses died. Now it is time for his work to begin. So after the death of Moses, God said to Joshua:

> My servant Moses is dead. Arise, therefore, and cross over the Jordan. Everywhere you walk in the land will be yours, just as I promised through Moses, from the Negev in the south to Lebanon in the north, from the great river Euphrates even to the Great Sea to the west, these will be your borders.
>
> No one will be able to stand against you as long as you live. As I was with Moses, so I will be with you. Be courageous and do not be afraid, because you will lead the people to inherit this land. The one requirement is that you must be very careful to do everything the law says. Do not turn from it to the right or to the left. You must let your words and your actions be continually guided by what is written in the law, because then your way will be prosperous, then you will succeed.
>
> Have I not commanded you? Be strong and courageous! Do not tremble nor be dismayed, for the Lord your God is with you wherever you go.

## Preparations for crossing the Jordan (Josh. 1:10-18):

Joshua moved promptly to prepare to cross the river. He told the officers to go through the camp and tell the people to prepare provisions because in three days they would pass over the Jordan.

Joshua reminded the tribes who already had their inheritance on the eastern side of the Jordan of the commitment they had made to cross the river and help their brethren take the land: "Remember what Moses, God's servant, commanded you when he said that Jehovah will give you rest, and will give you this land. The understanding was that your families and possessions would remain here on the east side of Jordan, but that your armed men would cross over and help your brethren take the land of Canaan. Afterward you can return to your own land."

The armed warriors of Reuben, Gad, and half the tribe of Manasseh answered: "We have agreed to all that you have said and we will do it. Just as we obeyed Moses in all things, we will obey you, and wherever you send us we will go, and we trust that Jehovah your God will be with you as He was with Moses. Whoever rebels against your word shall be put to death. Only be strong and courageous."

***Chronology note:*** *There is a slight chronology problem here:*

- *They are still encamped at Shittim on the plains of Moab in 1:1 when Joshua says they will be crossing the Jordan in three days.*
    - *In 3:1-2 they move from Shittim to the Jordan's edge where they wait, and after three days the officers go through the camp with instructions for the crossing.*
    - *In chapter 2 we have the story of the spies' visit to Jericho and the three days they stayed in the mountains before returning across the Jordan.*
    - *How do all these periods of three days fit together?*

*There is more than one possible explanation:*

- *The simplest explanation is that the three days the spies were gone were actually before Joshua's statement that in three days the crossing would take place.*
    - *The Hebrew language had no special past perfect tense; the simple past tense often served in that capacity. Therefore chapter two could be perfectly well translated: "Now Joshua the son of Nun had sent two men as spies...," that is, before 1:10-11.*
    - *We know that the crossing was completed on the tenth of the month (4:19). Therefore this explanation is that the spies were sent on the third of Nisan. They returned on the sixth, and Joshua's orders were given on the seventh. The children of Israel moved down to the river's edge in about one day. They waited two more days. With the three days of 1:11 now passed, the officers pass throughout the camp giving their immediate instructions about following the priests bearing the ark*
- *The other explanation is that the three days the spies were gone were the same three days mentioned in 1:11. This explanation is not as likely, however, for it would have required Joshua to foretell what would happen to the spies, and there is no evidence that he did.*

## Two spies to Jericho (Josh. 2:1-24):

Joshua chose two men and sent them secretly across the Jordan, telling them, "Go, view the land, especially Jericho."

Crossing the river, the spies made their way to Jericho. They went to the house of a harlot named Rahab, intending to spend the night there. In spite of the efforts of the spies to avoid notice, their presence became known, and word came to the king of Jericho: "Men have come into the city tonight from the Israelites to spy out the area."

The king sent soldiers to Rahab's house. "Bring out those men who have come to your house," they said, "because they are spies."

Now Rahab had hidden the men on the roof under some stalks of flax which had been spread out to dry. She said to the soldiers, "Yes, the men did come here, but I did not know where they were from. And about dark, when the gate is shut, they got up and went out, but I don't know where they went. Perhaps if you hurry you can overtake them." The king's men hurried away on the trail of the spies, thinking that they were headed for the Jordan. As soon as the soldiers were out of the city, the gates were shut, in an effort to trap the spies if they were still inside the city.

Rahab went to the spies who were hiding under the flax, and she said, "I know that the Lord has given you this land. Everyone is afraid of you, because all of us have heard how the Lord dried up the waters of the Red Sea when you left Egypt, and how you defeated Sihon and Og and completely annihilated them. As soon as we heard, there was no courage left in any of us because Jehovah your God is God in heaven above and in the earth beneath. And now I beg of you, swear to me by the Lord above: since I have been kind to you, please be kind to me. Swear that you will save the lives of my father, my mother, my brothers, and my sisters, and all that they have. Give me some token that you will do so."

The spies replied, "Our life for yours: if you do not tell anyone what we are doing, then we will show mercy to you and to your family."

Rahab set out to deliver the men. The gates of Jericho were shut, but that was no obstacle because Rahab's house was built on the wall of the city. She let the spies down the outside of the wall, through a window of her house that overlooked the wall. "Go to the mountain so the king's men will not find you. Hide there for three days, and then return to your people," she said.

As the spies were leaving, they told Rahab: "We want to be sure we can keep the oath we have sworn. When we come to take the city, tie this line of scarlet cord, by which you are letting us down, in your window. Gather into your house your father and mother, your brothers, and all your father's family. If anyone goes out of the house, then he will be responsible for his own death. If no one goes from your house, and we harm someone, we will bear the blame for it. If you tell anyone about this business, then we will not be bound by our oath."

Rahab agreed to the spies' conditions and urged them to depart. They fled to the mountains where they waited for three days. The king's men searched for the spies all over the plain of the Jordan, but could not find them.

Finally the spies returned to Joshua and told him everything that had happened to them. They said, "Truly Jehovah has delivered the land into our hands. All the inhabitants of the land melt before us."

*The Hebrew text indicates that Joshua gave the spies their instructions and sent them out secretly. Various estimates place Jericho two to three hours' walk from the Jordan. The danger the spies faced was that they would be quickly recognized as strangers, and surely the city would be quick to suspect that they were spies. By going to the house of a harlot, they hoped to allay the suspicions of the people of the city.*

*Rahab was not a "kadeshah," a prostitute who practiced fornication as an act of worship, but a "zonah," a harlot. Some have affirmed that Rahab was only an innkeeper, but zonah means a harlot (cf. James 2:25).*

## Israel crosses the Jordan (Josh. 3:1-17):

Early the next morning, Joshua rose up and moved his people from Shittim, down the slope, closer to the Jordan, where they waited to cross the river.

At the end of the three days, the officers went through the camp to give the people their instructions: "When you see the ark of the covenant carried before you by the Levitical priests, get up and follow after, but stay back 3,000 feet. Don't come any nearer because you do not know which way to go since you have never been this way before."

Joshua told the people, "Consecrate yourselves, for tomorrow the Lord will do wonders among you."

Joshua gave the priests their instruction: "Take up the ark of the covenant and pass over before the people." The priests picked up the ark of the covenant and led the way.

Jehovah said to Joshua, "Today I will begin to exalt you in the sight of all Israel, so that they will know that just as I have been with Moses, I will be with you. Therefore, command the priests who carry the ark: 'When you get to the brink of the waters of the Jordan, stand still in the river.'"

Joshua addressed the people, saying: "Come here and listen to the word of God. Hereby you will know that the living God is among you, and that, without fail, He will drive out from before you the Canaanite, the Hittite, the Hivite, the Perizzite, the Girgashite, the Amorite, and the Jebusite. Behold, you see the ark of the covenant is passing before you into the Jordan. Therefore choose a man from each tribe. When the feet of the priests who carry the ark of the Lord, the Lord of all the earth, shall rest in the waters of the Jordan, the waters of the river will be cut off, and the waters which are flowing down from upriver will stand in one heap."

When the people moved out of their tents, the priests went before with the ark, and when they stepped into the waters of the Jordan, the waters which came down from the north stopped and began to pile up a long way off by a city called Adam. The water that was in the river at Jericho flowed on out into the Salt Sea, and the people crossed over against Jericho. The priests stood firm on dry ground in the midst of the Jordan until all Israel was passed over. It was flood season, and the Jordan overflows all its banks all the days of harvest.

*The waters of the Jordan piled up. They would pile up if there were any kind of obstruction. There have been occasions when cliffs have caved off into the Jordan and blocked its flow, and there is nothing which would exclude such an obstruction as the way God chose to block the Jordan on this occasion. The miracle would then be the prediction of the blockage, and the timing of it —just as the priests' feet touched the edge of the water. It may have been that God held the waters of the Jordan back with an invisible wall — as He held them on either side of the people in the Red Sea. There is no way and no need for us to know how God accomplished the miracle. God used the wind to divide the waters of the Red Sea (Exod. 14:21). All the passage here says is that the water rose up in a heap.*

*Our understanding of this miracle is enhanced by the knowledge that the Jordan was in flood stage at this time. At other times of the year, this spot in the river was a good fording place because the water was shallow. But during flood time, the river ran ten to twelve feet deep, and the current was fast and strong. The spies had to be extraordinary swimmers to cross the Jordan during a flood. It is typical of God to try men's faith by requiring them to do what seems to be impossible, or to require them to do a thing which, at certain times, would be feasible, but at other times would be out of the question. With God all things are possible.*

## Memorial stones (Josh. 4:1-24):

As soon as the entire company of Israel was across the Jordan, God told Joshua: "Take twelve men, one from each tribe, and let each man pick up a rock from the midst of the Jordan, from the place where the priests stood, and let them carry the rocks to the place where you will camp tonight."

So Joshua called the twelve men who had been chosen, and said: "Go into the Jordan where the priests are standing with the ark of Jehovah, and each one of you pick up a stone which we will use to make a monument. The monument will be for a sign among you, so that, with the passing of time, when your children see these rocks, and they ask, 'What are these rocks for?' you can tell them: 'They remind us of the time that God cut off the waters of the Jordan before the ark of covenant of Jehovah, so that we could cross the river on dry ground.' So shall these stones become a memorial to the sons of Israel forever."

The men of Israel did as Jehovah commanded Joshua, and they carried the rocks to their camping place for the evening and put them down there. Also Joshua set up twelve stones on the spot where the priests stood in the midst of the river while they held the ark. The priests continued to stand where they were until the nation was completely over the Jordan. The soldiers of Reuben, Gad and half the tribe of Manasseh also crossed over, armed and ready for war, about forty thousand of them.

On that day Jehovah made Joshua great in the eyes of all Israel, and they revered him as they had revered Moses all the days of his life. When the people were all across, Jehovah told Joshua to tell the priests to come up out of the river, and, when they had done so, the river returned and flowed out over its banks as it had before.

It was on the tenth day of the first month when the people came up out of the Jordan, and they encamped in Gilgal which was a little east of Jericho. They took the twelve stones which they had taken from the Jordan and set them up as a memorial at Gilgal, and Joshua told the people, "When your children ask their fathers in time to come, 'What are these stones?,' then tell them, 'God dried up the waters of the Jordan until we were all across the river, just as He had done at the Red Sea, which He dried up until we had crossed, so that all peoples of the earth may know that the hand of Jehovah is mighty, so that you may fear Jehovah your God for ever.'"

*Remember there were 601,730 soldiers by now (Num. 26:51), plus women, children, and others who would not fit into the category of soldiers. It took a long time for all of them to cross the river. The priests stood still in the middle of the river bed the whole time they were crossing, plus during the time the men were gathering the stones for the memorials. It was a long day for the priests — but a glorious day.*

***Map assignment:***

- *Be sure the Jordan River and Jericho are labeled on your map.*
- *Label Gilgal near Jericho, east of Jericho, but west of the Jordan River.*
- *Complete the line of the route from Egypt to Canaan.*

***Chronology note:***

- *The new year has started. They cross the river on the 10th day of the 1st month.*
- *What is supposed to take place on the 14th day of the 1st month of each year?*

# Events at Gilgal
## (Joshua 5:1-12)

### The men are circumcised (Josh. 5:1-9):

When the kings of the Amorites who dwelt west of the Jordan, and the kings of the Canaanites who were by the sea, heard how Jehovah had dried up the waters of the Jordan, they were filled with fear and had no hope that they would be able to resist the Israelites.

With the people encamped at Gilgal after crossing the river, Jehovah said to Joshua, "Make knives of flint and circumcise the sons of Israel."

So Joshua made knives of flint and circumcised the men of Israel at the hill of the foreskins *(Gibeath-haaraloth)*. And this is the reason Joshua circumcised them: All the men who had come out of Egypt had been circumcised, but those who had been born in the wilderness had not been. When the men of war who had come from Egypt refused to go up and fight to take the land, they were forced to wander the wilderness for forty years until that generation died. Jehovah swore that He would not bring them into the land flowing with milk and honey. The children of these men, born in the wilderness, had not been circumcised, for they had not circumcised them along the way.

When the circumcising had all been done at Gilgal, everyone remained in camp until they were well. Jehovah said, "I have this day rolled away the reproach of Egypt from you." Therefore the place was called Gilgal *(Rolling)*.

*Why were the Israelites not circumcised in the wilderness?*

- *Since male infants would have been circumcised on the eighth day after birth, according to the law, there is no evident reason why they could not have been circumcised even while traveling.*
- *One explanation might be that the older generation did not have the necessary faith to carry out the demands of the law based upon the promises of God to the fathers. But that explanation seems to have some flaws:*
  - *Not every family among the Israelites was lacking in faith (for example, Joshua, Caleb, Phinehas, and others), so many families would have circumcised their babies if that had been the explanation.*
  - *God was severe in His punishments when they did not obey His law.*
  - *They had followed the ordinance of circumcision that had been given to their fathers (see Gen. 17) even while they were slaves, because the text here specifically says that the men who came out of Egypt had been circumcised.*
  - *So it seems illogical to think they had stopped the practice on their own initiative during these forty years in the wilderness.*
- *Though the Bible does not give the reason, it seems most reasonable to think that God Himself had told them not to circumcise their sons as part of the reproach of Egypt and of the wilderness.*
  - *When they refused to enter the land at Kadesh-barnea, that generation no longer had the right to say they were heirs to the promises made to Abraham —and therefore, circumcision would have been an empty gesture.*
  - *This explanation fits with the naming of the campsite "Gilgal," because by circumcising the men who had been born in the wilderness, they "rolled away the reproach of Egypt."*

*In what way did this act roll away the reproach of Egypt? The generation of circumcised men who left Egypt was not brought into the land of promise because of their unbelief. Since they left Egypt to go into the land promised unto their fathers, it was failure on their part not to be able to do so. For this they bore the reproach, the taunts of Egypt. That generation is gone now. The new generation has entered the land of promise. With their circumcision, the last vestige of Israel's failure and shame is erased. Israel is now a nation standing in a proper relationship with her covenant God.*

*Notice one more point about this circumcising of the men. They had been camped for weeks on the Plains of Moab, yet God did not demand that they take the action there. Now they have crossed into Canaan and are in the midst of their enemies — and God demands that they fix this problem that had existed for years. In order to do so, the men will be sore and unable to fight for a few days. It was a test of faith for them to obey God. This generation was not like the one before them — they passed the test God gave them.*

## Time to observe the Passover; The forty years are complete (Josh. 5:10-12):

The people crossed the Jordan on the tenth day of the first month (4:19). On the fourteenth day of the month, at evening, they kept the Passover. It had been exactly forty years since the first Passover. On the day after the Passover, they ate of the produce of the land, unleavened cakes and parched grain. After they had eaten the produce of the land, the manna ceased.

*Did God stop blessing His people when He stopped the manna after they ate the produce of the land? No, the land itself was the great blessing from God. For Israel to receive the land and its produce was a blessing from God just as surely as the manna. It just was not a miraculous one. A basic principle of God's dealings with mankind is exemplified here. Many times in history, God began a phase by blessing men through miracles. This phase would be succeeded by one in which by law, or through natural arrangement, men could continue to enjoy God's blessings, but not in a miraculous way.*

***Chronology note:***

- *On the evening of the 14th day of the 1st month, the firstborn of Egypt were killed while the firstborn of Israel were saved. It was the first month of the very first year of this monumental journey. (See Exodus 12.)*
- *Now it is the 14th day of the 1st month of the 41st year — to the day, a full forty years since their firstborn were spared and the Egyptians ordered them to leave the land.*
- *God makes no mistakes.*

## *The journey is complete:*

*The story of the deliverance from Egypt is complete. The group of Israelites who were slaves in Egypt were delivered from that bondage by the mighty hand of Jehovah. They crossed the Red Sea by that same great power, and they traveled south in the wilderness by God's guidance. At Mount Sinai, God spoke with these people and made them His covenant people. He gave them a law and He organized them as a separate, distinct nation. The promise to Abraham that God would make a great nation of his descendants was completely fulfilled at that time (Gen. 12:2).*

*The Israelites left Mount Sinai and traveled north, ready to inherit the land God was planning to give them. At Kadesh-barnea they sent twelve spies into the land to see what it was like and to see what its cities and people were like. The spies returned saying that the land was very good, but that it would be too hard for them to take the walled cities and to fight the giants they had seen there. The people did not have enough faith to overcome the bad report and to move forward with trust in Jehovah's ability to fulfill His promise.*

## Journey's End

*Therefore, they were forced to turn back and wander a year for every day the spies had been gone, until all that generation of soldiers were dead.*

*In the last year of that time, God directed them to travel to the east side of the Jordan. They defeated Sihon and Og — two mighty kings of the Amorites. Israel encamped at the plains of Moab just a few miles north of the Dead Sea. Moses died at the close of their time there, and the Israelites remained in camp. until they had mourned for him thirty days.*

*Now Joshua is their new leader and he has led them as they crossed the Jordan on dry land. They are encamped at Gilgal, they have rolled away the reproach of Egypt, they have observed the Passover to celebrate the full forty years since the night they were ordered out of Egypt, and they have eaten of the produce of the new land.*

*The rest of the book of Joshua tells the exciting story of how the Israelites conquer the land with the help of Jehovah. No enemy can stand against them. By the end of the book, God's promise that He would give the land of Canaan to Abraham's descendants is fulfilled (Josh. 21:43-45; 23:14). Not one promise God made to these people failed. Now it will be their task to remain faithful and hold their land. The choice is theirs. The rest of the Bible tells the story of the Israelites and the choices they made.*

# APPENDIX

## How Long Were the Israelites in Egypt?

Appendix

*How long were the Israelites in Egypt?

*Date of the Exodus

*The Hyksos Kings

Abraham was seventy five years old when he first came into the land of Canaan at God's command (Gen. 12:4). God had promised to bless him personally, to make a great nation through his descendants, and to bless all nations through a particular descendant of his. After Abraham arrived in the land of Canaan, God spoke to him again and promised to give that land to his descendants. These promises are recorded in Genesis 12:1-7. About ten years later, God appeared to Abraham again and made the promise into a covenant (Gen. 15). As part of God's statement on that occasion, He said,

> Know of a surety that thy seed shall be a stranger in a land that is not their's, and shall serve them; and they shall afflict them *four hundred years*; and also that nation, whom they shall serve, will I judge: and afterward shall they come out with great substance. And thou shalt go to thy fathers in peace; thou shalt be buried in a good old age. But *in the fourth generation* they shall come hither again: for the iniquity of the Amorites is not yet full. (Gen. 15:13-16.)

When Genesis closes, the children of Israel (Jacob) had moved into Egypt to escape a dreadful famine; Jacob had died, and so had Joseph and all his brothers. Before his death Joseph assured the Israelites that God would surely come to their rescue and take them back to the land of Canaan.

As the book of Exodus opens, time has obviously passed, but there is nothing in the first chapters to indicate how long the Israelites had been in Egypt or how long they had been slaves. It is not until they are leaving Egypt after the last plague that a number of years is given. Exodus 12:40-41 says:

> Now the sojourning of the children of Israel, who dwelt in Egypt, was four hundred and thirty years. And it

> came to pass at the end of the four hundred and thirty years, even the selfsame day it came to pass, that all the hosts of the Lord went out from the land of Egypt.

Exodus 6:16-20 gives the lineage of the family of Moses: Levi had a son named Kohath, who had a son named Amram, who had a son named Moses. Thus four generations: Levi, Kohath, Amram, and Moses. The number of generations fits with the prediction in Genesis 15. So the question of how long the Israelites were in Egypt sounds as if it is an easy one to answer: they were there four generations, just as God had predicted in Genesis 15. The difference between the 430 years of Exodus 12 and the 400 years of Genesis 15 is easily explained. Four hundred years was a round figure, and it corresponds to the exact figure of Exodus 12.

However, the question is not as easy to answer as it might first appear. There is another scripture that must be considered also. In Galatians 3:16-17, Paul says:

> Now to Abraham and his seed were the promises made... And this I say, that the covenant, that was confirmed before of God in Christ, the law, which was *four hundred and thirty years after,* cannot disannul....

Read the passages carefully. In Genesis 15, it sounds as if Abraham's descendants will live in a land not their own for *four hundred years* before they are brought out by the hand of God. Exodus 12 sounds as if they were in Egypt itself for *four hundred and thirty years*. But read Galatians 3 again: Paul makes the four hundred and thirty years reach all the way from the time the covenant was given to Abraham in Genesis 15 until the law was given a few months after the Israelites came out of the land of Egypt (see Exod. 12:40-41; 19:1). This means Paul was including the stories of Abraham, Isaac, and Jacob, that took place before Jacob's family went to Egypt to join Joseph (see Gen. 46) as part of the 430 years. If these stories are included, then the Israelites were in Egypt itself only about 215 years, instead of the full 430 years.

The question is not a matter of rejecting what the scriptures say, because both positions appear to be supported by scripture. We must be careful to avoid any position that implies we are unconcerned about the scriptures. The question is not of great importance in and of itself — but we want to know how the scriptures fit together. The Holy Spirit inspired both Moses and Paul as they wrote their information, so the answer is not that one of the men made a mistake. Therefore, let us look at the information, and see possible explanations, but there is no need to spend time seeking for more information than there is available on the subject. This is not a question that affects our soul's salvation — and we seek the answer only so that we can be informed and, therefore, not be upset when someone tries to say the Bible is "full of contradictions."

**It is difficult to date all very early events of history.**

- Every ancient civilization had its own way of counting time.
  - Some of their calendars were remarkably accurate, others very poor.
  - And since each group had its own calendar, basing its beginning upon some important event in their own history, it is very difficult to blend the calendars together.
  - The date of the Exodus is certainly not the only early historical event that is difficult to date.

**Many Egyptian records exist, so why not look there?**

- The Egyptians recorded their history carefully, but they did not choose to record the story of their humiliation at the hands of a group of slaves.

- They erased uncomplimentary bits of history from their records. (See our short article about the Hyksos kings. Their story was erased, and remains a mystery in many respects to this day.)

**The name of the Pharaoh of the exodus is not given:**

- From their earliest recorded history, Egyptian rulers took the title of Pharaoh when they came to the throne. But each man had his own personal name also. Many historical records have been found from the early Egyptians, so it is possible to know the dates of many of the Pharaohs.
  - Therefore the personal name of even one Egyptian Pharaoh in the history of Abraham, Isaac, Jacob, Joseph, or Moses would help immensely in dating the events, but no such personal name appears in the Bible record.
  - Moses does not tell us the name of the Pharaoh who tried to take Sarah as his wife in Abraham's day (Gen. 12:10-20), nor the one who dreamed dreams that Joseph interpreted (Gen. 41), nor the one who made the Israelites slaves (Exod. 1), nor the one who refused to let Israel go and suffered the plagues from God (Exod. 2:23).
    - But enough years passed between those events, it is evident that each of those was a different man.

The question about the 430 years arises because of the difference found in the wording of Exodus 12:40 in two ancient versions of the Old Testament.

- The Masoretic text of the Hebrew Old Testament is translated (Exod. 12:40): "Now the time that the children of Israel dwelt in Egypt was four hundred and thirty years" (*The Holy Scriptures According to the Masoretic Text*, p. 88).
- The Septuagint (Greek) translation of Exodus 12:40 adds some words: "And the sojourning of the children of Israel, while they sojourned in the land of Egypt *and the land of Canaan*, was four hundred and thirty years" (*The Septuagint Version*, p. 86).

To deal with this question about the manuscripts, it is necessary to have a little background about such matters. Almost all of the Old Testament was originally written in the Hebrew language. Copyists worked very carefully to preserve correct copies of each original. It is important to know that not one single original manuscript of any book of the Bible remains in existence today. Therefore, every copy we have of the Bible is a copy of copies that have been made again and again through the years. It is by God's providence that we have it preserved for us today.

After Moses wrote the first five books of the Old Testament, the centuries passed, and even before the last of the Old Testament was written, the people spoke the languages of Mesopotamia as freely — or perhaps even more freely — than they spoke their own Hebrew language. The people spoke the Aramaic language in their homes and in their business affairs. Parts of the books of Ezra and Daniel were written in Aramaic rather than in Hebrew. Then, during the years between Malachi and Matthew, the Greek language became the predominant language that was used throughout the Mediterranean world — including the land of the Israelites. By then, the Jews were scattered all over the then-known world, and they spoke and read Greek easily, but many of them had trouble reading their ancient scriptures in the Hebrew tongue.

Different efforts were made to translate the scriptures into the language of the people (Greek), but the translation that became the most widely accepted was made in Egypt by a group of scholars in the years between 285 and 250 B.C. It was called the Septuagint version of the Old Testament, and the name was abbreviated by the symbols "LXX" because of the number of scholars who worked on it. This translation was a tremendous blessing. For the first time in all history, people who were not Israelites by race could read the mighty works of Jehovah. No matter where the Jews were living, now they had their scriptures in the language they were accustomed to reading on a regular basis. It is evident that Jesus approved of the translation, and that the other writers of the New Testament did the same, because nearly every quotation in the New Testament comes directly from the Septuagint instead of from the original Hebrew text. Therefore we can rely upon it as an acceptable translation.

As our English versions began to be translated, however, the scholars went back to the best original texts that could be found. That is the desired policy in any effort to find the correct wording of any ancient literary work. The Masoretes were Hebrew scholars who studied the Hebrew Old Testament very diligently. Their work was done from about A.D. 600-1000. They noted variant readings and amassed a tremendous body of notes about the writing of the Hebrew Old Testament. They prepared what is considered to be the standard text of the Hebrew scriptures of the Old Testament. When the Old Testament is translated into English today, it is translated from the Hebrew text of the Masoretes.

**Which one of these versions is correct in its rendering of Exodus 12:40-41?**

- Since the only reference to a period of 430 years in the Old Testament is Exodus 12:40-41, it is to this reference that Paul was alluding in Galatians 3:17.
- And, since he makes the period of 430 years extend from the covenant God gave to Abraham (Gen. 12, 15) until the giving of the law (Exod. 12:40-41; 19-24), it is obvious that Paul's quote was from the Septuagint Version (LXX).

**In attempting to answer the question we are studying, we need to look at two primary positions:**

1. It was 430 years from the time the promise was given to Abraham until the giving of the law.
    - Therefore the 430 years are divided into two periods:
        - The years in Canaan during the stories of Abraham, Isaac, and Jacob — about 215 years;
        - And the time the children of Israel were in Egypt itself — about 215 years.
2. The children of Israel were in Egypt the full 430 years.
    - In this case, none of the stories of Genesis would be included in the figure until after Jacob took his family to Egypt in chapter 46.

Our only interest should be to determine what the truth is, and to arrive at a position which will reconcile passages on the subject, and which will reflect our reverence for the inspired text. Therefore we set forth both positions and present the arguments for and against each.

## Position one: In Egypt itself for 215 years:

From Galatians 3:17 it appears that it was 430 years from the time God confirmed the covenant with Abraham in Genesis 15 to the exodus from Egypt in Exodus 12:40-41, and to the giving of the law that took place in the same year the Israelites left Egypt (Exod. 19-24). If this is true then obviously Israel was not literally in Egypt itself for the full 430 years.

Rawlinson sets forth the most commonly accepted plan for figuring the time and the arguments for this position (See *Pulpit Commentary,* Vol. 1, pp. xvii).

- According to this position, how long was Israel in Egypt?
    - From the entrance of Abraham into Canaan to the birth of Isaac — 25 years (Gen. 12:4; 21:5).
    - From Isaac's birth to Jacob's birth — 60 years (Gen. 25:26).
    - From Jacob's birth until he went into Egypt — 130 years (Gen. 47:9).

    - Thus making a total of 215 years for the history of Abraham, Isaac, and Jacob before the family moved to Egypt.
  - That would leave 215 years in Egypt itself to complete the 430 years.

- The genealogies of Moses and Aaron fit the shorter number of years better.
  - Four generations are listed from Levi to Moses: Levi, Kohath, Amram, and, Moses (Exod. 6:16, 18, 20).
  - Four generations could not have covered 430 years.
  - If the time were 215 years, then each generation would have been slightly over 50 years each, which would be a more feasible estimate.

- If the early date of the Exodus is accepted, about 1450 B.C., 430 years earlier would have been 1880 B.C. — the time when Jacob and his family moved to Egypt.
  - If the 430 years were the time Israel spent in Egypt itself, then we would have to add 215 years to get to the time when Abraham entered Canaan, making it about 2095 B.C.
    - According to Rawlinson, this date would be too early for Abraham, based upon other information available.

## Position 2: In Egypt itself the full 430 years:

- In Genesis 15, when God appeared to Abram to confirm His covenant with him, He said, "Know of a surety that thy seed shall be a stranger in a land that is not theirs, and shall serve them; and they shall afflict them *four hundred years*" (Gen. 15:13).
  - According to Exodus 12:40-41, Israel was in Egypt 430 years *(according to the Masoretic text, and nearly all English translations).*

- The chief objection to this view is based on Galatians 3:17. Therefore, in setting forth position 2, it is necessary to deal primarily with the passage in Galatians.
  - In Paul's quotation, he alludes to the Septuagint version which renders the verse in Exodus 12:40: "while they sojourned in the land of Egypt *and the land of Canaan.*"
    - Based on these added words in the Septuagint, the tradition was widely accepted in the synagogues that the 430 years covered the time from Abraham until the Exodus.
  - Paul's use of the LXX in this reference may be explained by saying that the number of years more than 430 from the giving of the covenant to Abraham until the giving of the law at Mount Sinai is not important at all for Paul's argument.
    - Paul was making the point that the law of Moses came many years after the covenant was made with Abraham, and therefore the law did nothing to change that promise from God.
    - It was at least 430 years, and this figure was completely adequate for Paul to make his point that the law came *long after* the promise to Abraham. Therefore the Spirit did not see any necessity to straighten out this rather indefinite estimate.
  - The Galatian Christians already had access to the LXX version, and could read it for themselves, since it was written in Greek. The value of their being able to refer to the LXX themselves, and the adequacy of the reference in the LXX for Paul's use, easily outweighed the fact that, in that version, a clause was added to the Hebrew text.
  - In a similar way, if we were quoting the context of Isaiah 52:15 in the KJV, which says, "So shall he sprinkle many nations," we might make our point without necessarily dealing with whether

sprinkle could be more clearly translated as "sprinkle" or "startle." Whether we dealt specifically with the meaning of sprinkle would depend upon whether we were emphasizing the word or not.
  - Likewise, if it had been Paul's emphasis to show specifically how long it was from the covenant given to Abraham until the law of Moses, he would have set the matter forth carefully.

- Some might ask: "Is it possible that the words found in the LXX may have been dropped from the Hebrew text at the time of one of the copies?"
  - The copyists were very careful in their work, and great pains were taken to be sure of their accuracy, but such a thing is possible.
  - It is possible that the scholars who translated the LXX had much earlier manuscripts to work from than we have access to today.
  - Since this possibility exists, we cannot afford to be dogmatic about this point.

**A related question arises:**

Look back to Genesis 15. God says Abraham's descendants will serve another nation *for four hundred years*, but that He will bring them out *in the fourth generation*:

- The figure for the number of years was a round number, so the exact number of 430 years would correspond with the 400 years with no difficulty.

But the question of the "four generations" does raise some questions:

- Four literal generations of Levi, Kohath, Amram, and Moses, may be stretched to cover 215 years, but it would be impossible for them to cover 430 years.
- Evidence indicates that the four generations of Levi, Kohath, Amram, and Moses were not intended to say that only four literal generations spanned the years in Egypt.
  - Throughout the Bible, genealogy lists are given in order to show lineage, not to show a number of years.
    - Compare Ezra 7:1-5 with 1 Chronicles 6:2-15; compare Matthew 1:1-17 with the list of the kings of Judah who were in the direct lineage of Jesus; compare Luke 3:35-38 with Genesis 10:21-25.

- Difficulties arise with counting them as four literal generations either way we go with the number of years in Egypt. Look at the facts regarding the generations of Levi (Exod. 6:16-26):
  - Levi had three sons: Kohath, Gershon, and Merari.
  - Kohath had four sons: Amram, Izhar, Hebron, and Uzziel.
  - By the time the children of Israel reached Mount Sinai, Levi's male descendants numbered 22,000 (Num. 3:39).
    - Of those, 8,600 were direct descendants of Kohath (Num. 3:27-28).
  - But count the number of people in each generation if all the details are included in the Bible text:
    - Starting with Levi, there is one man.
    - Add his three sons of the second generation, and we have a total of four.
    - In the third generation: there were four sons in Kohath's family, two sons in Gershon's family and two in Merari's family (Num. 3:17-20).
      - Thus we have a total of eight sons of the third generation, making a grand total of twelve.

- In the fourth generation, of Kohath's sons, we know Amram had two sons, plus a daughter: Aaron and Moses, with their sister Miriam. All these children were born eighty years or more before the Exodus.
- The Bible does not give enough details to follow each generation after that.
  - But if the sons of the third generation all had three children each, then the children of the fourth generation would number thirty-six, making a grand total of forty seven males. (Daughters such as Miriam were not counted in the census of the Levite males.)
- By this time, of course, some of the earlier members of the family would be dead, thus reducing the total somewhat.
- There would have been time for at least three generations more to be born during the time Moses was growing up and during his stay in the land of Midian.

- Nevertheless, no later than a year after Israel left Egypt, the tribe of Levi numbered 22,000 males, and the clan of Kohath, consisting of four families or clans, numbered 8,600 males (Num. 3:27-28, 39).
  - If all the names and details are given, then most of these 8,600 did not come from Amram, Moses' father, because he had only three children (two sons).
    - Only two sons of Moses are named (Exod. 18:1-4); Aaron had four sons (Exod. 28:1); and none of Miriam's are named.
    - So most of that 8,600 would have had to be the children of Izhar, Hebron, and Uzziel, Amram's brothers. Therefore, Moses, Miriam, and Aaron must have had close to 8,600 first cousins!

- Even though Exodus 1:7 indicates that the Israelites were growing at a phenomenal rate, clearly, it could not be as we have described here.
  - Of course, there were multiple wives in that day, and there were likely some very large families, but even then it is difficult to see growth that rapid in four literal generations.

- In Genesis 15, God ties the figure of *four hundred years* and the expression *in the fourth generation* together.
  - God must, therefore, have been using the expression of "a generation" as a round figure to approximate one hundred years each.

- In considering which position is true, it needs to be borne in mind that if the 430 years includes the time of Abraham, Isaac, and Jacob, then how is it that their generations are not figured in with Levi, Kohath, Amram, and Moses? The four generations listed are the generations that went to and lived in Egypt itself.

For a much fuller discussion of the question of the generations, see the quotation from Tiele's book, *Chronology of the Old Testament,* p. 36, that is found in *Keil and Delitzsch* in their comments on Exodus 6.

**Date for the story of Abraham:**

- Some object to the idea that the children of Israel were actually in the land of Egypt for 430 years because, according to them, such a date pushes the time of Abraham back too far.
  - If we take the approximate date of 1450 B.C. for the Exodus, and add 430 years to it, we arrive at the date of 1880 for the time when Jacob and his family went down into Egypt.
  - One hundred and thirty years earlier, when Jacob was born, would have been 2010.

  - Sixty years earlier, when Isaac was born would have been 2070 B.C.
  - Twenty-five years earlier, when Abraham entered Canaan, would have been 2095 B.C.

- Scholars differ, however, on the best estimate for the date of the beginning of Abraham's story:
  - Millar Burrows estimates Abraham's time at 2,000 B.C. (*What Mean These Stones?*, p. 71).
  - J. A. Thompson says, "It is generally agreed, however, that we must place the days of the patriarchs in the period 2000-1700 B.C., perhaps rather earlier than later" (*The Bible and Archaeology,* p. 15).
  - Merrill F. Unger, using facts to which we have alluded, calculates that Abraham entered Canaan in 2086 B.C. and was born in 2161 B.C. (*Archaeology and the Old Testament,* p. 107; cf. pp. 105-106).

- If, on the other hand, we say that the 430 years spanned the time from the Exodus backward to the time when Abraham received the covenant from God, then we would come up with the date 1880 B.C., which is later than most authorities estimate for the date when Abraham entered Canaan.

No explanation is completely satisfactory. Remember that this is a detail concerning where we should begin counting the four hundred years under consideration. It has nothing to do with our soul's salvation. We do not have a contradiction here. We have a situation in which we do not know for sure which is the correct explanation. There are many such places in the Biblical record that cannot be explained with perfect certainty, and most of them have to do with numbers. It would be better in our classes simply to say in the words of the Bible that the end of the four hundred years had arrived, when the children of Israel should leave the land of Egypt. Material of this kind is provided for the teachers to have at their disposal— not as information that should necessarily be included in a presentation to a class. You need to be familiar with the problem for your own knowledge. If a student should raise a question about the subject, you will be prepared.

# Date of the Exodus

As we said regarding the question of how long the Israelites were in Egypt, the exact date of the exodus makes no difference in and of itself. The significance of the two dates is in the degree to which they give proper respect to all the facts given in the Bible. The two dates suggested are about 1450 B.C. or about 1290 B.C. It is very important to remember that, with all numbers labeled "B.C.," the number grows bigger as it refers to the number of years *before* the birth of Christ. Therefore, the date 1450 B.C. is 240 years before 1290 B.C. When we speak of the "early date" we are referring to 1450, and the "late date" is 1290.

Through the years, conservative scholars have taken the position that the Exodus was near 1450 B.C., while liberal scholars have taken the date 1290 B.C. The reason for these differences is interesting. The primary evidence for the early date is Biblical, while the only evidence for the later date is archaeological. Our tendency is to say, "Well, the Bible is right, so throw out the archaeological evidence." While we maintain the inspiration of the scriptures as strongly as anyone, honesty compels us to deal with the archaeological evidence as well as the scriptural evidence. In our setting forth the position on the early date of the Exodus, we will therefore have to present the evidence *for* the early date, but we will also have to deal with the archaeological evidence arrayed *against* that date. We are willing to accept any date which will not do violence to the Bible and its credibility or to *known* facts.

**There are a few things that would be seriously affected by the acceptance of the late date.**

- The late date would virtually demand that the 430 years of Exodus 12:40 were years that Israel spent actually in Egypt because otherwise the time when Abraham entered Canaan would be 1720 (1290+430), entirely too late to fit other historical evidence.

- The late date would contradict three primary passages that cannot be explained otherwise:
  - Judges 11:26 says that the children of Israel had dwelt in Transjordan (Heshbon and its suburbs, and in Aroer and its suburbs) for 300 years. This figure is given in a letter that Jephthah wrote to the king of the Ammonites.
    - If the Exodus were about 1290, and the conquest were in 1250, then Jephthah (a judge) would fit at 950 B.C. (1250-300=950) — which would make it early in the reign of King Solomon!
      - By Solomon's day, there is enough comparison between the events of the Bible and the events that can be dated from historical records to make the date of his reign fairly definite (from about 960 B.C. to about 920 B.C.).
  - There would be basically the same problem with Acts 13:19 which speaks of 450 years between the conquest and the kings.
  - The late date would flatly contradict the scripture in 1 Kings 6:1 which says that Solomon began to build the temple 480 years after Israel came out of Egypt.
    - The temple was begun in the fourth year of Solomon's reign, making it about 956 B.C. When we add 480 to that figure, we come up with the date of about 1440 — which fits the early date easily, but would not fit the late date at all.
  - Because of the conflicts with these three passages, we take the position in all our books that the exodus took place at the early date (about 1450 B.C.).
    - But, as a teacher, you need to know the evidence that is available about both dates.

- The question of the date also affects the relationship of the history of the Israelites in Egypt with the history of the Hyksos kings. We will deal with this point in the next section of the appendix. The history of the Hyksos kings is uncertain, and their relationship with the Israelites is uncertain, so no one can base an argument either way on their history — but their story seems to fit with the Biblical story of Joseph and the slavery of the Israelites.

Let us present the arguments for both dates so the student can clearly see the evidence and make up his own mind.

## The late date: About 1290 B.C.:

- Evidence indicates that Pharaoh's residence was near the Israelites at the time of the Exodus since he was obviously close enough to supervise their work, and close enough to be immediately available to Moses and Aaron (see Exodus 5-12).
  - The Israelites lived in the part of Egypt known as Goshen, so if Pharaoh lived nearby, then his palace was in the delta region of the land or "Lower Egypt."
    - *(Note: We speak of the upper and lower regions of a land based upon the maps we now use. "Upper" part of a land tends to be the northern part and "lower" is the southern part, because our maps are set up with north at the top and south at the bottom. But ancient countries did not use our maps. "Lower Egypt," consisting primarily of the Nile Delta, was so called because it lay farther down the Nile — away from its source — than "Upper Egypt," which consisted of the southern valley of the Nile River.)*

- There were two periods of history when the Pharaohs had their capital in the Delta, near Goshen:
  - During the time of the Hyksos kings of the Fifteenth and Sixteenth Dynasties (1750 B.C. — 1550 B.C.),
  - And in the days of the Pharaohs of the Nineteenth Dynasty (1319 B.C. —1200 B.C.).

- According to the early date theory, the ruling Egyptian dynasty would have been the Eighteenth.
  - But during the days of the Eighteenth Dynasty, the Pharaohs had their capital in the south at Thebes (Thompson, *The Bible and Archaeology,* pp. 56-57).
  - The Nineteenth Dynasty, having its capital near Goshen, would fit the circumstances of the Israelites better.
  - Therefore the late date is preferable. (We will answer this point later.)

- The capital of Egypt during the years of the Nineteenth Dynasty was called, "House of Raamses."
  - It was built on the site of the old Hyksos capital of Avaris, formerly Tanis. The new city was begun by Seti I and was continued by his son, Rameses II (1290-1224 B.C.).
  - Since the city of Raamses is listed as one of the cities the Israelites helped build (Exod. 1:11), then according to the argument for the late date, they must have still been in Egypt as late as 1310 B.C. (when the building of Raamses began) (Thompson, pp. 57-58).

- It is seldom, if ever, noted by advocates of the late date that the note about the Israelites working on the city of Raamses is given at the *beginning* of the book of Exodus, before the birth of Moses, hence over eighty years before the Exodus itself.
  - If Rameses II ruled from 1290-1224, and the reference in Exodus 1:11 to Raamses proves that Israel was there during his reign, then the time of the Exodus would be pushed 80 years (the 80 years

between Moses birth and the Exodus) later to 1210 B.C., with the invasion of Canaan taking place in 1170 (1210-40=1170), entirely too late to fit clear archeological evidence for other events.

- Two possible solutions are given for this problem:
  - Moses, in discussing the building of the city formerly called Avaris or Tanis, uses the name Raamses, because by his day that is what the city was called.
  - The passage in Exodus 1:11 might not be chronologically arranged. The verse is not meant to say that these cities were built by the Israelites before Moses was born. They merely state that these cities were built by the Israelites, but the time of the building of them actually fits in the days of the exodus itself. But this explanation does not fit the context of 1:11.

- Another argument for the late date is made on the basis of the excavations of Nelson Glueck. According to him, it seems that Edom and Moab did not develop into powerful kingdoms with border fortifications until around 1300 B.C. If Israel had passed through the territories of Edom and Moab earlier, they would have been unopposed (Pfeiffer, *Egypt and the Exodus,* pp. 84-85).

- Others argue that between 1850 and 1300 B.C., practically all of Transjordan was given over to semi-nomads who did not build walled cities (Thompson, p. 59). Therefore the Israelites would not have found a kingdom with sixty walled cities between 1850 and 1300 B.C. as the Bible says they did (Deut. 3:4, 5; cf. 2:32-3:6).

- Archaeological evidence indicates that Jericho was destroyed between 1250 and 1200 B.C. (Pfeiffer, p. 86).
  - Burrows lists cities such as Bethel, Lachish, and Kiriath-sepher (Debir) and says excavations show they were all destroyed in the thirteenth century (Burrows, pp. 76-77).
  - Thompson also speaks of general destruction throughout Palestine about 1250 B.C. (Thompson, p. 59).
  - All of these arguments assume that the Israelites were the cause of the destructions found about 1250 to 1200 in all these sites.
  - One point they do not make is that cities of that era were fought for and destroyed on more than one occasion. If the archeologists have found one destruction on one level, could there not be another one on a lower level that would be an earlier date?

## The early date: About 1450 B.C.

- Jephthah said that by his day Israel had dwelt in Transjordan about 300 years (Judges 11:26).
  - If the Exodus were 1450, the invasion of Transjordan would have been about 1410 (1450-40=1410).
  - Three hundred years later it would be 1110, which would fit the situation quite well.
  - If we take the late date for the conquest, about 1290, and the invasion about 1250, then 300 years later would place Jephthah in the early part of Solomon's reign.
- The Bible says that in the fourth year of the reign of Solomon, 480 years after the children of Israel were come out of Egypt, he began to build the house of Jehovah (1 Kings 6:1).
  - If Solomon began his rule about 960 B.C., then his fourth year would be 956. Adding 480 years to this date gives us 1436 B.C.
- Thus the scriptural evidence is squarely in favor of the early date.

- This would be a good place to deal with the way in which advocates of the late date deal with the scriptural evidence.
  - To some of them, the evidence of scripture carries no weight at all.
  - Those who do have at least some regard for scripture take the position that the number of years in 1 Kings 6:1 is simply wrong. They point to variations in different texts. A few variations exist, but none of them helps the late date.
    - We need to point out, however, that when there is correlation between figures given in different passages (1 Kings 6:1; Judges 11:26), the possibility of error is greatly diminished. Therefore we are unwilling to concede error in the text.

The rest of our argument for the early date is archaeological. We will show a couple of archaeological reasons for accepting the early date, and then we will answer the arguments of those who advocate the late date. Most of the information we will use can be found summarized in *Archaeology and the Old Testament* by Merrill Unger in his chapter titled "The Date of the Exodus."

- Unger makes a good argument that the Egyptian Pharaoh Amenhotep II (1450-1425 B.C.) was the Pharaoh of the Exodus.
  - His father Thutmose III (1482-1450) was a famous conqueror and empire builder. He would have been the Pharaoh of the oppression.
  - If Amenhotep II were the Pharaoh of the Exodus, then his firstborn son was slain in the last plague (Exod. 12:29).
    - Interestingly, contrary to normal practice, the eldest son of Amenhotep II did *not* follow him upon the throne.
    - In the so-called "Dream Inscription of Thutmose IV," inscribed in rock near the sphinx at Gizeh, Thutmose IV is said to have fallen asleep under the shadow of the sphinx. In a dream, the sphinx appeared to him telling him the surprising news that he would be the king of Egypt and asking him to clear away the sand from her feet in gratitude (Unger, pp. 142-143). Obviously he had no hope before of becoming Pharaoh, and therefore was not the elder son, to whom the throne would normally have gone. This story fits well into the situation required by the Bible story.

- Unger goes on to show how the broader history of the Seventeenth and Eighteenth Dynasties would have fit the scenario described in Exodus 1-15 (Unger, pp. 144-145). We will not go into all that he says, but the student would be advised to see Unger's book for a full presentation of his argument.

- We are not taking the position that the Pharaoh of the Exodus was definitely Amenhotep II, but rather showing that a very good case can be made for it.
  - History and archaeology do not favor just one candidate — Rameses II.
  - Some recent estimates of the time of Rameses II place him in the years 1188 - 1156 B.C. (Isaac Asimov, *Asimov's Chronology of the World,* p. 44). Such a date would be too late by far for him to be the Pharaoh of the Exodus.

- But, we are told, the Eighteenth Dynasty had its capital at Thebes in Upper (southern) Egypt, away from the Delta and the land of Goshen.
  - While this is true, it is unlikely that the Eighteenth Dynasty would have abandoned the critical area in the eastern Delta.

- Unger cites the fact that Amenhotep II was born at Memphis, not far from Goshen.
- It is therefore reasonable to suppose that Thutmose III, and, later, Amenhotep II, had a royal residence in the area of Goshen near Rameses or old Avaris (Tanis) (Unger, p. 150).
- Most kings throughout history have had more than one royal residence.

- The name of one of the cities the Israelites helped to build was called Raamses (a variation of the spelling of Rameses). It is argued that this city thus named proves that the Exodus was in the days of Rameses II. We have already shown the difficulty of this theory and a possible solution.

- In contending for the early date, *we* also have a problem.
  - How do we explain that a city was named Raamses over 150 years before the great Egyptian Pharaoh by that name?
    - We could say that Raamses was an updated name for an old city, except that it would have had to be updated by someone besides Moses since, if the Exodus was in 1450, he died long before 1290, the beginning of the reign of Rameses II.
  - The greater likelihood is that the name Raamses was from an earlier Pharaoh.
    - When Israel came into Egypt long before Rameses II, they settled in *the land of Rameses* (Gen. 47:1.
    - This reference indicates that the city was called by the name of an older Pharaoh named Rameses.
    - Several Pharaohs were named Rameses during the eighteenth, nineteenth, and twentieth dynasties (*McClintock and Strong,* Vol. VIII, p. 899).
  - All things considered, this explanation is the best that can be given of the store-city, Raamses, which the children of Israel built (Exod. 1:11).

- Let us deal with the argument of Nelson Glueck that there were no strong governments and no border fortifications in the area of Edom and Moab until 1300 B.C.
  - The situation set forth in Numbers 20:14-21 did not require border fortifications or well-developed urban centers.
  - The text merely says that "Edom came out against him with much people" (Num. 20:20). This argument for the late date carries no weight at all.

- Other arguments for the late date are that the Transjordan was inhabited only by semi-nomads during the period from 1850-1300 B.C.; that Jericho was destroyed around 1250 B.C.; and that excavations show that there was general destruction throughout Palestine around 1250-1200 B.C., but not in 1400 B.C.
  - Unger points out that "the validity of Glueck's methods of surface exploration have been questioned by several archaeologists" (Unger, p. 152).
  - We can illustrate Unger's statement even further. In an article by Bryant G. Wood in *the Biblical Archaeology Review* he says, "Scholars by and large have written off the Biblical record as so much folklore and religious rhetoric" (March/April 1990, p. 49).
  - In the same article, Wood discusses evidence that the destruction of Jericho was about 1400 B.C., which would place it about the time the Bible says.

- Archaeologists are as influenced by their bias (whether belief or unbelief) as anyone else is.
  - The difference is that, whereas believers freely concede their belief in the scriptures, and the influence that belief has upon them, unbelievers refuse to admit that their bias against the supernatural has any influence upon them.

- The work of the archaeologist is not as precise in determining dates as he would like it to be, as we can see in the case of Jericho. Dates have swung from about 1400 B.C., in the estimate of John Garstang, to the later date, in the estimate of Kathleen Kenyon, and now back again to 1400 B.C., in the estimate of Bryant Wood.

- The conclusion of the matter is that the archaeological evidence is not certain enough to convince us that the texts of 1 Kings 6:1 and of Judges 11:26 are in error.
  - The archaeological evidence itself is conflicting.
  - For further reading, consult the chapter to which we have referred in Unger's book.

# The Hyksos Kings

In the sections above, we have shown that there is no way to be sure of the exact date of the exodus, nor exactly how long the Israelites lived in Goshen in Egypt. That means we cannot go back to Egyptian records and be sure which part of their history fits with these particular Bible events. Human curiosity makes us wish we knew exactly what was happening in Egypt at this point in time. We have already said that Moses did not record the personal name of a single Pharaoh during this whole period of early Bible history, making it impossible to pinpoint the exact dates for the events. However, there are some fascinating facts of Egyptian history that fit into this era, facts that we need to include in our information, because they might play a part in the Biblical record.

The information recorded below about the Hyksos kings is not found in the older commentaries such as Keil and Delitzsch because very little was known about the role of the Hyksos in Egypt at the time they wrote their books. Now, however, enough information has been found to make it certain that there were foreign kings who ruled Egypt from about 1750 to 1550 B.C. (dates vary slightly). In 1954 a stela (a stone post or slab) was found in Egypt which contained an inscription which is a sort of open letter to the Hyksos ruler Apophis by the Egyptian Kamose (*The Ancient Near East*, Vol II, pp. 89-93). Such information documents the reality of the Hyksos kings in Egyptian history.

The Egyptians kept very detailed records of their activities; and their land is so dry the records have been remarkably well preserved. The earliest records that have been found date from about 3,000 B.C. They continue through the years until, suddenly, about 1750 B.C., the records stop, to begin again about 200 years later.

Josephus, the Jewish historian who lived during the first century after Christ (37/38 to c.95 A.D.), quotes from an Egyptian historian named Manetho:

> There was a king of ours whose name was Timaus. Under him it came to pass, I know not how, that God was opposed to us, and there came in most surprising manner, men of ignoble birth out of the East, who were bold enough to make an expedition into our country, and with ease subdue it by force, yet without our hazarding a battle with them. So, when they had those that governed us under their power, they burned down our cities, demolished the temples of the gods, and treated the people most barbarously.... At length they made one of their number king, whose name was Salatis. He also lived at Memphis, and put both Upper and Lower Egypt under tribute, and left garrisons at all strategic places. (Josephus, *Against Apion, 1, 14.*)

Josephus was trying to tie this description of Egyptian invaders to the moving of the Israelites into the land of Egypt. That conclusion does not fit the Biblical record at all, however, because Jacob did not enter as any sort of conqueror. But indeed, modern archaeologists have proven that Egypt was invaded by Semitic people about 1750 B.C. No one knows their exact origin. Josephus continues his quoting of Manetho to give them the name of HYCSOS (or Hyksos) meaning Shepherd-Kings according to the Egyptian language (*Hyc*-king; *Sos*-shepherd). Manetho goes on to say it is thought they were Arabians.

The Hyksos may have been of the same race as the Amorites, who came from the Arabian Desert and invaded Aram, Northern Mesopotamia, and Canaan about 2,000 B.C. Gradually they moved south in Mesopotamia and established a kingdom centered around Babylon under the mighty king Hammurabi (1728-1686 B.C.). The Hyksos rulers date from about the same period as Hammurabi's Babylon (c.1750-1550 B.C.). They used the same basic type of weapons, chariots, and other tools.

These Hyksos invaders took many of the Egyptian customs as their own in order to appease Egyptian anger — for example, the use of the Egyptian title of Pharaoh for their rulers. But they kept their own particular trades (shepherds) and their own products, such as the horse-drawn chariots and the Asiatic bow. It seems from archaeological evidence that many Asiatic people moved into the Nile Delta during this period.

The native Egyptians bitterly resented these foreigners who ruled their land. An Egyptian prince named Sekenenre seems to have been the first to resist. His mummy shows five major skull wounds, so he must have met an untimely death! His son Ahmose (1580 B.C.) succeeded in putting the Hyksos out of the land. The next several years were spent trying to hunt the remaining Hyksos out of the cities and destroying them.

The proud Egyptians kept the new products their enemies had introduced, but they sought to destroy all historical records of their humiliation. They seem to have destroyed all Hyksos written records in existence (at least none have been found to date). They went so far as to chisel the Hyksos names out of monuments. It is only within modern times that the archaeologists have begun to piece together the puzzle of the history of the Hyksos.

It is therefore no wonder the native Egyptian dynasties hated the Semitic people living in their delta. They were not Hyksos, but they, too, were "foreigners." At some point, no one knows the date, a Pharaoh decided to use these foreigners for the welfare of the State. Probably, the Hebrews were not the only people forced to work in building whatever the whim of the Pharaoh dictated.

It has been argued that the explanations both of Joseph's coming to power and of the Pharaoh who "knew not Joseph" center around the rule of the Hyksos kings. The Pharaoh who exalted Joseph obviously had flocks and herds of his own, because he asked that Joseph's brethren be put in charge of them (Gen. 47:6). He was especially considerate of these shepherds from Canaan and gave them a fertile region particularly valuable as pasture land. Yet the text is specific in saying that "every shepherd is an abomination unto the Egyptians" (Gen. 46:34). Thus, Joseph may have risen to power under a dynasty more favorably inclined toward people from Canaan than the usual Egyptian kings would have been, and it may be that the king that "knew not Joseph" was a native Egyptian ruler who had come to the throne following the Hyksos rule and did not honor anyone who had been part of the previous dynasty.

If, however, the Israelites were actually in Egypt for 430 years, then the early date for the Exodus (c. 1450) would mean that the Hyksos kings invaded Egypt (1750 B. C.) over a hundred years *after* the family of Jacob moved into Egypt (about 1880 B. C.) and were driven out (1550 B. C.) a little over a hundred years before the exodus (1450 B. C.). The presence of the Hyksos kings would have had little, or nothing, to do with the story of Joseph. But that would make no difference to the story itself, because Joseph rose to power because he interpreted the dreams of Pharaoh, and was given his position to prepare for the predicted famine, not because some king happened to like him.

If, on the other hand, we base our thinking on Galatians 3:17, and divide the 430 years into two periods of 215 years each, then the Israelites would have been actually in Egypt only 215 years. Again, taking the early date for the Exodus (c. 1450), 215 years earlier would be 1665 B.C., about a hundred years into Hyksos rule. According to this explanation, the presence of the Hyksos kings when Joseph came to Egypt would fit very nicely with the Bible story of Joseph.

Whichever position one takes regarding how long Israel was actually in Egypt, there is good evidence from chronology that the beginning of the oppression of the Israelites coincided with the expulsion of the Hyksos kings from Egypt. If the Exodus were about 1450 B.C., when Moses was eighty, his birth would have been in 1530 B.C. The Hyksos kings would have been gone by then (from about 1550), but the oppression of the Israelites began *before* Moses was born, and reached its height in severity just before Moses was born (see Exod. 1).

## Appendix

Whichever explanation is adopted, some problems remain. Therefore, as usual in cases like this, it is best to confine ourselves to teaching the facts given in the Bible. With older students, it is appropriate to give them a brief look at the alternatives, but let the emphasis be upon the accounts given in the inspired text.

# Selected Bibliography


Aharoni, Yohanan, and Avi-Yonah, Michael. *The Macmillan Bible Atlas*. Revised ed. New York: Macmillan Publishing Company, 1977.

Alexander, David, and Alexander, Pat (eds.). *Eerdman's Handbook to the Bible*. Grand Rapids: Wm. B. Eerdmans Publishing Company, 1973.

Asimov, Isaac. *Asimov's Chronology of the World*. New York: Harper Collins, Publishers, 1991.

Burrows, Millar. *What Mean These Stones?* New Haven, Connecticut: American Schools of Oriental Research, 1941.

Church, Alfred J. *Stories of the East From Herodotus*. New York: Dodd, Mead, and Company, n.d.

Edersheim, Alfred. *The Temple.* Grand Rapids: Wm. B. Eerdmans Publishing Company, n.d.

*Holy Scriptures According to the Masoretic Text.* Philadelphia: The Jewish Publication Society of America, 1955.

Josephus, Flavius. *Against Apion.* Trans. William Whiston, Grand Rapids: Associated Publishers and Authors, Inc., n.d.

Josephus, Flavius. *Antiquities of the Jews.* Trans. William Whiston, Grand Rapids: Associated Publishers and Authors, Inc., n.d.

Keil, Carl, and Delitzsch, Franz. *Biblical Commentary on the Old Testament,* Vol. I. Reprint. Grand Rapids: Associated Publishers and Authors, Inc., n.d.

Keyes, Nelson Beecher. *Story of the Bible World.* Maplewood, N. J.: C. S. Hammond & Company, 1959.

McClintock, John, and Strong, James. *Cyclopaedia of Biblical, Theological, and Ecclesiastical Literature,* 12 vols. Reprint. Grand Rapids: Baker Book House, 1969.

Pfeiffer, Charles. *Baker's Bible Atlas.* Revised ed. Grand Rapids: Baker Book House, 1973.

Pfeiffer, Charles. *Egypt and the Exodus.* Grand Rapids: Baker Book House, 1964.

Pritchard, James B. (ed.). *The Ancient Near East,* Vol. II. Princeton, N. J.: Princeton University Press, 1975.

*Septuagint Version.* Originally published by Samuel Bagster and Sons, London, 1851. Reprinted by Zondervan, 1978.

Spense, H. D. M., and Exell, Joseph. *The Pulpit Commentary.* F. Meyrick, commentator: Leviticus. Grand Rapids: Wm. B. Eerdmans Publishing Company, n.d.

Spense, H. D. M., and Exell, Joseph. *The Pulpit Commentary.* George Rawlinson, commentator: Exodus. Grand Rapids. Wm. B. Eerdmans Publishing Company, n.d.

Spense, H. D. M., and Exell, Joseph. *The Pulpit Commentary.* R. Winterbotham, commentator: Numbers. Grand Rapids. Wm. B. Eerdmans Publishing Company, n.d.

Spense, H. D. M., and Exell, Joseph. *The Pulpit Commentary.* Thomas Whitelaw, commentator: Genesis. Grand Rapids. Wm. B. Eerdmans Publishing Company, n.d.

Tacitus. *The Annals of Imperial Rome.* Baltimore: Penguin Books, 1971.

Thompson, J. A. *The Bible and Archaeology.* Grand Rapids: Wm. B. Eerdmans Publishing Company, 1962.

Unger, Merrill. *Archaeology and the Old Testament.* Grand Rapids: Zondervan Publishing House, 1954.

Waldron, Bob, and Waldron, Sandra. *History and Geography of the Bible Story.* Fairmont, IN: Guardian of Truth, 1984.

Waldron, Bob, and Waldron, Sandra. *Christ In You.* Bowling Green, KY: JRB Publications, 1988.

Wood, Bryant. "Did the Israelites Conquer Jericho?" *Biblical Archaeology Review,* March/April, 1990, pp. 44-59.